# Housing
# America

# Housing America

## Building Out of a Crisis

*Edited by*
**Randall G. Holcombe & Benjamin Powell**

Transaction Publishers
New Brunswick (U.S.A.) and London (U.K.)

This book is printed on acid-free paper that meets the American National Standard for Permanence of Paper for Printed Library Materials.

Library of Congress Catalog Number: 2009005976
ISBN: 978-1-4128-1020-3 (cloth); 978-1-4128-1046-3 (paper)
Printed in the United States of America
Cover Design: Christopher Chambers
Cover Photo: © iStockphoto

Library of Congress Cataloging-in-Publication Data

Housing America : building out of a crisis / Randall G. Holcombe and
    Benjamin Powell, editors.
        p. cm.
    Includes bibliographical references and index.
    ISBN 978-1-4128-1020-3 (alk. paper)
    1.  Housing--United States--Planning. 2.  Housing policy--United
    States. I. Holcombe, Randall G. II. Powell, Benjamin, 1978-

HD7293.H572 2009
333.33'80973--dc22

                                                            2009005976

# Contents

# Preface

This volume is a joint project of the Independent Institute and the DeVoe Moore Center at Florida State University. The project began in 2005 as we approached the chapter authors and asked them to write on some specific aspects of the housing market. Popular opinion at the time was that there were a number of problems with the housing market, and our objective was to show that in many cases those problems could be traced directly to some government interference in the housing market. The perception of problems in the housing market remains in 2009, but much has changed since we began the project.

The timing is noteworthy because most of the chapters were completed in 2006 when the housing boom across much of the country was reaching its peak. One chapter in particular that deserves mention in this regard is Mark Thornton's, because he was discussing the inevitable collapse of the housing market bubble at a time when many observers were arguing that house prices could continue rising indefinitely. Thornton's chapter does a good job of explaining the collapse of housing prices in hindsight, and it is worth noting that Thornton's hindsight was actually foresight: he was talking about the collapse before it actually occurred. Similarly, the chapter on Fannie Mae and Freddie Mac, by Lawrence White, was completed in 2006, well before the collapse of those institutions in 2008. Thornton and White both wrote brief post-scripts to their chapters in August of 2008 that were added to this volume shortly before it went to press, but their original contributions remain unchanged otherwise.

The only chapter not written in 2006 is Stan Liebowitz's chapter on the 2008 mortgage meltdown. When the book was started the housing boom was in full swing and reaching its peak. By the time the book was going to press, we wanted to add a separate chapter on the events occurring at the time, and the government policies that led to the mortgage meltdown. But while Liebowitz had the advantage of some hindsight in describing the events that actually occurred, he, like Thornton, saw problems on the horizon well before they actually materialized, and wrote an article on the problems with subprime lending back in 1998. Public policies that seem well intentioned at the time can lay the foundation for problems that may not manifest themselves for a decade or more.

Many of the other policies analyzed in the volume continue to have long-run impacts on America's housing market that often go unrecognized. Rent controls, eminent domain, zoning, and comprehensive land use planning all have substantial impacts on the housing market that are sometimes difficult to see, and that often have larger impacts in the long run than immediately. After all, the housing stock is durable and changes relatively little from year to year, so impacts of policies implemented today are likely to have their largest impacts decades later. When negative impacts show up there is the impulse to say, "The government should do something." What people too often fail to recognize is that the problem is likely due to something the government did in the past.

Our motivation in assembling this volume has been to catalog many of these policy decisions and their effects in one place to demonstrate that the problems in housing markets are not typically the problem of a "market failure," where markets do an inadequate job of allocating the resources to provide housing for Americans, but rather are the result of government failure: the effects of government policies that raise the cost of housing, that generate inefficient patterns of development, that make it difficult for people to find housing, and that create financial difficulties. In general, markets allocate resources well, and governments do not. The housing market is no exception.

We are grateful to DeVoe Moore and the DeVoe Moore Center at Florida State University for financial support for this project, and to Keith Ihlanfeldt, Director of the DeVoe Moore Center, for his support. We are also grateful to the Independent Institute Staff members who helped bring this project to completion. In particular, Independent Institute President, David Theroux, provided valuable encouragement that got this project started and Research Director Alexander Tabarrok provided guidance and feedback throughout the entire process. We thank Peter Gordon for reviewing an early draft of the manuscript. Finally, we thank Andrew Nuemann and Nick Currott for valuable research and manuscript preparation assistance.

# 1

# Introduction: Is There a Housing Crisis?

*Randall G. Holcombe and Benjamin Powell*

About 70 percent of American households own their own homes, and for most of them their homes represent the majority of their net worth. For them, housing policy not only affects the quality of life in their communities but also has a direct impact on their financial wellbeing. The same is true for renters, except that often the direct financial incentives for renters work in the opposite direction than for homeowners. Increases in housing prices raise the wealth of homeowners, but raise the expenditures of renters. Even the small minority of Americans who are homeless are affected by housing policy—directly, in terms of housing options specifically targeted to low-income individuals, for example, and indirectly: If housing policies raise the cost of housing, some people will find housing unaffordable, while if housing policies lower the cost of housing, the homeless may have an opportunity to find a place to live on the income from a low-paying job. Most housing in the United States is allocated in the private market, but that market is heavily regulated and government policies dictate whether people can build new housing on their land, what type of housing they are allowed to build, the terms allowed in rental contracts, and much more. A small percentage of housing is also directly provided by government public housing projects. The chapters in this volume critically analyze government housing policies in the United States. They show that many of the problems in housing markets are the result of government policies, and that many housing policies actually make the problems they are nominally intended to address worse.

Looking at the big picture, America's housing market is not facing a crisis. Most Americans have more-than-adequate shelter, and the size of the average new house grew from about 1,600 square feet in 1980 to about 2,300 square feet in 2004. In 2005, 60 percent of all homes had three or more bedrooms and at least 1.5 bathrooms. Compare that to 1970 when fewer than half of homes had three or more bedrooms and only 30 percent had 1.5 or more bathrooms. Housing amenities have also improved. In 2005, 77 percent of homes had a washing machine, 74 percent a dryer, 60 percent a dishwasher, and 47 percent a kitchen sink garbage disposal. Sixty percent of homes had a garage and 84 percent an outdoor deck or patio. In 2005, 86 percent of homes had some form of air conditioning and 60 percent had central air. Back in 1970, only 36 percent of homes had air conditioning and only 11 percent had central air.

Housing for poorer individuals has improved as well. University of California Berkeley professors Quigley and Raphael (2003) report that the percentage of homes occupied by the poorest fifth of income earners that have incomplete plumbing fell from 40 percent in 1963 to essentially zero percent today. Meanwhile, the homeless population is estimated at about 750,000, less than half a percent of the total population. Many of the homeless suffer from mental illness, drug addiction, or alcoholism, and their homelessness has more to do with their personal problems than with the housing market. But while almost all Americans live in very comfortable housing—especially by world standards, or even when compared to American housing a few decades ago—many Americans also perceive some significant problems with the nation's housing market.

One issue of concern was escalating housing prices, especially in the northeast and on the west coast. After adjusting for inflation, real housing prices rose 210 percent in Boston from 1980 to 2004, and in that same time rose 158 percent in White Plains, New York, 138 percent in San Francisco, 129 percent in Santa Barbara, and 109 percent in San Diego (Glaeser, Schuetz, and Ward, 2006: 6). This has made affordable housing a hot-button issue, not just for lower-income Americans, but also for working-class people. There was an increasing concern that schoolteachers, police officers, and many service workers cannot afford to live in the areas where they can find jobs. However, since the recent housing market meltdown now many are concerned about falling real estate prices. According to the Case Shiller National Home Price Index prices have fallen approximately 16 percent from a high in the second quarter of 2006 through the first quarter of 2008. The price decline has led to increased foreclosures, bank failures, and new government interventions into the mortgage market. As the chapters in this volume illustrate, whether housing values are rising or falling there are continuous calls for increased government intervention.

Another issue is the sprawling nature of the development that has occurred since World War II. While many people like to live in single-family detached homes with big yards in the suburbs, critics argue that this type of development has created an automobile-centric society, causes traffic congestion, increases pollution, and consumes green space. Sustainable development has become a mantra to some critics of sprawling development, and even though sustainable development may mean different things to different people, communities are increasingly engaging in land use planning. Policies extend beyond localities: many states have also produced state-wide land use planning policies, along with the accompanying bureaucracies that carry out those policies that, to varying degrees, are intended to counteract what critics see as the negative effects of post-World War II urban sprawl.

As is often the case, when people perceive problems they petition the government to do something about them, and the government has. New York was the first city to establish zoning regulations, in 1916, nominally to prevent incompatible uses of property. New York's zoning ordinances were a reaction to the construction of the Equitable Building, completed in 1915 and still standing at 120 Broadway, which cast long shadows over the residential properties of its neighbors. Today, "smart growth" encourages mixed-use development, but as Bernard Siegan notes in his chapter on zoning, the original goal of urban planning was to preserve neighborhoods with single-family detached homes from the encroachment of what planners then believed were less desirable types of development. Ironically, the type of development urban planners work to prevent in the early twenty-first century was just the type of development they tried to preserve throughout most of the twentieth century.

Cities also established building codes more than a century ago, and the primary reason for their original establishment was fire prevention. Obviously (as the Great Chicago Fire of 1871 dramatically demonstrated), a fire in one building can have substantial negative consequences for the owners and occupants of neighboring buildings. The combination of zoning regulations and building codes completely specifies what people can construct on their property and how anything they construct can be used.

Zoning regulations have expanded into growth management, which goes beyond merely trying to prevent conflicting uses of property to taking a broader look at developing more desirable communities in the eyes of the planners. Meanwhile, building codes extend to every aspect of construction, from construction materials and methods to standards for plumbing, electrical work, and even the amount of insulation and the width of doorways. People perceived problems with housing, and in response the government has acted, but perceived problems remain, prompting the public to demand more government action. That may be reasonable if, as the nation evolves, new problems arise demanding new solutions. But many of the chapters that follow suggest that the new problems people perceive are the result of past government policies, not the product of market forces in the housing market. As is often the case, government interference with market forces in one area has secondary effects that create other problems, which prompt people to call for more government interference, leading to more secondary effects. If so, the appropriate policy may be less government interference in markets.

## 1. Growth Management and Land Use Planning

At the beginning of the twenty-first century, growth management and land use planning are the most visible housing policy issues, because they have been changing so rapidly in recent decades. Almost all cities have zoning laws, and few citizens would quarrel with their desirability. Who would want to have a cement plant or a warehouse built next to their house? Zoning protects against these types of incompatible property uses. But Bernard Siegan shows in his chapter that zoning is not necessary to provide such protections. Restrictive covenants can be used with more effectiveness, and Siegan builds on his past work to show that land use patterns in Houston, the largest city in the United States without zoning, are indistinguishable from land use patterns in cities that use zoning.

While at first this conclusion might make it appear that zoning makes no difference, that is not quite true, because zoning turns what should be an economic decision into a political decision. People are rightly concerned about how their neighbors use their property, and without zoning, such issues remain very local. With zoning, people who are completely unaffected by land use decisions gain standing to participate in those decisions simply because they are a part of the political jurisdiction that oversees the zoning. This distorts land use decisions, but another longer-run result is that after decades of experience with zoning regulations, which make land use decisions a part of the political process, that process has been radically extended to more comprehensive land use regulation.

Oregon began an era of state-wide growth management legislation in 1973, followed by Florida in 1985. Since then many states have followed suit, establishing state-wide land use goals and policies. Typically, the actual land use planning is done at the local level, with requirements that local governments conform to state policies, methods, and goals. By the late 1990s those goals, under the banner of "smart growth," tended to support the containing of urban sprawl, more compact high-density development, the promotion of alternative means of transportation rather than automobile travel, and the provision of affordable housing.

As governments became more proactive in land use planning, they have increasingly used eminent domain as a method of obtaining property to fulfill their plans. Eminent domain allows governments to force owners to sell their property against their will. Traditionally, eminent domain has been reserved for public works projects such as building roads, but with the Supreme Court's 2005 decision in *Kelo v. The City of New London*, eminent domain may now be used to seize private property for other private uses if a government body determines that doing so will increase its tax base or promote some other public purpose.

Eminent domain is supposed to promote efficiency by overcoming transaction cost barriers to large-scale development problems. However, Randall Holcombe's chapter shows how the use of eminent domain fails to fully compensate residents who lose their home, leads to inefficient land use patterns, and is unnecessary to assemble large tracts of land for development.

An economic analysis of growth management programs illustrates how the secondary effects of government regulation lead to problems that create the demand for more regulation. As Samuel Staley demonstrates in his chapter, growth management policies nation-wide have worked to restrict the amount of development, reducing the supply of housing, and following the laws of supply and demand, increasing the price of housing. The smart growth policies of containing urban sprawl and promoting more compact urban development were responsible for rising housing prices, which led to the demand for policies that would create affordable housing. Meanwhile, Randal O'Toole's chapter provides further evidence of these points and also shows the smart growth emphasis on alternative means of transportation has led to expensive mass transit programs while de-emphasizing the road network that supports most transportation, leading to increased traffic congestion. Policies designed to increase population density in those areas that are already the most congested further exacerbate the problem—again leading to a public demand that government do something. Ironically, because land use policies tend to be complex and relatively invisible to the general public, most people do not realize that the problems that bother them the most are the direct result of past government policies.

## 2. Housing Prices

One result of smart growth policies that have restricted the supply of housing is higher housing prices, but other government policies have led to higher housing prices as well. Building codes raise housing prices, partly because they mandate a minimum quality of housing, but also because they require a specific type of construction that may not be the most cost-effective. Building codes vary substantially from one locality to another, making it costly for builders to expand across multiple markets. Even if the provisions in building codes may have had a reasonable rationale when they were established, they tend to change more slowly than the state of the art (as is true of many regulatory responses to perceived problems), rendering construction methods increasingly less cost-effective over time. Meanwhile, those in the construction industry have a vested interest in maintaining the existing codes, which they know how to deal with, and which provide a barrier to entry for potential competitors.

One twenty-first century answer to rising housing prices is inclusionary zoning—the requirement that developers build "affordable" housing as a part of their developments. As the chapter by Powell and Stringham notes, inclusionary zoning actually produces less affordable housing. It imposes costs on developers, reducing the supply of housing and thereby raising the price of all housing. Meanwhile, as inclusionary zoning drives up the price of all housing, only a small fraction of all housing is "affordable" according to the regulation's definition. But that affordable housing comes with strings attached, making it less valuable, and it is never affordable to those who need inexpensive housing the most anyway. Inclusionary zoning is yet another example of a policy that has effects that are the opposite of its stated intentions.

Government has directly attacked the affordable housing issue by providing public housing, and the chapter by Joshua Hall and Matthew Ryan shows that public housing programs have been such a well-recognized failure that governments have ceased building public housing.

The federal government has also gotten involved in the mortgage market. Lawrence White explains how Fannie Mae and Freddie Mac have encouraged overconsumption of housing by wealthier people while doing less to assist poorer individuals achieve homeownership. He recommends privatizing Fannie Mae and Freddie Mac to end this subsidy and the socialization of investment risk that government backing of these companies creates. Meanwhile, Mark Thornton shows how the Federal Reserve's monetary policy contributed to a housing bubble in the early twenty-first century, demonstrating how even programs that at first appear to have little relation to housing ultimately can make housing less affordable and a more risky investment. Since the collapse of the bubble, foreclosures have increased, major mortgage banks like Countrywide and IndyMac have failed, and the government has bailed out Fannie Mae and Freddie Mac. Stan Liebowitz analyzes how the government contributed to the mortgage market meltdown by encouraging the weakening of underwriting standards. He finds that the mortgage market collapse is a direct result of prior government policies that aimed to increase rates of home-ownership, particularly among minorities and the less affluent.

One reason why policies like these can garner political support is that they do provide some benefits to some people. Policies that restrict the supply of housing and increase housing prices benefit existing homeowners who see the value of their homes rise. In addition, in many communities people oppose the way that development changes the character of their communities, and policies that stop development can both prevent these changes and at the same time increase the market value of people's homes. Furthermore, one of the most visible by-products of development is traffic congestion, creating even more support for government-mandated growth controls. No wonder restrictive land use policies are widely supported. This is even truer when one recognizes that homeowners tend to participate more in the political process, and that while current residents have the option to participate, future residents who will face higher home prices due to restrictive growth management policies are completely disenfranchised from these decisions that will have a large effect on them.

The incentives of renters are different from the incentives of homeowners, because the higher housing prices that increase the net worth of homeowners translate into higher rents for renters. One reaction to higher rents has been rent controls, described in Matthew Brown's chapter. Again looking at the political incentives, rent controls can benefit current renters by reducing their rents, creating political support among renters. But rent controls reduce the supply of rental housing, imposing costs on future renters who, again, do not have a say in the political process. Policies that falter based on any economic rationale often can be understood when one looks at who gains and who loses from them, and comparing the relative political power of the gainers versus the losers. When looking at housing policies, typically it is the rich who benefit at the expense of the poor.

## 3. Market-Based Alternatives

The government policies that are critically examined in this volume all have been aimed at problems that people perceive exist in housing markets. As already noted—and discussed in more detail in the following chapters—many of these problems have actually been caused by government policies, and the solution is to remove those policies rather than enact more policies to try to offset the effects of existing policies. Markets can be very responsive to perceived problems, if they are given a chance. Bernard Siegan's chapter on zoning, and his earlier research going back decades, shows that the actual mix of land uses without zoning is indistinguishable from the mix under zoning. Siegan goes on to show how private contractual mechanisms can be used to provide protections to landowners in the absence of zoning. The narrow point is that private contractual arrangements to control land use and prevent conflicts work better than government zoning; the larger point is that market mechanisms work better than government planning in land use, as in other areas of the market. With markets, all participants have an incentive to bargain to an efficient outcome, and people who are not directly affected by outcomes are prevented from interfering with the process. The political process makes it easier for some people to benefit by imposing costs on others.

Jack Estill, Benjamin Powell and Edward Stringham pick up on this theme by describing how development impact fees are used by current residents to impose costs on new development in order to build infrastructure that could be more efficiently privately provided. Fred Foldvary expands on this by explaining how neighborhood associations can provide many of the functions that people associate with governments, and Robert Nelson builds on this theme by showing how neighborhood associations have grown, and how they can be established not only with newly-developed neighborhoods but also in existing neighborhoods. Government housing policy often results in government failure and makes housing problems worse, while reliance on market mechanisms leads to more efficient resource allocation.

Mostly, this volume deals with specific housing and land use policies and issues, and examines both how government policies address those issues and how market mechanisms can work as an alternative to government policy. In the background, however, is a larger issue that should be kept in mind when thinking about housing and land use policies. The organization of urban areas is the result of individuals making land use decisions that work to solve particular problems and overcome obstacles in economic and social organization. Market forces organize land uses to avoid conflicting land uses and negative externalities, as Bernard Siegan's work emphasizes, and at the same time exploit positive externalities.

Cities exist because there are advantages to some people and some businesses to being in close proximity to others. One can see economic forces at work in the agglomeration economies that lead cities to specialize, and to have unique characters. New York is a financial center, Detroit produces automobiles, and Silicon Valley has a concentration of high-tech electronics firms. These same economic forces that differentiate land use among different cities are also at work determining land use patterns in individual neighborhoods and individual parcels of land. These spatial arrangements are primarily market-determined, and are continually evolving as conditions in the economy evolve. No planner can have all the information that is coordinated through the use of the market mechanism, so there is good reason to be cautious about trying to substitute government planning for the forces of the market.

### 4. The Market Order

Throughout much of the twentieth century, there was an academic and policy debate on the merits of central economic planning versus the market system. That debate ended with the collapse of the Berlin Wall in 1989 followed by the demise of the Soviet Union in 1991. But even up through the 1980s there was a substantial amount of support in both academic and policy-making circles for the idea that central economic planning is a more effective way to run an economy than leaving things up to the uncertainties inherent in the market system. The debate was settled not by reasoned discourse, but by the events that provided real-world evidence on the inefficacy of central economic planning. Now, except for a few people at the fringes, everyone agrees in principle that markets allocate resources more effectively than government planning.

Despite the widespread acceptance of the idea that in principle markets allocate resources better than government planning, whenever people perceive problems in a market, they are prone to demand that government should do something to fix the problem, and those in government are only too happy to oblige with some new government program or policy. So while everyone agrees in principle that we should be using markets, not government, to allocate resources, little-by-little the influence of government over resource allocation grows as it responds to the specific demands for government to do something in particular cases. Since the collapse of the Berlin Wall, nowhere in the American economy has the demand that government do something been stronger than in housing markets and related land use issues.

The government's increasing involvement in housing markets, fed by the popular demand that government "do something" to address problems people perceive, provides good reason to look at what the government actually has done in housing markets, what the effects of its policies have been, and what can be done to make housing markets work better. Based on the chapters that follow, we believe that many of the problems people find in housing markets are actually the result of government policies, that the market mechanism will do as good a job of allocating resources in the housing market as it does in other markets, and that the appropriate policy response is to reduce the government's presence in housing markets. With that introduction to the subject, it is time to turn to the chapters that provide the supporting evidence for those views.

## References

Glaeser, Edward L., Jenny Schuetz, and Bryce Ward. "Regulation and the Rise of Housing Prices in Greater Boston." Cambridge: Rappaport Institute for Greater Boston, Harvard University and Boston: Pioneer Institute for Public Policy Research, 2006.

Quigley, John, and Raphael, Steven. (2004) "Is Housing Unaffordable? Why Isn't It More Affordable?" *Journal of Economic Perspectives,* Vol. 18, No. 1, pp. 191–214.

U.S. Census Bureau. (2005) *American Housing Survey for the United States: 2001.* Washington, DC: U.S. Census Bureau.

# 2

# Urban Planning, Housing Affordability, and Land Use

*Samuel R. Staley*

The anti-sprawl movement and its political progeny, Smart Growth, have ushered in a new wave of interest in and activity on urban planning. More and more communities are actively engaged in land use planning, and more and more states are requiring it. Unfortunately, popular and legislative support for land use planning is based more on hope and hype about its potential to improve local communities than on any serious analysis of its effects, particularly when it comes to real estate and housing affordability.

This chapter will delve into these issues in more depth. Space does not allow for a comprehensive summary of the academic literature, nor would this necessarily be productive. The lion's share of the research by mainstream academics and analysts concludes that planning has a significant impact on the housing market and prices (see Fischel, 2005). Most of this research also shows that the effect of land use planning has been to increase housing prices (see Green and Malpezzi, 2003; Staley, 1997a, 1997b).

The key policy issues, for citizen planners as well as ivory tower academics, has been how development regulations influence the market, whether higher housing prices are beneficial or negative, and what, if anything, public policy can do to make housing more affordable. Indeed, even supporters of strong, centralized approaches to land-use planning admit as much. For example, one recent review of the academic literature sympathetic to Smart Growth pointed out that growth management policies *should* increase housing prices, but not if the higher prices are due to supply constraints. "After all, if one of the primary purposes of growth management is to increase the desirability of the subject community, prices there should rise, but not because of supply-side constraints" (Nelson, Pendall, Dawkins and Knaap, 2004: 154).

The fallacy of this argument, however, lies in the practical application of growth management policies on the local level. Local planning boards and regional planning agencies simply don't have the kind of control over the housing market to make decisions so finely tuned that supply and demand effects can be disentangled in a way that avoids creating significant supply disruptions in the market (Staley, 2004b). Indeed, these disruptions are, to some extent, inevitable because the intent of growth management is to direct consumer choices toward a specific type of housing product, regardless of their true preferences.

## 1. A Thumbnail History of American Zoning and Urban Planning

Supporters of Smart Growth typically begin their presentations with a distinction between "growth management" and "growth control." Growth control, supporters of growth management claim, attempts to "limit" or "ration" development (Nelson, Pendall, Dawkins, and Knaap, 2004: 119). Growth controls included building caps, maximum population targets, moratoria on new residential permits, and other "hard" quotas on new growth. Growth management, in contrast, attempts to "influence the pattern of growth and development in order to meet projected needs" through integrated planning and regulation (Ibid). Growth management strategies would include density limits, urban growth boundaries, urban service areas, minimum lot size regulations, or agricultural zoning. In practice, the distinction between growth control and growth management is largely meaningless (see also Levy, 2000: 216).

At its core, the distinction confuses intent with effect. All development regulations and urban planning influences the pace, pattern, and form of land development. That's the intent—to generate or direct outcomes that are different from what would be produced by consumers and builders working in a free market. Policies such as permit caps and moratoria are simply more direct and transparent. For example, minimum lot size regulations are usually justified on the basis of preserving open space or maintaining a rural community character. Yet, the practical effect, and political intent, is often to stop new residential development altogether. A rural community outside a growing city in southwest Ohio, for example, established a minimum lot size of 1.75 acres for new residential development because that was the lot size necessary to push home costs high enough to make new residential development unprofitable.[1]

### A. *Getting Planning Off the Ground:* Euclid v. Ambler Realty

So-called growth controls really reflect a historical phase in the evolution of growth management rather than a fundamental difference "in kind" and intent. Most growth regulations are adopted as a response to politically undesirable market trends in the real estate market. In *Village of Euclid, Ohio v. Ambler Realty Co.* (1926), the U.S. Supreme Court upheld the village's zoning of land to prevent industrial uses in the village, essentially giving a national green light to zoning by local governments. Height, land use, and density regulations effectively eliminated the potential for Ambler Reality to develop its 68 acres. The Supreme Court upheld the village's zoning code (a relatively new tool at the time), even though there was no demonstrable harm proposed by the new use. Ironically, the Ambler property remained vacant for 20 years until General Motors built an aircraft factory (an industrial use) on the site during World War II.

The Supreme Court's decision in *Euclid* represented an ideological triumph of progressive political thinking over a property rights-based approach rooted in regulating nuisances and tangible externalities (Claeys, 2004; Staley and Claeys, 2005). The Supreme Court, following progressive and reformist thinking at the time, believed that professional planners and city administrators would be able to control and regulate development more effectively than real-estate markets or a property-rights based approach. This progressive thinking is still at the core of modern-day urban planning, particularly Smart Growth and the regional planning movement.

The Achilles heel of urban planning in the United States, however, is its political character. Zoning, like urban planning more generally, is nested in a political process. While it follows administrative procedures, policy decisions are made within a broader political framework that reflects local interests. Thus, the widespread use of zoning places land development solidly within the realm of political decision making, effectively collectivizing property rights of land uses (Nelson, 1977; Fischel, 1985).

One of the effects was using land-use policy as a way to bestow benefits on targeted groups of individuals, including wealthy homeowners who could now use zoning to exclude politically "undesirable uses" such as affordable housing and commercial uses. An empirical study of planning policy in 91 cities immediately following the *Euclid* decision found that the spread of zoning may have had as much to do with interest group politics as instilling professional city management or planning techniques. "Those reformers who denounced ward-based machine politics and lauded zoning," observes James Clingermayer, "must have been flabbergasted to discover that zoning was, in the early years, most popular among the cities where the ward-heelers were in office" (Clingermayer, 1993: 736).

Expanding local government authority beyond regulating broad land uses to include directing specific uses, housing types, and economic activity is a conceptually logical progression from these early years. "Euclidean zoning" notes law professor Eric Claeys, "institutes a centralized, command-and-control style of land-use regulation" (2004: 2739). Land uses are literally mapped onto the community based on density and type. The types can be very specific, and zones are commonly created for uses as narrowly defined as single-family housing with detached garages on lots of a certain acreage (e.g., half acre) or "neighborhood" businesses that include convenience stores, but not large grocery stores. While, as a practical matter, the initial zoning code and map grandfathers in existing uses, changes in land use have to be approved by a legislative majority on city council (often after a recommendation from a planning commission). Requests for changes in land use or type are almost always subject to public hearings, and the presumption is against the proposed change and in favor of the existing land use. (Scarlett and Staley, 1997; Staley and Claeys, 2005).

## B. Early Moves beyond Zoning

Dramatically higher household income in the post-World War II era prompted a wave of suburbanization and decentralization in most U.S. metropolitan areas. As suburban communities grew and became more diverse, residents of these small communities began to worry about the demographic, social, and cultural changes growth created. Citizens naturally turned to the political process to debate the future of their community. With zoning and urban planning enshrined as a public purpose, both in statute and judicial interpretation, communities used the planning process to try control growth.

The first wave of growth control, particularly on the west and east coasts, focused on the simple and direct methods—permit caps, moratoria on new development, and strict zoning. In some cases, particularly in California, comprehensive plans became binding documents that dramatically limited the ability of communities to spontaneously meet changing market conditions through the real-estate market. In cases such as the city of Petaluma outside of San Francisco, permit caps were instituted as a way to slow the demands of new growth on local infrastructure. In other cases, such as the city of Napa (also in the San Francisco Bay area), population caps were adopted and land use regulations were developed to support the broader policy goal. In most cases, however, these efforts failed. "The caps are typically imposed at time when the real estate market is hot," writes William Fulton in one of the leading textbooks on planning in California, "so the cap is set at a very high number" (Fulton, 1997: 193). Hot housing markets often cool down as some point, and housing development remains below the capped amount. In other cases, the city simply fails to grow at the levels predicted by planners.

The city of Napa, for example, established a population cap of 75,000 in 1975 (Staley, Edgens, and Mildner, 1999). At the time, planners expected the city's population to reach 150,000 by 1990. The city has since abandoned the cap, but growth has been well under the amount projected by planners. The U.S. Census Bureau reports that Napa's population was 72,500 in 2000 and peaked at 75,700 in 2003. Since then, the city's population has fallen to about 72,000 (and below the city's current forecast population of 78,800).

Local efforts to control growth, of course, have little impact on regional growth. If a cap were successful, it merely pushed development into other parts of the region, contributing to sprawl. In California, as in other parts of the nation, the failure of local and regional governments to invest in core infrastructure in a timely way often led to traffic congestion, higher air pollution, and lower quality of life.

Thus, as the 1990s unfolded, many communities were still experiencing the pangs of growth and development, but realized the simplistic notions of capping development or issuing moratoria on new development were unworkable or, in some cases, illegal. The traditional growth controls were rarely popular on a broad scale.

## C. Smart Growth and the Politicization of Planning

The next wave of growth control emerged in the 1980s and 1990s when more and more communities adopted growth management policies with less transparent impacts on housing and the real estate market. While not attempting to directly limit markets, the new growth management tools attempted to regulate markets through a negotiated, legislative process.

Unfortunately, many believe that because land use regulation is less visible, its impact on real estate markets is minimal. This is inaccurate. The regulatory process can impose significant costs, and these costs have direct impacts on the functioning of real estate markets.

Take the case of historic preservation. A 30-acre tract of vacant land in Ohio could potentially generate 60 homes based on a standard zoning density overlay of one half-acre per unit (Staley, 2002). The property, however, includes a historic farmhouse that reflects a cost to the developer of about $400,000. The developer would also have to forego the sale of two contemporary housing units, resulting in a total regulatory impact of $900,000. Thus, each new home will have to carry a $15,517 per unit burden (about 6.2 percent of the price of each new house) to carry out the historic preservation efforts of the community. In contrast, the farmhouse could have been preserved through a special citywide per unit assessment of just $97 per unit.

Similar dynamics are in play when communities impose inclusionary zoning requirements on new development. Inclusionary zoning provisions require developers to reserve a certain number of units for low-income families and households, and they are becoming increasingly popular. "The concept," writes Douglas Porter, "is based on the economic premise that developers' interest in building residential projects in strong housing markets offers an opportunity to exact contributions from the development industry to the stock of affordable housing" (Porter, 2004: 214). Inclusionary housing programs have been credited by advocates with producing 65,800 units in 585 cities (Porter, 2004: 239). The most active states are California, Massachusetts, and New Jersey, but Montgomery County, Maryland's program has received national attention for its success. By one estimate, 10 percent of all cities over 100,000 have inclusionary zoning requirements in place, and 20 percent of all California cities have some form of an inclusionary zoning policy (Powell and Stringham, 2004).

The success of these policies may be more apparent than real. Inclusionary zoning, sometimes called inclusionary housing, is an attempt by local governments to force the private sector to build housing targeted toward low-income households. Local governments accomplish this typically by requiring developers to set aside a certain number of housing units, often 10, 15, or 20 percent of the total planned production, for families below a particular income threshold. The threshold is typically around 80 percent of the median household income in city or county. Local governments usually do not dictate the type of housing that will be provided, but units have to be similar in architectural style and sold at below-market prices to qualifying households. In some cases, such as Montgomery County, Maryland, developers can transfer the ownership and deed of the housing units to the local (or state) housing authority. Some cities and counties also allow developers to contribute funds to an affordable housing fund in lieu of actually building the units.

## D. *Growth Management and Housing Supply*

In one of the few systematic studies of inclusionary zoning policies, economists Benjamin Powell and Edward Stringham examined housing supply and affordability in the San Francisco Bay area, Southern California, and Monterrey County, California. In each case, they found that inclusionary zoning policies led to a reduction in affordable housing supply.

In part, these programs simply aren't implementing on a scale sufficient to address the need. Fifty Bay Area cities have exclusionary zoning policies and have produced 7,000 "affordable" units since 1973, averaging about 228 units per year (Powell and Stringham, 2004a). The Association of Bay Area Governments, however, estimates that the region needs more than 24,000 units per year.

These data, however, may be underestimating the actual impact of real estate markets. Powell and Stringham found that housing production actually fell by 31 percent in the Bay area communities after inclusionary zoning was adopted (see also Chapter 10 in this volume). When they examined the effects of inclusionary zoning policies in 13 communities in Los Angeles and Orange County, Powell and Stringham found that 17,292 *fewer* homes were built in the seven years following the implementation of the inclusionary zoning program (Powell and Stringham, 2004b).

## 2. How Real Estate Markets React to Development Regulation

The reason why inclusionary zoning policies (and other growth management regulations) have a negative impact on housing production and builder expectations is pretty straightforward and follows directly from standard business management principles. By requiring builders to sell some units at prices below market, they incur two types of costs that they either pass on other homeowners or which force them to reduce the quantity of homes they supply.

### A. *Reducing the Bottom Line*

First, households buying market-rate housing have to cover the costs of the homes sold at a subsidized price. In a new subdivision, this can be a substantial new cost. Suppose a developer plans to build 100 homes in a city with a median household income of $50,000 and sell them at a market rate of $250,000. (This would require a household income of about $83,000 assuming a family can afford a mortgage three times their income, and they are not putting a down payment on the home.) Under normal market conditions, the developer would reasonably expect to generate revenue of $25 million.

The inclusionary zoning ordinance, however, requires the builder to set aside 15 percent of the units and sell them at a below-market price. Let's assume that the inclusionary zoning ordinance requires these homes to be sold at a price 80 percent of the median household income. Thus, a family earning $40,000 per year could purchase a home worth $120,000. Now, however, the developer's total anticipated revenue has fallen to $23.1 million. On this surface, this may not seem like a large hit—revenues are just 7.6 percent lower than what the developer expected. (In fact, this is the logic used by many planners and city officials.)

But the impact is much larger than the 7.6 percent. For many developers, this revenue reduction would eliminate any profit they would generate from the new development. To remain profitable, they would have to pass on the costs of the subsidized unit to market-rate homebuyers. Thus, the market-rate houses now have to sell for the original price ($250,000 per home) plus the subsidy to the lower-income households. The new price for the market-rate units is $272,941, a 9.2 percent increase in housing prices. This price increase might well significantly change the "price point" for the housing units—narrowing the size of the market for new homes in this category.

The effect is to raise the cost of building homes while limiting the revenue potential of the homes put on the market. This, in turn, reduces housing supply. Of course, the same process was at work in the earlier discussion of historic preservation.

## B. Uncertainty, Delay and Transaction Costs

But, there is a second effect that also influences the developers' bottom line—the time, resources, uncertainty, delay and negotiation required to comply with local regulations. These are the "transaction costs" associated with the development process, and inclusionary zoning is just one form of regulation on the local level that can influence housing production. Higher transaction costs raise the cost of doing business in a community, and this limits their development potential.

The financial costs of compliance with zoning and planning approval have long been recognized, but more recent research has paid closer attention to uncertainties and delays growth management has on the housing market (Staley, 2001; Lai, 1997; Staley, 1994). Many of these studies have examined the effects of regulatory delay and approval on the local and regional level. Regulatory processes that lengthen the development approval time, or significantly increase their complexity, tend to reduce levels of housing production. And the results can be dramatic. In a study of building activity in 44 metropolitan areas from 1985 to 1986, Christopher Mayer and Tsuriel Somerville found that the home building industry was less responsive to changes in demand when regulations were more burdensome. "An MSA with 4.5 months delay in approval where growth management actions have been introduced through two different approaches will have about 45 percent less new construction than an MSA with a minimal 1.5 month delay and no growth management policies" (Mayer and Somerville, 2000: 652–653).

In another widely cited study, economists Edward Glaeser and Joseph Gyourko (2002) found that most metropolitan areas were not faced with housing costs significantly higher than construction costs. However, for those that faced large differences, particularly urban areas on the east and west coasts, much of the discrepancy could likely be attributed to a planning double whammy. First, developers and builders had to incur high upfront costs to secure planning approval. Often, the permitting process can add months and even years to a project's timeline if it is subject to numerous public hearings and multiple approvals. Second, local zoning maps limit the land supply by, in effect, taking some land off the market because it is improperly zoned. In many cases, land may be zoned for densities too low to meet housing demand, ratcheting up housing costs and preventing the supply side of the market to produce the right kinds of houses for the rights types of consumers.

Many developers are critical of impact fees—costs imposed on new housing to cover the expenses of providing infrastructure such as water, sewer, roads, and parks. Yet, impact fees, while substantial in some parts of the country, are also predictable. Most impact fees are assessed based on formulas provided in local development regulations or subdivision ordinances. More often, the uncertainties surrounding the approval process impose greater burdens (and risks) for developers and builders. In an analysis of growth-related referenda in 63 Ohio cities, Staley (2001) found that the uncertainties related to ballot-box zoning created an annual "growth penalty" of between 19.4 and 28.7 housing permits per 1,000 residents. This penalty was equivalent to one quarter of the housing units actually built during the period.

## C. Throwing Housing Markets Out of Balance

Impacts on the overall supply of housing is just one part of the supply reduction equation. Regulation will also influence the types of housing produced. In some cases, as in Portland, Oregon and Minneapolis-St. Paul, this is an explicit goal of regional planning agencies. In both places, the intent of regional planning is to dramatically reduce the share of single-family houses on privately owned land and increase the amount of apartments and townhouses built in an effort to combat urban sprawl.

In Portland, the urban growth boundary has been largely successful in achieving this goal. Multifamily housing units increased from 25 percent of all building permits in 1992 to 49 percent in 1997 (Staley and Mildner, 2000; Staley, Edgens, and Mildner, 1999). Population densities also rose dramatically as average lot sizes fell from one fifth of an acre to one-eight of an acre during the same period (Staley and Mildner, 2000; Staley, Edgens, and Mildner, 1999). Growth management policies also influence the character of real estate submarkets. In Portland, as prices increased, households tended to buy larger homes on smaller lots (Staley, Edgen, and Mildner, 1999: 19).

This is more than a technical distinction. Recent supporters of more aggressive land use planning have argued that regions that aggressively regulate housing and land development do not experience higher housing prices compared to cities that are less restrictive (Nelson, Pendall, Downkins, and Knaap, 2004). In part, this is explained by fluctuations in the economic cycle as demand falls when urban areas experience economic recessions or slow growth. Higher prices can also be mitigated by increasing the number of units built in other sectors of the housing economy. In Portland, for example, the lack of housing for relatively large lot single-family homes was balanced with the increase in town-homes and apartments. Growth management policies, particularly those founded on Smart Growth principles, are explicitly designed to change the character and mix of the housing stock. Their intention is to shift housing development to higher density uses, more multifamily units, and into more traditionally urban forms.

## D. Regulation and Housing Quality

The change in housing mix, whether intended or accidental, represents an effective increase in the cost of housing. As a general analytical principle, economists examine housing prices for *equivalent units*. In other words, economists believe that changes in housing prices must reflect the same quality and type of housing—price changes for single-family homes should be compared to single-family homes of the same size and quality. In Portland, the price of single-family homes with private yards increased while the price for apartments and townhouses moderated as more units were built. This still represents an effective price increase because families are limited to buying a less desirable home and paying more for it.

Smart Growth advocates, or course, argue that high densities, smaller lots, and more urban development patterns create benefits that offset these other features of traditional housing. They also argue that other public policy goals justify limiting housing options. For example, a common Smart Growth goal is to revitalize central cities, even if it means limiting housing development and growth in suburban and rural areas. An analysis of 144 central cities found that those regions that had strong growth management laws that restricted development in suburban and rural areas experienced faster rates of growth and captured a larger share of residential and commercial development than those that were less restrictive (Nelson, Burby, Feser, Dwakins, Malizia, and Quercia, 2004). Another analysis of central city and suburban residential development in 452 urbanized areas in the United States found that regions with more dominant central cities had lower home prices and fewer homes in upper income tiers of the housing market (Wassmer and Baass, 2006). These studies, however, do not contradict the main point—growth controls and development regulations change the character and mix of the housing market. Paying the same or more for a less desirable product is still an effective price increase.

### 3. Development Regulation and Consumer Preferences

Of course, this begs the question, are growth controls or growth management policies distorting market supply and creating a larger and larger mismatch between supply and demand? This is a critical question for growth management advocates, particularly those that believe urban sprawl—low-density residential and commercial development—has detracted from the quality of urban life.

At first glance, critics of urban sprawl seem to have a point. When the actual behavior and purchasing patterns of households are examined, families seem to be buying homes on smaller lots. Lot sizes, for example, have fallen 10 percent since the mid- 1990s (Staley, 2001b), though this could be the result of higher land prices caused, in part, by growth restrictions. Meanwhile, the size of the average house has increased dramatically, rising from just 1,600 square feet in 1980 to 2,300 square feet in 2004 (see Figure 2.1). People seem to want bigger homes on smaller lots. Moreover, densities in suburban areas have increased dramatically as suburban communities have increasingly taken on an urban character (Staley, 1993; Kotkin, 2006).

**Figure 2.1**
**Size of New Single Family Homes Completed: 1991-2005.**

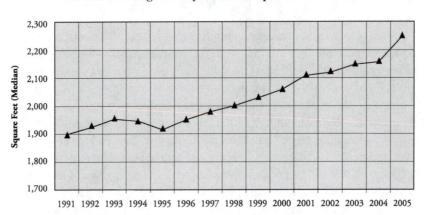

*A. Housing Is a "Bundle" of Many Different Characteristics*

Economists and housing policy analysts take a much more sophisticated approach to looking at consumer demand. Housing is not a mono-
lithic product. Homebuyers are looking for all sorts of specific features
that meet their household needs, including overall size, number of bathrooms, space for a home office, outdoor space large enough for a garden
or playground equipment, suitably sized kitchen, garage workspaces, air
conditioning, central heating, and other characteristics. Teasing out the
importance of each one of these factors in the decision to buy a house
is difficult. Homebuyers often look at dozens of homes before finally
deciding which one deserves making an offer, and each home has a
unique "bundle" of attributes that force homeowners to make trade-offs
about the relative importance of different characteristics of a home. Even
buyers of custom homes need to make trade-offs about materials, room
sizes, and other house features based on their budget.

The point, of course, is that housing choice is more than about choosing
a home with a quarter-acre lot or a half-acre lot, a two-story townhouse
or a one-floor ranch house. New homes come with dozens, sometimes
hundreds, of potential floor plans and designs, geared toward satisfying
every potential desire of the future homeowner. Moreover, the choice is
dynamic, depending on family life cycles.

Nevertheless, statistical techniques exist that allow analysts to determine which features of a home are valued more than others in the

real estate market based on what people really buy. More specifically, "hedonic" estimating techniques (see Green and Malpezzi, 2003, 41–50) can evaluate how various features are valued in the housing market. Rather than measure the value of a home as a single unit, the hedonic approach examines the characteristics of an individual home—the bundle of attributes that add to or subtract from its value. By looking at enough homes and sales prices, hedonic analysis can "de-bundle" the different characteristics of a house. This is useful for planners and policymakers because hedonic analysis permits theories about household housing preferences to be compared to the reality of "revealed preferences" in the actual purchases in the housing market.

A revealing application of this technique was done for the National Association of Realtors by Stacy Sirmans and David MacPherson. Focusing on 28,000 home sales in the Philadelphia metropolitan area, they were able to tease out which factors were more valuable to homebuyers (Table 2.1). The sample did not distinguish between new homes and existing homes, so their results are a good indicator of how different features are "capitalized" into the value of homes in the general real estate market. Unfortunately, their research on home characteristics did not include the size of the lot, but other research has shown that, all things equal, homes with larger lots or access to open space are valued more highly than those with less (Staley, Edgens, and Mildner, 1999).

Their results are consistent with trends showing real estate markets are responding to consumer preferences for bigger and more versatile homes. Each additional bathroom, for example, adds 24 percent to the price of a home. Even adding a half bath (not bathtub or shower) can add 15 percent to the value of a home. Other features that add significantly to the value (and size) of a home include a garage, basement, high ceilings, and bedrooms. Interestingly, proximity to a golf course (open space) factors prominently into the value of a home as well.

Notably, a professional office and an "in-law" suite reduce a home's value. While Sirmans and MacPherson do not speculate on why, the negative result is important. Given the rapid increase in telecommuting, intuition suggests that a professional office would be an asset to a new home. Yet, a dedicated room for office space may, in fact, be less desirable because it might commit a household to a particular use for that space. An extra bedroom, in contrast, has a wider number of potential uses that could be adapted to the changing needs of a family—home office, nursery, spare bedroom, or a playroom; it can be tailored or customized easily to the needs of a prospective family.

Table 2.1
Factors Influencing the Price of New Housing

| Added Characteristic | Added Value to Housing Price |
|---|---|
| Full bathroom | 24% |
| Partial bathroom | 15% |
| Garage | 13% |
| Central Air Conditioning | 12% |
| Fireplace | 12% |
| Basement | 9% |
| Close to golf course | 8% |
| Higher ceilings (9 ft.) | 6% |
| Additional bedroom | 4% |
| 1,000 sq feet added living space | 3% |
| Laundry | 2% |
| In ground swimming pool | 0% |
| In-Law Suite | -5.2% |
| Professional Office | -5.0% |

Source: G. Stacy Sirmans and David A. Macpherson, "The Value of Housing Characteristics," Research Brief, National Association of Realtors, December 2003.

From the perspective of planners, the negative impact of the in-law suite is more problematic. Planners have often recommended allowing "granny flats" as a way to defray housing costs by renting them to non-household members and increase the stock of affordable (small) housing. Yet, clearly, this feature comes with liabilities for most homebuyers.

### B. Meeting Consumer Preferences for Housing

Policies that attempt to shift production toward smaller, more compact housing units clearly work against the desires of most homebuyers (at least in this market). These results, which are consistent with other studies, should send a cautionary signal to planners, elected officials, and planning board members eager to embrace the view that older and smaller households are less interested in traditional homes and desire more urban, more compact homes. Little evidence of this as a general trend exists in the housing market, although certain niches may be developing for a highly segmented portion of the real estate market.

## 4. The Black Box of Growth Management

On the one hand, the problem of land use planning and housing may appear to be a technical one—using more and better refined data, planners and analysts should be able to calibrate housing goals and plans to match supply and demand. Reality, however, is much more complicated, and understanding this complexity is crucial for understanding why land use regulation negatively impacts the housing market in many communities. Taking a few minutes to go inside the "black box" of growth management and urban planning policy may help demonstrate how current practice creates the lags and market mismatches that inevitably raise prices and restrict housing choice. Chief among the observations that drive these outcomes is the recognition that growth management policies are not static. They can change because they are part of a politically driven legislative process. Even if they were consistent, the decisions do not apply to one point in time, but affect long-term investment decisions in the private investment and builder market.

## A. Central Planning Reborn: Smart Growth and the Community "Vision"

Modern planning is truly the progeny of its progressive predecessors. In fact, these progressive attributes have been reinforced by the current Smart Growth movement which emphasizes more land market regulation as a way for communities to "take control" of their future (Staley, 2004b). The comprehensive planning process begins with a "vision" that outlines what the "community" believes it should "look" like in 20, 30, or 50 years. Typically, the vision is sufficiently vague—"we" will be a "vibrant," "mixed use," economically "diverse," and a "tolerant" community—that setting goals and objectives is fairly loose.

Good planning, however, requires setting specific goals and objectives, and this often translates into specific plans for housing and certain areas of the city. So, the planning process might develop a detailed plan for a downtown that includes an entertainment complex or government center. Plans have also included objectives that limit so-called "big box" retailers like Home Depot, Circuit City, Best Buy, or Wal-Mart because the community planning process resulted in a vision that includes boutique retailers (even though they are higher cost and serve a narrow wealthy segment of most communities). The Comprehensive Plan will identify zones of the city that should be developed for commercial or industrial uses as well as areas set aside for residential development. In the context of housing, goals and objectives might include statements that the downtown should include and encourage apartments and townhomes, or allowing residential uses over commercial and retail uses on the first floor of buildings. In cities such as Portland, plans have called for transforming single-family residential neighborhoods into high-density transit-friendly city blocks.

Once these goals and objectives have been established, a comprehensive land use plan is adopted that specifies what kinds of uses will be allowed based on the designated districts and outlines the general criteria for what types of buildings are allowed in what zone. So, a residential zone might allow homes on quarter acre lots and with a height limit of 30 feet (three stories), but exclude apartments, duplexes, or commercial uses. Typically, a zoning map is also adopted that has detailed (and color coded) descriptions of permitted land uses for each parcel in the community. In short, the land market is centrally planned.

With the exception of particularly aggressive cities such as Portland, Oregon, most cities "grandfather" existing uses and rarely require a change in the character of neighborhoods. (That would be politically unpopular; it's easier to plan future residents than current ones.) Planning in practice applies to incremental adjustments in the land market—future development. The process also presumes that deviations from the plan will have a negative impact on the community, requiring specific approval from the city council for any change. In some states, such as California, land use changes can only be approved under very strict conditions and at certain times of the year.

Contemporary urban planning, then, effectively "collectivizes" the land market, a process begun with the adoption of zoning, by making decisions about use subject to legislative control and, in most circumstances, majority rule. This system can be characterized by four basic features (Staley, 2004b):

- *Closed systems and hierarchies* where land use and decisions are determined based on local political conditions and without direct explicit acknowledgement or information about changes or unfolding conditions in the market place;
- *End-state planning* where long-term visions of the community, as described in a vision statement in a comprehensive land-use plan, guide decisions about what kind of housing will be built when and where, subject to political control and the short-term interests of existing residents;
- *Assumption of complete knowledge* about the relevant market and housing conditions for implementing the plan, sometimes explicitly excluding economic conditions and embracing political criteria as the only relevant information for determining land use;
- *Political optimization* with a presumption that an open political process will generate all the relevant information necessary to make efficient and viable decisions about the future growth of the community.

## B. The Real World of Urban Planning

Of course, in the real world, the planning process is much less precise, accurate, and effective (Staley and Claeys, 2005). Ventura County, California, for example, has been engaged in aggressive Smart Growth planning for more than 30 years. Despite calls for higher residential densities and accommodating more housing production in its comprehensive plan, planning decisions have favored low-density patterns. Examining more than 12,000 housing units in 120 projects in ten cities, William Fulton and his colleagues (2001) found that approved densities were often 20 percent below zoned capacities and 45 percent below the plan's stated capacity. Attempts to approve higher densities couldn't be sustained because the general public failed to support higher density proposed despite the explicit (and presumably agreed upon) goals of the comprehensive plan (Fulton et al., 2003). Unfortunately, this kind of inconsistency is inevitable in a planning process that is rooted in an open, democratic, legislative approval process.

Indeed, in a neglected branch of research on the economics of zoning decisions on the local level, economists John McDonald and Daniel McMillen (1991) found that local communities used the political process to, in effect, "pick and choose" the land uses the majority decided were beneficial. They were using data from the Chicago metropolitan area and analyzed 260 ten-acre traces in suburban areas. "Our results suggest that these communities allow the desirable single-family residential land use to follow the market somewhat, but they actively interfere with the market for other uses" (McDonald and McMillen, 1991: 57). These results were also consistent with their previous investigations and studies (McMillen and McDonald, 1989; McMillen and McDonald, 1991b). Moreover, the use of the political process to choose "desirable uses" is not restricted to residential development. Asabere and Huffman (1991) found that zoning for industrial uses reduced land values, but zoning was slow to adjust to changing market conditions to restore balance in the land market.

Of course, proponents of Smart Growth and activist urban planning have used these studies and others demonstrating the bias for using zoning to exclude "undesirable" uses to justify intervention in favor of commercial and multifamily residential uses. But, little evidence suggests that the planning is more capable of restoring equilibrium or balance in the real estate market. In part, this is because the development approval process is slow and deliberate, befitting a democratic process rooted in constitutional limits (Staley, 2001c). But, this also reflects the dominance of alternative ideology of planning that favors a specific urban form that runs contrary to established preferences for low-density residential land development. The result, in both cases, is a politically driven imbalance in the real-estate market that dramatically increases transactions costs associated with housing development, reducing long-run production and supply while also exaggerating existing imbalances within particular housing market segments (e.g., too many apartments and too few single-family homes).

## 5. Conclusion

On a pure theoretical level, growth management does not have to reduce housing affordability. In principle, a land use planning system could be devised that focuses on minimizing the negative impacts of land development on neighbors and the environment while also minimizing the transaction costs associated with the approval process (Staley and Claeys, 2005). These policies would have to facilitate a better matching of housing characteristics with the preferences of consumers while also minimizing spillover costs imposed on neighbors and the communities from poorly regulated development. Thus, in principle, housing prices would be more aligned with market demand and housing prices would reflect the true costs of providing different types of homes so that consumers could make more informed tradeoffs about quality given the income they are willing to devote to housing. While these adjustments in the market could reduce affordability, this result is not inevitable (particularly if these policies lowered transaction costs and allowed spillover impacts to be mitigated).

Unfortunately, in the real world of planning, this outcome is unlikely. As Robert Lang (2004: 167) recently observed: "On a purely technical and mechanical level, growth management strategies can be devised that should have little impact on house prices. But in practice, growth management generally affects house prices." In reality, land-use planning and development regulations negatively impact the housing market, reducing supplies overall, creating mismatches between supply and demand for specific types of housing, and increasing the costs of building in heavily planned cities. Planners, no matter how well educated, simply don't have the data necessary to make the finely tuned decisions that lead to these market efficiencies. In many cases, the data is literally unknowable because consumers alter their housing preferences (and expectations) based on the actual opportunities presented to them by entrepreneurs in the housing market. Planning, particularly legislatively driven planning, is inherently limited in its ability to anticipate or accurately assess these preferences. Moreover, many regional planners aren't interested in these market efficiencies anyway since they believe that market preferences for certain types of housing (e.g., low-density residential housing) should be limited or even curtailed altogether.

The attempt by many supporters of development regulation to separate growth "management" from growth "control" is a theoretical fiction. Contemporary growth management includes a variety of strategies for achieving an ideal vision of what an urban area should look like and how it should function. Communities will use the tools that are available to them. Some of these tools, such as growth moratoria and permit caps, are notable for their transparency and explicit attempts to directly manipulate the housing market. Other growth management strategies, however, have pervasive impacts on the supply and type of housing provided in communities although their intent and impacts may not be as transparent. Inclusionary zoning is one example, but growth management strategies that direct certain types of development to specific places to create town centers, entertainment districts, transit-oriented developments, or even large lot housing subdivisions have measurable and palpable impacts on housing supply, housing quality, and housing affordability. The effects are real, even if they are more subtle and less obvious to the casual observer.

## Note

1.    Interview with planning consultants to Sugar Creek Township in Greene County, Ohio by the author.

## References

Asabere, Paul K. and Forrest E. Huffman. 1991. "Zoning and Industrial Land Values: The Case of Philadelphia," *AREUEA Journal,* Vol. 19, No. 2: 154–160.

Beal, Mary. 2004. "A Comparison of Land Use Regulation Between Leon and Wakulla Counties," Policy Brief Issue #12, DeVoe L. Moore Center, College of Social Sciences, Florida State University, July.

Carlson, Daniel and Shishir Mathur. 2004. "Does Growth Management Aid or Thwart the Provision of Affordable Housing?" in *Growth Management and Affordable Housing: Do They Conflict?* ed. Anthony Downs, pp. 20–66. (Washington, D.C.: Brookings Institution).

Claeys, Eric. R. 2004. *Euclid* Lives? The Uneasy Legacy of Progressivism and Zoning," *Fordham Law Review* Vol. 73, No. 2 (November): 731–770.

Clingermayer, James. 1993. "Distributional Politics, War Representation, and the Spread of Zoning," *Public Choice* Vol. 77, No. 4: 725–738.

Fischel, William A. 1985. *The Economics of Zoning Laws: A Property Rights Approach to American Land Use Controls* (Baltimore, Maryland: Johns Hopkins University Press).

Fischel, William A. 2004. "Comment on 'The Link Between Growth Management and Housing Affordability: The Academic Evidence,'" in *Growth Management and Housing Affordability: Do They Conflict?* ed. Anthony Downs, pp. 158–167 (Washington, D.C.: Brookings Institution).

Fulton, William. 1999. *Guide to California Planning,* 2nd ed. (Point Arena, California: Solano Press).

Fulton, William, Chris Williamson, Kathleen Mallory and Jeff Jones. 2001. "Smart Growth in Action: Housing Capacity and Development in Ventura, County," Policy Study No. 288 (Los Angeles: Reason Foundation, December), http://www.reason.org/ps288.pdf.

Fulton, William, Susan Weaver, Geoffrey Segal, and Lily Okamura. 2003. "Smart Growth in Action, Part 2: Case Studies in Housing Capacity and Development From Ventura County, California," Policy Study No. 311 (Los Angeles: Reason Foundation, May), http://www.reason.org/ps311.pdf.

Glaeser, Edward L. and Joseph Gyourko. 2002. "The Impact of Zoning on Housing Affordablity," *NBER Working Paper 8835* (Cambridge, MA: Harvard Institute of Economic Research, March).

Green, Richard K. and Stephen Malpezzi. 2003. *A Primer on U.S. Housing Markets and Policy* (Washington, D.C.: Urban Institute Press.

Holcombe, Randall G. and Samuel R. Staley, eds. 2001. *Smarter Growth: Market-Based Strategies for Land-Use Planning in the 21st Century* (Westport, CT: Greenwood Press).

Jud, Donald G. and Daniel T. Winkler. 2002. "The Dynamics of Metropolitan Housing Prices," *Journal of Real Estate Research* vol. nos. 1/2: 29–45.

Kahn, Matthew. 2001. "Does Sprawl Reduce the Black/White Housing Consumption Gap?" *Housing Policy Debate,* vol. 12, no 3: 77–86.

Land, Robert. 2004. "Comment on 'The Link Between Growth Management and Housing Affordability: The Academic Evidence,'" in *Growth Management and Housing Affordability: Do They Conflict?* ed. Anthony Downs, pp. 167–170 (Washington, D.C.: Brookings Institution).

Levy, John M. 2000. *Contemporary Urban Planning,* 5th ed. (Upper Saddle Rivers, NJ: Prentice Hall).

Mayer, Christopher J. and C. Tsuriel Somerville. 2000. "Land Use Regulation and New Construction," *Regional Science and Urban Economics,* Vol. 30 (2000): 639–662.

McMillen, Daniel P. and John F. McDonald. 1989. "Selectivity Bias in Urban Land Value Functions," Land Economics, Vol. 65: 341–351.

McMillen, Daniel P. and John F. McDonald. 1991a. "A Simultaneous Equatoisn Model of Zoning and Land Values," *Regional Science and Urban Economics* Vol. 21: 55–72.

McMillen, Daniel P. and John F. McDonald. 1991b. "Urban Land Value Functions With Endogenous Zoning," *Journal of Urban Economics* Vol. 29: 14–27.

Nelson, Arthur C., Raymond J. Burby, Edward Feser, et al. 2004. "Urban Containment and Central-City Revitalization," *Journal of the American Planning Association,* Vol. 70, No. 4 (Autumn): 411–425.

Nelson, Arthur C., Rolf Pendall, Casey J. Dawkins, and Gerrit J. Knaap. 2004. "The Link Between Growth Management and Housing Affordability: The Academic Evidence," in *Growth Management and Housing Affordability: Do They Conflict?* ed. Anthony Downs, pp. 117–158 (Washington, D.C.: Brookings Institution).

Nelson, Robert H. 1977. *Zoning and Property Rights: An Analysis of the American System of Land Use regulation* (Cambridge, MA: MIT Press).

O'Toole, Randal. 2006. *The Planning Penalty,* American Dream Coalition, March.

Porter, Douglass R. 2004. "The Promise and Practice of Inclusionary Zoning," in *Growth Management and Housing Affordability: Do They Conflict?* ed. Anthony Downs, pp. 212–248 (Washington, D.C.: Brookings Institution).

Powell, Benjamin and Edward Stringham. 2004a. "Housing Supply and Affordability: Do Affordable Housing Mandates Work?" *Policy Study No. 318* (Los Angeles: Reason Foundation, April), www.rppi.org/ps318.pdf.

Powell, Benjamin and Edward Stringham. 2004b. "Do Affordable Housing Mandates Work? Evidence from Los Angeles County and Orange County," *Policy Study No. 320* (Los Angeles: Reason Foundation, June), www.rppi.org/ps320.pdf.

Pozdena, Randall J. 2002. *Smart Growth and Its Effects on Housing Markets: The Risks of Portlandization,* QuantEcon, Inc., September.

Saks, Raven E. 2005. Job Creation and Housing Construction: Constraints on Metropolitan Area Employment Growth, *Finance and Economics Discussion Series,* Federal Reserve Board, Washington, D.C.

Staley, Samuel R. 1997a. "Growth Controls: An Overview of Their Impacts on Housing Values," Reason Foundation, Los Angeles, June, http://www.urbanfutures.org/r6897d.html.

Staley, Samuel R. 1997b. "Regulatory Impacts of Planning on Economic Development: An Overview," Reason Foundation, Los Angeles, June, http://www.urbanfutures.org/r6897c.html.

Staley, Samuel R. 2001a. Ballot Box Zoning, Transaction Costs and Urban Growth, *Journal of the American Planning Association,* vol. 67, no. 1 (Winter): 25–37.

Staley, Samuel R. 2001b. "On Overview of U.S. Urbanization and Land-Use Trends," in *Smarter Growth: Market-Based Strategies for Land-Use Planning in the 21st Century,* pp. 13–26. (Westport, CT: Greenwood Press).

Staley, Samuel R. 2001c. "Markets, Smart Growth, and the Limits of Policy," in *Smarter Growth: Market-Based Strategies for Land-Use Planning in the 21st Century,* pp. 201–217 (Westport, CT: Greenwood Press).

Staley, Samuel R. 2002. "Zoning, Smart Growth, and Regulatory Taxation," in *Politics, Taxation, and the Rule of Law: The Power to Tax in Constitutional Perspective,* ed. Donald P. Racheter and Richard E. Wagner, pp. 203–224 (Boston: Kluwer Academic Publishers).

Staley, Samuel R. 2004a. "Comment on 'Does Growth Management Aid or Thwart the Provision of Affordable Housing?'" in *Growth Management and Affordable Housing: Do They Conflict?,* ed. Anthony Downs, pp. 69–80 (Washington, D.C.: Brookings Institution).

Staley, Samuel R. 2004b. "Urban Planning, Smart Growth, and Economic Calculation: An Austrian Critique and Extension," *Review of Austrian Economics,* vol. 17, nos. 2/3: 265–283.

Staley, Samuel R. and Eric R. Claeys. 2005. "Is the Future of Development Regulation Based in the Past? Toward a Market-Oriented, Innovation Friendly Framework," *Journal of Urban Planning and Development,* vol. 131, no. 4 (December): 202–213.

Staley, Samuel R., Jefferson Edgens, and Gerard C.S. Mildner, 1999. *A Line in the Land: Urban Growth Boundaries, Smart Growth, and Housing Affordability,* Policy Study No. 263 (Los Angeles: Reason Foundation, November), http://www.reason.org/ps263.html.

Staley, Samuel R. and Leonard Gilroy. 2001. *Smart Growth and Housing Affordability: Lessons from Statewide Planning Laws,* Policy Study No. 287 (Los Angeles: Reason Foundation), www.rppi.org/ps287.pdf.

Staley, Samuel R. and Gerard C.S. Mildner. 2000. "The Price of Managing Growth," *Urban Land* (February): 18–23.

Steel, Brent S. and Nicholas P. Lovrich. 2000. Growth Management Policy and County Government: Correlates of Policy Adoption Across the United States, *State and local Government Review* Vol. 32, No. 1 (Winter): 7–19.

Wassmer, Robert W. and Michell C. Bass. 2006. Does A More Centralized Urban Form Raise Housing Prices? *Journal of Policy Analysis and Management* Vol. 25, No. 2: 439–462.

# 3

# The Benefits of Nonzoning

*Bernard H. Siegan[1]*

A major purpose for the establishment of zoning was to protect the exclusivity of single-family development. Supporters of zoning contended that single-family developments were frequently invaded by adverse and incompatible uses that were destructive to homeownership. The 6 to 3 U.S. Supreme Court decision in *Euclid v. Ambler* (1926), which ruled that zoning was a constitutionally valid limitation on the exercise of property rights,[2] was authored by Justice George Sutherland, who is usually identified as a staunch conservative. Apparently he set aside his ideological propensities because he was persuaded that zoning was required to preserve the integrity of homeownership. Very often, he wrote, "the apartment house is a mere parasite, constructed in order to take advantage of the open spaces and attractive surroundings created by the residential character of the district."[3]

The *Euclid* decision was strongly supported in the planning community. The protection of single-family exclusivity was a prime concern until the arrival in recent years of smart growth. In the belief that it greatly contributed to urban sprawl, urban planners attacked the protection and exclusivity accorded homeownership. Sutherland's parasites were now welcome in residential areas. To this extent, the security of homeownership and investment were left to the marketplace. However, while zoning was exclusionary, smart growth went further and virtually sanctified exclusion, a practice that in our diverse society is morally and legally offensive and economically unwise. To curb sprawl, smart growth walls cities by imposing urban growth boundaries and extinguishing, for many, personal choice in residence outside these boundaries. The cure is worse than the disease.

There is little that is scientific about urban planning. It is a discipline that is responsive to the predilections and propensities of its practitioners.

In the many years I practiced law in Chicago, I never had difficulty hiring a land planner who supported a client's proposed development, nor was I aware of any other lawyer who encountered this problem. This option was also available to government officials for they too readily found approval in the planning community for their rules and regulations. Inasmuch as each side in a zoning dispute can almost always obtain support in the planning community, it is hard to conclude that any particular plan is the product of "sound planning."

Smart growth is a plan that has attracted considerable national support. However, its permanence and longevity are uncertain. Law professors Ellickson and Been explain that schools of planning theory "have tended to rise and ebb within a period of no more than a decade or so." In the period from 1890 to 1989, it was possible to identify a number of periods in the history of planning, including The City Beautiful (1901–1915), The City Functional (1916–1939), The City Renewable (1937–1964) and The City Enterprising (1980–1989).[4] Although its success in changing land use patterns is doubtful, smart growth ideas have altered substantially the thinking of urban planners (Siegan, 2001a).

Contemporary land use experience illustrates the limited durability of land use planning. Until smart growth arrived, land use planners and regulators accorded single-family development the highest priority of any land use. In the *Euclid* case, the U.S. Supreme Court described the many harms that result from mixing single- and multiple-family housing, a position planners and regulators have long observed and which the smart growth advocates now decry.

To be sure, plans must change when they are no longer effective or become counterproductive. But comprehensive urban planning is not required for the viability of cities and towns or the pursuit of happiness by their residents. Substantially reducing or eliminating most zoning controls will not only eliminate its evils, but will achieve the important benefits for society that world experience shows inevitably accompany free markets, such as low prices, more production, competition and innovation. Indeed, the exclusionary controls accompanying land use regulation are repugnant to a free market. The former limit production and supply while the latter expands both.

The political processes in our cities and towns control the operation of land use regulation, a process inherently limited even in achieving public safeguards. Regrettably, some of our Supreme Court justices do not understand the limitation on local decision-making imposed by the local electorate. Consider for example this statement of Justice John Paul Stevens as part of his dissenting opinion in *Dolan v. Tigard:*

> In our changing world one thing is certain: uncertainty will characterize predictions about the impact of new urban developments on the risks of floods, earthquakes, traffic congestion, or environmental harms. When there is doubt concerning the magnitude of those impacts, the public intent in averting them must outweigh the private interest of the commercial entrepreneurs.[5]

To understand the error of such thinking with respect to earthquakes, for example, it is necessary to acknowledge that a city usually has the power to require construction standards that will make certain that all structures erected in the locality are able to withstand a major earthquake. Nevertheless, it is highly unlikely that it will enact such requirements because of the huge expense of complying with such mandates, which housing and commercial consumers will ultimately have to pay. Accordingly, the standard will have to be reduced to some lower level that will serve economic considerations at the expense of total safety. In the absence of earthquake protections, a private developer in an earthquake-prone area will have to satisfy both a mortgagor and an insurance company that it has provided substantial protections safeguarding the structure and its occupants from earthquake damage. It is doubtful that local government building controls will be more protective against earthquake damage than the private developer.

Houston is located in Harris County, the unincorporated section of which has never adopted a zoning ordinance or a conventional building code governing the construction and structure of improved real estate. The county's building ordinances control only flooding, drainage, and plotting of property proposed for development. The population of the unincorporated area is in excess of one million people. It is the site of many homes, and some high-rises 10 to 15 stories in height. Despite the absence of structural regulations, buildings in the unincorporated area are likely to be as soundly constructed and safe as those in Houston, which has adopted a conventional building code.[6] It is in the interest of private developers in the unincorporated sections that the structures they erect are soundly constructed because otherwise lenders will not provide financing. Savings and loan associations and other lenders approve the specification of the buildings on which they lend money or require builders to hire engineers to certify structural safety. They do not want their mortgage investment of twenty-five or more years to be jeopardized. Fire insurance companies refuse to cover firetraps, and the electric utility may refuse to extend service if it perceives a hazardous situation. Many portions of buildings come pre-assembled, and because they are mass-produced have to accommodate the bulk of builders and lenders who seek safe products. Moreover, manufacturers may be legally liable for hazards they create. Builders are no more careless about human life other than any other group. The vast number of people act with due consideration for the safety and well being of others. Furthermore, those in business who develop a bad reputation either among workers or customers are not likely to stay around very long.

Nonetheless, one might contend that building codes impose a level of safety not attainable in the private market. The problem is that this "safety" has come at great cost. Building codes are among the most abused regulations in the country. After an exhaustive study, a Presidential Commission, in a report published in 1968 (U.S. National Commission on Urban Problems, 1968: 266), concluded that "alarms sounded over the past years about the building code situation have been justified. If anything, the case has been understated. The situation calls for a drastic overhaul, both technically and intergovernmentally." The codes have required construction and installations far beyond the needs of safety. The municipalities start with the model codes and frequently add substantial numbers of extras. Building is consequently much more expensive than it should be.

Obviously, Justice Stevens is correct about the unpredictability of the future, but his confidence in government regulation is not warranted. Consider in this respect the zoning experience of New York City:

> The draftsmen of the 1916 zoning code of New York City began their work in 1913 and it lasted without substantial revision until 1939. Like all zoning plans it was drawn in the light of technology generally available some years earlier and it was addressed to problems set in motion decades or centuries earlier and then apparent. The decent motives of those draftsmen and their competence are unquestioned but their forward vision has to be small. Their image of the ideal city was heavily tinted by their memories of a more bucolic and less populous city of their youth. They were constrained to project the future as a virtually straight-line extension of the past. They simply could not (nor could anybody else) anticipate and plan for the tumultuous events of the next 23 years; United States entry into World War I, the virtual cessation of immigration after 1924, the Great Depression, the ubiquitous and ferocious automobile, air conditioning, the supermarket, penicillin (Mandel, 1971: 58–59).

## 1. Voting on Land Use Controls

The existence of zoning in almost all localities does not necessarily mean that it is fulfilling the wishes of the majority of people living there. Comprehensive zoning ordinances are adopted by local legislators usually without vote of the local residents. Only one major city, Houston, has voted on whether or not to adopt zoning. This city has the greatest population of any in the southwest United States and the fourth largest in the nation. In 1993, the voters of Houston rejected for the third time in its history the adoption of a zoning ordinance, leaving Houston as the only major city in the nation without zoning. The city had previously voted on the issue in 1948 and 1962. In 1948, only property owners were allowed to vote and the proposed zoning ordinance was defeated by a vote of 14,142 to 6,555.

The breakdown of the votes on zoning in 1993 and 1962 reveals a stark division based on socioeconomic factors. Less affluent persons vote against zoning while more affluent voters support it. The 1993 voting patterns were similar to those in 1962, except that unlike the prior vote, the most affluent group voted against zoning. The proposed 1962 zoning ordinance lost 57 percent to 43 percent; while the 1993 vote lost by 52 percent to 47 percent. Breakdowns according to socioeconomic groups, made by the Houston Post for each zoning vote, are shown in Tables 3.1 and 3.2.

Other, smaller municipalities in the nation have voted on adopting zoning, and, in many instances, the vote has gone against it. The socioeconomic breakdowns appear similar to Houston's (Siegan, 1976: 54–56). Whether the absence of zoning in Houston is desirable or not is controversial, of course. The judgment of the majority of people living there—probably as expert as anyone else on the subject—is favorable to the existing free-market system.

Although their properties generally were subject to restrictive covenants enforced by the city prohibiting incompatible or diverse uses within their subdivisions, middle-income property owners in Houston voted to obtain the further protection of zoning. As is evident from their high voting turnout, these owners were largely responsible for the city's

**Table 3.1**
**Houston's 1993 Vote on Zoning**

| Group | Turnout | For | Against |
| --- | --- | --- | --- |
| Low-income Black | 11.59% | 29.21% | 70.79% |
| Middle-income Black | 23.16% | 62.55% | 37.45% |
| Predominantly Hispanic | 13.72% | 41.05% | 58.95% |
| Low-Mid-income White | 17.63% | 31.82% | 68.18% |
| Middle-income White | 28.96% | 56.20% | 43.80% |
| Affluent | 34.52% | 43.83% | 56.17% |

**Table 3.2**
**Houston's 1962 Vote on Zoning**

| Area | Av. Annual Income | Owner-Occupied Housing | Turnout | For | Against |
|------|-------------------|------------------------|---------|-----|---------|
| Lindale, Melrose | $7200-$9700 | 52–55 | 43.1% | 15.7% | 84.3% |
| Little York, York | 8200-10000 | 61–62 | 49.3 | 17.3 | 82.7 |
| Magnolia Park | 6700-6900 | 44–47 | 30.7 | 20.2 | 79.8 |
| Heights | 7500-9000 | 47–60 | 42.3 | 23.5 | 76.5 |
| Negro | 6600-12000 | 42–80 | 28.3 | 27.7 | 72.3 |
| Park Place Pecan Place | 12300 | 75 | 51.9 | 38.0 | 62.0 |
| Mason Park Kensington | 9000 | 55–68 | 51.2 | 38.5 | 61.5 |
| Garden Oaks Oak Forest | 11300-12300 | 62–86 | 55.7 | 41.3 | 58.7 |
| Freeway Manor | 11300-12900 | 63–95 | 47.0 | 43.8 | 56.2 |
| Southland Hermann Park | 9300-16500 | 94–129 | 50.7 | 53.3 | 46.7 |
| Westheimer Post Oaks | 13800-25000+ | 78–132 | 63.3 | 58.1 | 41.9 |
| River Oaks Tanglewood | 25000+ | 107–132 | 60.5 | 58.9 | 41.1 |
| Memorial Spring Branch | 11700-25000+ | 85–171 | 59.8 | 60.7 | 39.3 |
| Westbury | 18300-22600 | 115–134 | 64.5 | 65.0 | 35.0 |
| Sharpstown | 15600-16600 | 123–124 | 65.3 | 68.3 | 31.7 |

efforts to adopt zoning. The view from the low-income areas that were not subject to covenants was entirely different. On each occasion, their voting turnout was relatively low, an event that is not unusual in elections in the poorer areas.

Socioeconomic factors have also generally been decisive in other land use elections. A breakdown of the 1972 vote on the California Coastal Zone Initiative in the city of San Diego reveals its supporters and opponents. (This initiative created the California Coastal Commission and gave it authority to control development of the California coast.) Contrary to what seems to be a widely held assumption, most opponents were in the lower income brackets, supposedly those most desirous or of coastal preservation. The most fervent supporters were students and wealthy people.

Table 3.3 is a breakdown showing median household income and votes on Proposition 20 (the Coastal Zone Conservation Initiative) and on two subsequent local propositions (A and C), both of which related to San Diego city's growth, and will be discussed subsequently. These results reveal that the Houston vote on zoning was not a unique experience: it seems the rich and poor have divergent views on land use regulation.

**Table 3.3**
**Breakdown of Vote Results on California Coastal Zone Conservation Initiative
and Two Subsequent Local Initiatives in San Diego**

| Selected Areas | 1970 Median Income | Yes on Prop 20 (1972) | Yes on Prop A (1985) | No on Prop C (1994) |
|---|---|---|---|---|
| San Diego City | 10,166 | 54% | 56% | 54% |
| *Student Areas* | | | | |
| Ocean Beach #500 | | 81 | 74 | 64 |
| #691 | | 84 | 74 | 68 |
| Mission Bay #000 | | 77 | | |
| #021 | | 79 | 72 | 64 |
| UCSD #000 | | 93 | 89 | 58 |
| #004 | | 94 | 63 | 61 |
| San Diego State #150 | | 89 | 171 | 84 |
| *High Income* | | | | |
| La Jolla | 19,249 | 57–81 | 54–77 | 57–73 |
| Mission Hills | 15,328 | 58–59 | 60–71 | 58–60 |
| University City | 14,979 | 57–63 | 63–68 | 56–61 |
| *White Blue Collar* | | | | |
| Encanto | 8,370 | 49 | 51 | 44 |
| Normal Heights | 7,568 | 46 | 54 | 49 |
| Paradise Hills | 9,204 | 46–48 | 41–52 | 46–49 |
| Nestor | 8,710 | 42–46 | 39–49 | 46–51 |
| South Park | 9,244 | 42–44 | | |
| *Mexican American* | | | | |
| Barrio Logan #150 | 6,495 | 39 | 37 | 38 |
| #500 | 6,255 | 39 | 49 | 36 |
| #521 | 6,859 | 46 | 40 | 39 |
| #570 | 5,859 | 38 | 40 | 34 |
| Otay Mesa #020 | 7,367 | 48 | 50 | 36 |
| San Ysidro #530 | 46 | 55 | 38 | |
| #500 | 7,367 | 48 | | |
| Centre City #200 | 7,150 | 49 | 49 | 37 |
| SE San Diego E #130 | 6,720 | 42 | | |
| SE San Diego W #500 | 6,073 | 39 | 36 | |
| SE San Diego W #510 | 7,029 | 50+ | | |
| SE San Diego W #520 | 7,029 | 46 | | |
| Golden Hill #630 | 5,679 | 43 | 36 | 45 |
| *African American* | | | | |
| SE San Diego E #060 | 5,965 | 36 | 44 | 28 |
| W #560 | 6,311 | 31 | | |
| #650 | 6,311 | 34 | | |
| Chollas Park #180 | 10,127 | 42 | | |
| #060 | 6,627 | 36 | 47 | 40 |
| #300 | 6,627 | 36 | | |
| #320 | 6,627 | 35 | 43 | 39 |
| West Encanto #500 | 9,530 | 37 | 33 | 42 |
| #530 | 9,530 | 38 | | |
| #590 | 10,149 | 42 | 32 | 55 |
| East Encanto #070 | 9,625 | 46 | 44 | 35 |
| #080 | 10,366 | 43 | 36 | 47 |
| Logan Heights #030 | 5,965 | | 33–4 | |

The election results shown in Table 3.3 disclose that the strongest support for the coastal initiative came from precincts containing mostly students living on college campuses and the adjoining areas. These precincts voted from 77 to 94 percent in favor. This return is quite understandable. Young people are the most frequent users of beaches and tend to support environmental measures. Running close behind youth dominated areas in support were the affluent communities of La Jolla, Mission Hills and University City with support from 57 to 81 percent.

Less affluent people, who could not afford to live on or close to the coast, opposed the coastal Initiative. Largely white, blue-collar precincts voted against it, with only 42 to 49 percent in favor. These voters live in Encanto, Normal Heights, Paradise Hills, and Nestor. Hispanic Americans also voted against, with only 38 to 50 percent favoring it. The strongest opposition came from African American voters who ranged from 31 to 46 percent favorable. Interestingly, Democratic registration in the nation among African Americans is over 90 percent, for Hispanic Americans it is over 80 percent, and in blue-collar white precincts about 55 percent. Yet most Democratic Party leaders usually support measures that the major environmental organizations favor.

Subsequent to the vote on the coastal initiative, San Diego city voters considered two growth measures and a breakdown of the results do not appear to differ appreciably from those in the coastal initiative. In November, 1985 San Diego voters approved Proposition A, a measure that barred land use changes in the city's northern tier unless specifically approved by voters in an election. Nearly a decade later, they rejected Proposition C that sought to amend Proposition A to allow development of lower-density housing and commercial centers in the northern tier without the necessity of voter approval. Anti-growth forces supported Proposition A and opposed Proposition C. Voters approved Proposition A by a 56 to 44 percent margin and rejected Proposition C by 54 to 46 percent. In both instances, the student and higher-income areas strongly voted in favor of no-growth and the racial minorities substantially opposed it. White blue-collar voters apparently split their vote on the two propositions, voting by small margins to approve Proposition A (anti-growth), but approved with a greater margin Proposition C (pro-growth).

The pattern of voting in all three elections corresponds to what occurred in Houston's zoning elections. That is, significant correlation exists in both San Diego and Houston between one's wealth and position on land use controls. As one descends the economic ladder, he or she is more likely to oppose land use controls. Students are an exception to the pattern because they usually have very little income. However, many come from the wealthy classes that support land use regulation. The greatest opposition to zoning in Houston came from lower-income African Americans, Hispanic Americans, and white Americans, and the same held true with respect to the three development-control propositions voted on in San Diego.

## 2. Protecting Private Property

Private ownership of property has for a very long time received strong protection in the English-speaking world, commencing with King John's approval of the Magna Carta in 1215. In my book, *Property Rights: From Magna Carta to the Fourteenth Amendment*, I report (Siegan, 2001b) that this high level of protection prevailed in the English common law, and prior to the Civil War, in the Supreme Court of the United States and in virtually every high state court in the Union. During this period, the common law courts of England as well as the federal and state high courts generally applied Blackstone's (1979: 134) assertion that the absolute right of property "consists of the free use, enjoyment, and disposal of all [the owner's] acquisitions without any control or diminution, save only by the laws of the land." Together with the protection of life and liberty, the early American judiciary effectively declared that the protection of private property was a fundamental tenet of this society.

Protection of property subsided in later years as illustrated by the *Mugler* case in 1887[7] (which held a prohibition on the use of property that the legislature declares is harmful to the community is not a taking of property) and the previously discussed *Euclid* case in 1926. But each of these victories for the police power were followed by decisions limiting government regulation of property rights. In 1922 in *Pennsylvania Coal Co. v. Mahon*, the U.S. Supreme Court struck down the Pennsylvania Kohler Act, which prohibited the mining of anthracite coal in such a manner that causes subsidence of any structure used as a human habitation.[8] It effectively overruled *Mugler* by adopting a legal standard balancing the police powers with the liberty guarantees of the Constitution. Two years after *Euclid*, the U.S. Supreme Court in 1928 unanimously in *Seattle Trust Co. v. Roberge* ruled unconstitutional a Seattle zoning provision that permitted in its First Residence District the erection of a philanthropic home for old people only "when the written consent shall have been obtained of the owners of two-thirds of the property within 400 feet of the proposed building."[9] In contrast to the deferential level of scrutiny of *Euclid*, the Supreme Court stated that legislatures may not under the guise of the police power, "impose restrictions that are unnecessary and unreasonable upon the use of private property or the pursuit of useful activities."[10] Delegation of the police power to a group of property owners violated the Constitution. The court asserted that the right of the plaintiff "to devote its land to any legitimate use is property within the protection of the constitution."[11] The city had no authority to prohibit construction of the new home since there was no evidence that the structure "would be a nuisance . . . or liable to work any injury, inconvenience, or annoyance to the community, the district, or any person."[12] The Roberge decision should be interpreted as a limitation upon the Euclid ruling. However, to the best of my knowledge, neither the judiciary nor the major constitutional law casebooks have acknowledged this.

Some subsequent decisions of the U.S. Supreme Court cast doubt on the primacy of private property. Such concerns were effectively erased by the court in a series of decisions that it made in and subsequent to 1987. For a long time in other areas of the law, the Supreme Court had applied scrutiny tests subjecting government regulation of noncommercial and commercial speech, religion, travel, gender and sexual privacy to judicial tests that a regulation must meet to pass constitutional muster. These tests originated in the common law and essentially require that the objective of the law must be compelling or legitimate and the means adopted must be narrowly tailored to advance that objective (Siegan, 1997: 111–115). The reasoning is that a law that does not accomplish its objective is futile and oppressive to those affected. In 1987, the Supreme Court applied these tests to the regulation of land use. The scrutiny test for property regulation has three prongs: (1) the objective of a restrictive government law must be legitimate; (2) it must substantially advance this objective; and (3) must not deprive the owner of economically viable use of its property. The high court applied this standard in the widely discussed cases of *Nollan v. California Coastal Commission*,[13] *Lucas v. South Carolina Coastal Council*,[14] *Dolan v. City of Tigard*,[15] and *City of Monterey v. Del Monte Dunes at Monterey, Ltd.*,[16] all of which brought back the protection of private property close to its original roots in American jurisprudence. The level of scrutiny is intermediate which is a lesser level than strict scrutiny and higher than minimal scrutiny. Pursuant to the separation of powers, the federal judiciary monitors legislative limitations on the exercise of this important right. The U.S. Constitution did not establish a majoritarian political system enabling local legislative bodies to control the use, acquisition, and transfer of private property. The U.S. Supreme Court is the final authority on constitutional interpretation, and all legislative decisions (which would include land use) are subject to its review.

That zoning is economically irrational is illustrated by the U.S. Supreme Court's 1926 *Euclid v. Ambler Co.*, decision. The property involved in that case consisted of 68 acres owned by the Ambler Realty Company in the Cleveland suburb of Euclid. This acreage fronted on Euclid Avenue, a major thoroughfare. The ordinance set forth rules that indirectly establish prices for vacant land. Euclid's zoning ordinance classified the property adjoining Euclid Avenue as R-2, permitting only single and two-family dwellings. The Ambler Company asserted that in the absence of zoning, the land in question had a value of $10,000 per acre and would be used for industrial and commercial purposes. However, under the R-2 zoning classification its value was only $2500 per acre. Despite Ambler's complaint that the zoning confiscated most of the value of its land, the U.S. Supreme Court upheld the zoning classification as a reasonable exercise of Euclid's police powers. The decision required the judiciary to give great deference to the zoning classifications imposed by the locality.

This position is devoid of merit. Ignoring prices eliminates this vital factor for satisfying public demand. The fact that the property was worth $10,000 per acre if it could be used for commercial and industrial purposes reflected a substantial demand for the erection of such structures on Euclid Avenue. By denying Ambler's request for a ruling that would allow the land to be used for commercial purposes, the Court in effect rejected the best measurement of community preferences. The reason that developers of stores or plants were willing to pay more for the land than the developers of single or two family homes is that measured by dollars the consumer's demand for their product was greater.

As economics professor Bruce Johnson (1977: 87) explains:

> [R]esource allocation decisions in every society must be conducted so that resources are directed toward satisfying the wants of individual members of society. Because the wants exceed the capacity to serve (given finite resources and the current state of technology) and because the various wants may be inconsistent with one another, some device must be used to assign relative valuations to the wants of individuals. In a decentralized economic system, individuals register their preferences by voluntarily bidding for goods and services with their dollars in open markets. ... The question is how best to satisfy current preferences in a world without certainty.
>
> In a market system the combination of competition among firms, free entry into industries, and private risk taking generates a process of trial and error that channels resources into those uses that most closely approximate the preferences exhibited by consumers; and the process channels the resources most efficiently....

As the price differentials caused by zoning for Ambler's land reveal, zoning is often not responsive to the economic preferences of consumers. Zoning decisions satisfy planning and political concerns much more than economic ones. However, in time, Euclid's zoning of the Ambler property succumbed to market forces. As of 1989, it had long been zoned for industry and occupied by General Motors Inland Plant with two gas stations, a restaurant and a medical center nearby (Harr and Wolf, 1989: 190).

The Euclid decision also deprived the community of a mechanism that automatically adjusts to both supply and demand changes. As commercial demands are met in the area, the price of the property will decrease, possibly to a figure lower than offered for residential property. Erecting stores and plants would also lead to more employment and availability of goods and services probably raising the demand for housing. Because it is governed by the political process, zoning is far less resilient to economic changes.

The private market is not devoid of "smart growth" controls. Consider land development in unzoned Houston. No large lot or snob zoning exists there because the builders and developers determine the size of most building lots, not the planners and politicians. There are very few regulatory curbs limiting density and height of residential or commercial structure. No laws prohibit mixed uses in a subdivision or the erection of buildings containing both residential and commercial uses. Nor does Houston have growth controls, which cause builders to by-pass restricted areas in order to build further out in less restricted areas. No regulations prohibit builders from erecting "new urbanist" traditional town housing near jobs, schools, parks, shops, civil services and transit.[17]

To be sure, Houston has no urban boundary law and some may consider its absence a defect of proper land use regulation. My reply to these critics is that the Houston system has more than overcome its absence by its commitment to entry of people and land uses. Very few laws exist that exclude people or property. A nonzoned city is a cosmopolitan collection of property uses. The standard is supply and demand. If there is economic justification for the use, it is likely to be forthcoming. Zoning restricts the supply of uses, and thereby prevents some demands from being satisfied. It likewise impedes competition and innovation. In the absence of land use regulations, there are many builders in Houston fiercely competing with each other to obtain consumer acceptance.

Houston is a viable and prosperous city. Despite the absence of regulation, a substantial amount of separation of uses occurs in that city and others without zoning.[18] Moreover, Houston enjoys benefits not generally available in zoned cities. These include low housing prices, minimal exclusion of persons and properties, less urban sprawl, and little political control of land use. In the balance of the chapter, I shall explain these benefits.

## A. Zoning Increases Prices of Housing

The evidence is strong that a land use regulation that limits supply of housing raises its price. All other things being equal, the more severe the regulation the greater the increase in prices, which means that a city that has not adopted zoning is likely to have lower housing prices than one that has adopted it. According to the 1982 Report of the President's Commission on Housing (1982: 199), "[e]xcessive restrictions on housing production have driven up the price of housing generally" creating concern for "the plight of millions of Americans of average and lesser income who cannot now afford houses or apartments."

To determine the impact of local government regulation on the price of housing, the U.S. Department of Housing and Urban Development initiated a housing cost reduction demonstration project in 1980. Four communities across the country were selected to participate in the project, which used reduced local government regulations as the only variable. In these communities, zoning, building, and subdivision regulations were minimized. In the selected projects subject to the reduced regulations, the prices of new homes were reduced by 21 percent to 33 percent when compared to similar local developments that were subject to traditional regulations. In Shreveport, Louisiana, demonstration housing units had sales prices of $52,850 while homes in a comparable suburban project with conventional regulations and processing sold for $70,000. In Hayward California, the demonstration units ranged in price from $53,000 to $65,000. Comparable units subject to conventional regulation in the area sold for $79,500 to $97,500. In all instances, the builders sought to obtain a normal profit margin (Bjornseth 1983).

William Fischel (1991), a professor of economics at Dartmouth College, produced a highly persuasive study demonstrating that strong land-use controls greatly raise the cost of housing. The study is based on California housing prices in the 1970s. After many years of rapid population growth, the median value of owner-occupied housing in California in 1970 was 35 percent higher than that in the nation as a whole. By 1980, after ten years of the slowest rate of population growth in the state's history, this differential in median value of owner-occupied housing had more than doubled, to 79 percent. During the 1970s, California's housing values rose 267 percent, compared to a 176 percent increase for the entire nation. Fischel concluded that democracy in the suburbs accounted for the extraordinary housing price increase in California. Resident voters were able to restrict new development in order to maximize the value of their own homes and maintain neighborhood exclusivity:

In my opinion, the only remaining explanation for why California's home prices rose so rapidly during the 1970s is that, during that decade, the state was the pioneer in growth controls. By legally removing significant amounts of suburban land from development, by denying those who did have subdividable land essential services like water, and by imposing costly subdivision conditions unrelated to home buyers' demands, growth controls created an artificial scarcity of housing. I submit that politically established and judicially validated scarcity was the newly operative constraint, not physical limitations (Fischel, 1991: 1154).

In areas of high demand, land-use regulations operate to greatly curb housing production, particularly that which serves less-affluent people. Consider M.I.T. Urban Studies Professor Bernard Frieden's study of three proposals to develop housing projects in northern California. In the first proposal, a developer in 1972 proposed to build 2,200 housing units in the foothills of Oakland, divided about equally between homes and apartments. By 1976, the proposal had been whittled down to the sale of 100 lots for estate homes on a portion of the property and the construction of 150 to 200 single-family homes on the remainder. The second proposal involved acreage on the shoreland of the East Bay across from San Francisco. The plan, originally submitted in 1972, sought permission for the erection of 9,000 moderately priced homes. In 1976, the project was reduced to one-third of its original size. The third proposal involved a site on a mountaintop and adjoining foothills just south of San Francisco. This proposal originally called for 11,000 housing units, but the county supervisors reduced it to 2,200 units, which rendered the project no longer feasible.

Frieden (1979: 30) posed the critical question: developers may be able to make compromises that will get them political approval in these cases, but how much longer can they make these compromises and continue to sell houses to anyone but the very wealthy?

In a paper published in March 2002 by the National Bureau of Economic Research, economics professors Edward L. Glaeser of Harvard and Joseph E. Gyourko of Wharton Business School assert that much of the price of housing in the nation is quite close to the marginal, physical costs of new construction. The price of housing is significantly higher in a limited number of areas, such as California and New York City and some other cities. In these areas, the authors contend that zoning and other land use controls play the dominant role in making housing very expensive. Thus, a home on a quarter-acre lot in Chicago is likely to sell for about $140,000 more than its construction costs. In San Diego, it sells for $285,000 more than construction costs, in New York City $350,000 more and in San Francisco $700,000 more than construction costs. Strict zoning laws, the Harvard and Wharton professors conclude on the basis of their research, are mostly responsible for the huge difference between price and cost.

Consider in this respect the difference in housing prices between the areas of Texas that contain Houston and Dallas, its largest cities, which are 230 miles apart from each other. In my book, *Property and Freedom*, I report the rent and home prices in these two cities and the two counties in which they are located in the 1970s, the period between the first and last day of that period. Although making comparisons between any two localities is always difficult, I concluded that the 1970s were a suitable period for assessing how housing prices responded to conditions of high demand in an unzoned city (Houston) and in a zoned city (Dallas).

According to the United States Bureau of the Census, the population of Texas increased 27 percent between 1970 and 1980 with both the Houston and Dallas areas registering substantial growth. Harris County, in which Houston is located, grew 38 percent and Dallas County, in which Dallas is located, grew 17 percent. The growth rate for the entire country was 11 percent. During this period Houston was a major oil industry center and Dallas a major financial center. In the 1970s, Harris County did not have zoning in approximately 80 to 90 percent of the areas where residential building occurred. The reverse was the case for Dallas County where zoning existed in about 80 to 90 percent of the areas where residential construction took place.

Over the entire decade of the 1970s, the Houston and Dallas areas confronted serious population pressures. While Harris County's population increased about 38 percent, its builders created enough new structures to house these additional people without significantly increasing the price of rents and owner occupied residences. This was a remarkable achievement. Dallas County did not do as well; the population increase there was 17 percent and housing prices for both single and multiple family units rose much more significantly. While the price of new single-family construction in Harris County increased by 61 percent from 1973 to

1980 new home prices in Dallas County increased 225 percent (Siegan, 1997: 194).

Supporters of smart growth policies assert that unlike conventional zoning Portland's smart growth program does not significantly raise the price of housing. Their explanation is that the inclusionary effects of infilling existing developments will overcome the exclusionary effects of an urban growth boundary. The accuracy of this reasoning depends on the extent of infilling that will occur. The problem smart growth confronts is that existing residents will be more favorable to drawing urban lines than they will be to infilling which may change the character of their neighborhoods. After all, many residents bought their homes under the assumption that mixed uses would never be allowed in their areas. Indeed, their financial interests also will be better served by restricting rather than expanding supply. These reasons may explain why the infilling that has occurred in Portland has not been sufficient to offset the containment effects of its urban growth boundary.

In support of their position, the smart growth advocates rely on a recent study by Anthony Downs (2002) of housing price increases from 1975 to 2000 in which he finds no clear relationship between containment policies and housing prices. He found in his study that prices in the 1980s did not rise as fast in the Portland area as in many other areas, that housing prices rose faster in Portland only from 1990 to 1994 or 1996, and that home prices in several other areas without growth boundaries were also rising rapidly. Downs does not claim that growth boundaries never accelerate rates of housing price increase or that they inevitably do. "The truth," he states (2002: 30), "lies somewhere in between."

In commenting on Downs' Study, Professor Fischel (2002: 48) notes that Portland's housing prices as well as those of other cities in the Western United States have increased considerably as compared with cities in other regions. According to him, the 1975–2000 figures show that Portland has not been very successful in promoting infill housing. "A successful infilling program would have retarded housing price inflation."

Portland's experience has little relevancy to Houston, which has no growth boundary and very few growth restrictions. Moreover, infilling is an accepted and ongoing practice in areas of Houston not subject to restrictions contained in recorded covenants.

## B. Minimal Exclusion of Persons and Properties

Tables 3.1 and 3.2 disclose that most people at the lower portion of the income scale—low- and moderate-income African Americans,

Hispanic Americans, and white Americans—reject zoning. This is not necessarily solely a matter of zoning, as Table 3.3 indicates. Those who vote against zoning are also likely to vote against coastal controls and growth regulations. The less affluent homeowners vote against these measures by large margins. Most of the time they vote in much smaller numbers than people who have more wealth. If the poor voted in greater numbers, it is probable that their votes on land use measures would be more decisive.

The similarity of land use voting in Houston, the state of California, and San Diego confirms that the poorer portion of the nation's population reject land use regulations probably by large margins. In my discussions with real estate brokers and residents of the areas in Houston that voted against zoning, I concluded that most of these people are reasonably satisfied with their homes and neighborhoods. Unlike people of greater wealth, they are not disturbed by the higher density of nearby or adjoining residential structures or the existence nearby or adjoining of commercial uses. For example, they view nearby auto repair shops as benefits and not harmful. In higher income single-family areas, mixed uses are economically detrimental, while in lower-income single-family areas, they are economically beneficial.

As a general matter, democracy is the best system available to control the powers of government. But democracy in land use eliminates the desires of many, particularly poorer people, to exercise the freedom to live their lives as they deem best. Unfortunately, planners are oblivious to this. Pursuant to smart growth, planners may opt for a local grocery store, pharmacy, or tailor shop on interior streets, if such development meets their standard, but they seem almost revolted by, for example, the existence of local auto repair shops, as are most people of higher income. However, for poorer people a nearby auto repair shop is almost a necessity. Being in walking distance and relying on used parts, they offer a service not available at more distant car dealers. The best means for accommodating the land use preferences of lower-income persons is the private market.

The current favoritism among (smart growth) planners for mom and pop stores moves in that direction but requires government compulsion without recourse to actual and not theoretical consumer demand. In the absence of land use restrictions, if demand exists for a particular store or shop, it will likely be forthcoming. Planners tend to impose their own version of village life because they are reluctant to use the market as their guide. Only the inherent and automatic planning of the market will achieve a reasonable mix. It will allow for supermarkets as well as mom and pop stores. Portland, Oregon, smart growth's model city, bans Wal-Mart, Price Club, and Home Depot, all of whom require use of automobile transportation and compete with the mom and pop stores, but provide valuable services to many residents.

In my research on Houston, I questioned real estate brokers and residents in unrestricted areas about the acceptability of local auto repair shops, something which zoning forbids on interior streets of residential areas. Were these residents willing to sacrifice aesthetics and conformity that zoning offers for the sake of convenience and price. The answer was generally positive, and was reflected in their vote against zoning. I also learned that economics was not the only explanation for the rejection of zoning. Some—perhaps many—have settled in nonzoned areas to maintain control over their lifestyles: something now rarely obtainable elsewhere. In the perceptive words of Immanuel Kant (1999: 39), "every rational human being exists as an end in himself, and not merely to be arbitrarily used by this or that will." Some of these people as well as many of higher income voted against zoning because of fears that government would impose controls over their neighborhoods eliminating their "right to be left alone."[19]

The United States is a land of great differences and diversities. It is a nation composed of people of many different ethnic, racial, religious backgrounds who have varying desires and beliefs. Surely there is place in this nation for the people who reject the conformity and symmetry of lifestyle required by zoning codes. There are many people who for reasons having to do with economic or other personal concerns do not want to live in zoned areas. Society should have places where these desires can be achieved. But regrettably there are few such places.[20]

Although smart growth is quite authoritarian in concept, at least its position on the commingling of uses is not inconsistent with development that has occurred in Houston's unrestricted sections. Smart growth has changed the zoning equation. A diverse use (multiple family, local stores, or light plants) is no longer an adverse or incompatible use when located in or adjoining a predominantly single-family area. These are now acceptable additions to the neighborhood. Multiple-family buildings conserve land and thereby prevent urban sprawl, local stores reduce the necessity for owning automobiles or driving long distances, and light manufacturing plants serve all these purposes, and most important, provide employment for local residents. Pursuant to smart growth apparently only heavy industry and busy transportation centers qualify as adverse uses.

Given this "modern" view, there is little basis for prohibiting the erection of structures that do not constitute nuisances in the areas of Houston not controlled by restrictive covenants. These areas come closer to the objectives of smart growth than do areas zoned and maintained exclusively for homes. The "old" Euclid rules are no longer relevant to these areas.

Our social order has been in flux in recent years as more people claim they have been denied "equal" rights. Personal freedom has been a critical issue of our times. Nevertheless, a reverse course has been followed on the ownership of real property. Rights of many who want to be property owners have been steadily eroding due to greatly escalating zoning restrictions.

This is not the position of large developers who tend to view zoning as a game of politics and expediency. Their attitude reflects the pragmatic wisdom of our times that puts property rights on the block. Many small property owners live in a less sophisticated world, and for them zoning is anything but a game; it is more a tyranny of government. However you refer to it, there is something terribly wrong when persons have to appear before local officials and plead for the opportunity to use or continue to use their property for a benign purpose. Numerous property owners would be in this predicament if Houston adopted zoning.

But no matter how wicked, reprehensible, and confiscatory a land use regulation is, a bolt from heaven will not strike it dead. If the locality upholds the regulation, it can only be declared unconstitutional by a court of law, and this means that an owner must be in a position to use costly and lengthy court processes to obtain such a ruling.

The situation faced by affluent owners will be entirely different from that of the less affluent. Consider, for example, the case of wealthy and not-wealthy landowners, each confronted with a proposed harsh and probably unconstitutional regulation of their land. From the moment the regulation is proposed, those financially able will begin employing lawyers and experts to protect their interests. They will be in a far better position to defeat or modify the proposal than those who cannot afford representation and have to represent themselves (if at all). There are some public interest groups such as the Pacific Legal Foundation that are prepared to help small landowners fight city hall. Unfortunately, their calendars are very crowded.

Most civil liberties groups are usually not available for this purpose. Property rights are involved and these groups seem to have read the provisions safeguarding them out of the Bill of Rights. Nor, of course, would the public defender be authorized to intercede, even though an owner can lose as much money because of government land use restrictions as he or she could from being fined for committing a crime. The big owners and developers have the capability to defeat regulations. While the state authorities may find it difficult to overcome them, they will easily succeed against those who cannot fight back.

The areas of Houston that are not controlled by land use covenants appear about as stable as those that are controlled. Consider, for example, the area of the city known as Denver Harbor-Port Houston located east of downtown. It has never been subject to restrictive covenants and a large majority of its voters rejected zoning in both the 1962 and 1993 elections. According to the 1997 census figures it was home to more than 18,000 people, 89 percent of whom are Hispanic. Twenty-eight percent of households had incomes below $15,000 annually compared with 23 percent citywide. Fifty-two percent of residents age 25 years and older did not receive a high school diploma compared to 27 percent citywide. Its residents have formed a civic organization and boast that two international bus companies have located their headquarters there. While the area consists largely of single-family dwellings, it also includes multiple family dwellings, trailers, houses used commercially and industrial uses as well as stores and shops catering to local residents. It contains a public park, an elementary school and at least three churches.[21]

As previously reported, African Americans rejected zoning for Houston by a larger margin than any other identifiable group. They apparently are satisfied with the city's laissez faire land use program. I come to this conclusion in part from an article in the July 2001 issue of *Black Enterprise* magazine, a publication that claims a circulation of 400,000 and a readership of 3.1 million. A readers' choice survey reported in that issue selected Houston as the best city in the nation for African Americans, who number about 25 percent of its population. In the competition for the best city for blacks, the ten leading cities were ranked in the following order: Houston, Washington, D.C., Atlanta, Charlotte, Memphis, Detroit, Baltimore, Dallas, Chicago, and Philadelphia (Brown and Padgett 2001).

The magazine reveals this information about African Americans who live in Houston:

1.  The city has a low level of segregation, which enables African Americans to live throughout the city.
2.  Among the ten finalists, Houston's metropolitan statistical area (MSA) had the second lowest cost of living and housing indices ($108,500 for a typical three-bedroom home).

3. Forty-three percent of blacks are homeowners despite a home mortgage rejection rate of nearly 41 percent.
4. There are 29 black residents for every black business, the best ratio of any city on the list.

## C. Zoning Is a Major Cause of Urban Sprawl

Development of the United States occurred over the years as cities and towns sprung up either by chance or design over vast and unoccupied territory. As cities were organized, those not satisfied with what cities had to offer settled outside of existing boundaries. A large percentage of this country's population lives in small cities, towns and rural areas, exterior to major cities, the kind of development that is popularly referred to as urban "sprawl." Prior to zoning, normal market forces were largely responsible for urban sprawl. Zoning imposed regulations limiting use, density, area and height, considerably reducing land available for development within localities, and causing much greater sprawl than existed previous to its imposition.

The United States successfully developed in its early years because of man's "overwhelming dynamic[,] ... the lust to own land." "[F]or the first time in human history," writes historian Paul Johnson (1998: 35), "cheap, good land was available to the multitude...." The availability of land enabled the colonists to achieve a level of prosperity and contentment not readily available in the countries from which they migrated. The colonists achieved great commercial success in part because there was little restraint on the use of land.

The story in modern times is far different. While the freedoms of ownership and production have enormously benefited most people in the United States, these freedoms are presently under attack because it is alleged the land is being wasted, that is, too much of it is being used for urban purposes. There is no land crisis, nor can there be one when no more than six percent of the total land area of the United States is devoted to these uses.[22] This study shows that in 1969, cities, highways and airports occupied about 2.5 percent of the nation's land area. A more recent estimate states that urban areas use about 60 million acres, or 3.1 percent of the over 1.9 billion acres of land in the continental U.S. (not including Alaska and Hawaii). What makes the purported crisis very perplexing is that many people who now demand reform of land use policies are those most responsible for its excesses. The amount of land used for urban purposes is determined both by the private market and by government regulation. It is inevitable that the ordinary and benign practices of the private market will not always lead to consecutive development. There will invariably be gaps between private developments. It would require a massive coercive effort to change these practices. The enormous amount of regulation the land use community imposes on the private market is mostly responsible for the excessive use of land and energy that critics condemn as constituting urban sprawl.

Regulations restricting development in cities and towns cause developers to build homes in the suburbs or rural areas. Consider, for example, the impact of California's coastal controls. The California Coastal zone covers land along and within five miles of California's eleven hundred miles of shoreline. The California Coastal commission regulates the use of this land and substantially limits development of it. In my home city of San Diego, much development is limited to three stories and quite severe density, use and area restrictions. To bypass these restrictions, developers build outside of San Diego where they are less likely to exist and thereby create urban sprawl.

## D. The Houston Government Has Minimal Control Over Land Use

Unlike city councils generally, Houston's has relatively little authority over land use. Elsewhere, the strongest supporters of zoning and other land use regulations are the local legislators and for two reasons: First, they usually believe in such government involvement and second, the issue attracts political and financial support, both from opponents and proponents. Highly contentious issues such as zoning help fill a candidate's coffers. Legislators do not always represent public opinion on zoning. Thus, although a majority of Houston voters twice turned down proposed zoning ordinances, no member of the city council voted against it on either occasion. For Judge Posner and Professor Landes (1975: 877), such outcomes are not surprising. They describe the incentives for legislation often as "payments [that] take the form of campaign contributions, votes, implicit promises of future favors, and sometimes outright bribes."

The failings and infirmities of lawmakers were known to the Framers of the U.S. Constitution and caused them to protect individual liberties by separating and substantially limiting the powers of government. James Madison, the most influential framer of the U.S. Constitution, was concerned about the frailties of legislative bodies, which he observed as a member for three years of the Virginia House of Delegates. Far from being dedicated to the public good, he believed most of the legislators were pursuing their own political or financial interests. Madison (1987:

168) wrote that men seek public office to achieve ambition, personal interest, or public good.

> Unhappily, the two first are proved by experience to be most prevalent. Hence the candidates who feel them, particularly, the second, are most industrious, and most successful in pursuing their object; and forming often a majority in the legislative councils, with interested views, contrary to the interest, and views of their Constituents, join in a perfidious sacrifice of the latter to the former. A succeeding election, it might be supposed, would displace the offenders, and repair the mischief. But how easily are base and selfish measures, masked by pretexts of public good and apparent expediency? How frequently will a repetition of the same arts and industry which succeeded in the first instance again prevail on the unwary to misplace their confidence?

Urban planners cannot rescue us from the failings of democratic society. The role of the planner in the zoning process is quite limited. He is the paid employee of the locality and cannot be expected to espouse with any degree of consistency policies contrary to those of his employers. The basic rules are established by officials elected to govern. A planner who strongly advocates high-density housing in suburbia may not last much longer than his first paycheck. Confrontations are probably rare because a planner is not likely to be hired or seek employment if his basic orientation appears to differ substantially from that of his prospective employers. Disagreements will occur and be tolerated—within limitations.

Even if a proposed plan appears to accord with the general desires of the local legislators and may even have been commissioned by them, it still must be acceptable in significant respects after hearings and debates to at least a majority of the local council to be adopted. Amendments required for passage can easily change the meaning and impact of the legislation. The "perfect" plan may be quite imperfect by the time it emerges from the legislative process, whether it be on a local or higher governmental level, and it might be ravaged further as administered. And, it is possible, the courts ultimately may lay much of it to rest.

Planners are beset by the same intellectual limitations and dilemmas confronting the rest of society. How should land be used? There are many factors that are relevant in making such decisions. The problems have become even more complex with the advent of smart growth which rejects the idea that diverse uses must always be separated, long a major zoning premise. For many years, the country has been in the midst of a great controversy on the issues of growth and development, and the responses of these protagonists differ greatly. Much day-to-day planning revolves about the core issue of the extent to which government should protect the values and desires of homeowners as well as the rights of landowners. Thus, in a very detailed study of apartment zoning practices there, Mandelker (1971: 168) found that the planners and zoning agencies in King County, Washington, "were caught between a desire to handle what they saw as land use externalities, and a desire to implement a plan for the future of the physical environment." Jacob Ukeles (1964: 22) adds this further insight:

> Each category or type of decision includes a series of choices involving knowledge of the city as it presently is and as it is likely to become in the future. Most zoning issues cannot be resolved solely by knowledge of existing conditions and trends, but require the application of values and judgments. What a city ought to become is as relevant a zoning question as what a city is likely to become. Even so-called technical studies, especially the mapping of zones, involve many value judgments as well as judgments of fact. The question of the appropriateness of an area will appear differently to different observers depending on their view of what the city and the particular locality ought to become. The decision that a given commercial strip or factory area is a menace to neighboring residents while a second such area is not, is rarely a "technical" decision.

Economist Friedrich Hayek (1944: 36) writes that the best means for obtaining a plan or plans is the competition of the marketplace.

There would be no difficulty about efficient control or planning were conditions so simple that a single person or board could effectively survey all the relevant facts. It is only as the factors which have to be taken into account become so numerous that it is impossible to gain a synoptic view of them that decentralization becomes imperative.

My experience as an attorney representing homebuilders and as investor in vacant and improved real estate in the generally affluent suburbs northwest of Chicago provided me knowledge about the land use in those areas. The many newcomers to these areas from Chicago or other major cities moved to obtain a lifestyle different than they had previously experienced. They wanted to live in restricted single-family areas with people of similar financial means. They rejected neighbors who were renters and mobile-home occupants. Zoning in these areas accommodated their concerns. As a result, a large portion of these suburbs is confined to single-family development. It was almost always a battle to attempt to rezone property for any use other than homes. While I understand the concern that created this perspective, the use of such power over other people's property is socially undesirable and constitutionally excessive.

The exclusionary character of zoning is now generally recognized. To remedy the problem of exclusion, the President's Commission on Housing (1982: 200–201) urged state and local legislators to enact legislation that would greatly limit state and local zoning powers:

No zoning regulations denying or limiting the development of housing should be deemed valid unless their existence or adoption is necessary to achieve a vital and pressing governmental interest. In litigation, the governmental body seeking to maintain or impose the regulation should bear the burden of proving it complies with the foregoing standard....

The new standard of zoning is intended to limit substantially the imposition of exclusionary land-use policies, since exclusion is clearly not an acceptable governmental interest.

Homeowners who seek protections against diverse and adverse uses are served in Houston by privately imposed restrictive covenants applicable to their properties. Under the common law in England and the United States, an owner of land has the right to impose restrictions on the use of the land he sells or conveys to another person that apply to the land usually for fixed periods and on occasion in perpetuity. Landowners use this right to apply covenants and restrictions on land they develop. In the absence of zoning, these covenants and restrictions control the use of the land to which they are subject. About 25 percent of the land in Houston is used for single-family development and most of it is subject to land use covenants. Market preferences will determine the content of the restrictions. Because wealthy purchasers are most concerned about the character of their neighborhoods, the covenants in the most affluent areas are very restrictive and contain a large number of provisions. The covenants in the less affluent areas are less strict and contain fewer provisions. And, of course, there are no enforceable covenants in some areas because the original owner of the property never imposed them, or they have expired. In addition to covenants, market prices also reduce externalities. For example, homes at or near a subdivision boundary that is contiguous to vacant land will sell for less than properties on the interior because of concern about the future use of the vacant land.

In Houston, economic forces tend to make for a separation of uses even without zoning. Business uses will tend to locate in certain areas, residential in others, and industrial in still others. Apartments will tend to concentrate in certain areas and not in others. There is also a tendency for further separation within a category; light industrial uses do not want to adjoin heavy industrial uses, and vice-versa. Different kinds of business uses require different locations. The Houston experience reveals that zoning is not essential to control this process.

In the absence of zoning, municipalities will adopt ordinances to alleviate specific land use problems. Houston has adopted a relatively small number of ordinances for this purpose. These ordinances have little effect in the areas that are subject to covenants and restrictions. However, they are important in the areas not controlled by these restrictions. The ordinances ban nuisances and impose off-street parking and some relatively minor (by comparison with usual zoning requirements) minimum lot, density and use requirements. Moreover, under the common law, government has the power to abate uses that are grave threats to lives and property.

Because many of the early restrictive covenants in Houston were (1) limited in duration, or (b) legally insufficient, or (c) not enforced by owners, zoning would have kept more areas as strictly single-family. The covenants created subsequent to 1950 are more durable and as a practical matter most will remain in force for about 25 years. Since 1965 the city has enforced these covenants. They are as effective as zoning in maintaining single-family homogeneity. They are usually more restrictive than zoning with respect to use, density, area, and height.

When covenants expire, land and properties will be used as economic pressures dictate. In time, commercial uses, apartments and some (probably light) industrial uses will develop along the major thoroughfares. Most business uses will not locate on interior (residential) streets because they require favorable traffic conditions available only on heavily traveled streets. Commercial uses develop in interior areas that are not restricted consistent with the demands of the residents. In Houston, within recent years, a considerable amount of multiple family dwellings have been erected in those subdivisions in which the covenants have expired. Interestingly, residents in a number of single-family subdivisions confronted with covenants that have expired or are soon to expire have imposed new and long-term covenants.[23]

### 3. Conclusion

In Houston, persons who want to live in subdivisions that control use and development within their borders have little difficulty in finding them. Most residential subdivisions in the city are subject to restrictive covenants running with land and enforced by the city that protect the exclusivity of single-family use. These covenants usually enable residents to participate in administration of the rules the covenants establish. But unlike persons who live in zoned communities, they will have no authority over any property except that which is located within their subdivisions. Under zoning, the city council or other similar legislative body controls (subject to constitutional and state provisions) the use of every square inch of land in the locality. As a legislative body, it is elected by the residents and whose members in order to remain in office or seek higher office must respond to the will of the voters. Zoning thus grants enormous powers over land use to the forces in the community that are most politically influential.

Houston also offers a choice not available in any other major city and in very few smaller localities. For the many who value it, the right to be left alone, which U.S. Supreme Court Justice Louis Brandeis considered "the most comprehensive of rights and the right most valued by civilized men"[24] flourishes in Houston. Many homeowners in that city live their lives without the land use regimentation of governments. Houston also provides for those who insist on a lifestyle influenced by legally enforceable rules of use and development. Homeowners live in developments subject to the provision of covenants and restrictions, which are no less restrictive than zoning regulations. The Houston system also offers low housing prices and a highly inclusionary policy for the entry of people and uses. Very few other localities can claim these important benefits (Siegan, 1972).

Smart growth proponents have narrowed the gulf between zoning and nonzoning. Smart growth supports mixed uses, a position that the private market achieves in those areas that are not restricted by zoning or covenants. However, a large philosophical gap still exists between the smart growthers and the free market advocates in at least three important respects. First smart growth emphasizes exclusion while nonzoning promotes inclusion. Second, supporters of smart growth seek to impose mixed uses in areas that are zoned exclusively single-family. This outcome is essential if smart growth is ever to be a meaningful concept. The problem with achieving it is that most residents in these subdivisions purchased their homes in the belief that they would always be protected against mixed uses. Government should honor this commitment, which, of course, does not apply to the areas of the locality that have not been developed. As President Reagan's President's Commission on Housing Report (1982: 201) states:

> A possible problem of deregulation is that it may adversely affect those who in good faith made their purchase or investments in reliance on the old rules. A change to the proposed "vital and pressing" standard would pose such a problem. Persons who purchase a home or a lot for construction of a home near vacant land assume that it will not be arbitrarily reclassified to allow other uses. The reasonable investment expectations of these homeowners should be protected. When vacant land is proposed for a use that would have required rezoning, homeowners entitled to notice under the old rules should be protected under the requirements and procedures of the old rules.

Third, smart growth requires regulatory controls while freedom in the use and development of property is practiced in the uncontrolled areas of Houston.

A locality can obtain the benefits of nonzoning without disturbing any person's investment-backed expectations by removing controls over new development. Some developers will impose land use restrictions while others will not. To accommodate both those who demand land use controls as well as those who reject them, our society should rely on the restraints inherent in human freedom to control the use of land.

## Notes

1.  Bernard Seigan passed away March 27, 2006. The editors produced the final version of this chapter by doing a minimal amount of editing of a nearly complete draft they received from Professor Siegan prior to his death.
2.  *Euclid v. Ambler Realty Co.*, 272 U.S. 365 (1926).
3.  272 U.S. at 375. Sutherland's position can be explained by his observation in *Euclid:* "a nuisance may be merely a right thing in the wrong pleas like a pig in the parlor instead of the barnyard." While a multiple family building in a single-family area was not a nuisance at common law, he viewed it as tantamount to one. Applying a cost-benefit analysis, smart growthers believe that the damage sustained by homeowners from developments nearby, of apartment buildings is offset by the resulting reduction of urban sprawl.
4.  Ellickson and Been (2000), p. 64, citing Hall (1989).
5.  *Dolan v. Tigard*, 512 U.S. 374 (1994).
6.  This information is confirmed by Baha Valdie, chief plan checker of Harris County. Mr. Valdie advises me that during the 20 years he has been checking building plans, he is not aware of any structural failure in the unincorporated area. The city of Houston requires that all requests for building permits for land in Harris County that is within five miles of the city be submitted to it for information purposes.
7.  *Mugler v. Kansas*, 123 U.S. 623 (1887).
8.  *Pennsylvania Coal Co. v. Mahon*, 260 U.S. 393 (1922).
9.  278 U.S. 116 (1928).
10. 278 U.S. at 121–2.
11. 278 U.S. at 122.
12. 278 U.S. at 122.
13. 107 S.Ct. 3141 (1987).
14. 112 S.Ct. 2886 (1992).
15. 114 S.Ct. 2309 (1994).
16. 119 S.Ct. 1624 (1999). But see the more recent case of *Sierra Preservation Council v. Tahoe Regional Planning Agency*, 122 S.Ct. 1464 (2002) which upheld two moratoriums restricting for 32 months development on the Lake Tahoe Basin.
17. For a discussion of new urbanist planning which rejects conventional zoning regulations, see Ellickson and Been (2000), pp. 490, 722, 960, and 1082.

18.  I came to this conclusion partly on the basis of visual comparisons of land use maps of Dallas, Los Angeles and Houston that various students and I made. The observations about land use separation in other non-zoned municipalities, is confirmed by land use maps of Texas cities that were not zoned in the 1960s when the maps were drawn: Pasadena, Wichita Falls, Laredo, and Baytown.
19.  A widely used phrase that originated in Cooley (1907: 29).
20.  The analogy to home schooling is worth considering. Our society protects the rights of parents to educate their children in their own homes and not enroll them in public or private schools. Despite its commitment to compulsory school education, this nation has long recognized and permitted parents to educate their children as they choose. As of 1999, parents of 850,000 children exercise this right.
21.  See *Houston Chronicle* section E, pg. 1, col. 1 (June 26, 2002). See also my book *Land Use Without Zoning*, which contains a description of the area as it was in 1970 and 71. When I first surveyed the area in 1968, it was largely populated by poor white people.
22.  U.S. Department of Commerce, United States Statistical Abstract: 1996, at 229. This figure excludes Alaska and District of Columbia and includes urban and built-up areas in units of 10 acres or greater, and rural transportation. Based on the Census Bureau's statistics, the following figures explain my estimate that about six percent of the land is developed for urban purposes

| | |
|---|---|
| Total surface area | 1,940,011 (thousands of acres) |
| Amount of developed nonfederal land | 92,352 |
| Total amount of federal land | 407,969 |
| Five percent of federal land | 20,398 |
| estimate of amount developed) | |
| Approx. Total developed land | 112,750 |
| Percent of developed land | 5.81% |

(Alaska contains 385,482,000 acres of total surface area and the District of Columbia contains 39,000 acres. Including the amount of development in these two areas would lower the percentage of total developed land.)
23.  For illustrations of homeowners creating new covenants in areas of Houston where covenants have expired or were soon to expire, see Siegan (1972: 239–245).
24.  *Olmstead v. United States* 277 U.S. 438, 479 (1928) (Brandeis, J., dissenting). This case involved the use of wiretaps for certain houses, a practice that Brandeis found despicable to the occupants of the homes. One might well contend that laws prohibiting use of a home as desired by the owner is similarly oppressive.

## References

Bjornseth, Dick. "No-Code Comfort." *Reason* (July 1983): 44.

Blackstone, William. *Commentaries on the Laws of England: A Facsimile of the First Edition of 1765–1789.* Chicago: University of Chicago Press, 1979.

Brown, Monique R., and David Padgett. "The Results Are In. Here are Your Top Picks for Blacks to Live, Work and Play." *Black Enterprise* (July 2001) pp. 74–95.

Cooley, Thomas McIntyre. *A Treatise on the Law of Torts.* Chicago: Callaghan, 1907.

Downs, Anthony. "Have Housing Prices Risen Faster in Portland than Elsewhere?" *Housing Policy Debate* 13, no. 1 (2002): 7–30.

Ellickson, Robert C., and Vicki I. Been. *Land Use Controls: Cases and Material,* 2nd ed. New York: Aspen Publishers, 2000.

Fischel, William A. "Comment on Anthony Downs's "The Advisory Commission on Regulatory Barriers to Affordable Housing: Its Behavior and Accomplishments." *Housing Policy Debate* 2, no. 4 (1991): 1139–1160.

_____. "Comment on Anthony Downs's "Have Housing Prices Risen Faster in Portland Than Elsewhere?" *Housing Policy Debate* 13, no. 1 (2002): 43–50.

Frieden, Bernard J. *The Environmental Protection Hustle.* Cambridge, MA: MIT Press, 1979.

Glaeser, Edward L., and Joseph Gyourko. "The Impact of Zoning on Housing Affordability." Cambridge, MA: *National Bureau of Economic Research Working Paper* 8835, March 2002.

Hall, Peter. "The Turbulent Eighth Decade: Challenges to American City Planning." *Journal of the American Planning Association* 55, no. 3 (Summer 1989): 275–333.

Harr, Charles M., and Michael Allan Wolf. *Land Use Planning: A Casebook on the Use, Misuse, and Re-Use of Urban Land,* 4th ed. Boston: Aspen Publishers, 1989.

Hayek, Friedrich A. *The Road to Serfdom.* Chicago: University of Chicago Press, 1944.

Johnson, M. Bruce. "Planning Without Prices: A Discussion of Land Use Regulation Without Confiscation." in Bernard H. Siegan, ed. *Planning Without Prices: The Taking Clause as it Relates to Land Use Regulation Without Compensation.* Lexington, MA: Lexington Books, 1977.

Johnson, Paul. *A History of the American People.* New York: HarperCollins, 1998.

Kant, Emmanuel. "Foundations of the Metaphysics of Morals." in Louis Henkin et al., *Human Rights.* New York: Foundation Press, 1999.

Landes, William M., and Richard A. Posner. "The Independent Judiciary in an Interest-Group Perspective." *Journal of Law & Economics* 18, no. 3 (1975): 875–901.

Madison, James. "Vices of the Political System of the United States" (orig. 1787) in Philip B. Kurland and Ralph Lerner, eds. *The Founders' Constitution.* Chicago: University of Chicago Press, 1987.

Mandel, David J. "Zoning Laws—The Case for Repeal." *Architectural Forum* 135, no. 5 (December 1971): 58–59.

Mandelker, Daniel R. The Zoning Dilemma: A Legal Strategy for Urban Change. Indianapolis: Bobbs-Merrill, 1971.

President's Commission on Housing, Report. Washington, DC: U.S. Government Printing Office, 1982.

Siegan, Bernard H. Other People's Property. Lexington, MA: Lexington Books, 1976.

_____, ed. Planning Without Prices: The Taking Clause as it Relates to Land Use Regulation Without Compensation. Lexington, MA: Lexington Books, 1977.

_____. Property and Freedom. New Brunswick, NJ: Transaction, 1997.

_____. "Smart Growth and Other Infirmities of Land Use Controls." San Diego Law Review 38, no. 3 (Summer 2001a): 693–734.

_____. Property Rights: From Magna Carta to the Fourteenth Amendment. New Brunswick, NJ: Transaction, 2001b.

Ukeles, Jacob. The Consequences of Municipal Zoning. Washington, D.C.: The Urban Land Institute, 1964.

U.S. National Commission on Urban Problems. Building the American City. Washington, D.C.: U.S. Government. Printing Office, 1968.

# 4

# Building Codes, Housing Prices, and the Poor

*William Tucker*

When I was in college in the 1960s I spent a summer hitchhiking across America. I took a sleeping bag, stayed at missions, and once sneaked into a model trailer home for a good night's rest.

When I was in Chicago, I had no trouble finding accommodations. The downtown Loop was filled with "flophouses"—dollar-a-night hotels. Many were abandoned factories where the floors had been partitioned into small cubicles. There was very little privacy. The first night I paid my dollar I arrived very late and slipped into my room, letting the door shut behind me. "Why don't you slam it a little harder," growled a voice that seemed to be coming from my bed. It was the man sleeping on the other side of the thin partition. It wasn't the Ritz-Carlton, but it was better than sleeping in the street.

Such cheap lodging has all but disappeared from downtown areas, where the poor and marginal inevitably congregate. The reason is simple–building code enforcement. Inevitably, some politician has come along with a campaign to "clean up downtown" and "get rid of substandard housing." "Code enforcement" is always the tool of choice. The first housing to go is the cheapest—that inhabited by the most marginal citizens. Buildings are condemned as "firetraps," for not having adequate ventilation, not providing kitchen or bathroom facilities, and for not offering people "a decent place to live."

The promise is always that such code enforcement will improve living conditions for the poor. But the result is just the opposite. "Substandard" housing that was providing some kind of shelter for the poor is forced out of business. Better housing does not appear magically in its place. Instead, people are forced off the bottom rung of the housing ladder. They become "homeless." Although homeless populations did not attract much attention before 1980, by 1989 the Conference of Mayors estimated their number at more than a million. [The United States Conference of Mayors, "A Status Report on Hunger and Homelessness in America's Cities, 1988," January, 1989.] A large portion of this growth was very likely a product of the "housing reform" efforts of the previous two decades.

Sometimes the intent of reform was even deliberate. Urban Renewal of the 1950s and 1960s was a program designed to demolish poor people's housing in the hope that the people would just go away. If replacement housing were ever built, it came years later. Efforts to clean up "Skid Rows" and spark downtown revivals adopted similar strategies. Often times, these campaigns are undertaken with the best of intentions by eager idealists. It doesn't matter. The results are the same.

Strict code enforcement leads to severe reductions of housing opportunities for the poor. Working families are affected as well. Zoning laws have now precluded building codes as the tool of choice in excluding what is considered undesirable housing, but much of the best older housing—Old Law tenements in New York, three-decker flats in Boston—are now classified as "non-conforming uses." Zoning laws cannot touch them but building codes become the impediment to housing renewal. Many states require older, non-conforming structures to upgrade to contemporary codes whenever renovation takes place. This often proves difficult or impossible. Attempt to convert older factories, offices and hospitals into housing are stalled and older buildings are abandoned. In Massachusetts, for example, three major state mental hospitals occupying more than 1,000 acres were closed in the Boston area over the last two decades. State officials agree they are ideal parcels for residential development. Yet with various zoning disputes and arguments over the preservation of out-of-code buildings, nothing has been accomplished at all three sites. [Charles C. Euchner with Elizabeth Frieze, "Getting Home: Overcoming Barriers to Housing in Greater Boston," p. 10.] Much of the deterioration in urban areas over recent decades can be traced to unreasonable enforcement of building codes. [Ibid., pp. 19ff.]

Simultaneously the maze of code regulations makes new housing much more expensive. In a 2004 report entitled "Building Codes and Housing," David Listokin, of Rutgers University and David Hattis, of Building Technology, Inc., write:

> In theory, the building code could adversely affect housing production and could increase housing costs through both substantive (technical) and administrative impediments. The former includes, as examples, restriction of cost-saving material and technologies and barriers to mass production; the latter encompasses such barriers

as administrative conflicts between different administering parties (e.g., building and fire departments) and inadequately trained inspectors.

The literature on the subject of building codes and housing presents many examples of the above-mentioned impediments. The various studies find that code inadequacies increase the cost of new housing from roughly one percent to over 200 percent. The more quantitative analyses are at the lower end of the spectrum and find code-related housing cost increases of five percent or less... [David Listokin and David Hattis, "Building Codes and Housing," April 2004: 2].

However, the role of building codes should not be exaggerated. As Listokin and Hattis conclude:

In all likelihood, building codes have much less of an impact on new housing costs compared to other regulation, such as zoning and subdivision requirements.... Past research suggests, and we concur, that these other regulations are more consequential with respect to new construction than building codes—[but] that may not be the case with respect to rehabilitation of existing housing [Ibid.: 3].

The earliest attempts to standardize building construction came from the insurance industry, which was trying to prevent fires. In 1905, the National Board of Fire Underwriters published the first model building code in the United States, the *National Building Code,* which was updated continually until 1976. The insurance industry also regulated electrical installations, creating the first *National Electric Code* in 1897. The engineering profession and the construction industry made contributions—sometimes as a way of setting standards that might limit their competition. The National Association of Master Plumbers became interested in plumbing codes in the nineteenth century and finally published a model plumbing code in 1933.

The more common origin of municipal building codes, however, was housing reform. Often beginning with journalistic exposes or political campaigns against conditions in the slums, there was always an element of ambiguity to these efforts. Was it the housing or the people living in it that were the real problem?

This ambivalence can be seen in the pages of the first great tract of housing reform, Jacob Riis's *How the Other Half Lives*, published in 1890. Setting the scene for his efforts to improve conditions in Mulberry Bend, the worst slum in Lower Manhattan, Riis began as follows:

[T]he moment [an observer] turns the corner he finds spread out what might better be the marketplace in some town in Southern Italy that a street in New York.... When the sun shines the entire population seeks the street, carrying on its household work, its bargaining, its love-making on the street or sidewalk, or idling there when it has nothing better to do.... Along the curb women sit in rows, young and old alike with the odd head-covering, pad or turban, that is the badge of servitude.... The women do all the carrying, all the work that one sees going on in "the Bend." The men sit or stand in the streets, on trucks, or in the open doors of the saloons smoking black clay pipes, talking and gesticulating as if forever on the point of coming to blows. [Jacob Riis, *How the Other Half Lives*, New York, Hill and Wang, 1957, pp. 43–46.]

Obviously uneasy in this alien landscape, Riis attributes the squalor to inadequate housing, particularly the practice of taking old single-family homes and chopping them up into rooms.

The first tenement New York knew bore the mark of Cain.... It was the "rear house," infamous ever after in the city's history. There had been tenement-houses before, but they were not built for the purpose. Nothing would probably have shocked their original owners more than the idea of their harboring a promiscuous crowd; for they were the decorous homes of the old Knickerbockers, the proud aristocracy of Manhattan in the early days [Ibid.: 5].

What Riis was describing, of course, was the process of "filtering," where older housing is divided up and handed on to poorer people, while the wealthy move on to newer headquarters. It is, in fact, one of the surest guarantees that the poor will get reasonably decent housing, since housing for the affluent is usually built to much higher standards than housing built to the lowest common denominator. Riis, like many other reformers, however, regarded this process with a jaundiced eye.

Their "large rooms were partitioned into several smaller ones, without regard to light or ventilation, the rate of rent being lower in proportion to space or height from the street; and they soon became filled from cellar to garret with a class of tenantry living from hand to mouth, loose in morals, improvident in habits, degraded, and squalid as beggary itself" [Ibid.: 6].

So were the poor better off because they at least had roofs over their head or was it better to tear down the slums in pursuit of some utopian vision? Riis opted for the latter. When his efforts led in short order to the complete leveling of The Bend, Riis defended his work five years later in *The Review of Reviews:*

Are we better off scattering the poison and the poverty of the Bend? Yes. It is not scattered. The great and by far the worst part of it is destroyed with the slum. Such a slum as this is itself the poison. It taints whatever it touches.... Its poverty is hopeless, its vice bestiality, its crime desperation.... There is a connection between the rottenness of the house and that of the tenant that is patent and positive. There will never be another Mulberry Bend.... In its place will come trees and grass and flowers; for its dark hovels light and sunshine and air. [Riis, "The Clearing of Mulberry Bend," *Review of Reviews*, 12 (1895) 172,177.]

The trees and grass and flowers, of course, never materialized—nor would it help the poor find housing if they did. In this vision, however, we can already see the seeds of Urban Renewal, which would attempt to replace solid housing with high-rise apartments surrounded by grass and trees and flowers fifty years later.

One irony of which Riis was well aware was that some of the worst slum housing he witnessed was often the result of previous efforts at housing reform. In describing Gotham Court, a notorious hangout, Riis notes:

> It is curious to find that this notorious block, whose name was so long synonymous with all that was desperately bad, was originally built (in 1851) by a benevolent Quaker for the express purpose of rescuing the poor people from the dreadful rookeries they were then living in [Riis, op. cit., p. 27].

The Big Flat, another infamous Lower East Side magnet for prostitutes and drunks, had been built in 1855 by the New York Society for Improving the Condition of the Poor. Riis was on hand in 1885 to see it torn down.

Surveying the situation 75 years later, Anthony Downs took a more realistic assessment of the slums:

> [I]n very low-income areas, where many households live in extremely deteriorating units that clearly violate the law, housing codes are almost totally unenforced. This is not a conspiracy between evil landlords and the authorities. Rather it is an economic necessity resulting mainly from the poverty of the residents. They cannot afford enough rent to allow property owners to maintain their housing at legal quality levels and still obtain a reasonable return on their investment....

> Under these circumstances, rigorous enforcement of housing codes would require local authorities to evict thousands of households from illegally substandard units. But where would they go? ... These households would have to leave the area or lives in the streets, as in Calcutta. [Anthony Downs, *Opening up the Suburbs: An Urban Strategy for America*, New Haven, Yale University Press, 1973, pp. 6–7.]

Still, such efforts persist even today. In the 1970s, residents of Takoma Park, Maryland, an older Washington suburb with the reputation of a liberal bohemia, became obsessed with the practice of single-family homeowners renting accessory apartments and "granny flats." Researching the law, the "housing activists" discovered a 60-year-old Montgomery County statute that forbad rentals in a single-family zone. Since the practice had been going on for decades, a compromise was adopted in 1978 allowing anyone who had rented before 1954 to remain in place for ten years. When the exemption expired in 1988, however, an estimated 1,000 tenants, including families with children, were evicted from apartments that many had occupied for decades.

*

The elimination of acceptable housing through code enforcement was not the only outcome of Riis's work. *How the Other Half Lives* also led to the first wave of building codes on new construction. Fortunately, the results here were a little more satisfactory.

The first building codes in New York had originally been adopted after the cholera epidemic of 1867. The law required small airshafts in the middle of the building so that every interior room would have some access to fresh air. The standard design became the "railroad flat," a front-to-back apartment with the living room in front, a kitchen in back, and small bedrooms with airshafts in the middle. Then at an architectural competition in 1880, James Ware proposed the famous "dumbbell design," featuring two small four-room apartments front and back, with an air shaft in the middle providing all rooms with air and light.

In 1887, the city government adopted the dumbbell design in what eventually became known as the "Old Tenement Law." For the first time, all new apartments were required to have running water. By the time Riis's book started to have an impact, however, the Old Law was already regarded as inadequate—even a betrayal of reform. Airshafts had become conduits for noise and repositories of discarded refuse. Toilets were still not required for each apartment. And so, following upon Riis's efforts, the New Tenement Law was adopted in 1901, requiring complete plumbing, bigger airshafts, and small backyards.

The success of the New Law shows that, if by nothing else than blind luck, regulations can occasionally coincide with market shifts. Builders protested the law would make housing unaffordable, but rising affluence made it possible for tenants to afford such improved amenities. The new code was an astonishing success. Most of Upper Manhattan, the Bronx, and Brooklyn were built according to its requirements. By 1916, half a million people—one-third of the city's population—were living in New Law buildings and by 1931 the figure had swelled to 3 million. Duplicate laws were adopted in New Jersey, Connecticut, Indiana, and Wisconsin and by 1920 more than twenty cities—including Cleveland, St. Paul, Duluth, Portland, and Berkeley—had similar building requirements.

No sooner had housing reformers created the success of the New Law than they once again began using the law to pursue their own objectives. One thing that has always characterized housing reformers is an intense dislike of landlords. The landlord is a lowlife, a shyster, a parvenu—often an immigrant or a Jew—someone who sucks the blood of the poor while challenging the status of the reformer as well. Most housing reformers tend to be middle-class people who look down on both tenants and landlords, although they are usually able to muster some sympathy for the tenants. In the early 1900s reformers tended to be mainline Protestants often as concerned with immigration as dilapidated housing.

The marvelous thing about housing is that it offers a business opportunity at which poor and immigrant classes can succeed. Study after study has shown that landlords of the poor come from the ranks of the poor themselves. Often they are members of the building trades. Michael Dukakis, the 1988 Democratic candidate for president, became a landlord while lifting himself out of his Greek immigrant neighborhood in Boston. Donald Trump's father was a Swedish carpenter who founded the family empire by building a neighbor's garage. In the last half of the twentieth century, many petit bourgeois immigrants from Eastern Europe and other parts of the world became landlords because they had limited English and couldn't claim a place in the larger society.

Housing reformers tend to look down on this process, characterizing landlords as exploiters and fantasizing them as fabulously powerful and wealthy members of their own class. (The term "landlord" has always been a grotesque misnomer for the owners of dilapidated urban housing.) Of course it must be acknowledged that the poor often tend to hate their landlords as well. It is often said that, next to the relationship between husband and wife, the ties between landlord and tenant are the most emotionally explosive in the world.

Unfortunately, this precarious balance between poor tenants and almost-as-poor landlords can be poisonously disrupted when housing reform enters the picture. Tenants who are the most disruptive and destructive often become the biggest beneficiaries. Rent control laws have a disastrous effect. Activists claim they are helping poor tenants but the more common result is the triumph of the most unruly tenants and the destruction of private housing.

As an alternative to this "unfair and unequal" relationship between private tenants and landlords, housing reformers inevitably propose government ownership of housing. The government will build better housing because it has unlimited resources. The government will be a beneficent landlord because public officials do not work for a profit and are therefore not exploitative. The housing will be built to higher standards because urban planners and imaginative architects will be called into the process. As Jane Jacobs discovered in writing *The Death and Life of Great American Cities*, the stark and forbidding public housing projects that came to dominate the urban landscape of the 1950s had been conceived in the 1920s as Le Corbusier's "Garden Cities of Tomorrow."

In 1900, a group of charitable organizations formed the National Housing Association to try to improve housing for the poor. In 1914, Lawrence Villier, director of New York City's Tenement Housing Department, became its director. By 1916, delegates at the Association's second national convention were listening to Prescott Hall, a Boston housing reformer, present a paper entitled "The Menace of the Three Decker." [Prescott Hall, "The Menace of the Three Decker," *Housing Problems in America*, Proceedings of the Fifth National Conference on Housing, 1916: 133].

The three-decker—a three-story wooden frame house on a small lot with a railroad apartment on each floor—had already become the favorite of immigrant groups. Members of the working class, usually skilled in some area of building maintenance, could buy a three-decker, occupy one floor and rent the other two, often to other family members. It was an ideal situation for upwardly mobile working people, allowing them to accumulate capital with little more than a subsistence income.

But reformers didn't like it. Hall argued against "vertical as compared to horizontal housing of people." Massachusetts had already adopted a "town tenement act" in 1912, enabling municipalities to ban any "wooden tenement" in which "cooking shall be done above the second floor." Now Hall—who also headed the Immigration Restriction League—wanted to use the law to ban the three-decker, then spread the gospel to the rest of the country.

In place of three-deckers, housing reformers proposed public housing supplemented by single-family homes in the suburbs. The Association published a pamphlet entitled "One Million People in Small Homes," outlining a suburban vision of "wholesome homes for low-paid workers." In *Housing for the Unskilled Wage Earner* (1919), reformer Edith Elmer Wood admitted that trying to upgrade housing through building code enforcement was only putting people out in the street. Instead, she proposed that municipal governments build housing and become the landlords of the poor. As Howard Husock, of the Kennedy School of Government, points out, the reformers' agenda consisted of "public and subsidized housing in the cities and single-family homes in the suburbs, with precious little in between." [Howard Husock, "Rediscovering the Three-Decker House," *The Public Interest,* 1990.]

What this vision failed to recognize is that public housing deprives the poor of the chance of becoming landlords. Instead of gaining ownership of small, multi-family housing, the poor are condemned to become eternal tenants. In theory, of course, the subsidized rents could allow poor families to accumulate savings for homeownership, but without multifamily homes the leap to a single-family ownership in the suburbs becomes too wide to cross. Instead, the poor become locked into public housing, spending their money instead on cars, clothing, large consumer items and other things that have no equity value.

Despite the reforms, cities continued to build tenements and three-deckers throughout the 1920s. Then came the Depression. Although few people remember it, the era was one of sizable housing vacancies. Young couples delayed marriage, tenants doubled up, and people remained in small apartments. Landlords had fewer prospects and those tenants they had couldn't always pay the rent. Banks began foreclosing. Ironically, housing reformers saw this as yet another opportunity to "clear the slums!"

In New York, Mayor Fiorello LaGuardia was particularly galled that 67,000 Old Law tenements still housed almost a million people. With Depression-era vacancies as high as 10 percent, this indicated—if nothing else—that Old Law building were still more than habitable. Pursuing the reformer's letter-of-the-law approach, however, LaGuardia vowed to level every remaining Old Law building simply because they did not meet code standards. When Langdon W. Post, chairman of the Municipal Housing Authority, pointed out that the city government was already the largest owner of Old Law tenements through tax foreclosures, LaGuardia didn't flinch. "We'll tear them down, every last one of them," he blustered.

By 1936, savings banks in New York had foreclosed on more than 2,000 Old Law tenements and become their landlords. Fearing criminal prosecution by the city government for code violations, a group of banks notified LaGuardia they intended to close down their entire stock, putting tens of thousands of people into the streets. Sobered at last, LaGuardia offered a six-month exemption from prosecution.

> I must confess to you we have some 30,000 tenement buildings that are inhabited today that are in violation of law, that disregard every provision of the Multiple Dwelling Law as to safety and health, air and ventilation. And yet, I dare not vacate those houses. I cannot order them demolished. Why? Because there's no place that the people living in these houses can move to.

And so the Old Law buildings survived. Today they are among the most sought-after prizes for urban renovators.

Although cheap multifamily housing survived the reforms of the 1930s, its expansion was doomed by another reform of the 1920s—municipal zoning. As Jane Jacobs would note in *The Death and Life of Great American Cities* (1960), the favorite target of zoning was unplanned urban diversity. Mixed commercial and residential uses became unacceptable. The nineteenth and early twentieth centuries had built what old-fashioned urban officials used to called "taxpayers"—three- and four-story buildings with stores on the ground floor and apartments above. Taxpayers created street traffic and a sense of security in urban spaces. Now urban planners began to construct their "garden cities," the sterile, high-rise apartments surrounded by grass and trees where—as one resident told Jacobs—"you can't even find a place to buy a newspaper." By the 1940s, Boston had zoned out three-deckers. New York was replacing the dynamism of Times Square with the windy plazas of Sixth Avenue, the "Avenue of the Americas."

In the new zoning context, three-deckers and older tenements became "non-conforming uses." Courts generally ruled that zoning could not be retroactive. If a building was already in place, it could not be condemned for not conforming to the zoning law. But these "undesirables" could be attacked by aggressive code enforcement. Most disastrous of all, if the building were to undergo any kind of renovation, it could be required to meet contemporary standards. As the suburban migration began to stress the urban tax base, this proved to be the most destructive policy of all.

The classic target of code enforcement became the "SRO"—single-room occupancy hotels. SROs are just a step above the partition hotels where I stayed in Chicago. They have separate rooms but few amenities. Bathrooms are shared in the hall, kitchens may not exist, although people often cook on hot plates (a common source of electrical fires, it must be admitted). SROs are the signature of a "seedy neighborhood"—a place that attracts the unemployed, the unattached, the down-and-out. "The Hot-1 Baltimore," a successful play of the early 1970s, was built around the tragicomic encounters among the loners and losers who congregate in such places. "Baltimore used to be one of the most beautiful cities in America," opines one character at one point, to which another responds, "Every city used to be one of the most beautiful cities in America."

As American cities struggled through an era of decline, many declared war on the SRO. New York City under John Lindsay ran a highly publicized campaign against SROs that was heralded as "saving the Upper West Side." In *Rude Awakenings* (ICS Press, 1992), Richard White, Jr. a twenty-year veteran of federal anti-poverty programs, argues that code-enforcement closings of SRO hotels were probably the leading cause of the homeless populations that emerged at the end of the 1970s.

> To judge from local reports…, the frequent observation that nearly 50 percent of the remaining supply [of SRO housing] disappeared in the 1970s does not seem unrea-

sonable. In Chicago, for example, SRO units declined 80 percent between 1960 and 1980. Most of these units were lost before 1973, when about 36,000 remained in the city as a whole. By 1984, half the remaining units had been "converted, abandoned, or destroyed" [White, p. 118].

Unfortunately, it was not always market forces that supported these SROs. The broad expansion of the welfare system created a virulent dynamic that gave the most disorganized among the poor enormous buying power. At various times, hotels as distinguished as the Martinique in Herald Square, the Carter Hotel in Times Square, and the St. George in Brooklyn Heights did spells as "welfare hotels," filled with welfare mothers and their children who often terrorized surrounding neighborhoods. In conducting a series of interviews outside the Martinique in 1986, I found people who had migrated from as far away as Ohio and North Carolina to take advantage of the subsidies.

The deinstitutionalization of mental patients in the 1970s added to the mayhem. Although the mass release had been built around the concept of "halfway houses," few such places actually existed. As Richard White, Jr. reported:

> While some of these patients were placed in nursing homes and boarding houses, others joined the low-income workers and alcoholics living in the shrinking supply of SROs. By the mid-1970s it was reported that almost a quarter of the 100,000 persons living in New York City's SROs were "severely mentally dysfunctional" [White, p. 118].

Whole neighborhoods such as Coney Island were transformed in the process.

Still, the traditional SROs had provided lodging and a social network to people who were capable of taking care of themselves:

> [C]ensus data show ... that 68 percent of the SRO dwellers in Chicago of the 1950s had lived in the same apartment for two years or more. In a current survey, about nine out of ten Chicago SRO residents report they are satisfied with their living arrangements. Almost as many know the managers or desk clerks personally, and more than half know the owner.... Local retail establishments in SRO districts provide services valued by the residents.... Seen as blight by reformers, saloons are social centers, and second-hand stores and pawnshops are important economic supports [White, p. 121].

In 1968, President Lyndon Johnson attempted to reverse urban decline with his Model Cities program. The National Commission on Urban Problems, better known as the "Douglas Commission," was appointed to conduct an exhaustive survey of urban housing. Listokin and Hattis report the results:

[The Commission] found that unnecessary housing costs are inherent in building codes that delay construction, prevent the use of modern materials, mandate antiquated and outdated provisions, inhibit mass production (e.g., the marketing of mobile homes), prevent large-scale conventional construction, and are questionably administered.

One odd factor—reported by Charles Euchner and Elizabeth Frieze, of Boston's Pioneer Institute—is that the level of municipal corruption had declined with the disappearance of immigrant political machines and the rise of professional city management. Paradoxically, this often made it harder to get things done. The intricacy of municipal building codes invited corruption and political officials were often willing to take advantage. Paying off a building inspector was a routine way of getting things done. But while corruption declined, building codes remained equally labyrinthine and now there was no way to get past them.

Spurred by the criticism of the Douglas Report, many states moved to reform by adopting statewide building codes. But the law remained enforced at the local level. In their 2003 report, "Getting Home: Overcoming Barriers to Housing in Greater Boston, written for the Pioneer Institute, Charles C. Euchner, of the Kennedy School of Government, and Elizabeth Frieze, of Harvard, found no fewer than eleven state agencies with jurisdiction over apartments being built or renovated in Boston.

"Each board and commission establishes and adjusts its own specialty code in isolation from the others, without consideration of its impact on the overall universe of codes," the authors concluded.

Moreover, leaving enforcement in the hands of local officials effectively undid the reform. "An unpublished document of the Board

**Table 4.1**
**Massachusetts State Agencies with Building Code Jurisdiction**

| State Body Promulgator | Codes and Regulations |
| --- | --- |
| Board of Building Regulation and Standards | State Building Code |
| Board of Registration of Plumbers and Gas Fitters | State Plumbing Code |
| Board of state Examiners of Electricians | Electric Code |
| Board of Fire Prevention Regulation | Fire Prevention Regulations |
| Board of Boilers Rules | Boiler Regulations |
| Board of Elevator Regulations | Elevator Code |
| Department of Public Health | Sanitary Code |
| Dept. of Environmental Protection | Drinking Water Regulations |
| Dept. of Environmental Protection | Title 5 |
| Dept. of Environmental Protection | Wetlands Protection Act |
| Architectural Access Board | Handicap Accessibility Code |

of Building Regulations and Standards details the ways in which local officials create de facto local codes," they noted. "As part of their everyday implementation of the state rules, local officials often take it upon themselves to upgrade the state standards."

As Anthony Downs notes in an introduction to the paper, this practice inevitably translates into higher costs:

> Developers, realtors, and other housing professionals say that local officials can increase the time and expense associated with building and selling homes. Idiosyncratic interpretation of state standards introduces a level of risk that gets translated into added costs to developers and ultimately the buyer [Euchner and Frieze, p. vii].

As problematic as building codes in general was the "25–50 law," which required that older buildings be brought up to contemporary standards code when renovated. If 25–50 percent were being rebuilt, that portion must conform. If more than 50 percent were being renovated, the entire structure must meet current code requirements.

"The major conceptual problem with the requirement of total overhaul is that many elements of the buildings were safe even if they did not meet new building standards," noted Euchner and Frieze. "Ceiling heights, window sizes, door widths, stair risers, emergency exits, fire alarm systems, and floor sags do not profoundly affect a building's health or safety, but new building standards might require a total gutting of the building.

> For instance, in the late 1970s developers sought to transform the property at 175 Commonwealth Avenue in Boston from a church into a five-unit dwelling…. [A]ccording to the 25–50 percent rule, the entire structure would need to be brought into compliance with the code for new residential buildings…. [T]he code for new construction would not permit the existing connecting balconies to be used as a means of egress. Normally buildings could construct a fire escape as an alternative…, but the building was located in an historic district where the special commission in charge had explicitly forbidden fire escapes [Ibid.: 23].

Because of these complications, many renovations were never undertaken. Euchner and Frieze cite the effort to convert three abandoned state properties—Boston State Hospital (175 acres), Danvers State Hospital (500 acres), and Metropolitan State Hospital (338 acres)—that had already stalled for more than a decade because of wrangling with various state agencies.

In other states, recognition of these problems has led to the adoption of "smart codes" that attempt to be business-friendly in encouraging urban renovations. New Jersey and Maryland are considered the best examples. "In the 1990s, it became clear that this form of regulation was often arbitrary, unpredictable, and constrained the reuse of older properties," write Listokin and Hattis.

Beginning with the State of New Jersey, states and local jurisdictions began to develop new ways to regulate work in existing structures, using what came to be know as rehabilitation codes, and in some jurisdictions as smart codes.... [S]mart codes have [since] been adopted by several states and local jurisdictions, including Maryland,; New York State, Rhode Island, Minnesota, Wilmington, Delaware; and Wichita, Kansas. The overall goal ... is to encourage the reuse of older buildings [Listokin and Hattis, op. cit., p. 10].

Failure to reform building codes in Massachusetts, on the other hand, has left Boston with the third highest per-unit construction costs in the country, behind only San Francisco and Nashville. Housing permits in the state have risen only 3 percent since 1980 as opposed to 37 percent in the rest of the country. Prices have increased 440 percent, as opposed to 182 percent in the rest of the states. Vacancy rates in single-family homes, normally 2 percent, have fallen to .6 percent and rental vacancies, normally 7 percent, are at 2 percent. Euchner and Frieze call housing costs "the single most important factor in the state's high cost of living," creating a tremendous damper on the state's economy.

"Look at the list of the National Home Builders Association," real estate lawyer John Smolak told the authors. "Massachusetts firms are almost never mentioned." Benjamin Fierro of the Massachusetts Home Builders Association added, "It's virtually impossible for a young builder to get involved in this business [in Massachusetts]. There are a lot of talented builders who are idle or nearly idle. The atmosphere is so hostile that people say, 'I don't need this.'"

Since Jack Kemp's tenure as secretary of housing and urban development, the emphasis at the Department of Housing and Urban Development (HUD) has turned to eliminating barriers to housing at the local level. Surprisingly, HUD has become one of the biggest critics of state and local building codes.

It has now become commonly recognized—at the national level at least—that the elimination of SROs and other forms of cheap urban housing are the cause of much homelessness. One city that tried early to undo the damage was San Diego, which found the gentrification of its downtown Gaslight District threatened by people living in the street. "Several SRO hotels were lost and charitable organizations serving the indigent were really getting kicked around down there," reported Frank Landerville, director of the Regional Task Force on the Homeless.

At first the city responded with a law that required builders who razed an SRO to replace it with another. This only discouraged new construction. The law expired in three years and by that time public officials had decided the real problem was building codes.

"We realized the law had created a gap in personal accommodations," said Judy Lenthal, a senior planner for the city government. "An SRO was less than people wanted but a studio apartment was more than they could afford." Instead, the city allowed a "living unit"—a one-room apartment that shared either a common kitchen or bathroom with other tenants. A boom in such units followed. In 2004, The Association for Community Housing Solutions won the $25,000 MetLife Foundation Award for Excellence in Affordable Housing for Del Mar Apartments, a 33-unit development to accommodate permanently homeless people under the new code.

Pursuing this line of approach, the Bush Administration has achieved some remarkable, if unheralded, success in reducing nation's urban homeless population. In 2006, for the first time in decades, a large number of cities reported simultaneous reductions in their homeless populations. The origin of the change lies in "Housing First," a program implemented through the Interagency Council on Homelessness. "Were conspiring to undo what we've been told for so many years, that this is an intractable issue," says Philip Mangano, former director of the Massachusetts Housing and Shelter Alliance, who now heads the Interagency Council.

The new approach returns full circle to the 1980s argument that the solution to the problem is "Housing, housing, housing." At the time, however, advocates blamed the Reagan Administration, arguing that "cutbacks in federal housing construction" were the source of the problem. This argument had two fatal weaknesses:

- There was no cutback in federal housing construction during the Reagan years. Most of the housing was already in the pipeline. The cutbacks came on authorizations of new funding, which would not have an effect for many years hence.
- While future construction was being scaled back, this was more than compensated by the expansion of federal Section-8 housing vouchers. The voucher system was much cheaper and reached far more people.

Vouchers could do very little, however, if there were no increase in the supply of cheap housing. Increased spending power in the hands of the poor would only inflate the price of existing housing. The solution lay in persuading municipal governments to adopt policies that make more housing available.

"Housing, housing, housing" eventually came under attack from Andrew Cuomo, the son of New York Governor Mario Cuomo. In 1986

Cuomo founded Housing Enterprises for the Less Privileged (HELP), an elaborately subsidized program that put small numbers of homeless people into full-service facilities dubbed "hospitals," where they underwent intensive therapy and counseling for various types of addiction before being moved to permanently subsidized housing. (The "hospital" designation was adopted so the HELP could skirt New York tenant laws, which would make it difficult to remove residents once they had occupied their quarters for 30 days.)

In 1991, while serving as commissioner of homeless services under New York Mayor David Dinkins, Cuomo raised hackles among housing advocates by publishing "The Way Home: A New Direction in Social Policy," which challenged accepted orthodoxies. Cuomo argued that housing was not the problem and that personal dysfunction was what put people in the streets. "For too long, we did not want to admit the truth, because to admit the truth could be seen as criticism of [the homeless]," Cuomo wrote. "The problem has many roots, [including] troubled family histories, drug or alcohol problems, and premature deinstitutionalization from mental hospitals.... The very term 'homeless' is a misnomer. An apartment doesn't cure a crack addiction."

When Cuomo became secretary of housing and urban development under President Bill Clinton, he pursued this strategy nationwide. Instead of offering only "three hots and a cot," more expensive shelters were designed to address homeless people's psychological problems as well. Meanwhile, the old shelter system persisted—even though many hard-core homeless people refused to enter them. What the Clinton administration never asked is why the market couldn't provide bare-minimum lodgings that would serve as a much cheaper platform for providing social services.

In 2004, Mangano instituted a completely different approach. Initiated in 2004, Housing First essentially recreates the SRO hotel as the safety net of last resort. Homeless people with severe personal problems are moved into these minimal living quarters and are allowed to live rent-free for the first few weeks. Some people insist on bring their shopping carts. As they are routed into job programs or detoxification facilities, they are required to pay small rents. What is avoided is the fruitless pattern of people shuffling back and forth between the street, soup kitchens, and temporary shelters. Studies have found 80 percent of the participants remained in their minimal living quarters a year later.

Housing First is unique in its recognition that local housing policies are at the root of the problem. The program requires cities to enter a ten-year contract to make various efforts, including reducing opposition to bare-minimum housing. So far more than 200 cities and counties have undertaken ten-year planning initiatives. So far the results have been promising.

Building codes have become a way of trying to drive cheap housing off the market. Unfortunately, the consequences are perverse—higher housing costs and greater homelessness, followed by ridiculously expensive programs to try to cure it. Letting the market do the work is the best way.

After fifty years, we have returned to the old SRO hotel—maybe even the partition hotel that once offered minimal accommodations in cities like Chicago. I hope to stay in one again next time I visit.

## References

Anderson, Martin. The Federal Bulldozer: A Critical Analysis of Urban Renewal Policies, 1949–1962, Cambridge, MA: The MIT Press, 1964.

Commission on Homeless Services, Andrew Cuomo, Chairman. "The Way Home: A New Direction in Social Policy," New York, 1991.

Downs, Anthony. Opening up the Suburbs: An Urban Strategy for America, New Haven, CT: Yale University Press, 1973.

Euchner, Charles C. with Frieze, Elizabeth. "Getting Home: Overcoming Barriers to Housing in Greater Boston," Pioneer Institute for Policy Research and Rappaport Institue for Greater Boston, 2003, http://www.pioneerinstitute.org/pdf/wp21.pdf.

Frieden, Bernard. The Environmental Protection Hustle. Cambridge, MA: The MIT Press, 1979.

Glaeser, Edward L., Gyourko, Joseph, and Saks, Raven E. "Why Have Housing Prices Gone Up?" Harvard Institute of Economic Research, Discussion Paper Number 2061, Cambridge, Mass., February 2005, http://post.economics.harvard.edu/hier/2005papers/HIER2061.pdf.

Glaeser, Edward L., Schuetz, Jenny, and Ward, Bryce. "Regulation and the Rise of Housing Prices in Greater Boston," Pioneer Institute, Boston, 2006, http://www.ksg.harvard.edu/rappaport/downloads/housing_regulations/regulation_housingprices.pdf.

Hall, Prescott. "The Menace of the Three Decker," Housing Problems in America, Proceedings of the Fifth National Conference on Housing, 1916.

Hopper, Kim and Hamberg, Jill. The Faces of Homelessness: From Skid Row to the New Poor. New York: Community Service Society, 1984.

Husock, Howard. "Rediscovering the Three-Decker House," The Public Interest, 1990.

Jacobs, Jane. The Death and Life of Great American Cities, New York: Random House, 1961.

Lipman, Barbara J. "Something's Gotta Give: Working Families and the Cost of Housing, Center for Housing Policy, Volume, Issue 2, Washington, D.C., 2005, http://www.nhc.org/pdf/pub_nc_sgg_04_05.pdf.

Listokin, David and Hattis, David. "Building Codes and Housing," Paper presented at the Workshop on Regulatory Barriers to Affordable Housing, U.S. Department of Housing and Urban Development, Washington D.C., April 22, 2004, http://www.planning.org/japa/pdf/JAPABurby06.pdf.

National Academy of Sciences. "Homelessness, Health, and Human Needs." Washington: National Academy Press, 1988.

National Coalition for the Homeless. "The Homeless and the Economic Recovery." New York: National Coalition for the Homeless, 1988.

Riis, Jacob. "The Clearing of Mulberry Bend," Review of Reviews, 12 (1895) 172, 177.

Riis, Jacob. How the Other Half Lives, New York, Hill and Wang, 1957.

Rossi, Peter. Down and Out in America: The Origins of Homelessness. Chicago: University of Chicago Press, 1989.

Siegen, Bernard. Land Use Without Zoning. Lexington, MA: D.C. Heath, 1972.

Sternlieb, George and Hughes, James. W. The Future of Rental Housing. New Brunswick, NJ: Center for Urban Policy Research, 1981.

Torry, Fuller E. Nowhere to Go: The Tragic Odyssey of the Homeless Mentally Ill. New York: Harper and Row, 1988.

Tucker, William. The Excluded Americans: Homelessness and Housing Policies, Washington, DC: Regnery Gateway, 1990.

Tucker, William, "Give 'Em Shelter: Good News for the Homeless." Washington. The Weekly Standard, July 3, 2006.

United States Conference of Mayors, "A Status Report on Hunger and Homelessness in America's Cities, 1988," January, 1989.

White, Richard W., Jr. Rude Awakenings: What the Homeless Crisis Tells Us, San Francisco, Institute for Contemporary Studies, 1992.

Wood, Edith Elmer. The Housing of the Unskilled Wage Earner: America's Next Problem, New York: Macmillan, 1919.

# 5

# Smart Growth and Housing

*Randal O'Toole*

Smart growth is a land-use and transportation planning concept that calls for higher-density, compact urban areas, mixing commercial with residential uses, and emphasizing pedestrian-friendly design and transit-oriented development over automobile-oriented development.[1] Smart-growth advocates believe that Americans are too "auto-dependent" and that their plans will allow people to reach jobs, shops, recreation, and other destinations without driving as much as they do today.

In actual practice, smart-growth advocates have badly mistaken the causal relationships that lead people to drive rather than walk or ride transit. The design features that smart growth would impose on urban areas have little effect on people's travel habits. They do, however, have a large effect on housing prices; namely, they make single-family housing unaffordable for all but the elite members of society.

The term *smart growth* was first applied to these ideas by the administration of Maryland Governor Parris Glendening in 1996. Prior to that time, they were most often called *New Urbanism*. While some architects and planners believe there are subtle differences between New Urbanism and smart growth, for the purposes of this chapter the terms are interchangeable. As noted by one member of Glendening's staff, the main significance of the term *smart growth* is it branded these planning concepts "with a name people would recognize and that would be hard to oppose." Anyone who questioned the wisdom of smart growth could immediately be labeled as favoring "dumb growth."[2]

There is clearly a market of people who want to live in high-density, mixed-use developments, but it appears to be mainly limited to young, single, or double-income no-children households—and not even a majority of those groups.[3] Surveys indicate that the vast majority of Americans still aspire to live in a single-family home with a yard, and less than 20 percent are eager to live in New Urban neighborhoods. For example, a 2002 opinion poll done for the National Association of Realtors and National Association of Home Builders found that:

- 64 percent of Americans would like to live in a larger home;
- Only 17 to 23 percent wanted to live closer to work, shopping, entertainment, and restaurants; and
- Only 7 to 9 percent wanted to live closer to "the city" or public transportation;[4]
- 82 percent preferred a single-family home in the suburbs while only 18 percent wanted a "home in the city, close to work, public transportation, and shopping."[5]

Yet most smart-growth advocates are not content to build to the market. As Urban Land Institute researcher Douglas Porter notes, there is a "gap between the daily mode of living desired by most Americans and the mode that most city planners ... believe is most appropriate." While most Americans "want a house on a large lot and three cars in every garage," planners believe this leads to a urban development pattern "that is expensive in terms of public and private infrastructure costs, quality of life, and environmental damage."[6]

To ensure that planners would have their way, in 1991 the founders of New Urbanism called for having "government take charge of the planning process" rather than allow "developer-initiated, piecemeal development."[7] They went on to form the Congress for the New Urbanism, whose goals included that "All development should be in the form of compact, walkable neighborhoods" and "A diverse mix of activities (residences, shops, schools, workplaces, and parks, etc.) should occur in proximity."[8] Not only does the group think that all new development should follow its model, it believes in "the reconfiguration of sprawling suburbs into communities of real neighborhoods and diverse districts."[9] In other words, if they had their way, no one except a few rural residents would be allowed to live anywhere but in New Urban neighborhoods.

The problem with government, observes Porter, is that democratically elected local officials are unwilling to try to impose huge lifestyle changes on their constituents. So Porter, the Brookings Institution's Anthony Downs, and other have recommended that planners use regional governments to impose smart growth on urban areas. As Downs says, regional governments "can take controversial stands without making its individual members commit themselves to those stands. Each member can claim that 'the organization' did it or blame all the other members."[10]

Officially known as metropolitan planning organizations, regional governments were imposed on urban areas by the federal government in 1965. Sometimes called councils or associations of governments, the original purpose of these regional governments was not to govern but to submit housing and transportation grant proposals on behalf of urban areas to the federal government and in turn to distribute those federal funds to local governments in each urban area. Each council of governments is supposed to be overseen by mayors or city councilors representing a majority of the people in the urban area. Over time, some regional governments have gained actual planning and governing powers over their regions, most often through their power to deny federal funds to local governments that refuse to cooperate with the rest of the region.

Mostly through the power of their regional governments, a number of urban areas in the United States have applied New Urbanism or smart-growth principles to their regions. Portland (Oregon), Minneapolis, San Jose, and San Diego are the most comprehensive examples, but some smart-growth principles have been tested in such varying regions as Baltimore, Denver, Austin, and Missoula.

## 1. Smart Growth and Transportation

One of the main goals of smart growth is to save people money and time while cleaning the air by reducing the amount of driving people have to do, so a brief review of smart growth's effects on transportation is worthwhile. From a transport point of view, the main result of smart growth is a significant increase in traffic congestion. This wastes people's time, fuel, and—because cars pollute more in stop-and-go traffic—makes the air dirtier rather than cleaner. Smart growth only slightly reduces driving's share of total travel and may not reduce per-capita driving at all.

Smart-growth advocates point to studies showing that people who live in high-density, mixed-use neighborhoods tend to drive less than people who live in conventional suburbs. But these studies fail to account for the fact that people who want to drive less—mainly young people without children—will tend to locate in pedestrian- and transit-friendly neighborhoods. This does not mean that forcing families with children to live in such neighborhoods will suddenly reduce the need to drive to discount grocery stores, soccer fields, or distant employment centers.

The idea that compact, mixed-use development would reduce driving was suggested and supposedly proven by the Land Use-Transportation-

Air Quality (LUTRAQ) study that was begun by 1000 Friends of Oregon in 1989.[11] But, as University of Southern California planning Professor Genevieve Giuliano observed, the higher densities required by smart growth more than made up for any per-capita reductions in driving.[12] If a 100-percent increase in density is required to reduce per-capita driving by 10 percent, the result is a 90-percent increase in driving per square mile. Unless more roads are built, which smart growth would oppose, that means more congestion.

More thorough studies by Portland-area planners found that LUTRAQ had overestimated the effects of smart growth on per-capita driving. Metro, Portland's regional planning agency, predicted that, after implementing the most comprehensive smart-growth plan in the nation, per-capita driving would increase, driving's share of travel would decrease by no more than 5 percent, and the amount of time Portland-area residents waste sitting in traffic would more than quintuple.[13]

The 2000 census asked people how they usually traveled to work, and their answers can be compared with population densities in the nation's 400 urban areas. As shown in the "Density and Commuting" figure, more than 89 percent of commuters take autos to work in the vast majority of regions. This group ranges from Kingsport, Tennessee, with a density of less than 1,000 people per square mile, where 98.3 percent of people drive to work, to Los Angeles, surprisingly the nation's densest urban area at more than 7,000 people per square mile, where 89.6 percent of people drive to work. If density is a factor at all in these urban areas, it appears that density must be increased by seven times to get 8 percent of commuters out of their cars.

Only about 50 of the 400 urban areas have less than 89 percent auto commuters. These almost exclusively fell into one of two groups. Either they were university towns with large percentages of young people, including Ithaca, New York; State College, Pennsylvania, and Davis, California; or they were major cities with large concentrations of downtown jobs, such as New York, San Francisco, and Boston.[14] Smart growth does not propose to do anything about the age composition of an urban area. But its prescription for job distribution is exactly the opposite of what these data suggest is needed to reduce driving. Instead of concentrating jobs in a central location, smart growth calls for achieving a jobs-housing balance among the communities in an urban area.

The hypothesis is that such a balance will allow people to live close to work. But it turns out that most people do not want to live particularly close to work. Surveys by University of California researchers have found

**Figure 5.1**
**Density and Commuting**

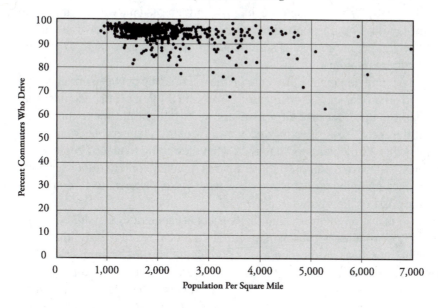

*Source: 2000 Census*

that people prefer an average commute time of 16 minutes—only a little less than the actual average of 22 minutes.[15] The researchers speculate that people want to use that time to prepare for work, depressurize on the way home.

So it was no surprise when University of California planning Professor Robert Cervero found that, in many communities in the San Francisco Bay Area, jobs and housing "are nearly perfectly balanced, yet fewer than a third of their workers reside locally, and even smaller shares of residents work locally." Thus, "even if jobs-housing balance is attained," says Cervero, "it does not guarantee self-containment or reduced external commuting."[16] So the smart-growth prescription for job distribution will at best have no effect on driving and could actually increase driving if it contributes to decentralization of downtown jobs.

In essence, smart-growth advocates have confused cause and effect in the relationship between land use and transportation. Before autos and streetcars, urban residents crowded in dense neighborhoods so they could reach jobs and shops on foot. Urban densities began to decline

when streetcars were developed in 1890 and this decline was accelerated as the automobile became popular in the 1920s and ubiquitous in
the 1950s. While transport technology influences land use, the influence
of land use on transportation is far weaker than smart growth assumes.
Forcing people to live in high densities will not cause them to give up
their automobiles.

After reviewing the literature on the relationship between urban design
and urban transportation, planning historian Sir Peter Hall concludes that
"all the different urban forms of the world might not make that much
difference." Yet, reflecting the views of many planners, he went on to
say that "Still, planners should do what they could to make people virtuous."[17] This self-imposed imperative to "make people virtuous" is what
makes planning so dangerous and what leads planners to lose sight of
the costs of their policies.

It is a supreme irony that the densest urban area in the United States
is Los Angeles because smart-growth advocates often argue that their
planning ideas are needed to save urban areas from becoming like Los
Angeles. When Cisco Systems proposed to expand San Jose's urban-
growth boundary in 1999, Janet Gray Hayes, who had been mayor of
San Jose when the urban-growth boundary was first established, argued
that this would lead to "the Los Angelization of San Jose."[18]

In fact, Los Angeles is the epitome of smart growth:

- It has the highest population density of any U.S. urban area, and is a
  third denser than the New York City urban area;
- It has the fewest miles of freeway per capita of any major U.S. urban
  area, with only about 53 miles per million people vs. an average of
  more than twice that many in other urban areas;
- It has an excellent jobs-housing balance with jobs distributed among
  more than 100 different major employment centers;
- It has spent billions of dollars building rail transit lines throughout the
  region and promoting transit-oriented developments along those lines.

Los Angeles is considered undesirable by many because it is the
most congested and has the most polluted air of any urban area in the
United States. Yet it congested because it is so dense with so few miles
of freeway per capita and it is polluted because people are stuck in so
much stop-and-go traffic. If smart growth worked, none of these problems would exist.

When Portland's Metro was preparing its land-use plan for the region,
planners observed, "In public discussions we gather the general impres-

sion that Los Angeles represents a future to be avoided." Yet "with respect to density and road per capita mileage it displays an investment pattern we desire to replicate" in Portland."[19] It never occurred to them that this might mean there was something wrong with their plan.

## 2. Smart Growth and Housing

Other than traffic congestion, the most important cost of smart growth is its huge effect on housing prices. Smart-growth policies effectively constrain the ability of homebuilders to meet the demand for new homes. Because housing demand in desirable areas is inelastic, a small reduction in supply translates to a large increase in price.[20]

In this respect, smart growth is similar to earlier planning policies collectively known as growth management. Many American cities and urban areas grew rapidly in the 1950s and 1960s, but growing environmental concerns in the 1970s inspired many planners to try to manage growth so that it would have fewer environmental effects. A 1999 book on growth management cataloged at least thirty different techniques for managing growth.[21]

Growth management began when the city of Ramapo, New York, passed the first adequate public facilities ordinance in 1970. Instead of allowing developers to build homes and commercial areas and then providing the sewer, water, and other urban services needed by those areas, Ramapo decided that it would only approve new developments once the capital improvements needed for the development were fully financed.[22]

In 1972, the city of Petaluma, California took a different approach. Instead of conditioning growth on urban finances, the city simply decided to allow no more than 500 residential building permits a year.[23] Boulder, Colorado and other cities soon followed, often limiting the number of building permits to a specified percentage of existing residences.[24] Boulder also began large-scale purchases of open space, eventually circling the city with a wide greenbelt that prevents any development outside the city limits.

Petaluma overtly set out to slow growth, but other growth-management policies claimed to seek only to control where growth would take place. In 1974, the city of San Jose and Santa Clara County agreed to draw an urban-growth boundary outside of which development could not take place. Inside the boundary growth could continue unabated, but outside it would be strictly limited. East of San Jose are tens of thousands of acres of marginal agricultural land, and the growth boundary effectively placed these lands off limits to development. Since most other cities in the San Jose urban area are land-locked by San Jose or other cities, this boundary effectively constrained the entire San Jose urban area.

Taking after Ramapo, San Jose said it would add land to the growth boundary when financing could be assured for the urban services needed for new developments. But in 1978, California voters passed Proposition 13, which strictly limited the property taxes cities could collect for urban services. This made California cities dependent on sales taxes and therefore reluctant to devote more land to residential areas.[25] As a result, San Jose has never expanded its urban-growth boundary.

Even before Proposition 13, cities throughout the San Francisco Bay Area had approved a variety of growth-management policies, including growth boundaries, density limits, and purchases of land for open space. While growth-management planning is supposedly aimed at protecting environmental quality, it is exceedingly vulnerable to manipulation by not-in-my-backyard (NIMBY) advocates whose real goal is to boost their property values by limiting the supply of housing for others. Bernard Frieden notes in his 1979 book, *The Environmental Protection Hustle,* one important limit to growth was a public involvement process that made it so easy for people to challenge proposed developments that "even a lone boy scout doing an ecology project was able to bring construction to a halt on a 200-unit condominium project."[26]

David Dowall's 1984 book, *The Suburban Squeeze,* points out that people living in a neighborhood of $200,000 homes will fear that an adjacent development of $100,000 homes will bring down their property values, while they would welcome a development of $300,000 homes. When NIMBYs object to plans, developers respond by eliminating affordable housing and proposing only expensive homes. For example, one 1979 proposal to build 2,200 homes selling for $25,000 to $35,000 on 685 acres in Oakland was, due to public opposition, scaled back to a mere 150 homes that would sell for $175,000 to $200,000.[27]

Federal, state, county, city, and regional governments were able to tie up a huge amount of potential residential land in the Bay Area as open space. According to Dowall, by 1984 "Over 15 percent of the region's total land supply is in permanent open space controlled by" various government agencies.[28] Today, nearly a quarter of the region is reserved as parks, open space, or agricultural reserves.[29] Ostensibly this was for environmental protection, but the hilltops that were reserved tended to have the lowest values for fisheries, wildlife, and streams. The main effect of such reservations was to significantly boost land prices throughout the region.

Proposition 13 spurred city governments to go further than ever before in beggar-thy-neighbor efforts to force residential developments into adjacent cities while capturing retail developments, and the sales taxes they generated, for themselves. As one city put up barriers to growth, that growth would spill over into nearby cities, leading them to erect their own barriers. "Santa Clara County cities have become extremely combative," observed Dowall, "fighting back with a variety of growth-restricting mechanisms that have made each community a 'tight little island.'"[30]

Oregon also attempted to manage growth with a 1973 state law requiring every city and county to write a comprehensive plan that would follow rules established by the governor-appointed Land Conservation and Development Commission. These rules required all cities to have urban-growth boundaries and required counties to dedicate most land outside of the boundaries to zones limiting development to 40-acre minimum lot sizes—which would later be increased to 160 acres.

By 1979, Oregon cities had all drawn their urban-growth boundaries. Planners promised that the boundaries contained enough vacant land to accommodate twenty years of growth, but at first this was not an important issue. While much of California enjoyed a Reagan-era defense industry boom in the 1980s, Oregon suffered from a massive contraction of the timber industry early in the decade, and the populations of some major cities actually declined. It was not until 1990 that Oregon's economy had recovered to the point that developers began worrying whether the vacant lands would be used up. But between 1989's publication of LUTRAQ and 1993 Oregon's growth-management planning morphed into smart growth.

In 1991, 1000 Friends of Oregon used LUTRAQ to persuade the Land Conservation and Development Commission to issue a rule directing planners in all major Oregon urban areas to reduce per-capita driving by 10 percent in twenty years and 20 percent in thirty years. To reach these goals, the rule specified that planners must use mixed-use developments, pedestrian-friendly design, and other policies that would come to be known as smart growth.

By 1993, land prices were rapidly increasing and 1000 Friends of Oregon was lobbying for no additions to Portland's urban-growth boundary. Portland-area homebuilders went to the Oregon legislature seeking a law that would force planners to expand the urban-growth boundary to accommodate growth, as they had promised in 1979. But Metro, Portland's regional planning agency, opposed the measure until it was amended to allow Metro to accommodate that growth by rezoning existing neighborhoods to higher densities. After the law was passed, Metro gave the Portland region's twenty-four cities and three counties population targets and required them to rezone land to meet those targets.

The result was that many neighborhoods of single-family homes were rezoned to multi-family standards. While past zoning had specified maximum densities—so that homes could be built on half-acre lots in an area zoned for quarter-acre minimum lot sizes—the new zoning was minimum-density zoning, requiring that all development be at least 80 percent of the maximum density allowed by the zone. In some cases, this meant that if people's homes burned down, they would be required to replace them with apartments.

In 1997, Metro formally approved its fifty-year plan for the region. Because the term "smart growth" had only been coined the year before on the opposite side of the country, Portland planners did not call it smart growth. But that is what it was. It targeted two-dozen neighborhoods for redevelopment to much higher densities. While it proposed some small additions to the urban-growth boundary, it sought a 70-percent overall density increase within the urban-growth boundary. It mandated pedestrian-friendly design, requiring many stores to front directly on the sidewalk, for example, rather than be separated from the sidewalks by parking lots.[31] Though the plan was not formally approved until 1997, local planners were already busily implementing because of the 1994 population targets.

Other cities and urban areas also passed growth-management plans that became smart-growth plans in the 1990s. San Diego's regional government wrote a plan in 1980 that restricted development outside the existing urban fringe, imposed stiff system development charges for new homes in suburban areas, but waived any system development charges for infill in the urban core.

According to San Diego State University planning Professor Nico Calavita, this plan led to "frantic overbuilding ... in the urbanized tier. One after another, single-family neighborhoods were invaded by multifamily dwellings, many of them insensitively designed." Though the purpose of the plan was to "manage growth," in fact community facilities were "overwhelmed," Calavita says. "Freeway congestion and sewer breakdowns became commonplace" and by 1990 the city estimated that "it would cost over $1 billion to make up the infrastructure shortfall."[32] Despite the failure of this plan, by 1999 the regional government was approving an even more prescriptive smart-growth plan.[33]

Other regions that have written smart-growth plans include Denver, Minneapolis-St. Paul, Charleston, South Carolina; Salt Lake City, Missoula, Montana, and many others. The plans for Denver and Minneapolis-St. Paul use urban-service boundaries instead of urban-growth boundaries. These theoretically allow development outside of the boundary but refuse to allow sewer, water, or other infrastructure to such developments. Because they effectively prevent developers from doing subdivisions outside of those areas, they have the same effect on housing prices as urban-growth boundaries. Inside the boundaries, the regional governments use their power to distribute federal funds to local cities to force those cities to promote the high-density developments that smart growth demands.[34]

### 3. Effects on Housing Prices

Basic economic theory says that growth-management and smart-growth constraints on housing supply should lead to increases in housing prices. There is considerable anecdotal and systematic evidence that this is true. This evidence includes:

- Published reports about land prices in Portland, San Jose, and other regions;
- National Association of Realtor calculations of median sale prices for homes in close to 140 housing markets;
- Coldwell Banker estimates of the price of a standardized home in nearly 350 U.S. and Canadian housing markets;
- National Association of Home Builder estimates of housing affordability in nearly 200 housing markets;
- Census Bureau calculations of median home values and median family incomes in urban areas throughout the country;
- Home price indices published by the Federal Office of Housing Enterprise Oversight;
- Published research by economists Edward Glaeser, Joseph Gyourko, and others.

As previously indicated, the strongest smart-growth plans in America are in California and Oregon, perhaps followed by Minneapolis-St. Paul and Denver (with emphasis on the Boulder area). Planning restrictions of various sorts can also be found in the Boston-New York-Washington areas and Florida. On the other hand, the least-regulated housing markets are probably in Texas and other Sunbelt states, ranging from Arizona to Georgia. These patterns clearly show up in various measures of housing prices.

## A. Local Effects

Land suitable for residential development typically sells for $20,000 to $50,000 an acre in unregulated regions. In 2002, San Jose land for residential purposes was selling for $1.2 to $1.7 million an acre.[35] Such high prices drive up the cost of housing, but they also promote smart-growth goals of encouraging more people to live on smaller lots and in multi-family housing. With land prices this high, San Jose planners did not have to use subsidies to encourage developers to build high-density housing.

In Portland, the price of such an acre of land grew from $20,000 in 1989 to $150,000 in 1996.[36] Still, this was not enough to promote high-density housing. Portland had a surplus of multi-family housing, so in 1996 the city began offering developers ten years of property tax waivers for building high-density housing.

Yet by 2005, planners were elated to observe that Portland suburbs had reached a "tipping point": land prices had reached such high levels that developers were actively buying homes in low-density areas, tearing them down, and replacing them with higher-density housing. Metro planners had "envisioned" this in the 1997 plan for the region and the rezoning cities had done to meet Metro's 1994 population targets.[37]

One observed effect of smart-growth policies is that they are creating "childless cities." Nationwide, about 26 percent of the population is under 18 years of age. But the under-18 populations of San Francisco, Seattle, Portland, Boston, and other cities that have attempted to create high-density, New Urbanist environments is considerably smaller. Instead, growing proportions of those cities are singles and childless couples.[38] Portland's school district expects to close three to four schools a year for the next decade even as suburban school districts are building more schools.[39] Portland city officials admit that the problem is caused by high housing prices forcing young families who want yards for their children to seek housing in the suburbs, particularly in less-regulated Vancouver, Washington.[40]

## B. Median Home Prices

The National Association of Realtors regularly publishes the median price of homes sold in 130 to 140 major urban areas. Some urban areas that are considered separate in other analyses, such as San Francisco and San Jose, are lumped together in the Realtors' numbers.

In 2004, the Realtors report that the highest-priced housing was in the San Francisco Bay Area, Orange County, and San Diego, in all of which the median-priced home costs more than $500,000. Other regions that appear high on the list are Honolulu, New York, Boston, and Washington, but except for Honolulu the median price in all these regions is under $400,000.

By comparison, prices were much lower in relatively unregulated Sunbelt markets. Median prices were $157,000 in Atlanta, $136,000 in Houston, and $123,000 in San Antonio.

A problem with median home prices is that they do not necessarily reflect the same size and quality of homes. The $93,000 median price reported by the National Association of Realtors for Buffalo may not actually buy a home as palatial as the $640,000 needed to buy a median home in the San Francisco Bay Area.

Fortunately, the Coldwell Banker Real Estate Corporation publishes an annual *home price comparison index* estimating the price of a standardized home in each of about 350 housing markets in the United States and Canada. The standard home Coldwell Banker uses is a 2,200-square-foot, four-bedroom, two-bath house with a family room and two-car garage in a neighborhood that is "typical for corporate middle-management transferees."[41]

In 2005, the nine most expensive markets on Coldwell Banker's list were all in California. A home that would cost around $150,000 in Houston would cost $1.3 million in San Francisco, $1.2 million in San Jose, and $1.1 million in Oakland.[42]

Homes in Oregon had not reached these rarified levels, but they were still high priced. A standard home in the Portland market would cost more than $300,000, and prices in other Oregon cities also constrained by urban-growth boundaries were approaching $400,000.[43]

Prices in Colorado provided a special insight into the role of growth management. While a home in relatively unregulated Colorado Springs would cost only $212,000, a similar house inside the Denver urban-service boundary would cost $336,000 and a home inside Boulder's greenbelt would cost $546,000.[44]

## C. Housing Opportunity Index

Actual housing prices may be less relevant than housing *affordability*. If incomes are higher in San Jose than in Houston, then San Jose residents will be able to afford higher quality housing or housing with more amenities that might not even be reflected in Coldwell Banker's attempt to price a standardized house. If the market is working, differences in housing prices among regions should be no greater than differences in incomes.

To measure this, the National Association of Home Builders developed a *housing opportunity index* that estimated the percentage of homes affordable to a median-income family using standard lender criteria. For example, an index of 25 meant that a median-income family could afford only a quarter of the homes on the market.

In 1990, when the association began keeping track of this index, San Francisco and San Jose were the least affordable housing markets in the country, with indices of 10 to 25. Portland and other Oregon markets were in the middle of the pack, with indices in the mid-60s.[45] By 2000, San Francisco and San Jose indices had fallen slightly to 9 and 20. But indices for Oregon markets had fallen to well below 50, with Portland at 46, Eugene at 39, and Medford-Ashland at 29.[46] No markets outside of Oregon had fallen that much.

## D. Price-to-Income Ratios

The Home Builder's data can be confirmed using a similar measure of housing affordability based on decennial census data: median home price divided by median income, or price-to-income ratio for short. At a price-to-income ratio of 2, a family dedicating 25 percent of its income to a 5.5-percent mortgage would pay it off in 11 years, which is affordable. If the ratio climbs to 3, it would take a marginally affordable 22 years, while at 4 it would take 55 years, which is unaffordable. Both median home prices and median family incomes are estimated by the decennial census for the year before the census takes place.

In 1969,[47] the national average price-to-income ratio was a very affordable 1.8, while rising prices in some markets pushed the average 1979,[48] 1989,[49] and 1999[50] ratios to around 2.3. At that time, the California, Massachusetts, and other housing markets that are so unaffordable today were all affordable. The least affordable metropolitan area was Honolulu, with a price-to-income ratio of 3.2. Housing was similarly unaffordable elsewhere in Hawaii, which suffers from a genuine shortage of land available for private development.

After Hawaii, the next seven least affordable markets were in the greater New York City area. Stamford and Norwalk, CT had ratios of 2.9 to 3.1, while New York City, Paterson, NJ, Bridgeport, CT, Danbury, CT, and Newark, NJ all had ratios of 2.4 to 2.6. Salinas, CA; New Orleans; San Francisco; Santa Barbara; Anaheim; New Haven; Los Angeles; San Diego; and San Jose all had ratios of 2.2 to 2.3, which is average for today but among the least affordable in 1969. The ratio in Boston was 2.1 and most other Massachusetts markets were around 1.7 to 1.9.

During the 1970s, the affordability of California housing markets dramatically declined. Honolulu was still the least affordable metropolitan area in 1979, with a ratio of 5.5. It was followed by Santa Barbara, Santa Cruz, San Diego, Salinas, Los Angeles, Anaheim, Santa Rosa, San Jose, and San Francisco, all of which had ratios of 4.0 or more. Other than Honolulu, the only non-California region in the top-ten least-affordable markets is Stamford, CT, whose ratio is 4.3.

In 1989, California housing prices were peaking after ten to twenty years of growth-management planning. Not surprisingly, most of the nation's highest price-to-income ratios were still in California: 7.2 in Santa Barbara, 6.5 in Monterey, 6.1 in San Luis Obispo, 5.6 in Los Angeles, 5.5 in San Francisco-Oakland, and 5.3 in San Jose. Eleven more California urban areas had price-to-income ratios greater than 4. Only eight urban areas outside California had ratios of 4 or more, all of them in Hawaii and the Boston-New York corridor. Most urban areas in Oregon, where the effects of growth management had yet to kick in because of the 1980s recession, were around 2.

Between 1989 and 1994, the California housing bubble deflated as defense spending declined in the post-cold war era. By 1999, price-to-income ratios in most California regions were 5 to 15 percent lower than in 1989, but still remained in the unaffordable range. The four regions with the greatest gain in price-to-income ratios—that is, the greatest fall in housing affordability—were all in Oregon or on the border of Oregon and Washington. Other urban areas whose housing declined from affordable to marginally unaffordable or unaffordable include Boulder, Denver, and Longmont, Colorado; Salt Lake City, Ogden, and Provo, Utah; and Missoula, Montana.

The census data reveal the elitist nature of growth-management planning. In 1959, most of America's urban areas had about the same housing prices. While the most expensive metropolitan area was five times more expensive than the least, the housing prices in three-fourths of the urban areas ranged from $9,000 to $14,000—a spread of 55 percent. By 1999, prices in three-fourths of urban areas ranged from $59,000 to $130,000—a spread of 120 percent—and the most expensive markets were 11 times as costly as the least.

Income distributions broadened as well, though not by as much. In 1969, the highest-income metropolitan areas had median incomes that were 1.7 times the lowest. By 1999 this had increased to 3.5 times. Because the variation in housing prices grew by much more than the variation in incomes, the range of affordability levels also grew. In 1969, the least affordable market had a price-to-income ratio that was just 1.7 times the most affordable. By 1999, this had increased to 5.7 times.

Smart-growth advocates might argue that the increased incomes in regions using growth-management planning reflect the improved livability that attracted more desirable jobs. But growth management's effects on housing prices were far more extreme than its effects on incomes. By making the areas that use it more unaffordable, growth management only appears to increase incomes because it forces low-income workers to live outside of those areas. Just as growing numbers of Portland workers commute from Vancouver, Washington, many San Jose workers commute from Modesto and Los Angeles workers commute from San Bernardino.

### E. Home Price Indices

The Federal Office of Housing Enterprise Oversight, whose main job is to oversee Fannie Mae and Freddie Mac, maintains a quarterly index of home prices in as many as 400 housing markets going back as much as thirty years. The index is based on repeat sales of identical homes in each market, so it is independent of home size or quality. All it measures is the change in home values over time in each market.

The contrast between regulated and unregulated markets is stark. Between 1975 and 2005, home prices tripled in unregulated areas such as Houston. But in coastal California regions that have long practiced growth-management planning, such as Los Angeles and the San Francisco Bay Area, prices grew by 12 times. Regions with more recent smart-growth plans such as Portland, Denver, and Minneapolis saw prices grow by 6 times.

The index provides a remarkable guide to when growth management or other restrictions on homebuilders start to drive up housing prices. In unregulated markets, and in regulated markets before regulation began, home prices closely track inflation. After regulation, prices increase far faster than inflation.

In San Francisco and San Jose, prices were already growing faster than inflation in the earliest years data are available for those urban areas. In Portland, prices start growing in 1989. In Charleston, South Carolina, prices started growing in 1998, the year Charleston County passed a planning ordinance limiting development on agricultural lands. In Minneapolis-St. Paul, they begin growing in 1999, the year smart-growth advocate Ted Mondale became chair of the region's Metropolitan Council.

Las Vegas is the exception that proves the rule. The nation's fastest-growing major urban area for the past two decades, Las Vegas has remained a very affordable housing market for most of that time. The region does not use any form of growth-management planning but it has an effective urban-growth boundary in the form of federal lands that make up 92 percent of the state of Nevada. Until recently, Las Vegas' growth has been supported by sales of federal land to homebuilders, but sales recently slowed due to environmental challenges. In 2004, home prices started increasing at double-digit rates.

Las Vegas demonstrates that any restriction on land or new home supply can result in a dramatic increase in home prices. While some restrictions such as natural barriers or federal land boundaries are beyond the control of local officials, most growth-management policies, including smart growth, seem aimed at creating artificial barriers in order to boost land prices and discourage homeownership and growth.

### F. Other Research

Most of the above information is anecdotal in the sense that it is based on an observed correlation between the imposition of growth-management policies in selected regions and high or fast-growing housing prices in those regions. Harvard economist Edward Glaeser and Wharton economist Joseph Gyourko did a more systematic study by comparing a database of land-use regulations that had been developed by the Wharton Business School with housing prices.

Glaeser and Gyourko confirmed that, where land was relatively unregulated, homes were priced "at close to construction costs."[51] But in regulated areas, homes cost much more than the basic costs of construction. Glaeser and Gyourko concluded that the difference was due to various forms of regulation.

For example, they found that, when the time it takes to get a permit to build a subdivision of less than fifty homes doubles, "15 percent more of the housing stock becomes quite expensive."[52] This happens for two reasons. First, increasing the permit time adds to the developer's costs. Second, cities that require more time are more likely to also impose design codes, impact fees, and other requirements on homebuilders that increase housing prices.

"Government regulation is responsible for high housing costs where they exist," conclude Glaeser and Gyourko. In particular, "difficult zoning seems to be ubiquitous in high-cost areas."[53] They add that their findings indicate that only 10 percent of the differences in housing and land costs between high-cost and low-cost cities is due to intrinsic differences in the value of the land; the rest must be due to artificial or natural restrictions on housing supply.[54]

The results of the Harvard study were confirmed by a study by University of North Carolina researchers that examined changes in housing prices in various urban areas. The study found that housing prices were strongly influenced by population growth, changes in median incomes, construction costs, and interest rates. After correcting for all of these factors, the study found there were still real differences in housing price appreciation among urban areas and that these differences were strongly "correlated with restrictive growth management policies and limitations on land availability."[55]

Research in California by UC (Berkeley) professors John Quigley and Steven Raphael confirms these conclusions. They find "a positive relationship between the degree of regulatory stringency and housing prices" and "that new housing construction is lower in more regulated cities." As a result, housing prices grew fastest in more regulated cities.[56]

A recent *New York Times* article by economist Paul Krugman summarizes recent research by dividing the country into what Krugman calls the "Zoned Zone," where "land-use restrictions" make "it hard to build new houses," and what he calls "Flatland," meaning the parts of the country that may have zoning but do not have aggressive growth-management planning. Krugman says that prices are rapidly increasing in the Zoned Zone, but remain very affordable in Flatland.[57]

Other research has indirectly reached the same conclusions. Tufts University economist Matthew Kahn has found that "sprawling" urban areas tend to have more affordable housing and higher rates of minority homeownership.[58] In 2002 Oregon economist Randall Pozdena reviewed Portland-area growth policies and concluded that, if such policies had been in place throughout the nation for the previous decade, more than a quarter-million minority families who currently own their own homes would not have been able to afford to buy their homes. "Insidiously, the burden of site-supply restrictions will fall disproportionately on poor and minority families," says Pozdena. For this reason, Pozdena labels smart growth "the new segregation."[59]

Unaffordable housing is not confined to the United States. Wendell Cox observes that most housing markets in Australia and New Zealand have become severely unaffordable, and that these regions, like those in California and Oregon, practice various forms of growth management. Vancouver, British Columbia, is heralded for having Canada's strongest smart-growth plans, including agricultural land reserves and other restrictions on housing development, and not coincidentally it is also has Canada's least affordable housing. Cox notes that, "among the 'severely unaffordable' urban areas" from around the world, "23 of the 26 are subject to strong smart-growth policies."[60]

## 4. The Smart-Growth Response

Defenders of smart growth and other growth-management policies typically deny that these policies have any impact on home prices. Instead, they blame rapidly rising prices on demand or greedy homebuilders.

The demand issue is a red herring; homebuilders can easily keep up with the demand in the fastest growing regions provided land is available and government regulation does not get in their way. Yet smart-growth advocates believe that their policies make cities more livable, so naturally they assume people will be willing to pay more to live in such livable cities. They take higher housing prices as proof that their policies are working, not as evidence that something is wrong.

In terms of absolute numbers, the demand issue is easily refuted. Census data show that, during the 1990s, the Atlanta, Dallas-Ft. Worth, Houston, and Phoenix urban areas all grew by 900,000 people or more, while the Denver, Los Angeles, and Portland urban areas grew by only about 400,000, and San Jose grew by only about 100,000 people. In percentage terms, the relatively unregulated regions also grew faster than the regulated ones. Yet the former group of regions all maintained their housing affordability, while the latter group either remained very unaffordable or significantly lost affordability during the 1990s.

Portland is a particularly interesting case because one of the four counties in the Portland urban area is in the state of Washington. Clark County, Washington grew far faster in percentage terms and grew faster in absolute numbers than any of the Oregon counties in the region. While Washington passed a growth-management law in 1991, that law had little effect on Clark County plans during most of the 1990s.

Nor are the regulated regions attracting people with higher incomes who buy more expensive housing. As the price-to-income data show, housing prices in Portland and Denver both significantly increased relative to family incomes, while they did not in Atlanta, Dallas-Ft. Worth, Houston, or Phoenix.

While smart-growth advocates say that they are not interested in slowing growth, only in managing it, growth-management policies appear to have reduced growth in many of the regions that have adopted them.

The San Jose urban area grew by about 42,000 people a year during the 1950s and 1960s, but in the decade that San Jose adopted the 1974 urban-growth boundary growth slowed to 20,000 a year, and by the 1990s it slowed to 10,000 people a year.

In a study that cites and seems aimed at refuting the research by Glaeser, Gyourko, and Kahn, two California researchers claim to find that regions that are "more centralized" have lower housing prices than less centralized regions.[61] Smart-growth advocates who seek to impose higher densities on their regions are using this study to support their views. Yet the researchers' definition of "centralized" is based on the size of each urban area's central city relative to its suburbs. This is a political question that has nothing to do with smart-growth planning.

For example, Texas has granted cities strong powers of annexation without the consent of the people being annexed. As a result, cities such as Houston, Dallas, and San Antonio all contain a high percentage of their urban area's population. Annexation powers are much weaker in California and Oregon, so cities such as Portland and San Francisco have a much smaller percentage of their urban area's population.

Of the cities cited in the California study, relatively unregulated Phoenix and Las Vegas are considered the most centralized, while heavily-regulated Boston and Baltimore are among the least centralized, helping the researchers to conclude that more centralized cities are more affordable. The researchers fail to consider land-use regulation as a factor in housing prices at all. Most sprawl opponents would call Phoenix and Las Vegas far more sprawling than Boston and Baltimore. Any attempt to use the California study to support efforts to contain low-density suburbanization would be highly misleading.

Regardless of the cause, it is undeniable that housing in regions that adopt smart-growth policies quickly becomes unaffordable. Planning advocates then turn their attention to the "greedy developers" who are demanding higher prices for their homes and attempt to rectify the situation with inclusionary zoning requirements that require developers to sell a percentage of their products at below-cost prices in order to provide a few people with affordable housing. But home prices are a tide that lifts all boats: as the cost of new homes increases for whatever reason, including the need of developers to recover their losses from mandatory affordable houses, owners of existing houses take advantage by increasing the prices of their homes when they sell them. The result is that inclusionary zoning actually makes housing even less affordable for all but the lucky few who get to buy some of the below-cost housing.[62] "If policy advocates are interested in reducing housing costs," Glaeser and Gyourko observe, "they would do well to start with zoning reform," not affordable housing mandates.[63]

## 5. Conclusions

Smart growth and other growth-management policies can greatly increase housing prices in the regions and communities that adopt them. Since 1975, California regions that have used various forms of growth management have seen housing prices increase by 12 times, while Portland, Denver, and other cities that have more recently used urban-growth boundaries and other smart-growth policies to obtain more compact urban development have seen housing prices grow by six times. By comparison, regions that remain relatively unregulated have seen housing prices grow by only about three times, which is approximately the rate of inflation.

Higher housing prices benefit the residents of regions adopting smart-growth policies who already own their own homes. Yet, from society's viewpoint this is at best a zero-sum game, since every family that sells its home for a higher price is offset by another family that must pay more for that home. More likely, it is a negative-sum game as it reduces the number of families who can take advantage of the benefits of owning their own homes. In addition, wealth increases among existing homeowners are partly or fully balanced by wealth losses among owners of land whose development is restricted by growth boundaries or other rules.

Smart growth makes traffic congestion worse and requires major intrusions by government officials into people's private lives. But its most costly effect may be the huge increase in housing prices and reduction in the number of people who can afford to own their own homes. For this effect alone, when historians write the history of turn-of-the-twenty-first-century urban planning, they will find it to be as bad for cities and possibly as racist as the urban renewal and public housing projects of the mid-twentieth century.

## Notes

1. Smart Growth Network, "About Smart Growth," www.smartgrowth.org/about/default.asp.
2. John W. Frece, "Twenty Lessons from Maryland's Smart Growth Initiative," *Vermont Journal of Environmental Law,* volume 6 (September, 2005), www.vjel.org/articles/articles/Frece11FIN.htm.
3. Timothy Egan, "Vibrant Cities Find One Thing Missing: Children," *New York Times,* March 24, 2005, page A1.
4. National Family Opinion, *Consumers Survey Conducted by NAR and NAHB* (Washington, DC: National Association of Realtors, 2002), p. 3, www.

realtor.org/publicaffairsweb.nsf/ca2dae5fa466338d862567e6004ad5ff/
cbf4f1aebd322cc985256ba30065ae7a/$FILE/survey-results.doc.

5.  Ibid, p. 6.
6.  Douglas Porter, "Regional Governance of Metropolitan Form: The Missing Link
    in Relating Land Use and Transportation," *in* Transportation Research Board,
    *Transportation, Urban Form, and the Environment* (Washington, DC: TRB, 1991),
    p. 65.
7.  Ahwahnee Principles, 1991, www.tbrpc.org/livable/ahwahnee.htm.
8.  Congress for the New Urbanism, "New Urbanism Basics," www.ub.es/escult/
    docus2/NEW_URBANISM_%20BASICS.doc.
9.  Congress for the New Urbanism, "Charter of the New Urbanism" (Chicago, IL:
    CNU, 1998), www.cnu.org/aboutcnu/index.cfm?formAction=charter.
10. Anthony Downs, Stuck in Traffic: Coping with Peak-Hour Traffic Congestion
    (Washington, DC: Brookings, 1992), p. 133.
11. 1000 Friends of Oregon, *Making the Connections: A Summary of the LUTRAQ
    Project* (Portland, Oregon: 1000 Friends, 1997), pp. 8–10.
12. Genevieve Giuliano, "The Weakening Transportation-Land Use Connection,"
    *Access* 6 (Spring, 1995): p. 8.
13. Metro, Region *2040 Technical Appendix* (Portland, OR: Metro, 1994), transpor-
    tation tables; Metro, *1999 Regional Transportation Plan* (Portland, OR: Metro,
    1999), tables 2.7, 2.9, 5.9, and 5.11.
14. Census Bureau, "Census 2000 Summary File 3, Journey to Work," table QT-P23,
    2002.
15. Patricia Mokhtarian and Ilam Salomon, "Travel for the Fun of It," *Access,* 15 (Fall
    1999): 29.
16. Robert Cervero, "Jobs-Housing Balance Revisited," *Journal of the American
    Planning Association,* 62(4): 492.
17. Peter Hall, *Cities of Tomorrow: An Intellectual History of Urban Planning and
    Design in the Twentieth Century* (Maldan, MA: Blackwell, 2002), p. 415.
18. Santa Clara Valley Audubon Society, "Former South Bay Public Officials Criticize
    Cisco's Expansion Plan; Unite with Environmentalists in Call for Major Revisions,"
    press release, 1999.
19. Metro, *Metro Measured* (Portland, OR: Metro, May 1994), p. 7.
20. Eric A. Hanushek and John M. Quigley, "What Is the Price Elasticity of Hous-
    ing Demand?" *The Review of Economics and Statistics,* 62(3): 449–454, tinyurl.
    com/766wq.
21. Irving Schiffman, *Alternative Techniques for Managing Growth* (Berkeley, CA:
    IGS Press, 1999), p. 165.
22. Ibid, p. 6.
23. Ibid; City of Petaluma, *Draft Petaluma General Plan 2025* (Petaluma, CA: City
    of Petaluma, 2004), p. 57, cityofpetaluma.net/genplan/pdf/06growthmngmt10–
    11rsv2.pdf.
24. Peter Pollack, "Controlling Sprawl in Boulder: Benefits and Pitfalls," *Proceedings
    of the 1998 National Planning Conference* (Chicago, IL: AICP, 1999), www.asu.
    edu/caed/proceedings98/Pollock/pollock.html.
25. John M. Quigley and Steven Raphael, "Regulation and the High Cost of Housing
    in California," *American Economic Review,* 94(2), 2005, forthcoming.
26. Bernard J. Frieden, *The Environmental Protection Hustle* (Cambridge, MA: MIT,
    1979), p. 6.
27. David E. Dowall, *The Suburban Squeeze: Land Conservation and Regulation in
    the San Francisco Bay Area* (Berkeley, CA: UC Press, 1984), p. 15.

28.  Ibid, pp. 141–142.
29.  Peter Fimrite, "Bay Area's open space tightrope," *San Francisco Chronicle,* June 5, 2005, p. A-17, tinyurl.com/91cx3.
30.  Ibid., p. 143.
31.  Metro, *Region 2040 Plan* (Portland, OR: Metro, 1997).
32.  Nico Calavita, "Vale of Tiers: San Diego's much-lauded growth management system may not be as good as it looks," *Planning magazine,* March 1997, pp. 18–21.
33.  SANDAG, "2020 Cities/County Forecast Land Use Alternatives," SANDAG Board of Directors Report #99–2–7, February 26, 1999.
34.  David Peterson, "Mondale says Met Council has big plans," *Minneapolis Star Tribune,* October 11, 1999.
35.  Tracey Kaplan and Sue McAllister, "Cost of land drives home prices," *San Jose Mercury News* August 4, 2002; Timothy Roberts and Andrew F. Hamm, "VTA selling land to meet payroll," *San Jose Business Journal,* November 22, 2002, sanjose.bizjournals.com/sanjose/stories/2002/11/25/story1.html.
36.  Alex Pulaski, "Land Is Dwindling and the Hunt Is On," *The Oregonian* December 22, 1996, p. A-1.
37.  Dana Tims, "Land value 'tipping point' hits suburbs," *The Oregonian* October 20, 2005, Lake Oswego supplement, p. 1.
38.  NewsMax.com, "U.S. Cities Have Fewer Kids, More Singles," June 13, 2001, www.newsmax.com/archives/articles/2001/6/13/52513.shtml.
39.  Paige Parker, "Enrollment falls further in Portland schools," *The Oregonian* October 8, 2005, p. B-1.
40.  Clifton R. Chestnut and Shirley Dang, "Suburbs drain city schools," *The Oregonian,* October 12, 2003, p. A-1.
41.  Coldwell Banker, "Study Evaluates Cost Variances in 319 U.S. Markets," press release, September 22, 2005, hpci.coldwellbanker.com/hpci_press.aspx.
42.  Coldwell Banker, "Home Price Comparison Index," hpci.coldwellbanker.com/hpci_full.aspx.
43.  Ibid.
44.  Ibid.
45.  National Association of Home Builders, "Housing Opportunity Index," fourth quarter, 1990.
46.  Ibid., fourth quarter 2000.
47.  *1970 Census of Housing Volume 1 Housing Characteristics for States, Cities, and Counties part 1 United States Summary,* table 17, "Financial Characteristics for Areas and Places; *1970 Census of the Population volume 1 Characteristics of the Population part 1 United States Summary section 2,* table 366, "Median income in 1969 of Families by Type of Family and Race of Head for Standard Metropolitan Statistical Areas of 250,000 or More."
48.  *1980 Census of Population Volume 1 Characteristics of the Population Chapter C General Social and Economic Characteristics Part 1 United States Summary (PC80–1-C1),* table 247, "Summary of Economic Characteristics for Areas and Places"; *1980 Census of Housing Volume 1 Characteristics of Housing Units Chapter A General Housing Characteristics Part 1 United States Summary (HC80–1-A1),* table 76, "Financial Characteristics for SCSA's and SMSA's."
49.  *1990 Census of Population,* tables P107A and H061A, available at www.census.gov.
50.  *2000 Census of Population,* tables P77 and H85, available at www.census.gov.
51.  Edward L. Glaeser and Joseph Gyourko, *The Impact of Zoning on Housing Affordability* (Cambridge, MA: Harvard Institute of Economic Research, 2002), p. 3.

52.  Ibid., p. 20.
53.  Ibid.
54.  Edward Glaeser and Joseph Gyourko, "Zoning's Steep Price," *Regulation,* 25(3): 24–30.
55.  G. Donald Jud and Daniel T. Winkler, "The Dynamics of Metropolitan Housing Prices," *Journal of Real Estate Research,* 23(1/2): 29–45.
56.  Quigley & Raphael, ibid.
57.  Paul Krugman, "That Hissing Sound," *New York Times* August 8, 2005, tinyurl. com/91wmp.
58.  Matthew E. Kahn, "Does Sprawl Reduce the Black/White Housing Consumption Gap?" *Housing Policy Debate* 12(1): 77–86.
59.  Randall Pozdena, *Smart Growth and Its Effects on Housing Markets: The New Segregation* (Washington, DC: National Center for Public Policy Research, 2002), p. 32.
60.  Wendell Cox, "Unprecedented Housing Unaffordability Strongly Associated with Smart Growth Policies," demographia.com/dhi-200502.htm; see demographia. com/dhi-rank200502.htm for data.
61.  Robert W. Wassmer and Michelle C. Baass, "Does a More Centralized Urban Form Raise Housing Prices?" 2005, forthcoming in *Journal of Housing and Policy Analysis and Management.*
62.  Jerald W. Johnson, *Issues Associated with the Imposition of Inclusionary Zoning in the Portland Metropolitan Area* (Portland, OR: Hobson Johnson & Associates, 1997), 13 pp.; Benjamin Powell and Edward Stringham, *Do Affordable Housing Mandates Work? Evidence from Los Angeles County and Orange County* (Los Angeles, CA: Reason Foundation, 2004).
63.  Glaeser and Gyourko, pp. 21–22.

## References

Ahwahnee Principles, 1991, www.tbrpc.org/livable/ahwahnee.htm.

Calavita, Nico. "Vale of Tiers: San Diego's much-lauded growth management system may not be as good as it looks," *Planning magazine,* March 1997.

Census Bureau, "Census 2000 Summary File 3, Journey to Work," table QT-P23, 2002.

Cervero, Robert. "Jobs-Housing Balance Revisited," *Journal of the American Planning Association,* 62(4).

Chestnut, Clifton R. and Dang, Shirley. "Suburbs drain city schools," *The Oregonian,* October 12, 2003.

City of Petaluma, *Draft Petaluma General Plan 2025* (Petaluma, CA: City of Petaluma, 2004), cityofpetaluma.net/genplan/pdf/06growthmngmt10–11rsv2.pdf.

Coldwell Banker. "Study Evaluates Cost Variances in 319 U.S. Markets," press release, September 22, 2005, hpci.coldwellbanker.com/hpci_press.aspx.

Coldwell Banker. "Home Price Comparison Index," hpci.coldwellbanker.com/hpci_full. aspx.

Congress for the New Urbanism, "New Urbanism Basics," www.ub.es/escult/docus2/ NEW_URBANISM_%20BASICS.doc.

Congress for the New Urbanism, "Charter of the New Urbanism" (Chicago, IL: CNU, 1998), www.cnu.org/aboutcnu/index.cfm?formAction=charter.

Cox, Wendell. "Unprecedented Housing Unaffordability Strongly Associated with Smart Growth Policies," demographia.com/dhi-200502.htm.

Dowall, David E. *The Suburban Squeeze: Land Conservation and Regulation in the San Francisco Bay Area* (Berkeley, CA: UC Press, 1984).

Downs, Anthony. Stuck in Traffic: Coping with Peak-Hour Traffic Congestion (Washington, DC: Brookings, 1992).

Egan, Timothy. "Vibrant Cities Find One Thing Missing: Children," *New York Times,* March 24, 2005.

Fimrite, Peter. "Bay Area's open space tightrope," *San Francisco Chronicle,* June 5, 2005, tinyurl.com/91cx3.

Frece, John W. "Twenty Lessons from Maryland's Smart Growth Initiative," *Vermont Journal of Environmental Law,* volume 6 (September, 2005), www.vjel.org/articles/ articles/Frece11FIN.htm.

Frieden, Bernard J. *The Environmental Protection Hustle* (Cambridge, MA: MIT, 1979).

Glaeser, Edward and Gyourko, Joseph. *The Impact of Zoning on Housing Affordability* (Cambridge, MA: Harvard Institute of Economic Research, 2002).

Glaeser, Edward Glaeser and Gyourko, Joseph. "Zoning's Steep Price," *Regulation,* 25(3).

Giuliano, Genevieve. "The Weakening Transportation-Land Use Connection," *Access* 6 (Spring, 1995).

Hall, Peter. *Cities of Tomorrow: An Intellectual History of Urban Planning and Design in the Twentieth Century* (Maldan, MA: Blackwell, 2002).

Hanushek, Eric A. and Quigley, John M. "What Is the Price Elasticity of Housing Demand?" *The Review of Economics and Statistics,* 62(3), tinyurl. com/766wq.

Johnson, Jerald W. *Issues Associated with the Imposition of Inclusionary Zoning in the Portland Metropolitan Area* (Portland, OR: Hobson Johnson & Associates, 1997).

Jud, G. Donald and Winkler, Daniel T. "The Dynamics of Metropolitan Housing Prices," *Journal of Real Estate Research,* 23(1/2).

Kaplan, Tracey and McAllister, Sue. "Cost of land drives home prices," *San Jose Mercury News* August 4, 2002.

Kahn, Matthew E. "Does Sprawl Reduce the Black/White Housing Consumption Gap?" *Housing Policy Debate* 12(1).

Krugman, Paul. "That Hissing Sound," *New York Times* August 8, 2005, tinyurl. com/91wmp.

Metro, *Metro Measured* (Portland, OR: Metro, May 1994).

Metro, *Region 2040 Technical Appendix* (Portland, OR: Metro, 1994).

Metro, *Region 2040 Plan* (Portland, OR: Metro, 1997).

Metro, *1999 Regional Transportation Plan* (Portland, OR: Metro, 1999).

Mokhtarian, Patricia and Salomon, Ilam. "Travel for the Fun of It," *Access,* 15 (Fall 1999).

National Association of Home Builders, "Housing Opportunity Index," fourth quarter, 1990.

National Association of Home Builders, fourth quarter 2000.

National Family Opinion, *Consumers Survey Conducted by NAR and NAHB* (Washington, DC: National Association of Realtors, 2002), www.realtor.org/publicaffairsweb.nsf/ ca2dae5fa466338d862567e6004ad5ff/cbf4f1aebd322cc985256ba30065ae7a/$FILE/ survey-results.doc.

NewsMax.com. "U.S. Cities Have Fewer Kids, More Singles," June 13, 2001, www. newsmax.com/archives/articles/2001/6/13/52513.shtml.

Parker, Paige. "Enrollment falls further in Portland schools," *The Oregonian* October 8, 2005.

Peterson, David. "Mondale says Met Council has big plans," *Minneapolis Star Tribune,* October 11, 1999.

Pollack, Peter. "Controlling Sprawl in Boulder: Benefits and Pitfalls," *Proceedings of the 1998 National Planning Conference* (Chicago, IL: AICP, 1999), www.asu.edu/caed/proceedings98/Pollock/pollock.html.

Porter, Douglas. "Regional Governance of Metropolitan Form: The Missing Link in Relating Land Use and Transportation," *in* Transportation Research Board, *Transportation, Urban Form, and the Environment* (Washington, DC: TRB, 1991).

Powell, Benjamin and Stringham, Edward. *Do Affordable Housing Mandates Work? Evidence from Los Angeles County and Orange County* (Los Angeles, CA: Reason Foundation, 2004).

Pozdena, Randall. *Smart Growth and Its Effects on Housing Markets: The New Segregation* (Washington, DC: National Center for Public Policy Research, 2002).

Pulaski, Alex. "Land Is Dwindling and the Hunt Is On," *The Oregonian* December 22, 1996.

Quigley, John M. and Raphael Steven. "Regulation and the High Cost of Housing in California," *American Economic Review,* 94(2), 2005, forthcoming.

Roberts, Timothy and Hamm, Andrew F. "VTA selling land to meet payroll," *San Jose Business Journal,* November 22, 2002, sanjose.bizjournals.com/sanjose/stories/2002/11/25/story1.html.

SANDAG, "2020 Cities/County Forecast Land Use Alternatives," SANDAG Board of Directors Report #99–2–7, February 26, 1999.

Santa Clara Valley Audubon Society, "Former South Bay Public Officials Criticize Cisco's Expansion Plan; Unite with Environmentalists in Call for Major Revisions," press release, 1999.

Schiffman, Irving. *Alternative Techniques for Managing Growth* (Berkeley, CA: IGS Press, 1999).

Smart Growth Network, "About Smart Growth," www.smartgrowth.org/about/default.asp.

Tims, Dana. "Land value 'tipping point' hits suburbs," *The Oregonian* October 20, 2005, Lake Oswego supplement.

Wassmer, Robert W. and Baass, Michelle C., "Does a More Centralized Urban Form Raise Housing Prices?" 2005, forthcoming in *Journal of Housing and Policy Analysis and Management.*

1000 Friends of Oregon, *Making the Connections: A Summary of the LUTRAQ Project* (Portland, Oregon: 1000 Friends, 1997).

*1970 Census of Housing Volume 1 Housing Characteristics for States, Cities, and Counties part 1 United States Summary,* table 17, "Financial Characteristics for Areas and Places.

*1970 Census of the Population volume 1 Characteristics of the Population part 1 United States Summary section 2,* table 366, "Median income in 1969 of Families by Type of Family and Race of Head for Standard Metropolitan Statistical Areas of 250,000 or More."

*1980 Census of Population Volume 1 Characteristics of the Population Chapter C General Social and Economic Characteristics Part 1 United States Summary (PC80–1-C1),* table 247, "Summary of Economic Characteristics for Areas and Places"; *1980 Census of Housing Volume 1 Characteristics of Housing Units Chapter A General Housing Characteristics Part 1 United States Summary (HC80–1-A1),* table 76, "Financial Characteristics for SCSA's and SMSA's."

*1990 Census of Population,* tables P107A and H061A, available at www.census.gov.

*2000 Census of Population,* tables P77 and H85, available at www.censu.gov.

# 6

# Inclusionary Zoning[1]

*Benjamin Powell and Edward P. Stringham*

Many areas of the United States are facing a housing affordability crisis. A family with average earnings cannot afford the median priced home in any of the 30 least affordable housing markets (Simon, 2005: D4), and prices in the most expensive markets continue to rise. Between 1995 and 2002 median home prices rose by 62 percent in Boston, 49 percent in Denver, 54 percent in San Diego, and 65 percent in the San Francisco Bay Area (Quigley and Raphael, 2004). This precludes many people from being able to own a home. What can be done? To deal with high housing costs many local governments are implementing a price control program referred to as inclusionary zoning or affordable housing mandates (California Coalition for Rural Housing et al., 2003; Calavita, Grime, and Mallach, 1997). As practiced in California, inclusionary zoning ordinances place a price control on a percentage of new development, requiring builders to sell or rent those homes at prices deemed affordable to low- or moderate-income households, in order for them to get permission to build.[2]

Details vary by city but most require that 5 to 35 percent of new homes be sold at price-controlled rates, which in the median city is more than $300,000 below the market price.[3] These specifics also vary but ordinances require the price-controlled units to be of similar size and quality as the market-rate units and require them to be spread throughout the project in order to create integration and avoid "ghettoization" (Burchel and Galley, 2003: 27–31). Some jurisdictions allow offsite construction or allow developers to pay a fee in-lieu of building a below-market unit, but the intent of inclusionary zoning is to have the below-market units "included" among the market-rate units.[4] To ensure that the units remain affordable cities then require that these units remain under price controls for a period of time typically fifty-five years or more (and each time the unit is resold that clock is reset for the new owner). Jurisdictions sometimes offer compensating incentives such as density bonuses, fast track permitting, or fee waivers but the value of these offsetting benefits is often small.

Inclusionary zoning dates back to the early 1970s[5] and it has become most prevalent over the past fifteen years. In California, cities such as Palo Alto first mandated their ordinance in 1973 and since then over one hundred Californian jurisdictions have followed suit. Today affordable housing mandates in varying forms are found in parts of Colorado, Connecticut, Delaware, Florida, Illinois, Massachusetts, New Jersey, New Mexico, New York, Oregon, and Washington (Powell and Stringham, 2003: 2). Goetz (1991: 341) found that nine percent cities of U.S. with populations over 100,000 had inclusionary zoning ordinances and the number is growing.

But are these programs a good idea? Although the number of communities with inclusionary zoning ordinances has been increasing, evidence that these ordinances are beneficial remains elusive. Advocates of these laws cite the very fact that the laws exist, or that some units have been built, as proof of their success. But economic reasoning requires us to not only take account of the obvious things that are seen but also what is unseen. Specifically we need to consider the effects these ordinances have on the supply of housing and overall affordability. Does enacting price controls on a percentage of units have any unintended consequences that the advocates of inclusionary zoning have not considered?

Despite its attractive sounding name inclusionary zoning as practiced in California is essentially a price control on a percentage of units and a tax on the remaining market-rate units and it leads to decreased production and increased prices for the vast majority of buyers. This chapter discusses the economics of inclusionary zoning ordinances and then examines evidence in California to look at the track record of its performance. After discussing how affordable housing mandates are equivalent to a tax on the housing industry, the chapter then estimates the size of the tax in California cities and discusses how that affects the supply of both market-rate units and price-controlled units. Ultimately inclusionary zoning fails to make housing more affordable and it is likely to lead a number of other long-term problems.

## 1. Economics of Inclusionary Zoning

How should housing prices be determined? Prices can be determined by relying on supply and demand or by using government price controls. Inclusionary zoning opts for a combination of the two. The economics of inclusionary zoning is a bit more complicated than the economics of rent control but not by much. One can think of inclusionary zoning as creating two markets for new homes, a percentage of units are price-controlled homes (the below-market homes) and the remainder are non-price-controlled homes (the market-rate homes) The price-controlled portion of the market will have many of the same characteristics of markets with rent control such as shortages and discouragement of production.

The twist of inclusionary zoning is that if builders want to produce non-price-controlled units they must also provide a certain number of price-controlled units. Unless these units are subsidized by government or some private charity, these price-controlled units become an obligation (or an economic burden) on a development. The cost, which economists refer to as an opportunity cost, is the difference between the level of the price control and the level that the units could fetch on the market. For example, if a builder could have sold a unit for $800,000 but they must sell it for $200,000 then they are losing $600,000 that they could have earned. In theory, governments could offer a subsidy equal to the cost of the unit, but in practice they rarely do. In fact, advocates of affordable housing mandates tout their programs saying, "A vast inclusionary program need not spend a public dime" (Dietderich, 1996: 41).

To the extent that subsidies do not cover the costs of below-market units, inclusionary zoning, much like development impact fees, will act like a tax on market-rate development.[6] Although the builders may appear to bear the burden of paying for the below-market units, they will likely end up passing part or all of this effective tax onto homebuyers or sellers of undeveloped land. Examining the economics of an inclusionary tax will help us determine how the burden is likely to be split between the builders, market-rate homebuyers, or owners of undeveloped land.

Figure 6.1 shows the supply and demand for the below-market units. One of the most important lessons from economics is that at lower prices fewer goods are supplied. Since inclusionary zoning restricts how much builders can charge for a portion of their development while not altering costs, expected revenues go down.[7] Builders decide to develop property based on expected profits so one should expect builders to invest less in housing with inclusionary zoning than if government allowed prices to adjust to market conditions. In this way, restricting how much builders can charge will lead to less housing, not more. Analyzing the interaction between consumers and sellers in Figure 6.1 shows how setting the price of housing below-market creates a shortage where demand for housing exceeds supply.

**Figure 6.1**
**Supply and Demand of Housing with Affordability Controls**

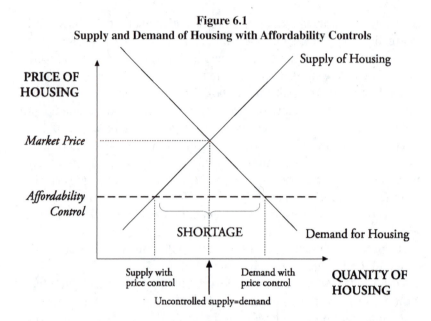

Studies show that restricting housing prices to below-market rates creates a situation in which only a few people can find units at the low price, which of course does not benefit the majority of the consumers (Tucker, 1990). An example of this shortage is the affordable housing complex Rich Sorro Commons near AT&T Park in San Francisco. It had 2,700 applicants for only 100 units. A family had to be fortunate enough to be living in the city, apply, and then win a lottery to get one of the 100 units (Stoll, 2002). The other 2,600 families, as well as low-income families who were unable to apply, did not benefit from programs that gave benefits to a select few. Thus, price-controlled units created by inclusionary zoning benefit a select few and create shortages for others.

The initial shortage described above is only the beginning of the economic consequences of inclusionary zoning. Figure 6.2 shows the supply and demand diagram for the non-price-controlled market to illustrate how a tax on housing impacts the price and quantity of new housing.[8] When government places a tax, like an inclusionary ordinance, on new development it will affect the price and quantity of new development. Suppose that a development company would have been willing to provide 10 units at $500,000 per unit, and now it has to pay an effective tax of $100,000 per unit. Now, rather than just receiving $5 million for those units the developer has to pay $1 million in taxes, so in order to continue to supply the same 10 units of housing, developers would need to receive the old price, $500,000/unit, plus the amount of the tax, $100,000/unit. Such a tax is represented in Figure 6.1 by the effective supply curve shifting directly up by the amount of the tax, which in the above example would be $100,000. Although developers would like to sell 10 units at $600,000/unit, buyers will demand fewer than 10 units at that higher price. The after tax price of market-rate homes will be at a point where the original supply curve plus the tax intersect with the demand curve (Point $P_{Tax}$ and $Q_{Tax}$ in Figure 6.2).

Even though developers are legally responsible for providing the below-market units, they will unlikely bear the entire burden or the cost of those units. The burden of the inclusionary zoning tax will end up being born by some combination of builders, landowners, and market-rate homebuyers. Exactly how the burden is split depends the relative elasticities of supply and demand in each community. Except in the extremely unlikely circumstance of a perfectly elastic demand curve or a perfectly inelastic supply curve, a tax on a good always leads to higher prices for consumers. This is reflected by the fact that $P_{Tax}$ is higher than $P_1$. In Figure 6.2 the burden of the tax is split evenly between buyers and sellers, but most estimates of the elasticity of the supply and demand of housing show that suppliers are more sensitive to changes in price and so are less likely to bear the burden than consumers (Green et al., 1999;

**Figure 6.2**
**Impact of an Inclusionary Zoning Tax on New Market-Rate Housing**

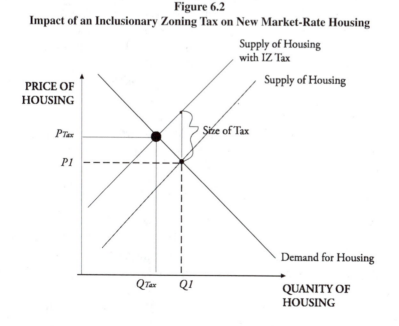

Hanoushek and Quigley, 1980; Glaeser and Gyourko, 2004). With the exception of a few unrealistic cases, taxes raise the price that buyers pay, decrease the price that sellers receive, lead to a decrease in quantity supplied and create a net deadweight loss for society.

Inclusionary zoning also affects the prices of existing homes given that new homes and existing homes are substitutes. Because inclusionary zoning restricts the supply of new homes many buyers who would have purchased new homes instead purchase from the existing stock. The increased demand for existing homes creates bidding wars and drives up prices.

The laws of economics clearly predict the consequences of inclusionary zoning. Restricting prices below market increases the quantity demanded and decreases supply. When units must be sold for a loss, someone must pay for that difference. Landowners and market-rate buyers are ultimately most likely to have to pay the cost of the subsidized units. Unfortunately, this tax makes housing less affordable for everyone but a few. Inclusionary zoning only exacerbates the affordability problem by increasing market prices and further discouraging supply.

## 2. California's Experience with Inclusionary Zoning

With more than 100 ordinances and 30 years of experience, California has the most experience with inclusionary zoning. Advocates of inclusionary zoning often hold California up as a success story, giving reports names like *Inclusionary Housing in California: 30 Years of Innovation* (California Coalition for Rural Housing et al., 2003), yet most advocates measure success based on the number of ordinances rather the number of affordable units actually built. But a proper analysis requires looking at costs and results rather than just intentions. Our research, which we summarize here, looked at inclusionary zoning in Los Angeles County, Orange County, and the San Francisco Bay Area, and found that the programs are extremely costly and lead to few affordable units being built. First let us consider the some of the costs.

### A. *Size of the Inclusionary Tax*

Economic theory shows that inclusionary zoning acts as a tax on new housing production but exactly how big are these taxes in California? We estimated the losses imposed by the below-market units by comparing market prices to price-controlled prices and next estimated the size of the tax on each market-rate unit by looking at the percentage of market-rate units that would absorb the burdens of the below-market units. Each ordinance targets different income levels, so we used Census data, looked at target income levels by city, and calculated sample price controls by city. For example, if a city in Alameda County required that a percentage of new units be affordable to "very low" income the price control would be $130,429 per home. Or if a city in Alameda County required that homes be affordable to "low" or "moderate" income families, the levels of the price controls would be $208,752 or $299,287. Once we estimated price control for each city, we then subtracted it from the market price for each city.[9] For example, we estimate that a new home in Tiburon could be sold for $1,426,997, and Tiburon requires that 5 percent of homes be priced at "low" and 5 percent at "moderate," which we conservatively estimate at $294,728 and $357,581, an average of $326,155. That means 10 percent of homes would need to be sold for $1,100,842 less than market price. In other words, the cost of providing a single inclusionary unit in Tiburon is $1.1 million.[10]

Figure 6.3 shows the costs imposed per below-market unit are quite considerable. In cities with more restrictive price controls and higher land values, the cost is higher. In the median city the cost of providing each inclusionary unit is $346,212. In one fourth of the jurisdictions the cost exceeds $500,000 per unit.

**Figure 6.3**
**Average Cost Associated with Selling Each Price-Controlled Unit**

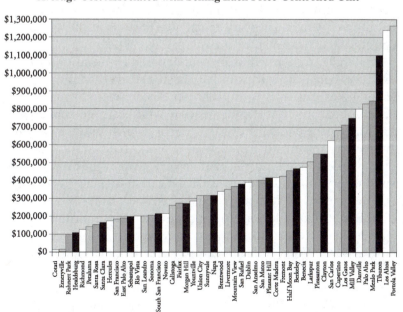

Once we calculated the average cost or average loss associated with the below-market units we could calculate the size of the tax on non-price-controlled units. To calculate the effective tax in each city we look at the average loss associated with each inclusionary unit and the number of market-priced units over which the loss must be spread. To do this we multiply the loss of each inclusionary unit times the percentage attained by each city and then divide by the percentage of market-rate homes. To illustrate, for Mill Valley each price-controlled unit has an associated loss of $747,899 (Figure 6.3) and 10 percent of units must be sold at those price controls. To make it more concrete, if a project had 10 units, one must be sold at a loss of $747,899. Spreading the loss over the remaining nine units gives a loss of $83,100 per market-rate unit.

Figure 6.4 shows the effective tax on new home purchases imposed by inclusionary zoning in the San Francisco Bay Area. Inclusionary zoning imposes sizeable taxes on each newly constructed home. The median city with inclusionary zoning is effectively imposing $45,721 of taxes on each market-rate home. In the seven cities with the most restrictive programs, inclusionary zoning imposes an equivalent tax of more than $100,000 per home. In Portola Valley the equivalent tax if a developer built and sold an affordable home is well over $200,000 per newly constructed home. Our findings in Southern California were similar. In Los Angeles and Orange counties the cost of providing a single inclusionary unit in the median city was $577,000 dollars. The median tax per market-rate unit in cities with inclusionary zoning was $66,000 and it ranged up to almost $500,000 per market-rate unit in Laguna Beach.

The large tax on new development imposed by inclusionary zoning will have significant effects in the housing market. Economic theory demonstrates that taxes such as this will increase prices and decrease the total quantity of housing produced. Who bears the burden of the tax? Many people assume that the cost of below-market units will be absorbed by abnormally high developer profits but this is not the case. Local market conditions will determine exactly how the burden is split, but all theory and evidence suggest that the costs of inclusionary zoning will be borne by new homebuyers and landowners rather than builders.[11] Why? Because construction is a competitive industry with relatively free entry, builders are least likely to bear the burden.

If builder profits were abnormally high, other builders would enter the market and undercut prices, thus bringing profits down. Conversely, if profits were abnormally low it would drive would-be-builders to invest in other endeavors. When a tax like inclusionary zoning is placed on

**Figure 6.4**
**Effective Tax Imposed on New Market-Rate Units Caused by**
**Inclusionary Zoning**

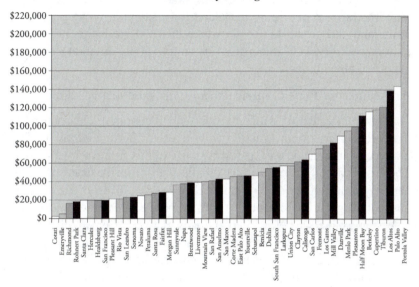

builders, it decreases the number of profitable projects that they want to undertake in that jurisdiction. Builders will vote with their feet and undertake fewer projects in jurisdictions with price controls and more in neighboring jurisdictions without price controls. Building will decrease in locations with price controls and increase in locations without price controls, pushing some homebuyers away from their first choice of locations, but for developers, profit rates at the margin will remain the same.[12]

Price controls may not stop all development, but will discourage building at the margin. In order for development in a price-controlled city to be profitable enough to attract builders, one of two things has to happen. Either market-rate home prices must increase, or land prices must decrease to compensate the builder for his losses due to price controls. Because land cannot move and buyers are often attached to living in a particular locale, landowners and new homebuyers are the most likely candidates to end up paying for the subsidy for the price-controlled units.

When landowners and homebuyers bear the burden of the tax, the quantity of new housing will decrease because fewer market-rate buyers will be able to afford to purchase a home or landowners will supply less land for residential development. Raising home prices for other new homebuyers creates a paradox because the alleged goal of inclusionary zoning is to make housing more affordable, not less. Decreasing land prices decreases the quantity of new housing because it discourages landowners from providing their land for residential projects. Instead, more land will be put to uses in which the final product is not subject to price controls. Thus, the restriction on the supply of land restricts the supply of new homes.

## B. The Effect of Price Controls on Housing Construction

How do price controls affect production? Economics clearly predicts that the quantity of construction will be lower after the adoption of inclusionary zoning and we can see evidence of this from various sources. The experience of the city of Watsonville, California illustrates what can happen on the supply side of the market. In 1990 Watsonville passed a law requiring that 25 percent of all new homes be sold to low- and moderate-income buyers at below-market prices. Between 1990 and 1999, with the exception of a few small non-profit developments, almost no new construction occurred. The law was finally revised in 1999. In the words of Watsonville Mayor Judy Doering-Nielsen, "There was an incredible pent-up demand. Our inclusionary housing ordinance was so onerous that developers wouldn't come in" (Morgan, 2003).[13] Jan Davison, the city's redevelopment and housing department directory commented "It [the inclusionary zoning law] was so stringent, and land costs were so high that few units were produced," but then "It was completely redone in 2000, and we got more units produced" (Morgan, 2003).

The change in 2000 lowered affordable housing requirements from 25 percent to 20 percent for larger developments and lowered requirements to 15 percent for developments with between 7 and 50 units. After almost a decade with no residential construction, a 114-unit development, a 351-home development, a 389-unit development, and a number of smaller developments began construction after the lowering of affordable housing requirements. Overall, the number of projects approved and pending approval from 2000 to 2003 was set to increase the city's housing stock by 12 percent. All of this development occurred with just a slight decrease in affordable housing requirements. If affordable housing laws were further rolled back even more units would come to market. Watsonville is an extreme example of how burdensome inclusionary zoning requirements can completely kill development.

San Jose had a similar experience when the city offered a two-year exemption on its 20 percent affordability requirement for redevelopment areas (Simonson, 2004). The rollback quickly generated proposals for three new high-rise buildings that have the potential to provide an additional 533 downtown units, a significant accomplishment for a downtown that as of 2006 does not have a single residential high-rise.

Both Watsonville and San Jose provide some evidence about how much building will increase as ordinances are rolled back. This effect is also suggested by the data on housing construction. To see the overall effect inclusionary zoning ordinances have had throughout the San Francisco Bay Area we looked at the amount of new construction in years prior and years following the adoption of an inclusionary zoning law in each city that has adopted an ordinance. We examined Construction Industry Research Board yearly housing permit data to compute average construction pre- and post-ordinance. For example, Larkspur adopted its ordinance in 1990 and Union City adopted its ordinance in 2001. We would thus compare Larkspur housing construction in 1989 and 1991, and Union City housing construction in 2000 and 2002. We also looked at three-, five-, and seven-year averages before and after the ordinances and found similar results.

The data indicate that inclusionary zoning does lead to a decrease in new construction. In the year prior to the adoption of inclusionary zoning, the average city added 213 new residences, whereas in the year following the adoption of inclusionary zoning, the average city only added 147 units. For the 45 cities in the sample, that amounted to 9,618 units the year prior to the inclusionary ordinance and 6,636 units the year following the inclusionary ordinance. New construction fell by 31 percent in the year following the adoption of the inclusionary zoning ordinance.

To check if one-year results were not coincidental, we examined construction for the seven years prior and seven years following the ordinance and found similar results.[14] This fourteen-year data exists for 33 cities. In those cities we found that in the seven years following the adoption of inclusionary zoning housing, production decreased by 10,662 units.

Examining Los Angeles and Orange Counties produced similar results. Average housing production in the cities with inclusionary ordinances fell in the one-, three-, five-, and seven-year time periods after an ordinance was passed. In the cities where the full data was available for the seven-year time period housing production fell from over 28,000 homes before an ordinance was passed to only 11,000 in the seven years afterward—a decrease in housing production of 61 percent.

Additional econometric work on the supply restriction caused by inclusionary zoning is needed. Difference in difference tests would provide better indicators of exactly how changes in the policy variable affect changes in output, but all theory and our first look at the data indicate price controls on a percentage of new homes and effective taxes on the remainder lead the quantity of construction to decrease.[15]

## C. Inclusionary Production

Not only does economic theory predict that price controls and taxes will increase price of market-rate homes, but it also predicts inclusionary zoning is bound to fail to produce many price-controlled units because of the very nature of the program. The experience of the San Francisco Bay Area illustrates how few units these ordinances produce. Because inclusionary zoning discourages construction of both price-controlled units and non-price-controlled units, few price-controlled units have ended up getting produced. Let us consider the numbers.

The Association of Bay Area Governments (2001) estimated the 2001–2006 5.5-year period need for very low, low, and moderate priced units to be 133,195 units, or 24,217 per year. Yet in the thirty plus years that inclusionary zoning has been implemented in the San Francisco Bay Area, inclusionary zoning has resulted in the production of only 6,836 affordable units or 228 units per year (Powell and Stringham, 2004b: 5). Controlling for the length of time each program has been in effect, the average jurisdiction has produced only 14.7 units for each year since adoption of its inclusionary zoning requirement. The number of units expected from inclusionary zoning pales in comparison to the regional need. The program would have to be twenty times more effective each year before it could be relied on to meet the area's five-year affordable housing needs.

The disparity between the regional housing need and inclusionary zoning production is shown in Figure 6.5. In Figure 6.5, the front columns represent the average yearly production of affordable housing reported by cities (only for years when cities had inclusionary zoning) multiplied times 5.5, and the back columns represent the five and a half year need for affordable housing in the cities with inclusionary zoning. The number of units expected from inclusionary zoning hardly even put a dent in the problem.

From an overall production standpoint, inclusionary zoning has been unmistakably ineffective. Some advocates of inclusionary zoning respond to this poor record by calling for more vigorous and numerous restrictions. Yet because price controls discourage housing production, more burdensome ordinances would only further drive out development

**Figure 6.5**
**Housing Needs versus Expected Units Produced under Inclusionary Zoning.**
**(5.5-Year Housing Needs According to the report "Regional Housing Needs Determination" by the Association of Bay Area Governments.**
**5.5-Year Average for Production of Inclusionary Zoning.)**

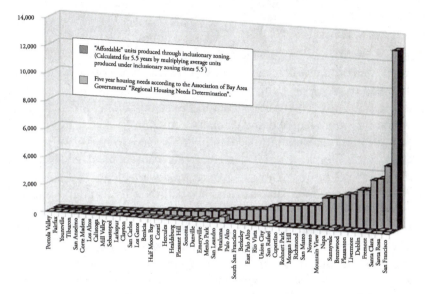

and hence the very price-controlled units these ordinances are intended to create.

## 3. Effect of Long-Term Affordability Controls

In addition to restricting supply and increasing prices on the vast majority of homes, affordable housing mandates have some other important flaws. The program is not even that good of a deal for those people who get the price-controlled homes. At the tip of the iceberg is the fact that almost all inclusionary zoning ordinances impose resale price controls on the "owners" of the affordable units. In the median California city, subsequent buyers cannot sell the unit at market rates unless they live in the unit for 55 years and each time the unit changes hands that clock is reset. Even though they have to pay the value of the mortgage plus interest, the level of the price control is only allowed to appreciate at the rate of inflation or the rate of increase of low-income salaries in a city. The rationale is to keep those units affordable for future buyers and to prevent current residents from making windfall profits by immediately flipping the homes once they buy. Unfortunately these resale restrictions devalue homes and create unintended incentives that undermine the goals of inclusionary zoning. This says nothing of the incentives it creates for "owners" to try to get around the price controls and the government administrative costs of keeping the price controls in place.

## A. Incentives for Mobility and Improvements

Why have resale price restrictions on a home? The hope is that once they are in place eventually the home will be sold to another low-income family and the unit will remain affordable over the long run. One advocate summed the reasoning for resale restrictions: "In order to ensure that affordable units remain affordable to the same income population for whom they were targeted, inclusionary zoning ordinances must include provisions for maintaining affordability for a specified period" (Rawson, et al., 2002). Despite their good intent, resale restrictions adversely impact the incentives for residents to move as well as maintain their property.

Under the free-market, many people sell their first starter home and move to larger homes as their earnings increase over their lifetime, but price controls create incentives for families to stay in their homes long after they need them. And one of the main benefits of homeownership is building equity in a home that can appreciate in value. Inclusionary zoning removes this benefit because it controls resale prices. Because appreciation is limited, owners of price-controlled units often cannot build up the necessary equity to afford a down payment on a larger market-rate home. So even as incomes rise, a disproportionate percentage of those in price-controlled units will remain in them longer than they would otherwise choose. While families may initially feel lucky to have received a subsidized home, in the longer term the wealth constraint imposed by limiting appreciation actually may serve to trap them in a lower quality of housing by limiting their ability to upgrade.

Also, because owners of restricted units are not permitted to sell at market price, much of the incentive to maintain the property is taken away. This makes it more likely that price-controlled units will deteriorate over time. Even the owner of a less well-maintained property would be able to find buyers if the legally mandated price is significantly below the market equilibrium price. Owners of restricted units who spend resources maintaining their home have to pay all of the costs and receive few of the benefits. In addition, because the potential for the sweat-equity gains of home improvement are taken away, improvements are less likely to be made.

Consider the case of Richard Fontius a resident of Palm Springs, who did not realize his inclusionary zoning home had resale price restrictions placed on it over two decades ago. He recently remodeled the home, adding a swimming pool and 400-square-foot addition, and planned on selling it after the improvements. Now the city is considering enforcing the resale price restrictions. Richard Fontius says, "If I knew about it to begin with I would not have bought it" (quoted in Joseph, 2003). The many residents aware of their resale restrictions will be less likely to improve their homes or spend resources to prevent deterioration. The problems will worsen over time as already pricey market-rate homes increase in value but homes under price controls do not. Occupants of price-controlled homes may feel like second-class citizens because the government prevents them from gaining in equity.

Some government agencies realize the problems created by resale restrictions. One city's report assessing their inclusionary zoning program noted, "Failure to consider improvements in the calculation of resale value may discourage property owners from investing in improvements." It also wrote that, "The question of resale value highlights the conflict between preserving the stock of affordable units and allowing the build-up of equity for the owners' use." (Monterey Staff Report, 2003: 63–4) Other jurisdictions are more blunt. Dennis Lalor, the executive director of the non-profit that manages the city of Hollister's resale restrictions, said simply, "The idea of wealth creation was never part of this [inclusionary zoning]" (Paton, 2003). Unfortunately, the unintended consequence of preventing wealth creation is that families remain in the price-controlled units even after their incomes rise, thus preventing other low-income families from moving in. In addition, the properties deteriorate because there is less incentive for maintenance and improvement. Homeownership is often considered the American dream; unfortunately, homeownership with little or no potential of appreciation is not the same thing.

## B. Inclusionary Zoning Is Costly to Administer and Police

As market-rate homes continue to appreciate, owners of price-controlled units have a tremendous incentive to get around their resale restrictions and sell for market rates. Unless local jurisdictions spend time and money monitoring units carefully, some owners may attempt to sell or sublet them at market prices even though this is in violation of inclusionary zoning. The Niguel Beach Terrace condominiums on the Dana Point Coast illustrate the problem. More than 200 units were sold at below-market rates with resale restrictions during the early 1980s and price controls set in place for two decades. Just as the resale restrictions were about to expire in 2003, the California Coastal Commission issued 143 cease and desist orders (38 of which have been retracted) to owners thought to have either sold or rented out their units for market rates. Some owners reportedly have rented out their units for more than $1,000 per week while they moved out-of-state. If the charges are accurate, more than 50 percent of the owners of subsidized units in this complex violated their resale restrictions (Weikel, 2003).

Although some residents may have purposefully ignored their restrictions because of the huge potential gains, others tried to play by the rules but were frustrated by poor administration. Homeowners claim that administration of the ordinance was so poor that they could not find out which agencies to contact about selling or renting out their units, so they had no choice but to go out on their own. At least three different agencies have monitored the program since the condominiums were sold in the early eighties, and one admittedly had neither the staff nor the money to handle the program. The current nonprofit managing the restrictions, Civic Center Barrio Housing Corporation, was reportedly notified that many of the units were being rented out improperly in the early nineties but did nothing (Weikel, 2003).

The condominiums at Dana Point are not the only ones with a poor enforcement record. In another case in the city of Hollister, a real estate agent involved in a resale violating the price controls wrote to city officials about her seller's intent. The city government never even responded (Paton, 2003). Officials now admit that they received the letter but did not respond because they had no system in place to prevent owners from selling at market rates.

Programs that do monitor resale are often costly to administer. Running and monitoring the program in Palo Alto costs $40,000 to $60,000 in annual administration costs alone. But in the previous thirty years only 152 for sale units and 101 rental units have been produced (*Bay Area Economics*, 2003: 55–6). These administration costs of inclusionary zoning could have been passed on to housing consumers in the form of housing assistance. A report by *Bay Area Economics* notes:

> In general, program managers characterized monitoring of inclusionary requirements as a challenging process. One Sunnyvale Housing Division staff person described the monitoring requirements as 'time consuming' and 'cumbersome.' Complications regularly arise from unit resales, owners renting out their units, and tenants and owners losing their qualifications as their incomes grow, among other issues (*Bay Area Economics*, 2003: 60).

The debate on inclusionary zoning often ignores the consequences of long-term price controls and the associated administrative costs. Advocates of inclusionary zoning leave out important details such as how the property will be maintained and whether long-term, in-kind subsidies are the best way to help those earning low income. Our evidence suggests that these problems and their costs are quite significant.

In addition, inclusionary zoning creates other administrative costs because the price-controlled units are far more difficult to sell than market-rate homes. One of the biggest challenges for builders of price-controlled units is qualifying buyers. Some builders estimate that the administrative cost of selling price-controlled homes is about double that spent on market-rate homes. One builder described to us the costs of qualifying buyers for a current development in Novato.

> For the 40 buyers we have to date, we have processed over 270 applicants. The conversion ratio is so low that we are hiring additional staff to process the workload. The city also required us to have a custom software program developed to manage the list of applicants. The procedure is so complex that the software costs over $400,000 to develop. This cost is for only 352 homes. (Personal correspondence March 3, 2004.)

The process also takes time. The same builder says that at the Meadow Park development in Novato, "The process, as mandated by the city, is so cumbersome that we have only been able to sell 40 homes in 6 months. We started with over 2,600 prequalified buyers and have only been able to process 270 potential buyers netting 40 sales in 6 months. We literally can build the homes faster than we can process sales." Both the direct administrative costs and the financing cost of carrying unsold inventory while searching for qualified buyers are additional administrative burdens created by inclusionary zoning ordinances.

## 4. Conclusion

Despite the increasing popularity of inclusionary zoning, it is a failed public policy. Its stated intent is to make housing more affordable, yet they produce few affordable units, increased prices of new market-rate homes, decreased construction, and thus increased demand and higher prices for existing homes. Affordable housing mandates make housing less affordable for the vast majority of consumers, and even the "lucky few" recipients of price-controlled units do not receive the full benefits of homeownership. Is government monitoring and preventing people from gaining appreciation really what homeownership is all about?

It is hard to square the dismal record of inclusionary zoning with its increased popularity if one believes that the political process is meant to help people. The policy fails to achieve its stated purpose and if the real goal is increasing affordability, inclusionary zoning should have been weeded out long ago. However, if one takes a more cynical view of politics the popularity of inclusionary zoning is less surprising. Robert Ellickson (1982) has argued that inclusionary zoning allows communities to appear to favor making housing more affordable yet in reality it helps restrict the amount of new building and it prevents low-income people from actually being able to move in. Having restrictive price controls through inclusionary zoning might be an effective way to promote exclusionary zoning while using the rhetoric of affordability. Is it an accident that many environmental activist groups favor inclusionary zoning even though their organizations are not dedicated to low cost housing? Maybe they do understand the economics behind the program and realize that these ordinances will help kill development. Robert Ellickson (1982: 167) pointed out that communities that were known to be exclusionary were some of the earliest adopters of affordable housing mandates because they knew how much it would stifle production.

Does a better alternative to affordable housing mandates exist? For communities really interested in making housing more affordable the most effective way is not price controls but to allow increases in the supply of new homes. As other chapters in this book document intrinsically scarce land is not the main cause of high housing prices. The scarce resource is government permission to build. Increasing the supply of homes is the best method to drive down prices and make them more affordable. Price controls implemented through inclusionary zoning ordinances are perhaps the worst way to address the problem.

## Notes

1.  This chapter draws heavily on our prior research on inclusionary zoning. In particular it draws most from Powell and Stringham (2004a, 2004b, and 2006).
2.  Most California ordinances target a combination of Very Low, Low or Moderate incomes where "Very Low" income is classified as up to 50 percent of county median income, "Low" as 50–80 percent of median, and "moderate" as 80–120 percent of median (California Coalition for Rural Housing et al., 2003, p. iii, pp. 31–35).
3.  If the units are for lease, the present discounted value of the revenue stream from that property is equivalently decreased so the economics behind the price control are the same.
4.  Most ordinances are mandatory, so builders must participate in order to get permission to build, although about 6 percent of California ordinances are "voluntary" in that they offer incentives in exchange for a builder selling at price-controlled rates (California Affordable Housing Law Project et al., 2002, p. 10; California Coalition for Rural Housing et al., 2003, p. 8). But as Tetreault (2000), notes "The problem is that most of them, because of their voluntary nature, produce very few

units," and Kautz (2002, p.982) also points out the voluntary programs are ineffective at producing units. We argue below that this is because of the very nature of the economics of inclusionary zoning that these authors fail to understand.

5.    In 1971 Fairfax County, Virginia was the first city to enact inclusionary zoning by applying price controls to 15 percent of large multifamily dwellings. The Virginia Supreme Court ruled that the law was a takings because landowners were not compensated for the new regulation, thus Fairfax had to make it a voluntary ordinance. *Board of Supervisors of Fairfax County et al. v. DeGroff*, 1973. In 1973, Montgomery County, Maryland passed its "moderately priced dwelling unit" ordinance, requiring 12.5 percent to 15 percent of units (in developments of more than 50 units) be affordable to families with 50–80 percent of the median income. The ordinance in Montgomery County is still in effect today.

6.    Nico Calavita and Victoria Basolo (2004), two advocates of inclusionary zoning, recognize that "IH [inclusionary housing] is a development fee." Although in that article Calavita and Basolo argue against the theory that inclusionary zoning raises housing prices, Calavita's prior writing on development impact fees, however, unambiguously states, "Although the full amount is not necessarily passed on to consumers, high fees usually mean higher housing costs" (Calavita and Grimes, 1998). So although Calavita never directly admits that inclusionary zoning increases the price of market-rate housing, one must conclude this from his writings. This view on impact fees is also consistent with the California Department of Housing and Community Development (2001, p. 99) which wrote, "California's high residential development fees significantly contribute to its high housing costs and prices."

7.    In some cases costs may also go down when builders are allowed to substitute lower quality housing for the price-controlled units. Even in these cases though profits still go down because builders are forced to vary their product mix away from the optimal.

8.    The slopes of the curves vary by city so the *magnitudes* of the changes will vary by city, but the diagram shows that *directions* of effects of each change. In the rare market where housing in another jurisdiction without inclusionary zoning were a perfect substitute, the demand curve would be perfectly horizontal (or perfectly elastic) and the price of new homes would remain unchanged, although a tax on housing would still decrease quantity. One of the only ways that inclusionary zoning would not affect quantity is in an equally unrealistic situation where the supply curve for new housing were vertical (or perfectly inelastic). In this case suppliers (raw landowners) would bear the full burden of the tax. This is unlikely because it would require suppliers of raw land to supply the same amount of land to residential development regardless of what price they received. A final odd case would be if buyers demanded the same quantity of housing regardless of price (the demand was perfectly inelastic), then quantity would remain unchanged and market-rate homebuyers would bear the full burden of the inclusionary tax. All three of these cases are extremely unlikely in the real world.

9.    We estimate market price by city by comparing 2003 data of the average price of new homes by county compiled by First American Real Estate Solutions and 2000 Census median price of existing homes by city. Because new homes in the Bay Area sell for more than the 2000 median price of existing homes, and because new home price data by city is difficult to assemble, we adjust the 2000 Census city data based on each county's price differential for new homes. In Alameda, Contra Costa, Marin, Napa, San Francisco, San Mateo, Santa Clara, Solano, and Sonoma the ratio of the price of new homes to the price of existing homes is 1.8, 2.0, 1.4,

2.2, 1.2, 1.6, 1.5, 2.3, and 1.3 respectively. For example, the 2000 Census median price of existing homes in the City of Sonoma was $305,100, so we multiply that by 1.3 to estimate that a new home would be sold for closer to $400,000. We are implicitly assuming that the price-controlled units are of the same quality and cost to build as the market-rate units. To the extent that they are cheaper to build the actual losses will be slightly lower than the ones estimated above.

10.    We decided to make our estimates very conservative but in actuality, the cost for each price-controlled sale is much larger. Compared to our conservative assumptions (that diminish the costs of inclusionary zoning). Tiburon sets price controls for "affordability" much more strictly. Its ordinance assumes an interest rate of 9.5 percent, assumes 25 percent of income can be devoted to mortgage, and defines moderate as 80 percent of median rather than the standard 120 percent. According to Tiburon's ordinance, a "moderate" price-controlled home can be sold for no more than $109,800. That means the actual cost for each "moderate" price-controlled home in Tiburon is $1,317,197, not $1,100,842 per home as we estimate. Nevertheless, we want to err on the low side for our estimates of the costs of inclusionary zoning, so we present the data according to our conservative assumptions.

11.    Burchell and Galley (2003, p.29) correctly explain how builders will not bear the burden. "Who pays for inclusionary zoning? The requirement of subsidized housing has the same effect as a development tax. The developer makes zero economic profit with or without inclusionary zoning, so the implicit tax is passed on to consumers (housing price increases) and landowners (the price of vacant land decreases). In other words, housing consumers and landowners pay for inclusionary zoning."

12.    In the very short run, if builders own the land when the ordinance was passed, they would bear part of the burden. But in the long run, builders are most able to avoid the tax because they can simply move their construction to more profitable locations.

13.    Interestingly many advocates of affordable housing miss this completely. Bay Area Economics (2003:15) wrote, "The City of Watsonville adopted its inclusionary housing ordinance in 1991. To date, the program has directly created only thirteen affordable units. However, this low number is attributable to the lack of new development in Watsonville over the last 10 years." (*The City of Salinas Inclusionary Housing Program Feasibility Study* (2003) Berkeley: Bay Area Economics) The "however" in the above sentence is very telling. Bay Area Economics treats the lack of development as something that has no connection to the price controls. By ignoring the most important variable, namely price, it is easy to absolve price controls as the culprit that drove out builders.

14.    Our data is from 1970 to 2002, so we have data for seven-years-prior and seven-years-following for 33 cities that created their ordinances between 1977 and 1995.

15.    After more than 30 years of experience with inclusionary zoning advocates of these price controls have not produced a single serious study to show that the supply of new homes is unaffected by these ordinances. Instead, economic theory is usually ignored and success is measured by the passing of ordinances or the construction of a few price-controlled units.

# References

Association of Bay Area Governments (2001) "Regional Housing Needs Determination for the San Francisco Bay Area. 2001–2006 Housing Element Cycle." Oakland, CA: Association of Bay Area Governments.

Bay Area Economics (2003) "They Bay Area Case Studies, Report to the City of San Jose," pp. 53–62, in The California Inclusionary Housing Reader. Sacramento: Institute for Local Government.

Burchel, Robert and Galley, Catherine (2003) "Inclusionary Zoning: Pros and Cons" pp. 27–31 in The California Inclusionary Housing Reader. Sacramento: Institute for Local Government.

Calavita, Nico and Victoria Basolo (2004) "Policy Claims with Weak Evidence: A Critique of the Reason Foundation Study on Inclusionary Housing Policy in the San Francisco Bay Area." at 11 (Unpublished, June 2004).

Calavita, Nico and Kenneth Grimes, (1998) "Inclusionary Housing in California: The Experience of Two Decades" Journal of the American Planning Association 64: 150–169.

California Affordable Housing Law Project and Western Center on Law & Poverty (2002) Inclusionary zoning: Policy Considerations and Best Practices. Oakland, CA: California Affordable Housing Law Project.

California Coalition for Rural Housing and Non-Profit Housing Association of Northern California (2003) Inclusionary Housing in California: 30 Years of Innovation. Sacramento, CA: California Coalition for Rural Housing.

California Department of Housing and Community Development. (2001) Pay to Play: Residential Development Fees in California Cities and Counties, 1999. California Department of Housing and Community Development.

Dietderich Andrew (1996) "An Egalitarian's Market: The Economics of Inclusionary Zoning Reclaimed," Fordham Urb. L.J. 24: 22–104.

Ellickson, Robert C. (1982) "The Irony of 'Inclusionary Zoning'" in Resolving the Housing Crisis: Government Policy, Decontrol, and the Public Interest (edited by M. Bruce Johnson), pp. 135–87. San Francisco: Pacific Institute for Public Policy Research.

Glaeser, Edward L., Joseph Gyourko, Raven Saks (2004) "Why is Manhattan So Expensive? Regulation and the Rise in House Price" NBER Working Paper No. 10124, 2004.

Goetz, Edward, Promoting (1991) "Low-Income Housing Through Innovations in Land-use Regulations," Journal of Urban Affairs 13 (3): 337–351.

Green, Richard K., Stephen Malpezzi, and Stephen K. Mayo (1999) "Metropolitan-Specific Estimates of the Price Elasticity of Supply of Housing, and Their Sources" Wisconsin-Madison CULER working papers 99–16, 1999.

Hanushek, Eric and John Quigley (1980) "What is the Price Elasticity of Housing Demand?" Rev. Econ. & Statistics 62(3): 449–54.

Joseph, Brian "Palm Springs resale restriction pinches residents," The Desert Sun, June 23, 2003.

Kautz, Barbara (2002) "In Defense of Inclusionary Zoning: Successfully Creating Affordable Housing" University of San Francisco Law Review 36: 971–1026.

Monterey Staff Report (2003) "How Did We Do? 17 Recommendations for the Monterey County Inclusionary Program," pp. 63–76 in The California Inclusionary Housing Reader. Sacramento: Institute for Local Government.

Morgan, Terri "Loosened Rules Lure Developers to Watsonville" San Jose Mercury News, Sat Oct. 18, 2003.

Paton, Dean "The equity debate," The Pinnacle, Vol. 17, No. 52, September 25, 2003.

Powell, Benjamin and Stringham, Edward (2003) "'Affordable' Housing Laws Make Homes More Expensive" Economic Education Bulletin, Vol. 28, No. 12 (December 2003) 1–8.

Powell, Benjamin and Stringham, Edward (2004a) "Do Affordable Housing Mandates Work? Evidence from Los Angeles County and Orange County" Reason Foundation Policy Study 320. Los Angeles: Reason Public Policy Institute, June 2004, pp. i-v, pp. 1–26.

Powell, Benjamin and Stringham, Edward (2004b) "Supply and Affordability: Do Affordable Housing Mandates Work?" Reason Foundation Policy Study 318. Los Angeles: Reason Public Policy Institute, April 2004, pp. i-v, pp. 1–45.

Powell, Benjamin and Stringham, Edward (2006)"The Economics of Inclusionary Zoning Reclaimed: How Effective are Price Controls?" Florida State University Law Review Vol. 33 No. 2: 471 499.

Quigley, John and Raphael, Steven (2004) "Is housing Unaffordable? Why Isn't It More Affordable?" Journal of Economic Perspectives, 18: 191–214.

Rawson, Michael et al. (2002) "Inclusionary Zoning: Policy Considerations and Best Practices." Sacramento, CA: California Affordable Housing Law Project of the Public Interest Law Project.

Simon, Ruth (2005) "The Nation's Least Affordable Housing Markets," Wall St. J., January 12, 2005: D2.

Sharon Simonson (2004) "City eases rules to speed condo construction" Silicon Valley/San Jose Business Journal, July 23, p.1, p.40.

Stoll, Michael (2002) "Mission Bay Takes Shape," San Francisco Examiner, September 13, 2002.

Tetreault, Bernard, (2000) "Arguments Against Inclusionary Zoning You Can Anticipate Hearing." New Century Housing Vol. 1 No. 2: 17–20.

Tucker, William (1990) Zoning, Rent Control, and Affordable Housing, Washington, DC: Cato Institute.

Weikel, Dan "Coast Homes Battle Grows" LA Times, December 1, 2003.

# 7

# A Brief Survey of Rent Control in America: Past Mistakes and Future Directions

*Matthew E. Brown*

A two-bedroom apartment on New York's Lexington Avenue is not as spacious as Turkey's 285-room Dolmabahce Palace (currently a museum), but it is home to the man some consider to be the rightful occupant of the Palace, His Imperial Highness Prince Osman Ertugal, the 93-year-old grandson of the last sultan of the Ottoman Empire. The prince, who has lived at his current address since 1945, shares the apartment with his wife, the niece of Afghanistan's last king, and pays $350 a month in rent (Bernstein, 2006). Like many of New York's well-off or well-connected beneficiaries of rent control they enjoy huge discounts from prevailing market prices, while waging battle against their landlord over the need for repairs to the apartment. Their story is a fantastic, but in many ways common, example of the checkered history of rent control in the city of New York.

New York, with America's longest history of rent control, has had some form on the books continuously since World War II. Although instituted as a temporary emergency measure "it will probably be with us forever, or at least until the buildings crumble" (Rose, 2003: 670). Economist Thomas Sowell has appraised rent control as "a subject where insanity is the norm" (Sowell, 2000).

The form of rent controls that were initiated during World War II are variously known as first-generation rent controls, hard price controls, or simply rent control to distinguish them from the later forms more commonly known as rent stabilization. They fixed nominal rents at pre-war rates. With the exception of New York, rent control remained absent in America through the 1960s and started spreading again in the

• 1970s. During the heyday of faith in government planning and regulation, increasingly left-leaning local governments and political pressure
groups, which grew out of the anti-Vietnam War movement, took up rent
control as a response to the rising prices of the '70s and perceived social
injustice in the housing market. There was even a temporary nationwide
freeze on rents in 1971 as part of the Nixon administration's wage and
price controls. •

Matching other political trends at the time, rent controls were instituted
in a handful of traditionally liberal or progressive major cities such as
Boston, Los Angeles, San Francisco, and Washington, D.C., as well as
smaller cities in states on both costs including the intellectual centers
of Cambridge, Massachusetts and Berkeley, California. But unlike the
first-generation rent controls that fixed nominal rent levels in New York
and other places during World War II, the new wave of rent controls in
the 1970s, second generation controls, did not focus on nominal price
fixing but on a more complex regime of rent determination. Some regulations allowed rents to be raised between tenants but not on continuing
residents (vacancy decontrol-recontrol). Often controls fixed the rate at
which rates could rise (rent stabilization or tenancy control) tying them
to a cost of living index, still others allowed for the complete decontrol
of property once the existing tenants left (vacancy decontrol), while
some created provisions under which landlords could pass along costs
of improvements to their tenants in the form of higher rents. Table 7.1
contains a brief summary of major events in the history of rent control
in the United States.

In addition to increased control over financial arrangements, the new
laws also impacted a broader array of interactions between the tenant
and landlord that shifted the power or property rights (depending on
your perspective) away from property owners and to renters. These included provisions to make it more difficult to evict residents who paid
low controlled rates and regulations to control the type and frequency
of maintenance to prevent landlords from decreasing investments in less
profitable rent-controlled buildings. Changes were also instituted that
restricted the ability of building owners to convert their property from
rental units to potentially more lucrative forms such as condos. By the
mid-1980s rent control, in its various forms, had spread to cities and municipalities that were home to roughly 1 in 5 Americans (Tucker, 1997).
Since then the number has declined as some rent control laws, notably
those in Massachusetts, have been repealed.

Table 7.1
Rent Control History

| 1920 | New York adopts Emergency Rent Law of 1920 in response to rising evictions and lack of new housing following World War I. |
| 1929 | Increase in vacancy rates leads to repeal of 1920 rent controls in New York |
| 1943 | Federal rent control laws adopted as part of war price control efforts |
| 1951 | Federal rent control law expires, New York state continues state level controls |
| 1969 | New York "Rent Stabilization" law enacted |
| 1970 | Massachusetts allows cities to enact rent control |
| 1971 | Federal wage and price controls temporarily freeze rents nationwide |
| 1971 | New York adopts vacancy decontrol |
| 1973 | New Jersey Supreme Court allows local rent control laws |
| 1974 | New York's vacancy decontrol repealed |
| 1975 | District of Columbia establishes rent control |
| 1979 | Los Angeles and San Francisco enact rent stabilization |
| 1985 | San Diego voters reject rent control |
| 1993 | New York adopts "luxury decontrol" |
| 1994 | Massachusetts voters approve referendum eliminating rent control |
| 1995 | California passes Costa-Hawkins vacancy decontrol law |
| 2005 | Activists call for rent control in New Orleans following Katrina disaster |
| 2006 | District of Columbia strengthens local rent control law |

Source: Various, compiled by author

## 1. Rent Control and Its Discontents

Rent control seems to enjoy a special place in public sentiment, even in otherwise open markets; rent controls are often viewed as necessary protections of buyers at the hands of potentially merciless landlords who could prey upon them. In the foreword to Friedman and Stigler's classic 1946 Roofs or Ceilings essay, Leonard Read wrote that "even among those who oppose continuance of other forms of price and wage control, a large number make an exception in favor of rent control. It, at least, they say, should be retained." This was echoed in Friedman and Stigler's list of the commonly used arguments for retaining controls: 1) "the rich will get all the housing, and the poor none" (p. 10); 2) "landlords would benefit; and 3) "a rise in rents means an inflation, or leads to one" (p. 11). Yet, they point out, contrary to popular opinion, the use of rent control further tilts the playing field to the advantage of the well-off who can either pursue non-rental housing or pay the added costs of acquiring scarce rent-controlled housing. They tell the story of a newly released World War II Army veteran looking for housing in New York who finds an apartment available for rent at $300 per month if he is "prepared to pay

$5,000 for the furniture in the apartment" (p. 14). This type of payment is sometimes referred to as "key money"—extra payments made outside of the formal rental agreement and thus more difficult to regulate.

Economists have compiled a long list of theoretical arguments against, and empirical evidence on, the destructive effects and unintended consequences of rent control. Shortages of apartments for rent, decreases in quality and lack of maintenance, decreased construction of new apartments, long waiting times and high search costs, discrimination, homelessness, abandoned buildings, and labor market inefficiencies have all been pointed to as blights on the urban landscape caused by rent controls. A major one, which is often confused by advocates of rent control as proof that controls are needed, is higher prices for uncontrolled units in cities with rent control laws. Advocates for rent control point to the higher prices charged for units that are not regulated as proof positive that rent controls protect residents from being exploited by exorbitant market rents. However, economists have argued that it is rent control itself that causes such large increases in unregulated rents. By splitting the market in two, renters who can't find rent-controlled units are forced into the smaller unregulated market where increased demand drives prices higher than would be the case in a free market. Tucker (1997) surveyed rental listings in the newspapers of major American cities, both with and without rent control. He found that in cities without rent control a large number of rental units were advertised as available at prices below the cities average rent level and the distribution of rents on units available for leasing resembled a common bell curve. However, in cities with rent control the vast majority of rental units advertised were for high-end units renting for well above the average rent level. Rent control effectively "drives out affordable housing" as the name of his study suggests (Tucker, 1997; for a general overview of the economic arguments against rent control, see Block, 2002a).

Far from leading to more equitable housing allocations Friedman and Stigler concluded rent controls do just the opposite. Priority is given to current renters, friends and relatives of owners, and those who can afford a "cash supplement" above the rent-controlled price (1946: 14). Finally, the system works to the disadvantage of those who must work for a living, and thus cannot spend large amounts of time looking for apartments, and those with children, who are deemed less desirable tenants. Rent control in this way lowers the costs of discrimination. In a free market a landlord would have to measure the gain received from discrimination against the lost income from turning away a tenant who might be willing to pay a higher price. With rent control the severity of this trade-off is lessened or eliminated allowing landlords the ability to satisfy their prejudices with less financial punishment.

But while the poor and minorities are commonly pointed to as the beneficiaries of rent control, that is often not the case. Famous examples of well off residents who took advantage of rent controls in New York include mayor Ed Koch, who held onto a rent-controlled apartment even though he was provided housing in Gracie Mansion while mayor, actress Mia Farrow, the former president of the New York Stock Exchange, and pop singer Cindy Lauper.

Rent controls have also created something of a cottage industry for bureaucrats justifying the creation of various administrative and control boards as well as a whole new category of housing regulation in the form of anti-discrimination, or fair housing oversight. Additionally, rent control laws, as Friedman and Stigler pointed out, are self-perpetuating. Created to ease housing shortages during and following World War II rent controls lead to decreased turnover and decreased construction exacerbating the shortages. Thus, *as long as the shortage created by rent ceilings remains, there will be a clamor for continued rent controls. This is perhaps the strongest indictment of ceilings on rents. They, and the accompanying shortage of dwellings to rent, perpetuate themselves, and the progeny are even less attractive than the parents*" (Friedman and Stigler, 1946: 19–20).

A survey of economists' views published in the *American Economic Review* in 1992 showed that the question on rent control had the highest degree of agreement of any question. Asked to what extent they agreed with the statement "A ceiling on rents reduces the quantity and quality of housing available" over 93 percent agreed or partially agreed (Alston, Kearl, and Vaughan, 1992: 204). Block (2002b) writes: "this opposition to the measure ranges widely over members of the economic profession, and is representative of all shades of opinion on politics and ethics. Even economists with otherwise impeccable socialist credentials are on record as critics. For example, states Lindbeck (1972) "In many cases, rent control appears to be the most efficient technique presently known to destroy a city—except bombing" (p. 76).

However, there is an increasing movement toward support for some forms of rent control among housing economists, particularly based on theoretical models that suggest certain types of second-generation controls may be socially desirable. Arnott (1995) observes, "In recent years, however, there has been a wave (or at least a swell) of revisionism among housing economists on the subject of rent control. While few actually advocate controls, most are considerably more muted and qualified in their opposition. Perhaps a majority, at least among the younger generation, would agree with the statement that a well-designed rent control program can be beneficial" (Arnott, 1995: 99).

If this shift of opinion toward a more favorable view of rent control is real, it could help tip the balance that had been swinging away from rent control, back in favor of control. After a wave of new regulations in the 1970s and '80s some locations started eliminating or weakening rent control laws in the 1990s. But the return of the Era of Big Government during the Bush administration has coincided with some signs that the public's and politician's love of rent control is far from over.

## 2. Rent Control Today

Political support for rent control has fluctuated since the 1970s in tandem with the changing mood for economic regulation in general. The wave of rent regulation that swept the coasts in the 1970s was backed by a well-organized movement of politically savvy tenant organizations like the California Housing Action and Information Network and the New Jersey Tenants Organization many of whose members had been involved the political activism of the 1960s. By the time the political climate began to move away from regulation during the Reagan administration in the 1980s over 170 communities nationwide had passed some form of rent control laws. But during the 1980s the tenants associations began to lose power and become disorganized while landlords' organizations like the National Apartment Association and the National Council of the Multi Housing Industry began to mobilize to oppose rent controls and take advantage of a growing public and political opposition to regulation (Keating and Kahn, 2001). By the 1990s the political climate had swung decidedly away from the supporters of increased rent control and there were growing signs that opponents of rent control were on the ascendancy.

Currently, rent control in America is confined to stretches of the east and west coasts. Four states—California, Maryland, New Jersey, and New York, and the District of Columbia—have some form of rent control laws on the books. Thirty-five states have laws that preempt rent control by local governments, including Massachusetts, which eliminated rent control in a statewide referendum in 1994. These state laws take various forms. Outright prohibitions of rent control exist in states like South Dakota and Tennessee where the law reads "a local government unit shall not enact, maintain or enforce an ordinance or resolution that would have the effect of controlling the amount of rent charged for leasing private residential or commercial property." Some states such as Arizona have banned rent control at the local level, but maintain the state government's right to enact such rules in the future: "the state legislature determines that the imposition of rent control on private residential housing units ... is of statewide concern. Therefore, the power to control rents on private residential property is preempted by the state." Other states such as Florida and Texas have outlawed rent control except under emergency circumstances. In Texas the local government can impose rent control if it "finds that a housing emergency exists due to a disaster" and "the governor approves the ordinance" (NMHC, 2006). In Connecticut there is no rent control, but a system of "fair rent" laws allow tenants to challenge their rent on an individual case-by-case basis. A local agency is responsible for handling these claims and determining if a landlord has failed to meet health and safety codes or implemented excessive rental increases (Fair Rent Commission, 2006). Eleven other states have no rent control and no state preemption of such laws (NMHC, 2006). Table 7.2 summarizes the state-by-state breakdown of rent control laws.

The remainder of this chapter will provide an overview of America's major rent control laws and their evolution in New York, California, New Jersey, and Washington D.C., an account of the repeal of rent control in the state of Massachusetts as well as a summary of some of the findings that researchers have made regarding the impact of those laws, and in the case of Massachusetts their repeal.

### 3. New York

New York City's rent control laws are famous and have earned a place in many pop-culture representations of the city. The hit TV show *Friends* featured an ongoing story line where the characters were benefiting from a rent-controlled apartment that was supposed to be rented to one of the characters' grandparents. Rent control and the absurdities it creates for apartment seekers came up several times in the series *Seinfeld,* and *Sex and the City's* Carrie Bradshaw found herself engaged in a search for an affordable apartment with a closet big enough to store her designer shoe collection after her rent-controlled building went condo. In the Tom Hanks-Meg Ryan movie *You've Got Mail,* a character brags that he enjoys a large rent-controlled apartment for only $450 per month. This prompts the retort, "It's like bragging because you're tall," capturing the

**Table 7.2**
**State Rent Control Laws**

| Rent Control | State Preemption | No Control/No Preemption |
|---|---|---|
| California | Alabama | Alaska |
| Maryland | Arizona | Delaware |
| New Jersey | Arkansas | Hawaii |
| New York | Colorado | Maine |
|  | Connecticut | Montana |
| District of Columbia | Florida | Nebraska |
|  | Georgia | Nevada |
|  | Idaho | Ohio |
|  | Illinois | Pennsylvania |
|  | Indiana | Rhode Island |
|  | Iowa | West Virginia |
|  | Kansas |  |
|  | Kentucky |  |
|  | Louisiana |  |
|  | Massachusetts |  |
|  | Michigan |  |
|  | Minnesota |  |
|  | Missouri |  |
|  | Mississippi |  |
|  | Missouri |  |
|  | New Hampshire |  |
|  | New Mexico |  |
|  | North Dakota |  |
|  | Oklahoma |  |
|  | Oregon |  |
|  | South Carolina |  |
|  | South Dakota |  |
|  | Tennessee |  |
|  | Texas |  |
|  | Utah |  |
|  | Vermont |  |
|  | Virginia |  |
|  | Washington |  |
|  | Wisconsin |  |
|  | Wyoming |  |

Source: NMHC (2006).

popular impression that the city's rent control laws are both random and seemingly unfair in the benefits they bestow on a lucky few.

While rent control in New York is primarily a twentieth-century phenomenon, the involvement of the government in the regulation of rental housing goes back to the nineteenth century.[1] By the Civil War, overcrowded multi-family dwellings known as "tenements" had become the source of a large portion of the city's housing, as well as the locus of much unrest, disease, and violence. In 1867 the state of New York passed the Tenement House Act, which regulated fire escapes and the number of water closets per resident among other things. The 1901 Tenement House Act required that each floor of a tenement have running water and increased regulations for escape from fires. By 1904, and again in 1908, widespread protests concerning rental rates and conditions in tenements took place. In 1920, following World War I, the mayor of New York told the state legislature the best way to fight the growing popularity of socialism in the city was by preventing what the city's large working poor viewed as unfair rent increases. The state legislature passed rent control laws in April and September of 1920 that subjected rent increases to judicial review for "reasonableness." "Effectively, any increase over that of a prior year was presumed 'unjust, unreasonable and oppressive' unless an owner could demonstrate otherwise" (RGB, 2006a). Early on it was clear rent controls would do nothing but increase problems with post-war housing shortages and additional laws were passed exempting newly constructed buildings from property taxes and rent control laws. Rent control lasted throughout the boom years of the roaring twenties with "luxury decontrol" on units renting for more than $20 per month per room in 1926. Eventually complete decontrol, with the exception of certain eviction regulations, occurred in June 1929.

Rent control returned to New York City in 1943 following the passage a year earlier of the Emergency Price Control Act, which placed the power to control rents with the Administrator of the federal government's Office of Price Administration. On November 1, rental rates for apartments and houses in New York City were frozen at the level that had been in place on March 1, 1943. The rent control laws were extended through the 1940s with periodic adjustments to the allowable rates made by the OPA. Federal law governing rent control throughout the country expired in 1953. In anticipation, the state of New York adopted its own law establishing a similar system of controls set to take effect at the expiration of the federal law. Rent controls were continued on buildings constructed prior to 1947 and those constructed after that time were allowed to rent at market rates. The justification for continuing controls after the war was fear that returning soldiers would add pressure to rental markets and raise prices to unaffordable levels. This fear, like the fear that the end of the war would lead to a return to depression, quickly proved unwarranted as the post-war economy boomed along with the construction of new housing and movement to the suburbs. By the mid-1950s New York was the only place left in America with wartime rent controls.

During the 1960s, increasing political radicalism, combined with rising rents in new uncontrolled apartments and declining vacancy rates, led the mayor of New York to appoint a Rent Guidelines Board to study the city's rental housing market. The resulting Rent Stabilization Law of 1969 created a system of "rent stabilization" for the over 300,000 apartments that had been built after 1947 that were not subject to rent control. Under the law, the Rent Guidelines Board was given the authority to establish yearly acceptable rates of increase on rents in the city in buildings not subject to rent control. Since that time, New York City has had, in effect, a dual system of rent regulation, with rent control (real rate controls) on units built prior to 1947 and rent stabilization (controlled increases in rent) on units built after that time.

In a burst of *laissez faire* spirit in 1971, the state legislature enacted vacancy decontrol and vacancy destabilization, which would allow owners of both pre-war and post-war buildings to charge market rents following the lawful vacancy of an apartment. If it had remained in place, the law would have led to the elimination of all rent regulation in the city as natural turnover occurred. But by 1974, public outrage over rising rents, and indeed inflation in general, led to reestablishment of the system of rent regulation with the Emergency Tenant Protection Act of 1974 (RGB, 2006a).

"Rent *control*" in New York now applies to units in "residential buildings constructed before February 1947 in municipalities that have not declared an end to the postwar rental housing emergency." There are a total of 51 such communities including New York City, Albany, and Buffalo. To qualify for rent *control* the tenant, or their successor, must have been living in one of the pre-1947 buildings since before July 1971. If a rent-controlled tenant moves out and no legal successor (generally a spouse, child, or life partner) resides in the apartment, then the unit becomes subject to rent *stabilization*. However, if the vacant rent-controlled unit is in a small building (6 or fewer total units) it can be completely deregulated and rented for market rates (DHRC, 2006a). The number of rent-controlled units has been declining steadily as vacancies convert them to rent-stabilized units. In the 1950s there were over 2 million rent-controlled units in the city of New York, today there are fewer than 50,000 (RGB, 2006c). In addition to the changes due to conversion to rent stabilization, the rates of rent-controlled units can be altered for several reasons. The building's owner can apply for rent increases if major improvements are undertaken or operating costs increase, and they may be decreased if the owner fails to meet building code standards.

"Rent *stabilization*" laws apply to three broad categories of apartments in New York City: first, buildings constructed between 1947 and 1974 with more than 6 rental units; second, previously rent-*controlled* units (pre-1947 units) that have been vacated after 1971 with no legal successor; and third, buildings with 3 or more rental units which have taken advantage of special tax breaks to finance construction or extensive renovations since 1974 that require the owner to abide by rent stabilization during the period that the tax breaks are in effect (RGB, 2006b). There are four common ways that rent-stabilized rates can rise. First, a new tenant signs what is known as a "vacancy lease." These leases, as with renewals, are available for one- or two-year terms at the choice of the tenant. The rent on a vacancy lease is equal to the rent charged the previous regulated tenant's lease plus vacancy increases authorized by the Rent Guidelines Board (RGB). For leases signed between October 2005 and September 2006, the vacancy increase allowed is 17.75 percent for a one-year lease and 20 percent for a two-year lease. The second way a stabilized rent can increase is during the renewal of a lease. The renewal lease adjustment is also determined by RGB. For renewals between October 2005 and September 2006, the renewal increase is 2.25 percent for a one-year lease and 4.5 percent for a two-year lease.[2] The third common way stabilized rents are increased is through a major capital improvement (MCI), which consists of a major building renovation, such as installing a new boiler. The cost of the improvement is amortized over 7 years and is allocated to the units in the building on a per room basis and is permanently added to the legal rent of the units. Such improvement related increases are limited to 6 percent per year. Finally, stabilized rents may be raised for individual apartment improvements (IAI), which are unit-specific changes such as new appliances (DHRC, 2006b). This provision is discussed briefly in the next paragraph as part of the changes to rent regulations during the 1990s.

Rent regulation laws remained relatively stable in New York for the 20 years between 1974 and 1993. Deregulation was reintroduced in 1993 with "luxury decontrol." Under these provisions, rent-stabilized apartments whose rents rose legally above $2,000 per month were allowed to be destabilized (no longer subject to regulation) following a vacancy. Or units where the rent rose legally above $2,000 per month and the tenants had an annual income of over $250,000 for each of the previous two years were allowed to be deregulated. Also, the law allowed landlords to pass the costs of individual unit improvements, such as buying new appliances, on to tenants at a rate of $1/40^{th}$ of the cost of the improvement in increased monthly rent. For example, if a $320 appliance is installed in a rent-stabilized apartment which rents for $800 per month the landlord may increase the rent by $8 to $808 per month. Existing tenants are allowed to refuse such improvements (DHRC, 2006b).

Following a brief four day lapse in rent control laws in 1997 the state enacted the Rent Regulation Reform Act of 1997 which, among other things, lowered the required annual income for luxury decontrol to $175,000, and prevented nephews, nieces, aunts, and uncles from being allowed to "inherit" rent-*controlled* apartments of their relatives. Spouses, life partners, and children may still continue a family members rent control if they meet certain residency requirements.

A few landlords in the city are trying to get around rent regulation laws by having a plan approved for the demolition of their building; once approved the tenants can be evicted, even if the building is ultimately only renovated. An April 2006 article in the *New York Times* details several recent examples of such demolition evictions, including a case, ongoing at the time, of a building containing a 2,000 square-foot loft that under rent regulation rents for only $850 per month, but could bring in over $2 million dollars if sold on the open market (Barbanel, 2006). Although such evictions generate widespread media attention and public outcry they are imposed on a tiny fraction of the city's rentals.

In 2005 there were 3,261,000 housing units (rental and owner-occupied) in the city of New York, up just over 50,000 units since 2002. Of these 3 million, just over 2 million (2,028,000) are rental units. Just over 2 percent of those units, 43,000 are rent-controlled units and approximately half of all rental units, 1,044,000, are rent-stabilized. The rest are not regulated. The number of rent-*controlled* units decreases slightly each years with vacancy decontrol—as controlled units are vacated and no legal successor takes the controlled rent the unit is decontrolled and subject to rent stabilization. The number of rent-controlled units decontrolled varies from year to year, but between 2002 and 2005 16,000 units were decontrolled (Lee, 2006).

### Table 7.3
### Rental Statistics for New York City, 2005

| | |
|---|---|
| Total Housing Units | 3,260,856 |
| Total Rental Units | 2,092,363 |
| Rent-Controlled Units | 43,317 |
| Rent-Stabilized Units | 1,043,677 |
| Total Vacancies available to rent | 64,737 |
| Percent of Rents below $1,000 | 58.0% |
| Maximum increase on one-year renewal lease (10/05–9/06) | 2.25–2.75% (see note 2) |

Source: Lee (2006) "Selected Findings of the 2005 New York City Housing and Vacancy Survey," Tables 1, 2, 4, and 13; and DHRC (2006b).

Henry Pollakowski of the MIT Center for Real Estate, and the editor of the *Journal of Housing Economics,* studied the housing market in Manhattan to determine the impact of New York's system of rent control and rent stabilization on the rents paid by the city's residents and to estimate the effect of repealing the regulations. One of the primary arguments made against the repeal of the city's rent regulations is that the working-class and poor residents of the city could not afford the rent payments that would be required by an unregulated free market in rental housing, under the assumption that these middle- and lower-income renters are benefiting from the current system by paying substantially lower rents than would otherwise be available to them. But according to the results of Pollakowski's study this conventional wisdom may be incorrect.

The difference between what a renter pays for a rent-regulated unit and what that unit would rent for in an unregulated market is referred to as the renter's subsidy. According to Pollakowski, the subsidy for most people in New York is not very big. Once you take into account features that affect rents, like the location, age of building, square footage, and quality of the apartment, the difference in rents for regulated and unregulated units are quite small in most of the city, with the exception of the wealthier areas. While the average subsidy city-wide is estimated to be $42 per month, in Queens and Staten Island it is effectively zero, in Brooklyn and Upper Manhattan it is roughly $10 per month, in the Bronx it is $58 per month, and in the more affluent Lower Manhattan and Mid-Manhattan areas it is estimated to be $397 per month (Pollakowski, 2003a: 4–5). So the benefits of the current system, far from primarily going to the poor, accrue to residents of the city's wealthier areas.

Given the contentious history of rent control and the mounting evidence of its questionable and even unfair distribution of benefits it is sure to generate an enormous amount of public interest and political debate when the state of New York's entire rent stabilization system comes up for renewal again in 2011 (RGB, 2006c).

## 4. California

In the 1970s and early 1980s California experienced a statewide campaign to lobby local governments to adopt rent controls. Local measures were successful in several major cities, including San Francisco, Los Angeles, and San Jose, as well as smaller cities like Berkeley and Santa Monica. Ultimately about half of the state's renting population ended up living in cities with rent regulations on the books. The notable exception has been San Diego where voters defeated a rent control ballot measure in 1985. Currently, other California cities with some form of rent control include Beverly Hills, Campbell, East Palo Alto, Fremont, Hayward, Los Gatos, Oakland, Palm Springs, Thousand Oaks, and West Hollywood (NMHC, 2006).

Santa Monica is famous for having one of the most stringent rent control laws in the nation. Residents, it has been argued, use rent control, not as way to help low-income renters, but as a legal obstacle to keep development and increasing populations out of their beach side haven. The difficulty of finding a place to rent in Santa Monica is legendary as is its homelessness. According to Tucker (1997) Santa Monica "is often called the 'The Homeless Capital of the West.'"

While San Francisco, Berkeley, and Santa Monica represent the strongest forms of rent control and its negative consequences, Los Angeles has historically had a rent regulation regime that is relatively mild by comparison allowing rents to rise to market levels between renters. Vacancy rates in Los Angeles are far higher than other big cities in the state like San Francisco and San Jose, and because of the city's large size, Los Angeles' rent stabilization law impacts more renters than any other city ordinance in the state of California (Carlson, 2006). The city's Rent Stabilization Ordinance took effect on May 1, 1979 and primarily governs rents in buildings with certificates of occupancy issued before October 1978 and contains regulations regarding four categories: allowable rent increases, registrations of units, evictions, and causes that require relocation assistance (LAHD, 2006b). Los Angeles has typically

Table 7.4
Los Angeles and San Francisco Annual Rent Increases

| Year | Los Angeles | San Francisco |
|------|-------------|---------------|
| 2007 | 4 % | 1.7% |
| 2006 | 3 % | 1.2% |
| 2005 | 3 % | 0.6% |
| 2004 | 3 % | 0.8% |
| 2003 | 3 % | 2.7% |
| 2002 | 3 % | 2.8% |
| 2001 | 3 % | 2.9% |
| 2000 | 3 % | 1.7% |
| 1999 | 3 % | 2.2% |
| 1998 | 3 % | 1.8% |
| 1997 | 3 % | 1.0% |

Notes: Allowable increase in Los Angeles is for the 12-month period ending on June 30 of that year and in San Francisco for the 12-month period ending on February 28 of that year.
Sources: LAHD (2006a) and Rent Board (2006).

allowed higher annual rent increases than other major California cities like San Francisco, contributing to its less restricted housing market. For the period July 2006 to June 2007 the allowed increase was 4 percent (LAHD, 2006a).

San Francisco's rent control laws have historically been much more severe since their enactment in 1979. However, the city's experiences with the harmful side effects of rent control go back further. Friedman and Stigler (1946) used San Francisco as a natural experiment in how rent control and the free market each impact the availability of rental housing. They compare the availability of and demand for rental housing in the city immediately following the devastating earthquake of 1906 and forty years later at the end of World War II. Following the earthquake and subsequent fires that according to Freidman and Stigler eliminated over half of the city's housing, remaining units, after taking account of people who left the city, had to accommodate 40 percent more people than before the disaster. "Yet when one turns to the San Francisco Chronicle of May 24, 1906—the first available issue after the earthquake—*there is not a single mention of a housing shortage!*" (p. 7). And they go on to document how listings in the paper for units available for rent outpaced listings of people seeking units. At the end of World War II when as they observe "the use of higher rents to ration housing has been made illegal by the imposition of rent ceilings," the situation was reversed. "During the first five days of the year there were altogether only 4 advertisements offering houses or apartments for rent, as compared with 64 in one day in May 1906" only one month after the earthquake and fires had destroyed much of the city's infrastructure (Friedman and Stigler, 1946: 8).

Stanford economist Thomas Sowell took up the subject of rent control in San Francisco in a column over a half a century after Friedman and Stigler and observed that the problem only seems to have gotten worse after San Francisco passed a strong rent control law in 1979. Sowell pointed out another common problem with rent control: proponents of control rarely seem to have much regard for the negative consequences of rent control laws. "What has happened under stringent rent control laws in the city by the bay is what has happened in virtually every other city around the world where such laws have been passed. But it will still be news to rent control advocates, who seldom bother to get the facts.... The San Francisco Board of Supervisors recently commissioned the first official study ever done of the effects of rent control in the city. Imagine! San Francisco's first rent control law was passed in 1979 and has been amended more than 50 times in the two decades since then—usually tightening the controls—but nobody in government has yet bothered to find out what the actual effect has been" (Sowell, 2000). Tucker (1997) found a lack of advertised low-cost housing in San Francisco's papers, with fewer than 10 percent of units advertised for rents below the city's average. Sowell cites statistics that show construction of apartments decreased by over 30 percent in the decade following the passage of San Francisco's rent control law, and during the decade of the 1990s the number of apartments actually declined, vacancy rates have remained among the lowest in the nation, and rental prices have skyrocketed to among the highest in the nation.

San Francisco's Rent Board oversees annual increases on existing leases. The annual increases are limited to 60 percent of the urban consumer price index for the Bay Area (the allowable increase across the Bay under Berkeley's rent control law is also low, only 65 percent of the index). The maximum allowable increase for the year ending February 28, 2007 is 1.7 percent applicable to all units built before June 1979 (Rent Board 2006 and Rent Stabilization Board 2006). San Francisco has a relatively high amount of renters (65 percent) compared to the national average (34 percent) making the existence and impact of rent control particularly important to its residents' well-being. And like in many major cities, rent control is hardly limited to the poor. While the average income of San Francisco residents living in rent-controlled units is lower than the average of those paying market rates, both groups have the same percentage of residents who earn over $100,000 per year (SFBS, 2002: 4). The study commissioned by the San Francisco Board of Supervisors, mentioned by Sowell above, surveyed property owners (landlords) and found that for "all listed regulations with a comparable national category ... San Francisco respondents are more likely than respondents nationally to see the regulation as causing difficulty in operating the property" (SFBS, 2003: iv). And when asked, "If you own rent-controlled units, how much has rent control affected your financial ability to maintain those units?," 73 percent answered "much more difficult," 9 percent answered "slightly more difficult," 9 percent answered "not affected," and 7 indicated it was less difficult (SFSB, 2003: 44). While it is predictable that owners would take a chance like that to express their displeasure with rent control, the results when combined with the extremely limited annual increases and other regulations paint a picture of San Francisco as a city not at all hospitable to anyone interested in providing rental housing.

In a major reform the California legislature passed state-wide vacancy decontrols in 1995. Commonly known as the "Costa-Hawkins Act," the law supersedes local ordinances and requires that once a tenant voluntarily leaves an apartment or is legally evicted the rent on the unit can be raised to the market rate. The law also provides for the elimination of rent control on units constructed after 1995 and single-family homes (CAA, 2003). The law was phased in and took effect statewide by 1999. One response by the activists who favor rent control has been to advance other forms of rent regulation, strengthening laws that limit the ability of landlords to recoup operating costs or increasing regulations that govern tenant landlord relationships in other ways. Despite the evidence against rent control cited by Sowell and many others, voters in San Francisco passed an initiative in 2000 to limit increases in rents that landlords can enact because of capital improvements (traditionally one way cities with rent controls, like New York, try to deal with the adverse effects rent controls have on the incentives of landlords to maintain safe and modern buildings) (Keating and Kahn, 2001).

## 5. New Jersey

New Jersey experienced a boom in rent control regulations in the mid-1970s following a state Supreme Court decision in 1973 that allowed local governments the authority to enact rent control. By 1976 at least 97 communities in New Jersey had some form of rent control. And in the 1990s 60 cities in New Jersey with populations over 10,000 had rent control out of a total number of 125 cities with population over 10,000. Breaking the regulations down more finely Krol and Svorny (2005) find that in the year 2000 of the 1415 census tracts that they studied 733 were subject to some form of rent control (2005: 423).

According to Tucker (1997) rent controls in New Jersey have been effective as a way of keeping outsiders away from ethnically homogeneous communities. "Rent control has proved an effective tool for making sure that small, exclusionary minded communities do hot have to undergo change" (Tucker, 1997). Efforts to enact statewide restrictions on the ability of cities to impose rent control have not been effective like they were in the case of state wide vacancy decontrol in California and elimination of rent control in Massachusetts (discussed below). Efforts to eliminate rent control for apartments over $750 a month, and later to mandate statewide permanent vacancy decontrol, have been proposed by Republican state legislators in recent years but have not gained enough support for passage (Keating and Kahn, 2001).

While the regulations vary from location to location the general trend in New Jersey was in line with the national trend in the 1970s of second generation controls, namely some form of tenancy control rather than unit-specific real rent controls like those put in place in New York following World War II. Primarily the rate of increase on existing tenants was limited, some allowances were made for landlords to pass cost increases from tax increases and building renovations and repairs on to tenants, and new buildings were generally exempted. However, a great degree of variation in the laws governing inter-tenant regulations do exist from community to community in New Jersey. At one extreme an ordinance may allow the complete elimination of rent control on a unit once the occupant has moved out; this is known as "vacancy decontrol," and at the other extreme the same rental regulation may remain in place from one tenant to the next effectively eliminating the difference in rent due to turnover. In between there exist various levels of vacancy decontrol that allow rents to rise but less than to full market rates between tenants (limited vacancy decontrol), and regulations that allow rates to rise between tenants but re-impose tenancy controls once a new tenant is in place (decontrol-recontrol). Of the 733 New Jersey census tracts subject to rent control studied by Krol and Svorny (2005) the most common regime was one of vacancy decontrol and then control put in place again for new tenants, this occurred in 367 tracts. Next most common was no vacancy decontrol at all which occurred in 189 tracts. 152 tracts had limited vacancy decontrol, and 25 tracts had complete vacancy decontrol.

Vacancy decontrol was adopted in the 1990s by the cities of Bloomfield and Passaic (Keating and Kahn, 2001). The number of communities with rent control has remained relatively constant following the trend around the country where rent control came mostly in one large movement in the 1970s and then was relatively stable. "Between 1976 and 2000 we find that, of the 1415 census tracts with associated place names, ordinances were repealed in 63 and newly instituted in 110. There was no change in the remaining 1242 tracts" (Krol and Svorny, 2005: 423).

Krol and Svorny (2005) study the impact that rent control has on commute times in New Jersey, a growing concern in today's housing market among both consumers and urban planners because of increasing crowding on roads and recent increases in gas prices. Their results "show a positive and statistically significant relationship between rent control and the percent of the working population that has a long commute for 1980, 1990, and 2000" (435). Specifically, in 2000 rent control is estimated to have increased the number of commuters who reported a commute time of over 45 minutes by 48,000 people. These longer commutes induced by rent control have many negative consequences. In addition to the obvious costs associated with commute times such as increased automobile maintenance and increased gas consumption, there are others including increased driving-related accidents, pollution, and road congestion. Effects can also be felt farther from the road; as Krol and Svorny indicate "labor market matches will deteriorate as workers fail to move when they might otherwise benefit from a move, slowing economic activity and growth" (Krol and Svorny, 2005: 422).

## 6. Washington, DC

Washington, DC first passed rent control with the Rental Accommodations Act of 1975. The original law was updated by the Rental Housing Act of 1985, which governed the city's program of rent regulation through 2006. The law established rent ceilings and governed maximum allowable increases of rent for existing tenants and on units that have been vacated in buildings built before 1975. It also created regulations on eviction procedures and special provisions for elderly tenants. The DC regulation began with a "base rent," which is the amount of rent charged for a unit on September 1, 1983, from that the rent ceiling was determined by adding allowable yearly increases and other periodic adjustments, such as capital improvements (DCRA, 2006: 14–19). According to recent estimates 61 percent of the district's households live in rental units and of those about 74 percent (101,000 units) are subject to the city's rent

control system (NARPAC, 2005). However, the rent ceilings in most of
the rental units in the District did not directly determine what renters paid
because most rental units rented for amounts well below the maximum
allowable rent ceiling. Due to the city's high vacancy rate, crime, shrink-
ing population, and general impression that it is an undesirable place to
live, rental rates did not kept up with the rent ceiling, which increased
each year based on the CPI-W regardless of the rent the unit can actually
command. So, for example, a studio with a real rent of $1,200 per month
may have a rent ceiling of $4,400 (Weiss, 2006). While some buildings
in the more desirable neighborhoods of northwest Washington had rents
that kept up with the ceilings, most did not. By 2006, of the 101,000
units subject to rent control only 18,000 were renting at the rent ceiling
(NARPAC, 2005).

The DC financial control board, established by Congress to oversee
the often comically incompetent DC local government, was required to
undertake a study of the city's rent control system in 1997. The report,
released in 2000, recommended removing rent control because the city's
high vacancy rate would protect poor tenants from increases in rents under
decontrol. It estimated that units renting at the existing ceiling would see
increases of less than $40 per month (NARPAC, 2005). Not one to take
its subservient role lying down, the DC city council swiftly voted in the
fall of that year to extend the city's rent control laws.

Rent control was revisited by the District's government in 2006. Responding to pressure from renters and activists who claim the rent ceiling
program didn't do enough to keep rents low, the DC Council took up a
measure to eliminate the ceiling program and impose a new system of
yearly allowable increases, because according to the proposal's sponsor
"the very concept of rent control has become utterly meaningless" (Weiss,
2006). In May, the Council voted unanimously to give preliminary approval to a new rent control law that was given final approval and signed
into law by the mayor in June 2006. The new law, the Rent Control Reform Amendment Act of 2006, eliminates the rent ceiling program and
replaces it with a system that regulates how much rents are allowed to
be increased from their existing levels each year. Most vacant units will
be allowed to increase rent from the previous lease by 10 percent (but
by no more than 30 percent for special cases), existing leases will be
limited to yearly increases of 2 percent plus inflation (with a maximum
increase of 10 percent), and rents charged to the elderly and disabled
will have increases limited to inflation (capped at 5 percent) (RCRAA,
2006). Former mayor and current Council member Marion Barry has

expressed interest in extending the new bill to also cover buildings constructed after 1975.

## 7. Massachusetts

Boston and nearby cities adopted rent controls in the early 1970s following a 1970 decision by the state government (the Rent Control Enabling Act) to allow cities with populations over 50,000 to enact rent regulations. In addition to Boston, Cambridge, Lynn, Somerville, and Brookline adopted rent controls starting in 1971. Regulations were short lived in Lynn, which eliminated controls in 1974 and Somerville, which did the same in 1979. By the early 1990s, Cambridge was the only city not to significantly relax its controls (Pollakowski, 2003b: 1, 14). The measures were popular with many of the city's progressive voters. The mayor of Cambridge in the early 1990s even mentioned in his campaign ads the fact that he lived in a rent-controlled apartment he first obtained as a Harvard law student in the 1970s (Tucker, 1997).

In 1994 a statewide ballot measure advanced by Boston-area property owners put the legality of local rent control laws in front of the state's voters. The advocates for eliminating rent control in Boston, Cambridge, and Brookline, argued that voters in the rest of the state bore part of the burden of rent control by being forced to pay higher property taxes because rent control reduced the property values in, and thus tax revenues collected from, the rent-controlled cities. Opponents of the repeal argued, as rent control advocates have elsewhere, that the elimination of rent control would lead to skyrocketing rents and increasing homelessness resulting from increased evictions by greedy landlords eager to take advantage of higher rents. The state's voters ultimately approved of the measure to eliminate rent control by a thin 51 to 49 percent margin. Not surprisingly, voters in the only cities in the state with rent control laws, Boston, Cambridge, and Brookline, voted overwhelming in favor of keeping rent control (Tucker, 1997).

While the new state law called for the immediate elimination of local rent control laws, an agreement among landlords extended rent controls in certain "hardship cases" for two additional years. Owners further took efforts to address hardship cases by "setting up a bank of 200 apartments around the city [Boston] that are immediately available for emergencies" (Tucker, 1997). On January 1, 1995, when the majority of rent controls were eliminated, Massachusetts became the location of the first major rent decontrol in the nation since the expiration of federal wartime controls in the 1950s. Current Massachusetts law does actually allow for cities to impose rent control, but under conditions not likely to be found appealing. In addition to making the compliance voluntary, cities are required to compensate landlords for the difference between market and controlled rents, with the stipulation that "such compensation [come] from the municipality's general funds, so that the cost of any rent control shall be borne by all taxpayers of a municipality and not by the owners of regulated units only" (The General Laws of Massachusetts).

Rent decontrol has led to increases in housing investment at all levels of the market. A study by MIT housing economist Henry Pollakowski found that investment in Cambridge increased by 20 percent above and beyond what would have been expected if rent control had remained in place. And both high-income and lower-income neighborhoods benefited, supporting the typical economic argument that price controls on rental properties discourage investment and lead to decreased quality of rental housing. Pollakowski concluded that Cambridge's experience with de-control is "one of a tremendous boom in housing investment, leading to major gains in housing quality" (2003, 5). Special programs and funds set up to assist the needy displaced by decontrol have been vastly under-utilized. An aid to the mayor of Boston observed, "Frankly, we're a little surprised at how smoothly everything has gone" (SPOA various).

## 8. Conclusion

The 1990s may be looked back on as the golden age of rent decontrol, most notably with the elimination of rent control in Massachusetts and the imposition of vacancy decontrol in California. However, like the Era of Big Government, rent control is nowhere near its end. Strong economic growth in many large cities in recent years has led to rising urban housing costs, making rent control particularly alluring to the uninformed. Seattle activists have called for rent control in response to the rising rents that followed the city's urban renewal and technology led boom. However, the movement has enjoyed little success due to state laws that preempt local rent control. Following the devastation of New Orleans by Hurricane Katrina, there have been calls for rent control to be imposed in New Orleans to prevent residents from having to pay rising rents due to the city's depleted housing stock. And in the summer of 2006 Washington, DC enacted a major tightening of its rent control regulations.

An enormous amount of empirical research has been collected by economists over the years documenting the negative effects of rent regula-tion. And the negative consequences of rent control have been found in surveys of professional economists to garner more agreement than just about any other issue. Restricting the market's ability to allocate rental properties has decreased the incentives for landlords to maintain their buildings and forced developers to rethink plans about future housing construction, while making it harder for would be renters to find available units and discouraging existing renters from ever moving. Additionally, rent control has been identified as a contributor to a dizzying array of modern urban problems: homelessness, slums, abandoned buildings, urban depopulation, road congestion, labor market inefficiencies, and discrimination to name just a few. However, despite economist's pleadings to the contrary voters and local politicians seem intent on continuing their search for a free lunch in the housing market.

## Notes

1.  Rent control has been around for a long time outside the United States. In the twelfth century, Emperor Frederick Barbarossa established rent controls in Bologna following the influx of students and scholars to the city after the founding of the university there (RGB, 2006a).
2.  If the owner provides or is required to provide heat to the tenant at no additional charge, then the allowed increases are slightly higher: 2.75 percent and 5.5 percent respectively for the same time period.

## References

Alston, Richard M., J. R. Kearl, and Michael B. Vaughan. 1992. Is there a Consensus Among Economists in the 1990s? American Economic Review 82(2): 203–209.

Arnott, Richard. 1995. Time for Revisionism on Rent Control? *Journal of Political Economy* 9(1): 99–120.

Barbanel, Josh. 2006. A New Chapter in the Face-Off Between Tenants and Landlords. *New York Times.* April 2.

Basu, Kaushik and Patrick M. Emerson. 2000. The Economics of Tenancy Rent Control. *The Economic Journal.* 110 (October): 939–962.

Bernstein, Fred A. 2006. Not Quite a Castle, but It's Home. *New York Times.* March 26.

Block, Walter. 2002a. Rent Control. In *The Concise Ecyclopedia of Economics.* Ed. David Henderson. Liberty Fund. Online: http://www.econlib.org/library/Enc/RentControl. html (Cited: May 2006).

Block, Walter. 2002b. A Critique of the Legal and Philosophical Case for Rent Control. *Journal of Business Ethics.* 40: 75–90.

CAA (California Apartment Association). 2003. General Overview. Online: http://www. caanet.org/AM/Template.cfm?Section=Home1&CONTENTID=7224&TEMPLATE =/CM/ContentDisplay.cfm. Cited: May 2006.

Carlson, Kenneth. 2006. LA Rent Control Made Simple. California Tenant Law website. Online: http://www.caltenantlaw.com/LARSO.htm. Cited: March 2006.

DCRA (Department of Consumer and Regulatory Affairs). 2006. Tenant's Guide to Safe and Decent Housing. Government of the District of Columbia: Washington, DC.

DHCR (New York State Division of Housing and Community Renewal). 2006a. Fact Sheet #1: Rent Control and Rent Stabilization. Online: http://www.housingnyc. com/html/resources/dhcr/dhcr1.html. Cited May 2006.

DHCR (New York State Division of Housing and Community Renewal). 2006b. Fact Sheet # 26: Guide to Rent Increases for Rent Stabilized Apartments in New York City. Online: http://www.dhcr.state.ny.us/ora/pubs/html/orafac26.htm. Cited May 2006.

Fair Rent Commission. 2006. Website of the Norwalk, Connecticut Fair Rent Commission. http://www.norwalkct.org/FairRent/index.htm. Cited: May 2006.

Friedman, Milton and George J. Stigler. 1946. Roofs or Ceilings? The Current Housing Problem. *Popular Essays on Current Problems*. Foundation for Economic Education. Volume 1, Number 2.

General Laws of Massachusetts, The. Online: http://www.mass.gov/legis/laws/mgl/40p-4.htm. Cited: May 2006.

Keating, Dennis and Mitch Kahn. 2001. Rent Control in the New Millennium. Shelterforce Online. May/June. Online: http://www.nhi.org/online/issues/117/KeatingKanh.html. (cited May 2006).

Krol, Robert and Shirley Svorny. 2005. The Effect of Rent Control on Commute Times. *Journal of Urban Economics.* 25: 421–436.

LAHD (Los Angeles Housing Department). 2006a. Rent Stabilization: Allowable Rent Increases Bulletin. Online: http://www.lacity.org/lahd. Cited: May 2006.

LAHD (Los Angeles Housing Department). 2006b. Rent Stabilization Ordinance. Online: http://www.lacity.org/lahd/rso.htm. Cited: May 2006.

Lee, Moon Wha. 2006. Selected Findings of the 2005 New York City Housing and Vacancy Survey. New York City Department of Housing Preservation and Development. February 10.

Lindbeck, Assar. 1972. *The Political Economy of the New Left*. New York: Harper & Row.

NARPAC (National Association to Restore Pride in America's Capital). 2005. *DC's Economic Landscape*. Recent Analyses. Online: http://www.narpac.org/REXSCAPE. HTM. Cited: May 2006.

NMHC (National Multi Housing Council). 2006. Rent Control Laws by State. Online: http://www.nmhc.org (cited: May 2006).

Pollakowski, Henry O. 2003a. Who Really Benefits from New York City's Rent Regulation System? Civic Report, No. 34. Manhattan Institute: New York.

Pollakowski, Henry O. 2003b. Rent Control and Housing Investment: Evidence from Deregulation in Cambridge, Massachusetts. Civic Report, No. 36. Manhattan Institute: New York.

Raess, Pascal and Thomas von Ungern-Sternberg. 2002. A Model of Regulation in the Rental Housing Market. Regional Science and Urban Economics 32: 475–500.

Rent Board. 2006. This Year's Annual Allowable Increase Amount. City of San Francisco. Online: http://www.sfgov.org/site/rentboard_page.asp?id=3683. Cited: May 2006.

Rent Stabilization Board. 2006. Guide to Rent Control in Berkeley. Online: http://www.ci.berkeley.ca.us/rent/geninfo/guide/guide1–3.htm. Cited: May 2006.

RCRAA (Rent Control Reform Amendment Act of 2006) 2006. Online: http://www.dccouncil.washington.dc.us/images/00001/20060614160621.pdf (cited July 2006).

RGB (New York City Rent Guidelines Board). 2006a. An Introduction to the NYC Rent Guidelines Board. Online: http://www.housingnyc.com/html/about/intro/History(1).html. Cited May 2006.

RGB (New York City Rent Guidelines Board). 2006b. Rent Stabilization FAQs. Online: http://www.housingnyc.com/html/resources/faq/rentstab.html. Cited: May 2006.

RGB (New York City Rent Guidelines Board). 2006c. Rent Control FAQs. Online: http://www.housingnyc.com/html/resources/faq/rentcontrol.html. Cited: May 2006.

RGB (New York City Rent Guidelines Board). 2006d. When Can an Apartment Be Deregulated? Online: http://www.housingnyc.com/html/guidelines/decontrol.html. Cited May 2006.

RGB (New York City Rent Guidelines Board). 2006e. Mission Statement. Online: http://www.housingnyc.com/html/about/about.html. Cited May 2006.

Rose, Daniel. 2003. The Theology of Rent Control: History of Low Income Housing. *Vital Speeches of the Day.* August 15.

SFBS (San Francisco Board of Supervisors). 2002. San Francisco Housing Data Book. Bay Area Economics: Berkeley, CA.

SFBS (San Francisco Board of Supervisors). 2003. San Francisco Property Owners Survey: Summary Report. August. Bay Area Economics: Berkeley, CA.

Sowell, Thomas. 2000. Sanity in 'Frisco. Jewish World Review. August 21. Online: http://www.jewishworldreview.com/cols/sowe11082100.asp. Cited: May 2006.

SPOA (Small Property Owners of America). Various. Online: http://www.spoa.com/pages/rent-control.html. Cited: May 2006.

Tucker, William. 1997. How Rent Control Drives Out Affordable Housing. Cato Policy Analysis No. 274. Cato Institute: Washington, DC.

Weiss, Eric M. 2006. D.C. Rent Ceilings Set to Come Down. *Washington Post.* May 3: A01.

# 8

# The Economics of Government Housing Assistance for the Poor

*Joshua C. Hall and Matt E. Ryan*[1]

Since the 1930s, the federal government has undertaken several major efforts to provide housing assistance to low-income individuals. The government attempts to help low-income individuals reduce housing costs or improve the quality of housing consumed through a variety of programs, most of them administered through the U.S. Department of Housing and Urban Development (HUD). In the past, the majority of federal housing assistance occurred through the construction of public housing while today most federal housing aid occurs through rental assistance programs (U.S. House of Representatives, 2004). In constructing publicly owned and managed housing, government attempts to increase the quality of the housing stock available to low-income individuals. Rental assistance programs, on the other hand, try to increase the quality of low-income housing either through building or rehabilitation programs geared toward low-income households or through direct subsidies that allow low-income households to rent better private units than they otherwise would rent. These two types of housing assistance come under a variety of different programs and in various forms, but at the core they comprise two somewhat distinct approaches to providing housing assistance to the poor.

In real terms, total outlays for all housing programs administered by HUD have grown over the past quarter century (Table 8.1). From 1977 to 2002, total spending by HUD on all of its housing programs grew from $7.2 billion to $31.8 billion even after correcting for inflation. While HUD administers many different housing programs, according to the House Ways and Means Committee the majority of the increase in outlays is attributable to increased spending on rental assistance and other forms of direct housing assistance for low-income households (U.S. House of Representatives, 2004). This increase in assistance occurred primarily for two reasons. First, more individuals began receiving rental assistance through the Housing Choice Voucher Program (colloquially known as "Section 8") and other rental assistance programs during this period as funds were appropriated for around 2.7 million net new commitments (U.S. House of Representatives, 2004). Second, the size of the average subsidy per commitment increased over this period. The result of these two factors was that that spending on direct rental and housing increased fifteen fold over the period.

A breakdown of HUD outlays by broad program categories is presented in Table 8.2. Spending on Section 8 and other direct forms of rental and housing assistance for the poor (with the exception of public housing) has grown from around $1.3 billion in nominal terms in 1977 to over $20 billion dollars in 2002. The data presented in Table 8.2 show the recent transformation of federal housing policy towards the poor from constructing public housing to providing rental assistance. In 1977, 54 percent of HUD's outlays went towards government programs that directly provided housing for the poor such as Public Housing Capital, Public Housing Operating Subsidies, and Revitalization of Severely Distressed Public

**Table 8.1**
**Total HUD Outlays for All Housing Programs Administered by HUD, 1977-2002**
**(2002 dollars)**

| Fiscal Year | Total outlays (in millions) | Fiscal Year | Total outlays (in millions) |
|---|---|---|---|
| 1977 | $7,209 | 1990 | $20,668 |
| 1978 | 8,392 | 1991 | 21,303 |
| 1979 | 9,030 | 1992 | 22,245 |
| 1980 | 10,614 | 1993 | 24,699 |
| 1981 | 12,147 | 1994 | 26,827 |
| 1982 | 13,228 | 1995 | 28,900 |
| 1983 | 15,216 | 1996 | 29,976 |
| 1984 | 17,132 | 1997 | 29,258 |
| 1985 | 37,764 | 1998 | 29,188 |
| 1986 | 18,141 | 1999 | 28,952 |
| 1987 | 18,168 | 2000 | 28,878 |
| 1988 | 19,287 | 2001 | 29,369 |
| 1989 | 19,789 | 2002 | 31,866 |

Source: U.S. House of Representatives, Green Book (2004), Table 15-3.

Housing. In 1987, the percentage of HUD outlays going towards public housing dipped below 30 percent for the first time and in 2002 only 28 percent of direct federal housing assistance for low-income individuals goes towards public housing. This trend should only continue in the future as the production-oriented approach to providing low-income housing assistance has fallen out of favor in the face of evidence that rental assistance is more cost-effective (Olsen, 2000). As a result, most current federal spending on public housing is for maintenance and rehabilitation of current structures.

**Table 8.2**
**Direct Housing Assistance Administred by HUD, 1977-2002**
**( in millions of current dollars)**

| Fiscal Year | Section 8 and Other Assisted Housing | Public Housing | Other Outlays | Total Outlays |
|---|---|---|---|---|
| 1977 | $1,331 | $1,564 | $0 | $2,895 |
| 1978 | 1,824 | 1,779 | 0 | 3,603 |
| 1979 | 2,374 | 1,815 | 0 | 4,189 |
| 1980 | 3,146 | 2,218 | 0 | 5,364 |
| 1981 | 4,254 | 2,478 | 0 | 6,732 |
| 1982 | 5,293 | 2,553 | 0 | 7,846 |
| 1983 | 6,102 | 3,318 | 0 | 9,420 |
| 1984 | 7,068 | 3,932 | 0 | 11,000 |
| 1985 | 7,771 | 17,261 | 15 | 25,047 |
| 1986 | 8,320 | 3,859 | 142 | 12,321 |
| 1987 | 8,993 | 3,517 | 167 | 12,677 |
| 1988 | 9,985 | 3,699 | 217 | 13,901 |
| 1989 | 10,689 | 3,774 | 338 | 14,801 |
| 1990 | 11,357 | 4,331 | 361 | 16,049 |
| 1991 | 12,107 | 4,786 | 293 | 17,186 |
| 1992 | 13,052 | 5,182 | 185 | 18,419 |
| 1993 | 14,032 | 6,447 | 456 | 20,935 |
| 1994 | 15,289 | 6,857 | 1,087 | 23,233 |
| 1995 | 16,448 | 7,505 | 1,618 | 25,571 |
| 1996 | 17,496 | 7,668 | 1,889 | 27,053 |
| 1997 | 17,131 | 7,809 | 1,981 | 26,921 |
| 1998 | 16,975 | 8,028 | 2,232 | 27,235 |
| 1999 | 17,171 | 7,805 | 2,399 | 27,375 |
| 2000 | 17,359 | 7,860 | 2,610 | 27,829 |
| 2001 | 18,153 | 8,188 | 2,656 | 28,997 |
| 2002 | 20,037 | 8,926 | 2,903 | 31,866 |

Source: U.S. House of Representatives, Green Book (2004), Table 15-3.

In light of several decades of the U.S. government provision of housing assistance for low-income Americans and billions of taxpayer dollars expended, it is only appropriate to scrutinize these efforts from an economic perspective. The purpose of this chapter is not only to take a fresh look at the impact of federal intervention into the housing sector on behalf of low-income individuals, but also to critically evaluate the economic arguments put forth for housing assistance for the poor. The federal government provides both direct and indirect assistance to low-income individuals through a variety of programs administered through HUD and other federal agencies. Given the large number of federal agencies and programs involved in directly and indirectly providing housing assistance to the poor, we are not attempting to provide a comprehensive study of all government housing programs. In this essay we limit our analysis to: 1) the economic justifications for government intervention on behalf of low-income households and 2) the economics of public housing. We limit ourselves in this manner because the economic justifications generally apply to all government housing programs for the poor. Public housing is one of the largest federal housing programs for the poor and many of the insights we discover here apply to other forms of housing assistance such as rental vouchers.

An economic analysis of government intervention into the housing market on behalf of low-income individuals' yields important insights as to the efficacy and effectiveness of government attempts to improve housing for the poor. In addition, our analysis generates some insights into the secondary effects that housing assistance has on other individuals in society. The remainder of the chapter proceeds as follows. In Section 2, we present a brief history of the federal government's attempts to provide housing assistance for poor Americans. Section 3 discusses the economic arguments for government intervention into housing markets on behalf of low-income individuals. Section 4 looks at the economics of public housing in order to see the effect that government construction and operation of housing for low-income households has had on those households and society as a whole. Section 5 concludes with a summary of the findings.

## 1. A Brief History of Housing Subsidies to Low-Income Families

The first major federal policy regarding housing for the poor occurred during the Great Depression. Low-quality housing areas eroded into slums, providing a visible reminder of the suffering of the American public. The National Industrial Recovery Act of 1933 authorized the

President Roosevelt to establish the Federal Emergency Administration of Public Works (FEAPW), a temporary government organization that was to organize projects for the "general welfare" of the American public for two years after the passage of the Act. Secretary of the Interior Harold L. Ickes, the administrator appointed by the President Roosevelt to run FEAPW, was charged with preparing a comprehensive program of public works, including the construction or rehabilitation of low-income housing. During its first four years of existence FEAPW built only 25,000 units and soon saw its role in providing low-income public housing eliminated with the passage of the U.S. Housing Act of 1937.

The U.S. Housing Act of 1937 was enacted partly in response to constitutional restrictions on the federal government's ability to condemn private property in order to build new public housing units (Glasheen and McGovern, 2001). The act switched the federal government's role from being directly involved in the rehabilitation and construction of public housing to providing financial support for state and local governments. Under the Act, state legislatures were to provide for the establishment of local public housing authorities (PHAs) that would determine the location for all public housing developments. While the federal government would be responsible for the up-front capital costs—namely, the cost of building the physical structure—PHAs would own and operate the public housing development. (PHAs were also responsible for securing the land needed.) The first PHAs developed almost immediately; the first public housing development built under the U.S. Housing Act of 1937, Santa Rita Courts, opened in Austin, Texas in 1938. Led by the concerns of private developers over the increased supply of housing and its downward pressure on local rents, the construction of public housing was set to match the clearance of substandard units at the local level.

The subsequent decades saw public housing-related legislation as nearly an annual occurrence. Hardly a year passed without an additional housing program or an amendment to an existing Act. Nonetheless, the main objective of the federal government in providing housing assistance was through building large public housing projects in which low-income families could reside. This attitude slowly began to change with the passage of the Housing Act of 1965. The 1965 Housing Act created the Section 23 Leased Housing Program, which gave PHAs the option of leasing existing housing units from private landlords and subleasing them to program participants. Section 23 housing was an important first step that severed the tie between subsidized renter and the physical, government-produced public housing unit (Orlebeke, 2000).

The movement away from public construction and operation of housing projects that began with the Section 23 Leased Housing Program accelerated with the passage of the Housing and Community Development Act of 1974. This legislation established the Leased Housing Assistance Payment Program, otherwise known as the Section 8 Housing Program. In the Section 23 Leased Housing Program, the PHA acted as an intermediary between the private housing owners and the tenants subsidized by the government. The Section 8 Housing Program eliminated the middleman by giving eligible families a rental certificate at a subsidized price. The rental certificate was valued at the fair market rent for moderate-quality housing as determined by the government. Section 8 tenants generally contribute 30 percent of their income towards rent with the government covering the remaining difference up to the pre-determined fair market value for moderate-quality housing. Beginning in 1984, Congress began to experiment with a rental voucher program. The rental voucher program increased the flexibility of families in choosing their living quarters because rental vouchers did not have the fair market rent (FMR) stipulation that rental certificates had and allowed for situations where families could pay less than 30 percent of their income towards their subsidized rent. HUD, the Cabinet-level agency under which public housing programs reside, began the process of combining the rental certificate and rental voucher programs in 1994. The Quality Housing and Work Responsibility Act of 1998 finalized the merger of the two programs and created the Housing Choice Voucher Program. The vouchers administered through the program continue to be colloquially refereed to as "Section 8" vouchers after the section of the U.S. Housing Act that initially created rental certificates. In 2003, the Center on Budget and Policy Priorities reported that a network of over 2,600 PHAs distributed 2.1 million housing vouchers.

## 2. Rationales for Government Intervention

In general, markets operate efficiently, bringing self-interested individuals together in a manner that results in gains from exchange and drives economic progress. There are times, however, when markets do not allocate resources efficiently. In the presences of market failures, the private outcome can deviate from the socially efficient outcome and in such cases, government intervention might be able to increase efficiency. This section considers the economic arguments for government intervention into the low-income housing market.

An important thing to note before proceeding is that individuals will always prefer cash to any form of housing subsidy. Individuals prefer cash to any form of direct or indirect subsidy because a cash transfer not tied to housing consumption would allow an individual to be at least as well off and likely much better off than any type of housing subsidy. To see why, consider the actions of the typical low-income individual who is receiving the equivalent of a $400 monthly housing subsidy. Were that housing subsidy changed to a pure cash transfer, it is unlikely that the individual would continue to spend the entire $400 on housing and instead would purchase a bundle of other goods that they would prefer more. This implies that individuals would get higher utility from a direct cash transfer than from a housing subsidy. Thus, arguments for housing subsides cannot be based solely on the low-incomes of recipients, because the solution to individuals having low-incomes need not involve housing-related subsidies. Instead, economic justifications for housing assistance for low-income individuals must involve the existence of benefits flowing from increased consumption of housing by low income households.

A frequent argument for housing subsidies is that the underconsumption of housing by the poor is a public health threat because consumption of low-quality housing can increase the spread of communicable disease. The public health argument for low income housing subsidies goes back at least to the nineteenth century when public health advocates argued that slums were breeding grounds for communicable diseases and other social problems that imposed costs on the rest of society (Grigsby and Bourassa, 2003). The argument is that housing subsidies increase the health of low-income individuals by enticing them to move out of low-quality housing, thereby reducing the prevalence of communicable diseases. Because communicable diseases spread directly from person to person, all citizens have an incentive to help limit the spread of communicable diseases, because the proliferation of illness among low-income housing consumers has the potential to impose a significant cost on the rest of society.

The public health argument for low-income housing subsidies depends on the existence of negative external costs imposed on others in society. The effect of housing underconsumption on the health of the poor is not a public health issue unless it is shown to impose costs on others in society through the spread of communicable disease. Edgar Olsen (1982) summarized the available evidence in 1982 and states that negative externalities may exist but their magnitude seems to be small. Based on his reading of the literature, he concludes (1982: 214) that "[i]f the goal of housing subsidies is to make both recipients and taxpayers better off, it is doubtful that substantial expenditures can be justified on the basis of these externalities alone." In the 1970s HUD commissioned a review of the literature between poor-quality housing and mental and physical health. After reviewing over 175 studies on the topic, the author of the study concluded that the theorized link between housing quality and physical and mental well-being was not supported by the empirical evidence (Kasl, 1976). More recently, Whitehead (2003: 139) suggests that the "majority of direct externalities related to health in that poor housing can encourage the spread of disease, although generally only at standards well below those prevalent in advanced economies."

While it is possible and perhaps likely that poor-quality housing may worsen the health of low-income individuals, it does not appear that it generates a public health issue that requires government intervention into housing markets. To the extent that the substandard housing generates external costs, those costs appear to be inframarginal in that there may be some spillovers from the consumption of low-quality housing but there are no marginal costs to society at large given the current state of the housing stock.

In addition, Fertig and Reingold (2006) suggest there are three reasons why government interventions such as public housing might make low-income individuals less healthy. First, subsidized housing might be more environmentally contaminated than housing available on the private market. Second, the lumping together of individuals into large public housing developments often isolates them from access to cheap and accessible grocery stores that stock fresh fruits and vegetables necessary for good nutrition. Third, they argue that the close association between public housing and youth gangs and their concomitant violence might lead individuals to isolate themselves into their apartments, leading to a more sedentary lifestyle and possibly mental health difficulties. We raise these points not to debate their individual validity, but rather to point out that there is no theoretical reason why the health outcomes from a completely private low-income housing market might be worse than those resulting from government intervention.

Before proceeding further, it is worth noting that this is usually true of all arguments for government intervention in the marketplace. It is not sufficient to show that market production could be better in some respects to provide economic justification for intervention. It must also be shown that the government solution will be an improvement. The status quo must be compared not the ideal planned solution, but rather the solution that actually arises out of the political process. For example, one of the goals of the federal housing program was to improve the health of low-income individuals. Recent research on public housing residents relocated from public housing projects to subsidized private-market outcomes, however, finds that moving out of public housing is *beneficial*—not harmful—to their health (Acevedo-Garcia et al., 2004). Thus, the correct standard to apply from an economic perspective is market failure versus government failure.

In addition, it is important to take into account the market as a dynamic process. In some cases it may be that while the market failure might be slightly larger than the government failure in the short-run, government intervention might make things worse in the long run. For example, many housing advocates argue that markets neglect the poor in that few developers construct housing for the poor. While it is true that private developers generally do not produce housing for the poor (Baer, 1986), this perspective neglects how housing markets evolve over time. Much of today's housing occupied by the poor was occupied by the wealthy in some earlier time period (Rosenthal, 2006). The natural evolution of neighborhoods is to decline in economic status. Rosenthal (2006) finds that over two-thirds of neighborhoods were of "quite different" economic status in 2000 than they were in 1950, and that the average neighborhood's economic status declines at around 13 percent per decade as new neighborhoods come into existence.

One example of this filtering is in the area of Cleveland formerly known as "Millionaire's Row" because it was the home to many wealthy millionaires such as John D. Rockefeller. This area is now almost exclusively low-income housing. While some of the original homes of the wealthy families have been demolished, many of the large homes still exist and are either occupied by a large single family or have been subdivided into multi-family apartments. This same pattern can be observed in many other older inner-ring Cleveland neighborhoods as rising incomes lead families to purchase larger and newer homes in outer suburbs. Thus, the older homes filtered down to low-income residents who benefited in two ways: 1) the homes of the formerly wealthy were superior in size and quality to their previous residences, and 2) the increased housing supply created by the filtering process depressed rents for low-income individuals, making housing more affordable.

This neighborhood evolution occurs primarily because housing is a normal good; that is, as individuals' incomes rise over time, so too does their housing consumption. According to the Census Bureau, the average new home is 46.6 percent larger than the average new home in 1973 (Christie, 2006). Thus, even though today's houses for the wealthy will have deteriorated somewhat when they eventually filter down to low-income households, they will be of considerably higher quality than the houses consumed by the poor today. Once the housing market for the poor is viewed as a dynamic rather than a static process, it becomes apparent that the market does provide housing for the poor. Disrupting this process through limitations on new home construction may do more to harm the poor in the long-run than all direct governmental attempts to help the poor through direct subsidies.

Another often-mentioned argument for market failure involves interdependent utility functions. Also known as "paternalistic altruism," Olsen (1982, 2003) calls it the major rationale for housing subsidies. The general idea is that one individual's utility is dependent upon the actions of another individual and if that other individual undervalues housing, then that imposes a cost on others who care about her housing consumption. If individual A cares about the well-being of individual B and the poor quality of individual B's housing (as perceived by individual A) lowers individual A's utility, then individual A's utility will be lower as a result of individual B's consumption of low-quality housing. If the world consisted of only individual A and B it is likely that A would privately subsidize B's housing consumption. If many people care about B's housing consumption, however, many of those individuals might choose *not* to transfer resources to A because, if they don't, someone else will likely take care of the problem—a situation in which the benefit is enjoyed without having to incur the cost. Economists call this problem *free-riding,* and it may result in fewer charitable transfers than may be efficient given the interdependent nature of individuals' utility functions. This is a variation of the argument put forth by Hochman and Rodgers (1969) who argue that the existence of interdependent utility functions between rich and poor people requires government intervention as a corrective in order to overcome free-riding in the market for charity.

Olsen (1982) argues that this argument does not justify universal housing subsidies. Instead, it may justify select subsidies to certain low-income families. His reasoning is that many low-income families consume housing of higher quality than available through many housing programs. Olsen presents evidence from the Experimental Housing Allowance Program (an eleven-year study of housing subsidies conducted by HUD) showing that between one-quarter and one-half of eligible families occupied housing meeting model housing codes. From this he concludes (1982: 216):

> First, almost all low-income families are able to occupy housing meeting the standards embodied in model housing codes. Some choose not to do so. Second, low-income families are not as poorly housed as is widely believed. If these conclusions are accepted, it seems reasonable to believe that many taxpayers who favor housing subsidies have a distorted perception of the housing conditions of low-income households and of the reasons that families are poorly housed. Therefore, a reconsideration of the desirability of housing subsidies versus unconditional cash grants seems to be in order.

It could be argued that conditions have changed since the Experimental Housing Allowance Program was conducted and that many families cannot afford housing meeting model housing codes. Given that the housing stock tends to filter down over time, with the houses of the middle class thirty years ago now being occupied by the poor, this is unlikely to be the case however.

Olsen (2003) points out that many paternalistic altruists do not actually believe that families undervalue housing. He points out that many housing advocates suggest that spending too much of a household's income on rent (i.e., high rent-to-income ratio) is a rationale for housing subsidies because it implies that too little is being spent on other goods. This means that the paternalistic altruist is arguing that many individuals undervalue other goods in the households consumption bundle. Therefore, in order to attain an efficient allocation of resources, the paternalistic altruist should argue for subsidization of non-housing consumption for the poor such as food stamps and Medicaid, not housing subsidies. Thus interdependent utility functions do not seem to provide an accurate economic rationale for housing subsidies for the poor.

However, there is a larger problem with the argument about interdependent utility functions. Interdependent utility functions generate externalities that, while creating welfare losses on third parties, do not necessitate a public policy corrective because no resources are being allocated external to the market (Holcombe and Sobel, 2000). The reason why externalities generated by independent utility functions do not create inefficiency is because the externalities are pecuniary and thus do not affect household production. Only technological externalities that directly affect household production are relevant for public policy. The consumption of low-quality housing by poor individuals may lower the utility of higher-income individuals but that lower utility does not affect their household production as they can produce the same outputs with the same inputs. The decline in utility a high-income person may get from knowing poor individuals have to consume housing the high-income person would feel is inferior is analogous to the wealth losses a hardware store owner may suffer from a chain-retailer such as Lowe's or Home Depot opening next door. The welfare losses are real but are not relevant for public policy because no inefficiency is created.

Along these same lines, Ho (1988) suggests that a negative production externality may exist to the extent that substandard housing pushes low-income individuals, particularly children, out into the street where the probability of fighting and other forms of juvenile delinquency are increased. He admits, however, that the evidence does not seem to be in favor of there being any widespread benefits from better housing. While some studies have found that better housing reduces "deviant behavior" (Burns and Grebler, 1977), little empirical attention has been paid to the extent that these reductions in negative behaviors are socially beneficial. Many negative behaviors are largely internalized to the extent that the costs of the negative activity are borne by the individual engaging in the behavior and thus, while these activities are bad for them, they do not transmit any negative third-party effects requiring government intervention.

Even if such activities impose costs on third parties, recall that the key comparison is between the market failure and the outcome after government intervention. Looking at the history of public housing, it is clear that government intervention can lead to increased social costs as well. Consider the case of large public housing projects such as the Robert Wagner Homes in East Harlem. Husock (2003) argues that public housing creates social problems because it concentrates individuals prone to criminal activity into one central place, exacerbating social ills. Using data on youths in Boston neighborhoods, Case and Katz (1991) find that even after controlling for family and personal characteristics, living in a neighborhood where a lot of other teens engage in drug usage and crime (in their data set these neighborhoods tended to contain public housing projects) significantly increases the probability that a given youth will engage in these behaviors. They argue that "contagion" models, where having one's peers engage in an activity increases the likelihood of an individual engaging in the activity, provides a possible theoretical basis for how neighborhood effects can play a role in juvenile delinquency. On the other hand, basic economic theory would suggest that individuals move into public housing because they are better off in total then they were in the private marketplace. Thus, even if juvenile delinquency increases as a result, perhaps parents value benefits in the public housing bundle enough to offset the negative effects on the probability their kids engage in crime.

In sum, there are many theoretical arguments for why markets may fail. What is lacking is research measuring the extent of market failure. There are many articles showing how the outcomes of private markets might be "bad"—defined as an outcome that the author would find substandard—yet few empirical articles attempt to measure the external spillovers associated with the level of housing consumed by the poor in a free market. The strongest theoretical argument and the one most empirically tested is the public health argument. Given the empirical evidence and the current state of the U.S. housing stock, the existence of inframarginal positive externalities from replacing low-quality housing stock occupied by the poor seems to be in doubt. Once the issue of government failure is broached, the case against government intervention becomes even greater as it essentially raises the burden of proof for those wishing to intervene on behalf of low-income individuals. The remainder of this chapter discusses in detail the economics of public housing and housing vouchers and the accumulated empirical evidence on the effects of these interventions into the housing markets for low-income individuals.

### 3. The Economics of Public Housing

Historically, public housing has been the primary method for providing housing assistance to the poor in the United States. Based on the mistaken observation that unfettered markets did not provide adequate housing for the poor, federal involvement in the construction and operation of housing for low-income individuals began during the Great Depression (Olsen, 1983). The goal was to pick up where the market appeared to fail—providing safe and healthy housing for low-income families (Kraft and Kraft, 1979). This was done through federal construction of new housing units, some small apartment buildings and some high-rise tenements colloquially referred to as "projects." Once construction was completed, the public housing sites were turned over to local housing authorities who managed the sites and were responsible for maintenance and upkeep of the units out of rent paid by tenants and possibly local tax or state tax dollars. As of 2002, there were over 13,000 public housing developments managed by around 3,000 local public housing authorities (Stegman, 2002).

According to Olsen (1983), the federal government initially became involved in the construction of public housing in an attempt to stimulate employment during the Great Depression. While the ineffectiveness of housing programs with regard to employment stimulus became apparent, the argument that insufficient supply existed in the current market for low-income housing quickly took its place as the *raison d'être* of public housing. The basic economics of supply-side attempts to improve the level of housing consumed by low-income households can be seen in Figure 8.1. While this example is simplistic in that it ignores many of the secondary effects of public housing construction, it serves to illustrate the basic idea economics behind public housing. Figure 8.1 depicts the market for low-income housing units. In equilibrium, market prices (rents) per unit will be $P_0$ and there will be $Q_0$ units of housing. After the introduction of a federal public housing program in an area, the supply of housing shifts outward from $Supply_0$ to $Supply_1$. The increase in the supply of housing in the market causes housing prices (rents) to fall from $P_0$ to $P_1$. The current quality of housing can be purchased for lower rent, or alternatively, better housing can be purchased for the same level of housing expenditure. Thus, increasing the supply of housing would seem, in theory (if housing is a normal good), to increase housing consumption for all low-income households, regardless of whether they ended up in public housing. This is not the case, however, for two reasons which we will discuss.

The first reason why we cannot be sure that public housing makes low-income individuals consume better housing is that public housing could induce families to consume lower-quality housing. While families may be better off in terms of utility given the choice of public housing (based on their actions), recall that the justification for government intervention into housing markets is to increase the level of housing consumed by the poor because that is what generates the externality, not their lower utility. Consider Figure 8.2 drawn from Olsen (2003), which shows a possible budget space for a low-income individual under public housing as it has historically operated in the United States.

Here housing is measured on the x-axis and all other goods on the y-axis. For any level of income, points on the budget line represent the maximum combination of housing and other goods that the individual could afford. Absent the public housing program, the low-income individual could afford points A, B, or C and would choose the allocation that maximized their utility given the individuals preferences. So point C represents a low-income individual that prefers to spend a lot of money on housing and not a lot on other goods while point A represents an individual that highly values all other goods but not housing.

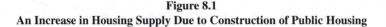

**Figure 8.1**
**An Increase in Housing Supply Due to Construction of Public Housing**

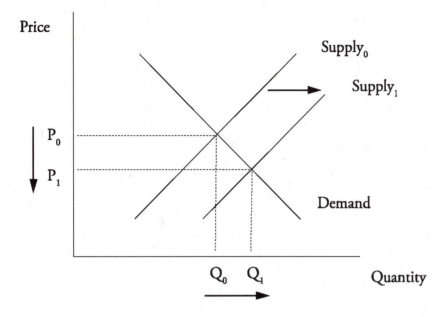

Now let us consider the offer presented to this individual when offered an apartment through a public housing program, represented by point PH. In the United States, public housing is not available to all that qualify. Instead, individuals have to get on a waiting list and get offered an appropriate apartment for their household size once one becomes available. Individuals can take or leave the apartment they are offered. If they reject it, sometimes they are given alternative choices, but if no suitable choices are presented, they are removed from the public housing list. Let us assume that an individual's utility is such that if offered PH, the individual will take it. If the individual was previously at point A, the public housing program definitely increased the household's consumption of housing. But for the individual at point C, the offer of public housing may increase her utility, but lower housing consumption. Given that the rationale for housing subsidies generally involves increasing housing consumption, this result is perverse. Depending on the low-income individuals preferences, a public housing program such as the one presented here can change an individual's consumption bundle

**Figure 8.2**
**Possible Budget Space under Public Housing**

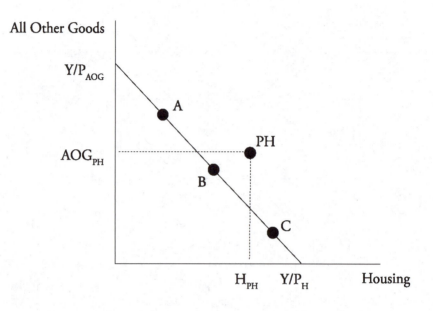

in every possible way, with the exception of reducing the individuals' consumption of both goods (Olsen, 2003).

Because it is theoretically ambiguous what effect public housing will have on individuals' housing consumption, we must rely on empirical estimates to see whether or not public housing increases the housing consumption of low-income households. Olsen (2003) summarizes the results of nine different studies on the effect of public housing. He concludes that the empirical evidence clearly shows that public housing increases the quality of housing consumed by low-income individuals. Hammond (1987), for example, finds that public housing increases housing consumption among participants by 41 percent. The estimates across studies range from 22 to 82 percent. A caveat to these estimates is that the extent to which they increase housing consumption is dependent upon the age of the housing units. New construction typically gives the highest increase in consumption because the quality of the units generally declines over time as the buildings depreciate relative to market housing. No new public housing projects have been started since the Carter administration (Green and Malpezzi, 2003). While the federal government has spent considerable dollars rehabilitating current units, the extent to which public housing improves housing consumption is likely to be towards the lower end of that range. Estimates of non-housing consumption find that public housing residents generally increase their non-housing consumption by up to 20 percent as the lower rent on public housing frees up income to be spent on other goods (Olsen, 2003).

Another reason why we cannot be sure that public housing makes people better off is because of crowding out of other low-income housing. The simple analysis presented above assumes that there is no demand change in response to the changes brought forth by the construction of public housing. If, however, we assume that at least some households entering into public housing previously were sharing housing with family members, then the introduction of new subsidized public housing will lead to an increase in demand, as extended families living under a single roof can now afford to set out on their own. In the extreme, if every household in public housing previously was living with a family member rent free, then there will be zero crowding out and the result will be as depicted in Figure 8.1. The increase in supply will lead to an increase in the housing stock. If, on the other hand, all new public housing residents previously rented unsubsidized units then crowding out will be 100 percent and demand will fall to exactly offset the increase in supply. The result will be a transfer of privately operated low-income housing to public housing, but no net increase in the housing stock. Thus, the questions of crowding out is really an empirical one because it depends on how many public housing recipients are coming from shared living arrangements.

Murray (1983) conducted the first study on crowding out and finds evidence of crowding out. He estimated that in the long run 85 percent of the effect of new public housing was offset by a decline in unsubsidized housing starts. In an update to his 1983 study, Murray (1999) comes to a different conclusion. He finds that subsidies for low-income public housing do not crowd out unsubsidized units, but that subsidization of housing for moderate-income individuals does crowd out private housing. Murray argues that the reason for the difference is that very few moderate-income families are becoming independent households for the first time upon receiving the subsidy, so subsidized housing for moderate-income families displaces unsubsidized housing. Conversely, many low-income public housing tenants previously lived with family or friends and thus the introduction of public housing does little to change the market demand for unsubsidized housing. The most recent study on crowding out by Sinai and Waldfogel (2005) finds that while subsidized housing does increase the total amount of housing in a city, for every three subsidized units constructed, two unsubsidized units are crowded out. They conclude that this is a positive effect of low-income housing subsidies, because the subsidies did increase the housing stock somewhat as many subsidized residents would not have occupied unsubsidized units absent the program.

Husock (1997b) states that 48 percent of public housing recipients entered public housing to live independently from family and friends, not to escape dangerous or debilitated housing. He suggests that this is actually a failure of public housing, implying that public housing is not correcting an externality but subsidizing a lifestyle choice. Perhaps more important, Husock argues that this choice that is negative for the recipients in the long-run because it builds a dependency on government and reduces incentive to engage in activities that will improve their lives in the long run. He argues that public housing disrupts the housing ladder, where low-income individuals live with family or in substandard conditions for a time before they can work and save enough to move to better housing. Public housing disrupts this process for many households because subsidized housing frees up income to be spent on other consumer goods and the gap between consumption bundles in public housing and in unsubsidized housing is so great it reduces incentive work to reach the next rung on the housing ladder. According to Husock (1997b), more that 25 percent of public housing recipients have been in public housing for more than a decade.

One reason why public housing might foster a dependence on government assistance is that it reduces incentives to work and earn income. Public housing is means-tested to the extent that the subsidy received by a low-income individual receiving public housing depends on its earned income (Olsen, 2003). Empirical estimates find what economic theory suggests—that public housing induces individuals to work less. Murray (1980) finds that public housing causes recipients to reduce labor earnings by around 4 percent. Painter (2001) estimates that the opportunity to live in subsidized housing raises the disincentives to work by 21 percent. Yelowitz (2001) looks at female-headed households and finds that a one-percent increase in the amount of subsidy conferred by housing programs reduces female labor force participation by around 4 percent. Thus, housing subsidies appear to reduce the incentive to work, preventing households from earning income and accumulating savings that would enable them to move out of public housing.

We have spent considerable time discussing the impact of public housing and housing subsidies on the participants to the programs. This is understandable because people generally want to make sure that government programs do what they are intended to do. While we think the evidence is clear that, on net, public housing recipients are better off having received the subsidy, it does not mean that public housing is efficient or desirable. After all, there is another side to the ledger in that taxpayers and other citizens in society are impacted by public housing either because they pay for it through taxes and/or because public housing indirectly impacts their life through changes in the housing market.

Unfortunately, almost no studies look at the impact of public housing on others in society, so it is difficult to estimate the full costs of public housing. In terms of taxpayer outlays, we have the direct costs of (the federal component) of public housing as laid out in Table 8.1. While not insignificant, it is important to remember that direct outlays do not represent the economic cost of a government program. There is also the deadweight loss of taxation occurring due to reduced exchange as a result of the taxes levied to fund the program in question. While estimates of the deadweight loss arising from taxation are quite varied, it is safe to say that they are in the range of 10 to 50 percent of every dollar raised (Vedder and Gallaway, 1999). Regardless of whether the high or the low end of that range is used, taking into account the deadweight loss of taxation for housing subsidies places a substantial additional burden on the operation of public housing when it is not clear that it is correcting any externality and instead merely represents a transfer of resources.

Some of the other indirect ways that public housing affects other members of society is through changes in the housing market. Public housing projects disrupt the regular rise and fall of neighborhoods that occurs as the housing stock gets older and gets sold to lower-income households, and then eventually gets demolished or rehabilitated as the neighborhood turns around again. Public housing designates certain neighborhoods where the projects are located as low-income, thereby disrupting the process of decline and redevelopment for neighborhoods where housing projects are located. In addition, proximity to public housing could affect other individuals through its effect on property values. Early studies on this issue such as Nourse (1963) generally found that public housing had zero effect on nearby housing values. More recent studies (Goetz, Lam, and Heitlinger, 1996; Lyons and Loverage, 1993; Santiago, Galster and Tatian, 2001) find that in certain circumstances subsidized housing can reduce nearby property values as homeowners do not like the location of public housing near their residences.

Finally, public housing is a failure because it is an inefficient way to provide housing assistance to the poor compared to alternative forms of housing assistance such as rental vouchers. Public housing exhibits numerous problems that exist because of the absence of private ownership. Consider the incentives faced by a low-quality apartment complex owner and a PHA operating a public project. Apartment owners are engaged in a voluntary agreement with their tenants; if owners do not provide a rental unit (and any accompanying services) that the tenant feels is satisfactory considering the rent paid, the tenant can terminate the agreement and seek housing elsewhere. Without tenants, apartment owners earn no income, and thus no profit, from their apartment complexes. Apartment owners have the incentive to make sure that their tenants—their customers—are satisfied with their living situations. If maintenance is not performed in a manner deemed timely by the tenant, tenants can pursue other housing options. In fact, much of the maintenance performed on low-quality housing is done by informal tradesmen connected, either socially or by living arrangement, to the apartment complex owners in an effort to keep rents low (Husock, 1997a).

Another advantage of private ownership is that private owners have the ability and the incentive to terminate housing agreements should the tenant not be upholding his end of the agreement. The clearest case is the failure to pay rent where owners can seek to evict those tenants that do not pay according to the terms of their rental contract. In addition, private ownership is superior to public management in dealing with inter-tenant externalities related to noise usage of common areas. Private landlords have a strong incentive to mediate disputes between tenants and to evict residents should tenants be unable to abide by the terms governing common resources. The owner/tenant relationship highlights the benefits of private property and voluntary, non-coercive contracting—if either side is unsatisfied with the terms of the agreement, they are free to terminate the relationship and pursue better situations. While federal policy has evolved over time to allow the screening out or removal of difficult families, the lack of a profit motive, combined with the bureaucracy associated with public management, makes the process far less efficient than private management.

Public housing exhibits little of the welfare-enhancing qualities outlined above. Apartment complex owners can be classified as *residual claimants;* that is, any profit derived from the efficient utilization of their assets will directly benefit the owners themselves. This is a properly aligned incentive. PHAs, however, do not face the same incentive structure in managing public housing projects. Since PHAs do not benefit from a project's efficient operation there is little incentive to maintain the condition of public housing units and to operate the projects in an efficient manner. For example, in 1992 the *Detroit Free Press* reported that around one-third of Detroit's public housing units were in such a state of disrepair that they had been vacated and boarded up (Ball and McGraw, 1992). Around the same time, Chicago's housing authority came under fire because thousands of units were deemed unlivable (Reardon, 1992). In the aggregate, the condition of U.S. housing projects became so bad in the 1980s that Congress felt it necessary to establish the National Commission on Severely Distressed Housing in 1989 (Schill, 1993).

While there are a examples of well-maintained and operated large-scale housing projects (see Vale, 2002 for one example) and many smaller projects are not in obvious disrepair, the fact that so many projects were virtually unlivable only a couple of decades after construction is strong evidence of the bad incentives associated with public housing. The massive Pruitt-Igoe housing project in St. Louis is but one example. Pruitt-Igoe, which consisted of over 2800 apartments, was in such disrepair that it had to be demolished just *sixteen* years after opening in 1956. Despite being designed by the architect who later would go on to design the World Trade Center, the Pruitt-Igoe housing project was an abysmal failure because it was not designed with customer demands in mind. To cite but one example, the elevators in the eleven-story buildings were designed with stops only on the fourth, seventh, and tenth floors. While the goal was to get residents to meet people on other floors while they transferred from the elevator to the stairs, the result was that no one wanted to live on a floor that was not the fourth, seventh or tenth floor. It is of little wonder why occupancy never rose above 60 percent (Newman, 1996). The buildings were also designed with ample common areas in an attempt to facilitate interaction among residents. These areas quickly became vandalized and filled with garbage and human waste. According to Newman (1996), the common areas became so dangerous that mothers needed to travel in groups in order to safely shop for food or to escort their children to school.

Similar tales of neglect and disrepair can be told of housing projects in other cities, such as the Cabrini Green and Robert Taylor housing projects in Chicago or Mulford Gardens housing project in New York. Changes brought about as a result of the National Commission on Severely Distressed Housing have led to the demolition of most of these large-scale housing projects that generated the most glaring problems. It should be noted that planners have learned, to some extent, from their past failure. Common areas in new or rehabilitated projects are being minimized in order to reduce the problems that can arise from communal ownership. Recognition of the importance of architecture on the amount of maintenance and upkeep in public housing will play an important role in the future cost-effectiveness of public housing.

Despite the teardown of the most distressed public housing projects, and recognition of the importance of minimizing commonly owned space, the fact remains that managers of small, well-designed PHAs still have poor incentives to manage projects efficiently. Why? *Because those who run the project do not benefit from increasing demand to live in the projects.* First of all, increases in demand do not result in higher rents as occurs in private markets. Second, the heavy subsidization of tenants means that demand generally outstrips supply at most public housing projects. Even if tenants became fed up enough to "vote with their feet" and move out, another household would quickly move in and the status quo is thus likely to remain in place. As a result of these poor incentives, it is little wonder that public housing is almost always more costly than other forms of housing assistance for the poor such as rental vouchers (Olsen, 2003). Thus it is easy to see why recent federal efforts to reform housing assistance for the poor have focused on housing vouchers and away from public housing.

## 4. Conclusion

Federal public housing policy has changed a lot in the past twenty-five years. According to Stegman (2002), national housing policy has improved considerably over the period as federal officials have learned from past mistakes. The shift from public housing to housing vouchers may be a clear example of government officials learning from past mistakes. Yet many housing projects continue to operate and thus it is important to examine the economics of public housing as well as the reasons for providing housing assistance to low-income individuals in the first place.

After reviewing the economic rationales for government intervention into the housing market for low-income individuals it is clear that little economic justification exists for low-income housing subsidies on the grounds of market failure. Paternalistic altruism arising from interdependent utility functions, even if they were widespread among citizens, are not Pareto-relevant because they do not produce efficiency losses. In addition, paternalistic altruism in the context of the "unaffordable housing" suggests non-housing subsidies, not housing subsidies. Finally, the public health argument for housing subsidies, to the extent it was once relevant, is no longer relevant as economic growth and the filtering down of homes in the housing market is continually leading to improved housing conditions in the United States. Regardless, the link between housing quality and poor health is tenuous at best. Supporters of public housing need to look elsewhere besides market failure to find economic justification for housing subsidies for the poor.

Finally, a review of the economics of public construction of housing does find that federal public housing at least increases housing consumption among the poor, so it is meeting the goal of getting the poor to consume more housing. Given that are not really any Pareto-relevant externalities from their consuming less housing, however, they would probably be better off were they just given unrestricted income transfers. At the very least, housing vouchers improve upon public housing because they eliminate many of the worst problems that come with government ownership and they distort the housing market far less than public housing. While federal policy seems to be moving in the proper direction in shifting away emphasis from public housing and towards housing vouchers, our analysis suggests that little economic justification exists for any federal government intervention on behalf of low-income individuals.

## Note

1.    The authors would like to acknowledge the support of the Kendrick Fund.

## References

Acevedo-Garcia, Dolores, et al. 2004. "Does Housing Mobility Improve Health?" *Housing Policy Debate* 15, no. 1: 49–97.

Baer, William. 1986. "The Shadow Market in Housing." *Scientific American* 255, no. 5 (November): 29–35.

Ball, Zachare, and Bill McGraw. October 30, 1992. "U.S. Threatens to Sue City Over Public Housing Woes." *Detroit Free Press.*

Burns, L., and Grebler, L. 1977. *The Housing of Nations: Analysis and Policy in a Comparative Framework.* New York, NY: Wiley.

Case, Anne C., Lawrence F. Katz. 1991. "The Company You Keep: The Effects of Family and Neighborhood on Disadvantaged Youths." NBER Working Paper No. 3075.

Center on Budget and Policy Priorities. 2003. *Introduction to the Housing Voucher Program.* Washington, DC: Center on Budget and Policy Priorities.

Christie, Les. 2006. "Honey, I Stretched the House—Again." *CNNMoney.com,* July 25. http://money.cnn.com/2006/07/24/real_estate/home_stretching/index.htm. Accessed 23 August 2006.

Fertig, Angela, and David Reingold. 2006. "Public Housing and Health: Is There a Connection?" University of Georgia, mimeo.

Glasheen, Megan, and Julie McGovern. 2001. "Mixed-Finance Development: Privatizing Public Housing through Public/Private Development Partnerships." In *Privatizing Governmental Functions* edited by Deborah Ballati. New York, NY: Law Journal Press.

Goetz, E., Lam, H., and Heitlinger, A. 1996. There Goes The Neighborhood? The Impact of Subsidized Multi-family Housing on Urban Neighborhoods. Minneapolis: Center for Urban and Regional Affairs.

Green, Richard K., and Stephen Malpezzi. 2003. *A Primer on U.S. Housing Markets and Housing Policy.* Washington, DC: Urban Institute Press.

Hammond, Claire H. 1987. *The Benefits of Subsidized Housing Programs: An Intertemporal Approach.* Cambridge: Cambridge University Press.

Hochman, Harold M., and James D. Rodgers. 1997. "Pareto Optimal Redistribution." *American Economic Review* 59, no. 4 (September): 542–47.

Holcombe, Randall G., and Russell S. Sobel. 2000. "Consumption Externalities and Economic Welfare." *Eastern Economic Journal* 26, no. 2 (Spring): 157–170.

Husock, Howard. 1997a. "We Don't Need Subsidized Housing." *City Journal* 7, no. 1 (Winter): 50–58.

Husock, Howard. 1997b. "Now Let's Put Time Limits on Public Housing." *American Enterprise* 8, no. 1 (January/February): 70–71.

Husock, Howard. 2003. "How Public Housing Harms Cities." *City Journal* 13, no. 1 (Winter): 70–79.

Kasl, Stanislav V. 1976. "Effects of Housing on Mental and Physical Health." In *Housing in the Seventies: Working Papers* 1. Washington, DC: Government Printing Office.

Kraft, John, and Arthur Kraft. 1979. "Benefits and Costs of Low Rent Public Housing." *Journal of Regional Science* 19, no. 3: 309–317.

Lyons, R.F., and Loveridge, S. 1993. "A Hedonic Estimation of the Effect of Federally Subsidized Housing on Nearby Residential Property Values." Staff Paper P93–6. St. Paul, MN: Department of Agriculture and Applied Economics, University of Minnesota.

Murray, Michael P. 1980. "A Reinterpretation of the Traditional Income-Leisure Model, With Application to In-Kind Subsidy Programs." *Journal of Public Economics* 14: 69–81.

Murray, Michael P. 1983. "Subsidized and Unsubsidized Housing Starts: 1961–1977." *Review of Economics and Statistics* 65, no. 4 (November): 590–97.

Newman, Oscar. 1996. *Creating Defensible Space.* Washington, DC: U.S. Department of Housing and Urban Development.

Nourse, Hugh O. 1963. "The Effect of Public Housing on Property Values in St. Louis." *Land Economics* 39, no. 4 (November): 433–441.

Olsen, Edgar O. 1971. "Subsidized Housing in a Competitive Market: Reply." *The American Economic Review* 61, no. 1 (March): 220–224.

Olsen, Edgar O. 1983. "The Role of Government in the Housing Sector." In *Reassessing the Role of Government in the Mixed Economy* edited by Herbert Giersch. Tubingen: Mohr.

Olsen, Edgar O. 2000. "The Cost-Effectiveness of Alternative Methods of Delivering Housing Subsidies." University of Virginia, mimeo.

Olsen, Edgar O. 2003. "Housing Programs for Low-Income Households." In *Means-Tested Transfer Programs in the United States* edited by Robert A. Moffitt. Chicago, IL: University of Chicago Press.

Orlebeke, Charles J. 2000. "The Evolution of Low-Income Housing Policy, 1949–1999." *Housing Policy Debate* 11, no. 2: 489–520.

Painter, Gary. 2001. "Low-Income Housing Assistance: Its Impact on Labor Force and Housing Program Participation." *Journal of Housing Research* 12, no. 1: 1–26.

Reardon, Patrick T. November 2, 2002. "CHA Reeling From Years of Maintenance Neglect." *Chicago Tribune.*

Rosenthal, Stuart. 2006. "Old Homes, Externalities, and Poor Neighborhoods: A Model of Urban Decline and Renewal." Mimeo.

Santiago, Anna M., George C. Galster, and Peter Tatian. 2001. "Assessing the Property Value Impacts of the Dispersed Housing Subsidy Program in Denver." *Journal of Policy Analysis and Management* 20, no. 1: 65–88.

Schill, Michael H. 1993. "Distressed Public Housing: Where Do We Go From Here?" *University of Chicago Law Review* 60, no. 2: 497–554.

Sinai, Todd, and Joel Waldfogel. 2005. "Do Low-Income Housing Subsidies Increase the Occupied Housing Stock?" *Journal of Public Economics* 89, no. 11–12 (December): 2137–64.

Stegman, Michael A. 2002. "The Fall and Rise of Public Housing." *Regulation* 25, no. 2 (Summer): 64–70.

U.S. House of Representatives, Committee on Ways and Means. 2004. *2004 Green Book.* Washington, DC: Government Printing Office.

Vedder, Richard K., and Lowell E. Gallaway. 1999. *Tax Reduction and Economic Welfare.* Washington, DC: Joint Economic Committee.

Vale, Lawrence J. 2002. *Reclaiming Public Housing: A Half Century of Struggle in Three Public Neighborhoods.* Cambridge, MA: Harvard University Press.

Whitehead, Christine M.E. 2003. "The Economics of Social Housing." In *Housing Economics & Public Policy: Essays in Honour of Duncan Maclennan* edited by Tony O'Sullivan and Kenneth Gibb. Malden, MA: Blackwell Science.

Yelowitz, Aaron W. 2001. "Public Housing and Labor Supply." Lexington, KY: University of Kentucky, mimeo.

# 9

# Eminent Domain

*Randall G. Holcombe*

Eminent domain is the government's power to expropriate private property without the owner's consent. The Constitution of the United States requires that any property expropriated by eminent domain be taken for public use, and that the owner be fairly compensated for the property. Eminent domain, which has always been recognized as a threat to private property in the United States, as indicated by the fact that its scope is limited by the U.S. Constitution, became a substantially more visible issue in 2005, when in the U.S. Supreme Court case of *Kelo v. New London* (268 Conn. 1, 843 A. 2d 500, affirmed) the Court supported the right of the city of New London, Connecticut, to take the homestead of Susette Kelo for the purpose of transferring it to another private owner to increase the city's tax base.

The brief facts in the *Kelo* case were that the city of New London, Connecticut, wanted to purchase a number of privately owned tracts of land, aggregate them, and sell them to private developers to redevelop the land to increase its value, "revitalize an economically distressed city,"[1] and thereby to increase the city's property tax base. At the time the property was taken, the city had not even identified the specific private buyer(s) to which it would sell the property it was acquiring. It simply believed that if the property were aggregated and redeveloped as a whole, it would enlarge the city's tax base and foster economic development. At issue was "whether the city's proposed disposition of this property qualifies as a 'public use' within the meaning of the Takings Clause of the Fifth Amendment to the Constitution." In a close 5–4 decision, the Court decided that the taking qualified as a public use, with the result that the Kelo property was allowed to be forcibly taken from one private owner (Susette Kelo) by the government, to be transferred to another private owner who in the city's view could make better use of the property.

From the time of its creation, a fundamental principle underlying American government has been the protection of individual rights, and the American Founders viewed government as the most serious threat to the rights of individuals. Bailyn (1992) notes the strong ideological foundations of the American Revolution, based heavily on John Locke's (1690) theory of rights. Following Locke, rights begin with the principle of self-ownership. People own themselves, and when people combine the labor they own with unowned resources, the product becomes their property. Thus, property rights have a philosophical foundation that predates the American Revolution and were an integral part of the rights the American Founders wanted to protect. Evidence that the Founders viewed government as a threat to private property rights is found in the Fifth Amendment to the United States Constitution, which states in part, "nor shall private property be taken for public use without just compensation." The Founders recognized the threat posed by government confiscation of private property and included in the Bill of Rights a provision to compensate property owners when their property was taken by the government for public use.

The idea that the government might take private property from its owner and give it (or sell it) to another private owner was not directly addressed by the Founders, because taking property from one person for the purpose of giving it to another is antithetical to the protection of rights that the Founders sought in designing their new government. A government designed to protect individual rights, and designed to have checks and balances on its power to prevent it from violating individual rights, would not be in a position to take property from one person and transfer ownership to another. Yet increasingly governments are using their power of eminent domain to do just that. In the name of economic development, governments have been forcibly transferring property from one private owner to another who the government believes can make better use of the property.

While the issue blossomed into prominence in 2005 with the *Kelo* case, similar cases in which eminent domain has been used to transfer property from one private owner to another have a long history. After a brief look at the reaction to the *Kelo* case and the history of eminent domain abuse that preceded it, this chapter considers why the weakening of private property rights through the use of eminent domain poses a threat to both individual liberty and to the private property foundations of a prosperous market economy.

## 1. The Backlash from *Kelo v. New London*

The Supreme Court's decision in the *Kelo* case created an immediate backlash. Prompted by citizen outrage, within six weeks of the *Kelo* decision bills were introduced in more than half of the state legislatures and in the U.S. Congress to restrict the use of eminent domain for private development.[2] By the beginning of 2006, thirty-eight states had either passed legislation restricting the use of eminent domain or were in the process of doing so.[3] In addition to government action, a wide range of negative responses came from the private sector.

Regional bank BB&T Corp., headquartered in Winston-Salem, North Carolina, and one of the nation's top 10 banks by assets, said that it would not make loans to developers to build commercial projects on land taken from private citizens by eminent domain, according to Nowell (2006). John Allison, the bank's president, said, "The idea that a citizen's property can be taken by the government solely for private use is extremely misguided, and in fact it's just plain wrong." Allison went on to say, "We do business with a large number of consumers and small businesses in our footprint. We are hearing from clients that this is an important philosophical issue." Mr. Allison's argument indicates that the bank's objection is partly on principle, but also in response to the popular belief that the Supreme Court erred in the *Kelo* decision.

A more amusing protest came from Logan Darrow Clements, a resident of California, who organized an attempt to use eminent domain to seize Justice David Souter's home in Weare, New Hampshire, to build a hotel to be named the "Lost Liberty Hotel." Justice Souter was one of the Supreme Court Justices who sided with the majority in the *Kelo* case, and Clements' argument for the use of eminent domain parallels the Court's decision. Clements claims that taking the property and redeveloping it as a hotel will increase Weare's tax base to revitalize the town's economy. He further claims that Souter's property is needed for the project because of its historical significance as the homestead of one of the justices that supported the decision. Because no other property in Weare has the historical significance to make it appropriate for the project, Clements argued that Weare's government should use eminent domain to take the property from Justice Souter and transfer it to Clements' group to build the hotel. Clements said that if he is successful, the hotel will contain a "Just Desserts Café" and a public museum with exhibits on the loss of freedom in America. Instead of a bible in each room, guests will be given a copy of Ayn Rand's novel, *Atlas Shrugged*.[4]

Clements' protest is amusing, but the wider recognition and popular support Clements received is part of an overall reaction that was overwhelmingly negative toward the Supreme Court's *Kelo* decision. Whether a decision is popular is not the ultimate test of whether it is correct, of course, but the public backlash against the *Kelo* decision has given the case an unusual prominence among recent Supreme Court cases.

All of the backlash was not aimed at reducing the taking of property through eminent domain, however. U.S. Senator John Cornyn (R-TX) noted, "Within hours of the decision, officials in many states and localities began filing paper to seize homes or businesses to make way for others" (2006: 14). Cornyn also notes that six months after the *Kelo* decision, lower courts had already been citing it as the legal basis for additional cases. While opponents of the decision have been mobilized to try to limit its impact, those who support the use of eminent domain to obtain property for private development projects have been able to use the decision to accelerate the forced transfer of private property from one owner to another private owner the government prefers.

## 2. *Kelo v. New London* Is Not Unique

While much attention was focused on the *Kelo* case, the use of eminent domain to transfer property from one private owner to another is far from unique, and the Supreme Court's approval of the use of eminent domain to take property for economic development has a history stretching back at least half a century, and possibly further. Epstein (1985: 170–175) discusses nineteenth-century mill acts, which allowed private property owners to dam waterways passing through their property to generate water power to run mills. The mill acts required that if the dams flooded upstream property, compensation had to be paid to the upstream property owners, but those building the dams had the unilateral right to do so without receiving permission from the owners of the flooded lands. This flooding of upstream land not owned by the dam builder was upheld by the courts. Effectively, the private property of one party was made available for the use of another, subject to the requirement that compensation be paid. The mill acts did not involve a complete transfer of property from one owner to another—the owner of the flooded property still retained title to it—but the acts did allow one person to use the property of another if compensation was paid.[5]

The 1954 case of *Berman v. Parker,* discussed by Epstein (1985: 161, 178–79), has much in common with *Kelo*. In the *Berman* case, the Supreme Court approved the condemnation of "blighted areas" in

Washington, D.C., for redevelopment. Berman owned a department store in the area to be redeveloped. The building was not structurally unsound or dangerous, but the Court allowed the DC government to use its power of eminent domain to take the property from Berman and transfer it to another private owner as a part of the redevelopment effort. In that case, the Court said, "The rights of these property owners are satisfied when they receive that just compensation which the Fifth Amendment exacts as the price of the taking." As with *Kelo,* private property was taken from one party and given to another private owner, against the wishes of the original owner, through the government's power of eminent domain. This case predates *Kelo* by half a century, showing that precedent for the *Kelo* decision has a long history.

In *Hawaii Housing Authority v. Midkiff,* a 1984 case, the state of Hawaii passed a land reform act that allowed a local commission to specify that the residents in certain rental properties would be given the opportunity to buy their residences from their landlords without the landlord's consent, regardless of the terms of the lease. The act further specified bounds within which the purchase price would be set. In affirming the state of Hawaii's power to permit this involuntary transfer of property from one private owner to another, the Court's opinion said, "where the exercise of the eminent domain power is rationally related to a conceivable public purpose, the court has never held a compensated taking to be proscribed by the Public Use Clause." Essentially, as long as compensation is to be paid, government has substantial latitude in determining whether the taking is for a public use.

Epstein (1985: 162) notes that constitutional scholars have worked to interpret the Constitution's takings clause as requiring only just compensation, and have pushed to interpret public use as meaning anything within the legal powers of government. Quoting an article by Bruce Ackerman in the journal Environmental Law, "any state purpose otherwise constitutional should qualify as sufficiently 'public' to justify a taking." Elsewhere, Ackerman (1977: 27) says, "it would be much better (but for the inconvenience involved in abandoning shorthand) to purge the legal language of all attempts to identify any particular person as 'the' owner of a piece of property." It is ignorant to view property law as defining ownership over things, Ackerman (1977: 26) says; rather, it "discusses the relationships that arise between people with respect to things." (original emphasis) Sometimes legal changes take some rights from particular individuals and transfer them to others, and in Ackerman's view all the Constitution's takings clause does is require compensation when that happens.

Following Ackerman's line of reasoning, there is little difference in principle between the mill acts, which involuntarily transferred some rights from one individual to another, and the Berman case which transferred ownership of the entire property. The difference is only one of degree, not principle, which explains the logic that might lead from the mill acts toward the use of eminent domain to involuntarily transfer the title of a property from one private owner to another. While Ackerman supports the government's right to engage in such takings, opponents of government-forced takings might also agree with Ackerman's conclusion that there is little difference in principle between the mill acts and the Court's decision in the Berman case.

A 1981 decision by the Michigan Supreme Court, *Poletown Neighborhood Council v. City of Detroit* (410 Mich 616, 304 N.W. 2d 455, 1981), also lays a foundation for the Kelo case. In the *Poletown* case, the Michigan Court affirmed the right of the City of Detroit to condemn a low-income neighborhood known as Poletown so that the city could sell the land to General Motors to build an automobile plant, under the justification that the jobs created, along with the additional income and tax revenue, constituted a public use. More than 1000 homes and 600 businesses were taken in this transfer of property from the former owners to General Motors.

The legal history of eminent domain shows that the courts have supported its use to transfer property ownership from one private individual to another well before the Kelo case. Seen in this light, Kelo is not an aberration; however, it was a close 5–4 decision, indicating that the legal principles behind it were not completely obvious to all members of the Court.

### 3. More Cases Coming

Despite the popular backlash against the *Kelo* decision, it affirmed the right of government to use eminent domain to take property from private owners for the purpose of economic development by other owners. The common element in many of these cases is that the government declares a property (or a whole area) to be "blighted," which then justifies taking the property for redevelopment. In one pending case, Joy and Carl Gamble, retirees in Norwood, Ohio, refused to sell the home they have owned for 35 years for a redevelopment project. Officials in Norwood then moved to take it by eminent domain for a $125 million project that would include offices, retail space, and condominiums. Ferguson (2006: A3) quotes Joy Gamble as saying, "It was a nice neighborhood. It was not a slum. We thought this was our home, and we'll fight to keep it."

Florida's Community Redevelopment Act gives a broad definition to the term blighted, and to declare that an area is blighted, a local government only needs to find the presence of two of a list of 13 characteristics, such as inadequate street layout, property assessments that have failed to show appreciable increases over five years, diversity of ownership, and emergency medical calls that are disproportionately higher than the rest of the community, according to Fernandez (2005). As a result, many Florida cities are in the process of using eminent domain to obtain property for redevelopment, including Boynton Beach, Daytona Beach, Jacksonville Beach, Riviera Beach, and West Palm Beach. In many of these projects, local officials want to forcibly take beachfront property for redevelopment, which in some cases would even reduce public use. For example, the beachfront boardwalk just north of Main Street in Daytona Beach currently has a series of game arcades, rides, and gift shops open to the public, but the city would like to use eminent domain to take this property and turn it over to private developers to build hotels and condominiums that could bring in more tax revenues. In an ironic twist of the term "public use," the use of eminent domain is being proposed to take property now open to the public and transfer it to new private owners for a use that would exclude public access.

Taking of private property via eminent domain to transfer to private owners for redevelopment is also widely used in New Jersey. Last (2006) reports the case of Long Branch, New Jersey, where a redevelopment plan first presented in 1995 was to redevelop 135.5 acres of this oceanfront community. Residents were led to believe that their existing residences would be safe from the bulldozer, and that new development would be integrated with existing neighborhoods, but by 2000, existing homes were being taken by eminent domain for redevelopment as condominiums and commercial establishments. While the question of public use raises significant issues in this case, Last (2006) presents credible evidence that compensation being offered to those homeowners being evicted from their own property was often half the fair market value, or less.

The property is being condemned because the government of Long Branch has declared it to be blighted, but after analyzing the facts, Last (2006) concludes that many of the condemned properties are far from blighted, and are "big, beautiful houses facing the ocean, with nothing between them and the beach except wide, rolling lawns." Cities are not going after property that is in poor condition, but rather property in a desirable location, regardless of what is built on it. Eminent domain is a way for cities to get that property at below-market prices. One Long Branch resident analyzed the situation in the following way. She had lived there as the area became increasingly run-down, and after sticking it out, the area was now redeveloping. Now that her property was becoming more desirable, the government wanted to take it by force. And, lest one think that the Long Branch case is exceptional, Last (2006) reports that 64 municipalities in New Jersey are currently in the process of using eminent domain for redevelopment projects that would forcibly transfer the property from its current private owner to other private owners.

Ultimately, these cases will be decided in the courts, but the *Kelo* case appears to have taken away considerable constitutional protection over individuals' property. Without additional legal protection, private owners are likely to lose their property as their governments, nominally charged with protecting their rights and their property, abdicate that responsibility and forcibly transfer their property to a new set of private owners.

## 4. Problems with Eminent Domain

The fact is that private property rights throughout the United States are threatened by the use of eminent domain. *Kelo* is not an isolated case. Why should this be viewed as a problem if the transfer is judged to be undertaken for a public purpose? There are two lines of reasoning that lead to the conclusion that the government's use of eminent domain is a problem. The first line of reasoning is that if the protection of property rights is viewed as a fundamental responsibility of government, this use of eminent domain undermines one of government's fundamental responsibilities. Government should protect property rights, not violate them, and it violates property rights when it takes property from one private owner and transfers it to another. The second line of reasoning is utilitarian. In fact, the use of eminent domain to transfer property from one private owner to another works against the public interest, so no public purpose is served. The next several sections consider these problems with eminent domain.

### A. The Protection of Property Rights

The United States government was created to protect the rights of its citizens, and the American Founders recognized that the greatest threat to individual rights is the power of government. The Declaration of Independence is largely a list of grievances that citizens of the colonies had with the king of England, and the new nation of the United States was created to protect the rights of its citizens against the abuses of government power. If one views the protection of property rights as a desirable goal in itself, and if one views it as government's constitutional responsibility to protect those rights, then taking property from one owner to transfer it to another turns government from a protector of property rights to a violator of property rights. Government is violating the very rights it was designed to protect. To support this argument requires that one recognizes that the protection of property rights is a fundamental responsibility of government, but this should not be controversial. It is a part of the American Constitution, and its moral foundations going back to John Locke were used to support the American Revolution and to create the United States government. Government violates one of its fundamental responsibilities when it forcibly takes property from one person to give to another.

Following this property rights approach to the issue, whether the forcible taking of property from a private owner would in some way produce a social benefit—because of increased economic development, or increased tax revenues, or the reduction of blight—is irrelevant. It is private property, and unless the owner agrees to the transfer, the role of the government should be to protect the owner's property right. A government that protects people's rights cannot reassign property ownership based on what some government officials perceive as the public good. The existence of private property means that the owner of the property—not some agent of the government—has the right to determine how the property will be used.

If governments are allowed to get away with such conjectures to use eminent domain to take property, there is no property owner who could present evidence to refute such a government's hypothetical claims. All rights to the ownership of property then become subject to the continuing approval of government, and government becomes the violator of property rights, not the protector of those rights.

Beginning in 2000, Zimbabwe President Robert Mugabe began confiscating privately owned farms in Zimbabwe to undertake land reform. Most private farms were owned by white farmers and Mugabe wanted to transfer ownership of what he called "stolen lands" from the white minority to the black majority. More than 80 percent of those white-owned farms had changed ownership since Mugabe assumed power in 1980, so most of those current owners paid the market price for their farms to acquire them (Richardson, 2005). Regardless of whether at some time those lands could have been viewed as stolen, their current owners bought them in voluntary transactions under the current property rights and legal regime that was sanctioned by Mugabe's existing government. Nevertheless, Mugabe undertook this forced transfer for what he argued was a public purpose.

There are significant differences between Mugabe's forced transfer of farmland in Zimbabwe and New London's forced taking of Susette Kelo's home, but there are also alarming similarities. One difference is that New London was required to compensate Kelo for her home, but by her reluctance to voluntarily agree to the transfer, it is apparent that the compensation offered was insufficient in Kelo's view.[6] The issue of compensation will be discussed further below, but note that in both cases, the government decided that private owners had to give up their property so it could be transferred to others, and in both cases, the government decided what was fair compensation to the previous owner. While Kelo was offered more for her property than the landowners in Zimbabwe, in both cases citizens were unhappy with the transfer and had to be forced to surrender their private property, and in both cases the government dictated the terms of the transfer.

Even when looked at from the vantage point of the new owner—whether the owner is in Zimbabwe or New London—if that owner came into possession of the property as a result of a forcible transfer because the government believed it would benefit from the transfer, the new owner risks having that same type of transfer occur, so the new owner's property rights are less secure because of the way the owner came into the possession of the property.

The very dichotomy of government versus citizen stated in the name of the case *Kelo v. New London* indicates the government's disregard for the rights of its citizens. Susette Kelo is a private citizen, and her government, the city of New London, should be the protector of her rights; yet it initiated action to forcibly take her property from her.

## B. Utilitarian Arguments

Some individuals place a high value on the government's role as a protector of property rights, and the use of eminent domain to forcibly transfer property from one private owner to another obviously weakens property rights. But others—including a majority of the Supreme Court justices in the *Kelo* case—believe that such transfers are constitutionally permitted and serve a public purpose. Why should property owners like Susette Kelo have the right to stand in the way of the public interest by refusing to sell her property to the government when the government demands it?

The next several sections take a utilitarian approach to eminent domain, and consider whether the benefits to those who gain from such a transfer outweigh the costs imposed on those who are forced to give up their property. If one takes the property rights approach, this utilitarian approach is invalid from the start. Nevertheless, might it somehow serve a public purpose to use eminent domain in this way? Could it be that the benefit to the gainers outweighs the costs imposed on others? Even if property rights are disregarded and a strict utilitarian approach to eminent domain is taken, there are many reasons to think that this use of eminent domain works against the public interest. The next several sections of this chapter consider a variety of reasons.

## C. What Public Purpose?

Who are the beneficiaries from a forced transfer of property like the one litigated in *Kelo?* One could hardly say that the beneficiary of the forced transfer is the city of New London, because cities are simply aggregations of people, of which Susette Kelo was one. Which citizens of New London would benefit from the city's stripping Susette Kelo of her property rights? The argument of an increased tax base and economic revitalization does not directly translate into benefits for any of Kelo's fellow citizens. For one thing, many of them were displaced by the same redevelopment that displaced Kelo, so they will not benefit. A larger tax base and economic revitalization may benefit some remaining citizens, but because the redevelopment project was undetermined when the property was taken, there is no telling whether all of the benefits might go solely to those residing in the redeveloped area, or even if the redevelopment might impose additional costs on those whose property was not included in the redevelopment effort.

One might argue that the new occupants (residents and/or businesses) of the redeveloped area might benefit, but if these occupants move in from outside New London, the project forcibly imposes costs on existing citizens to provide benefits to people (currently) outside the government's jurisdiction. It would be difficult to argue that a government serves a public purpose by using eminent domain to impose costs on its citizens for the benefit of outsiders. But if New London sells the aggregated property for its fair market value, it does not transfer much of a benefit to the new owners anyway. If they pay the fair market price, then their purchase would give them the same benefit as if they bought property elsewhere.

Citizens of New London who lie outside the area taken by eminent domain are not clear beneficiaries either. Although the city's intention is to increase its tax base, it may be that the new development also brings with it a demand for additional government services, and if the new taxes are insufficient to pay for those services, the remaining residents of New London could find themselves saddled with higher taxes and/or reduced services. While the disposition of the property in New London was undetermined at the time it was taken, it has not been uncommon for municipalities to offer economic development incentives to incoming businesses that include tax breaks, increases in public services, or both.

While the claim is that economic redevelopment and an increase in the tax base will serve a public purpose in New London, it is easy to identify specific citizens of New London who are negatively impacted by the city's use of eminent domain, and it is difficult to identify any specific citizens of New London who would find their welfare increased because of the use of eminent domain. Thus, it is a stretch to say that any public purpose is served, even if redevelopment takes place and tax revenues increase. Those who run the government may perceive a benefit to themselves in the form of more tax revenues they can spend, but—in theory anyway—governments exist for the benefit of their citizens; citizens do not exist for the benefit of their governments.

In many cases, as Last (2006) notes, the use of eminent domain for economic redevelopment involves assembling tracts of land in desirable locations where property values are already rising. Governments pay "fair market value" for property at its old market value, as if the property is blighted, and assemble a tract and sell the tract for more than they paid for it, pocketing the difference. Fair market value is the price at which the property is sold, and if the former property owners get less for their property than the government's sales price, the forced transfer has obviously exploited the property's former owners, and is an example of citizens existing for the benefit of their governments rather than governments acting for the benefit of their citizens.

At a minimum, if a government aggregates property through the use of eminent domain and sells the property for more than it paid the owners from whom it was forcibly taken, the difference should be returned to the original property owners. What argument would justify distributing the sales price of that land to anyone other than the owners from whom it was taken? This still does not justify the original taking, but if the economic value of the property remained with the owners who were forced to surrender their property, this would reduce the incentive for government to use eminent domain to profit from reselling property it acquired by force.

The use of eminent domain to transfer property from one private owner to another weakens the property rights of everyone, inflicts harm on specific individuals who can be identified because they do not want to give up their private property, and provides no readily identifiable benefits to any other specifically identifiable citizens. Perhaps they will benefit from the revitalized area; perhaps not. One cannot say that there is a benefit to the city of New London, for example, because only individuals can receive benefits or incur costs. To say that there is a public purpose involved would require identifying specific citizens within that jurisdiction who are beneficiaries, and with economic redevelopment projects, it is difficult to identify those beneficiaries.[7]

## D. Government Redevelopment Plans Often Do Not Meet Their Proponents' Expectations

The use of eminent domain for economic redevelopment is based on a projection that some future owner of a property will be able to make better use of it than the existing owner. Hindsight shows that in many cases governments were overly optimistic about the potential for economic redevelopment. In one example, the city of Rockville, Maryland, used eminent domain to clear a blighted area of about 15 acres and build a shopping mall, which was completed in 1972. The Rockville Mall struggled financially from the start. High vacancy rates led to an increased occupancy by government offices rather than the retail establishments the redevelopment originally envisioned, and most of the mall was demolished in 1995.[8] This is the very type of redevelopment proposed by New London in the *Kelo* case.

Other urban redevelopment projects have fared even worse. The St. Louis Pruitt-Igoe housing project is one of the more spectacular failures. Built in 1956, this high-rise low-income housing project was riddled with crime, damaged by vandals, and fell into disrepair to the extent that those it was targeted to help preferred to live elsewhere, leading to low occupancy rates. The project was demolished in 1972.[9] The Ida B. Wells housing project in Chicago offers a similar story. It was constructed in 1941, and after decades of crime, decay, and low occupancy rates, was slated for demolition in 2003.[10] These plans for government redevelopment differ from the New London case because the redevelopment was undertaken by the government itself rather than by private owners, as is the intention in New London, but they demonstrate that the promises of benefits from government-designed redevelopment projects do not always materialize. Of course, the same is true of private redevelopment, but the difference is that when private developments fail, the people who bear the costs are those who voluntarily agreed to engage in the market transactions that led to the redevelopment. Nobody is forced to give up their property.

Meanwhile, other cases show that when there is a potential for economic redevelopment, market forces can produce that redevelopment without forcing property owners to give up their property. A good example is the Georgetown area of Washington, DC. Established in 1751, Georgetown was one of Washington's better neighborhoods in the 1800s, but had fallen into disrepair by the beginning of the twentieth century, and after World War I became one of the city's worst slums. Because of its location, private individuals saw run-down homes, apartments, and commercial buildings in the area as a bargain, and economic redevelopment began in the 1930s as new private owners bought property in Georgetown and improved it.[11] It is now an upscale neighborhood, and one of the more desirable locations in the district, redeveloped by private owners without the use of eminent domain.

Long Branch, New Jersey, one of the eminent domain cases reviewed earlier, is likely in the same situation. Property owners bought into the area seeing a bargain, and the area began redevelopment. Now the city is using eminent domain to take property from existing owners at "blighted" prices, even though property values are rising and the area is becoming more desirable. After the fact, it is likely that what will exist in Long Branch if the city is successful with its eminent domain effort will be more desirable than what was there before. But that proves nothing. The area was already redeveloping, and would have become more desirable anyway, based on market forces. When locational advantages shift to favor an area, market forces will stimulate economic development without government planning. When locational advantages do not shift, government planning will not create economic development, as the urban renewal cases discussed earlier have shown.

With respect to *Kelo* and other similar cases, any economic development, improvement of the tax base, or removal of blight is purely speculative anyway. In the *Kelo* case, the city of New London did not even have a new buyer lined up, or a redevelopment project designed. The city simply conjectured that if it aggregated these properties in what it perceived of as a desirable location, it would be able to sell the property to a developer, appropriating the value of the property that rightfully should go to Susette Kelo and other owners, for its own benefit. In a good location, the likelihood of success is high, but as already noted, in a good location economic redevelopment will occur by market forces alone.

With the logic of the *Kelo* decision, all private property rights are in jeopardy. If governments have the right to transfer property from one private owner to another if such a transfer would increase a government's tax base, what property owner would be in a position to assert that no other owner could use that piece of property in a way that would generate greater tax revenues? The *Kelo* case is even more egregious than this, however, because in that case there was not even another owner waiting to take over the property or to pay higher taxes, or to promote economic development in New London. Rather, the city of New London was merely conjecturing that if they could take over and assemble a large tract of land, of which Susette Kelo happened to own a part, then it would be able to find a new private owner who could develop the property in such a way as to enhance the city's tax base. The analysis above shows that this may or may not happen, and that if it does happen as the city plans, it is likely that it also would have happened without government's use of eminent domain.

## E. Eminent Domain as a Part of the Social Contract

Some modern constitutional theories suggest that constitutional rights are not absolute, but rather are based on agreement by the governed. For example, Rawls (1971) would argue that if from behind a veil of ignorance where people did not know whether they would be one of the ones whose property would be confiscated by eminent domain, they would agree to a constitutional provision that would allow such confiscation to further the community's economic redevelopment, then such a taking would be in the public interest.[12] Whether any specific taking would be in the public interest is secondary; the main point is that a Rawlsian theory of justice says that in theory such takings can be justified if there is general agreement that the social benefits of such a transfer outweigh the costs borne by the owner who is forced to part with his or her property.

Richard Posner's pathbreaking *Economic Analysis of Law* (1972: 6) argues that "Economics turns out to be a powerful tool of normative analysis of law and legal institutions…. Since efficiency is a widely regarded value in our world of limited resources, a persuasive showing that one course of action is more efficient than the alternatives may be an important factor in shaping public choice." This was precisely the nature of the *Kelo* decision, which justified the transfer based on the argument that a new owner of the property in question would make more efficient use of it than the existing owner.

One might argue that if someone else places a higher value on the property than the existing owner, that person could buy the property at a mutually agreeable price such that both the old owner and the new owner would be better off. But the facts of the *Kelo* decision bring a new wrinkle to the argument, because the benefit from the transfer goes not just to the new owner, but to the general public through higher tax revenues, and the new owner has no incentive to consider the "benefit" of the higher tax revenues that would come along with the sale.

Even if the City of New London is able to determine which property owner would make more efficient use of a particular piece of property, that does not justify—even on utilitarian grounds—that the *Kelo* decision was correct from an economic standpoint. There are several issues that need to be considered to see why efficiency arguments do not justify the forced transfer of property from one private owner to another.

The first thing to recognize is that if new developers place a higher value on the property in an existing neighborhood than the existing property owners, the new developers can buy the property from the existing owners without resort to eminent domain. While the current owner has no incentive to consider the higher property taxes that might be paid by a new owner, the potential purchaser has every incentive to consider them, because those taxes would be a cost imposed on the purchaser. Thus, the purchaser would only want to buy the property if the purchase price were such that the benefits of owning the property were sufficient to compensate for both the price paid to the seller plus the present value of future expected property taxes. If that condition is met, then both the existing owner and the prospective purchaser should be able to voluntarily agree to terms and should consummate the transaction without government involvement.

But, as noted above, there are no clearly identifiable individuals who benefit from the use of eminent domain in economic redevelopment takings such as the *Kelo* case. The people whose property is taken away from them clearly are not in the category of beneficiaries. Perhaps the people who purchase the assembled tract from the government are beneficiaries, but if they buy the property at its fair market value, there is no greater benefit to them from purchasing that property than from making any other real estate investment. Even if the promise of economic redevelopment and an increased tax base is realized, that does not necessarily translate into any benefit to residents of New London: not those whose property is taken, and not those who remain in New London. Higher government tax revenues, along with a likely increase in government expenditures to service the new development, do not constitute an obvious benefit to citizens of New London, so the social contractarian view would suggest that from behind a Rawlsian veil of ignorance, this use of eminent domain would be rejected.

## F. Dealing with Holdouts

One argument supporting the use of eminent domain for economic redevelopment projects is that when a large tract of land would be needed by developers, holdouts can keep the acquisitions from taking place, so eminent domain is required for large projects. It is reasonable, then, to consider how large a tract one could assemble without eminent domain. One example is Walt Disney World in central Florida, which is 47 square miles of contiguous property, all assembled without the use of eminent domain. Disney set up its own real estate companies in Florida and bought all the property before it announced its plans to build Disney World as a strategy to avoid holdouts. Such a strategy should be generally feasible, and it is rare that one economic development project will be as large as 47 square miles.[13] If one could assemble the property for Disney World—which is approximately the size of the City of San Francisco—entirely using voluntary transactions, then it would appear feasible for most other private development projects too, and any argument for eminent domain goes away.

Of course, holdouts are always possible, but two observations are relevant to holdouts on economic development projects. First—except for projects such as the Lost Liberty Hotel—those projects do not have to be located in one specific, exact location. If people hold out in one location, the project can be moved a block or two, or a mile or two. Second, not only does this fact help avoid having to deal with the holdouts (by moving away from them), it gives people an incentive to participate, as long as they are fairly compensated. If people try to hold out, they may lose out altogether on a mutually beneficial transaction. The developer can write contingency contracts to buy projects at above-market value (sharing the gains from the increase in the value of the property due to its assembly with the existing owners) only if the entire tract is assembled, meaning that people who hold out lose, and their neighbors may lose too. People have an incentive to participate.

Looked at in this way, one can see an immediate problem with the *Kelo* decision. New London wanted to take the property at its present fair market value, assemble it into a higher value tract which could then be sold to a new developer, and keep all the gains in the property value for itself. Of course, people would be reluctant to sell under these circumstances. People own property because it is worth more than fair market value to them. If it were not, they could sell it on the market for fair market value. Eminent domain also gives people an incentive to hold out because it costs the government money to take eminent domain cases to court, leaving open the hope of a sweetened offer to avoid those costs. Finally, eminent domain creates holdouts because it places property owners in an adversarial relationship with the government. When the government tells people that if they do not agree to sell, the government will force them to, this will induce resistance, not cooperation.

While from the standpoint of global economic efficiency it may not matter whether a development is located at a particular location or a few miles away, the government involved in the eminent domain case cares about the specific location because its whole purpose is to redevelop that specific location. The benefit to the government comes partly through the increased tax base, as the Court noted in the *Kelo* case, but also through confiscating property at "fair market value" through eminent domain and selling the assembled parcels at a higher price to new owners. If a privately organized redevelopment were successful a few blocks away, while the implications for global economic efficiency would be about the same, it would be the private owners would receive the benefits for the redevelopment, not the government. Even if the tax base increased, the increase in the market value of the redeveloped property would remain with the private owner. With eminent domain, the government can force the owner to sell at the pre-development lower price, and then the government can resell the property at a higher price, also capturing the increase in the market value of the property.

## G. Long-Run Implications of Weakened Property Rights

While policies such as New London's that assemble tracts for redevelopment through eminent domain may appear to increase the value of property, those policies have the effect of blunting the long-run incentives for redevelopment, for several reasons. First, such policies interfere with the market activities of private developers who consider buying low-cost real estate with the forward-looking idea of eventually redeveloping it based on a desirable location. An investor who does so runs the risk that the government will eventually spot that same redevelopment possibility and take the property by eminent domain, eliminating the profit potential. Such forward-looking strategies of buying undervalued real estate help the market function to allocate resources efficiently, but are inherently risky. It may turn out the investor was mistaken and turns out to be unable to profit from the investment. With eminent domain, the government takes those properties that may be undervalued according to the "fair market value" criterion, extracting profits from property owners, but the government does not take those properties that turn out to be a poor investment. If the investor takes the risk and then the government takes the profits of the good investments but leaves private investors with the losses from the bad, the incentives for investing in real estate based on future development potential are seriously eroded, and the government's policy creates less efficient land uses.

Another problem with the use of eminent domain is that people who own property in neighborhoods that may be subject to forced redevelopment have limited incentive to maintain them. If they lie under the threat of eminent domain, owners might as well let their properties decay, and take the government offer when it comes along. Such an incentive means that the threat of eminent domain can cause blight, rather than eminent domain simply being a reaction to blight. If the threat of eminent domain did not exist, the property might be better maintained.

An efficiently functioning real estate market requires that land use be allocated by market forces, not by government mandate. The argument in favor of eminent domain looks at economic efficiency through a static framework. The argument is that at a particular point in time it would be more efficient for someone other than the existing owner to own the property. But especially with regard to real estate, because buildings last a long time, efficient allocation of resources is a dynamic process, and eminent domain interferes with that process. People invest in property looking ahead to how it will be used years, or decades, into the future, and if eminent domain threatens to take private property from one owner and transfer it to another, it blunts the incentive for private owners to react to market forces to channel real estate to its highest-valued use. Using eminent domain in this way is shortsighted, and results in inefficient land use because it takes away some of the incentive for property owners to plan ahead to maximize the value of their property.

There is a substantial academic literature showing that when property rights are poorly protected, economies fare worse than when they are well protected. Knack (1996) and Knack and Keefer (1995) show that countries with stronger property rights protections have higher rates of economic growth. Hernando de Soto (1990, 2000) has written two compelling books showing how the poor protection of property rights in less-developed economies keeps them from enjoying the kind of economic development that exists in countries where government protects and respects property. Acemoglu, Johnson, and Robinson (2001) show that nations with a history of property rights protection have higher incomes, and Berggren (2003) surveys a substantial literature reaching similar conclusions. The use of eminent domain for economic development purposes weakens property rights protections, so ironically, while its stated goal is to improve economic performance, a large literature suggests that its ultimate effect is to interfere with economic development and lower economic performance.

### H. Is Compensation at Fair Market Value Just?

The idea of just compensation in eminent domain cases has barely been mentioned up to this point because if the arguments given above are correct, the problem with eminent domain is not the amount of compensation paid, but rather that the government has the power to take the property to begin with. Nevertheless, it is important to note the substantial tendency for compensation to be underpaid in eminent domain cases. Typically, governments pay owners the fair market value of their property when it is confiscated through eminent domain. Fair market value always undercompensates property owners, because their very ownership of the property is evidence that the owner values the property more than its fair market value. An owner who would rather have the fair market value of a property rather than the property itself can sell the property at any time and receive the fair market value. The fact that people own the property shows that if they are forced to give it up in exchange for fair market value, they get less than the property is worth to them. Of course, fair market value is better than nothing, but just as when Mugabe forcibly takes the land of white farmers in Zimbabwe, in both cases the government confiscates property and pays the owner less than the value the owner places on the property. There is a difference in degree, but not in principle.

Some critics of eminent domain have made the opposite charge: that compensation to property owners exceeds what is fair. This can happen in some holdout situations, when rather than fight an eminent domain case the government pays well above fair market value. It is still possible, however, that the owner values the property more than the amount of compensation paid, because as noted above, all owners value their property above fair market value. An interesting case is landowner Jesse James Hardy, who owned 160 acres of swampland in the Florida Everglades. The 70-year-old Hardy did not want to give up his land, or the house on it, which he built himself. The state of Florida paid Hardy, a holdout in an Everglades restoration project, $4.95 million for his land, which some argued was well above the land's value.[14] Was Hardy overcompensated? Just because he was paid more for his land than he might have been able to get if he sold it on the market is no indication that he was paid more than the land was worth to him.

In other cases, people are able to manipulate the system to receive excess compensation under eminent domain. It is common for people with inside information about upcoming condemnation cases to buy the property to be condemned (at fair market value) prior to the announcement of the condemnation, for the sole purpose of holding out and profiting from the sale of the property once the condemnation begins. Eminent domain undercompensates many landowners whose properties are taken, but it also has the potential to overcompensate others.

## 5. Ideology and Eminent Domain

When one steps back from the eminent domain issue, the Supreme Court's ruling in *Kelo v. New London* is consistent with a more general shift in the way that Americans view their government. Holcombe (2002) argues that when the nation was founded, if one were to summarize the underlying philosophy of the new American government in one word, that word would be liberty. Two hundred years later, the way that Americans viewed their government had changed substantially, and if one were to summarize in one word the underlying philosophy of contemporary American government, that one word would be democracy. Modern Americans view their government as a democracy in which the role of government is to carry out the will of the majority, and an argument that most people are in favor of some policy or program is sufficient to support government intervention in that area.[15]

At the beginning of the twenty-first century it would be difficult to imagine that the courts would uphold a government program to take a person's automobile from him (even with compensation paid) in order to transfer it to someone else who the government believed could make better use of it. However, at the beginning of the twentieth century it would have been almost as difficult to imagine that the courts would uphold a government program to tax a person's money from her to transfer it to someone else who the government could make better use of it. Higgs (1987: 83–84) reports on President Grover Cleveland's veto of an 1887 bill to provide a small amount of federal funding to Texas farmers to buy seed, with Cleveland saying he could "find no warrant for such an appropriation in the Constitution," and going on to note that "though the people support the Government, the Government should not support the people." A century later, Cleveland's views on government taxes and transfers were completely at odds with not only the actual practice of government, but at odds with citizens' views on the appropriate role of government.

The prevailing ideology is that the role of government is to carry out programs and policies that most people favor. At the beginning of the twenty-first century, a majority of federal tax revenues are used to finance transfers from some people (taxpayers) to others (who, presumably, can make better use of the funds than the taxpayers from whom they were taken).[16] That is the contemporary view of democracy. Apparently, it is a small step to move from taking general purchasing power from some people and transferring it to others to taking specific pieces of property from some people and transferring ownership to others—or so it would appear with reference to the Supreme Court's decision in *Kelo v. New London*.

Seen in this way, the use of eminent domain to take private property from one individual and transfer it to another private owner is more than a narrow abuse of the government's power of eminent domain. It is indicative of a broader underlying philosophy that individual rights are subordinate to the public interest, where the public interest is determined by the outcome of a democratic decision-making process. Taking this broader perspective, the arguments against the use of eminent domain presented above are a part of a larger argument to curb the forces of democracy to prevent popular opinion from violating the very liberty our government was designed to protect.

## Notes

1.  This quotation and the following quotation are from the Court's majority opinion, written by Justice Stevens.
2.  http://legisweb.state.wy.us/PubResearch/2005/05FS021.pdf, accessed February 23, 2006.
3.  www.heartland.org/Article.cfm?artId=18253, accessed February 23, 2006.
4.  Some information on Clements' plan can be found at www.worldnetdaily.com/news/article.asp?ARTICLE_ID=45029, accessed February 1, 2006.
5.  The mill acts show a continuum from regulatory takings to confiscation of property through eminent domain. Regulatory taking is a worthwhile issue in itself and has been analyzed frequently. See, for example, Mercuro (1992) for a good introductory essay discussing the topic. The current chapter focuses more narrowly on the use of eminent domain to involuntarily transfer the title to property from one private individual (or group) to another.
6.  After losing her case in the Supreme Court, Susette Kelo did come to an agreement with the City of New London in June 2006 that the city would move her existing house to a nearby location, allowing her to retain ownership of the house, but on a different lot.

7.  Imposing costs on some for the benefit of others would require interpersonal utility comparisons to reach the conclusion that the gain to the gainers outweighed the cost imposed on the losers, and economists will point out that there is no valid way of making interpersonal utility comparisons. Even so, the point of this section is that while the losers in cases where eminent domain is used for economic development projects can be readily identified, it is difficult to even identify specific individuals who gain from this use of eminent domain.

8.  www.rockvillemd.gov/news/2004/06-June/06–09–04.htm, accessed May 22, 2006.

9.  www.soc.iastate.edu/soc130Sec1PruitIgoe.html, accessed May 22, 2006.

10. www.lafchicago.org/articles/hundreds_face_street_as_chicago_.htm, and www.thecha.org/housingdev/madden_wells.html, accessed May 22, 2006.

11. www.georgetowndc.com/aboutgeorgetown.php, accessed May 22, 2006.

12. Actually, Rawls would argue that it would be just and fair, precisely because people would agree to it independent of their own personal interest in the matter.

13. Some environmental preservation projects have been larger than this, but they raise a separate set of issues that are well addressed by Anderson and Leal (1991).

14. www.naplesnews.com/news/2006/jan/13/todays_deadline_hardy_leave_his_haven/?local_news, accessed May 22, 2006.

15. Higgs (1987) notes a change in ideology in the United States that came with the Progressive Era around the beginning of the twentieth century. Holcombe (2002) argues that the final triumph of democracy came with Lyndon Johnson's Great Society in the 1960s. Prior expansions of government power came in response to changing conditions and the perception of some outside threat to the existing order. Wars and depressions led to calls for more government intervention, for example. In contrast, the Great Society was supported even though areas in which it increased government involvement were areas that were already characterized by improvement. The War on Poverty was declared a despite substantial decline in poverty prior to the 1960s. Medicare and Medicaid were established despite substantial improvements in health and health care. The Great Society was not pushed in response to any crisis or decline in welfare, but rather because it was popular and people wanted it. This was the triumph of democracy, with democracy displacing liberty as the fundamental principle underlying American government.

16. According to the *Statistical Abstract of the United States,* 2006 edition, Table 460, 64 percent of federal outlays go to the broad category of human resources, which includes income transfer (including social security) programs, health care education, social services, and veterans' benefits. If only income security and health expenditures are included, transfers still comprise 57.4 percent of the federal budget.

# References

Acemoglu, Daron, Simon Johnson, and James A. Robinson. 2001. "The Colonial Origins of Comparative Development: An Empirical Investigation." *American Economic Review* 91, pp. 1369–1401.

Anderson, Terry L., and Donald R. Leal. 1991. *Free Market Environmentalism.* San Francisco: Pacific Research Institute.

Bailyn, Bernard. 1992. *The Ideological Origins of the American Revolution*, Enl. ed. Cambridge, MA: Belknap.

Berggren, Niclas. 2003. "The Benefits of Economic Freedom: A Survey." *Independent Review* 8, pp. 193–211.

Cornyn, John. 2006. "Restoring Private Property After Kelo." *Cato Policy Report* 28, no. 1 (January/February), pp. 14–15.

Epstein, Richard A. 1985. *Takings: Private Property and the Power of Eminent Domain.* Cambridge, MA: Harvard University Press.

Ferguson, Ellyn. 2006. "Eminent Domain Comes Under Scrutiny." *Tallahassee Democrat*, January 4, p. A3.

Higgs, Robert. 1987. *Crisis and Leviathan: Critical Episodes in the Growth of American Government.* New York: Oxford University Press.

Holcombe, Randall G. 2002. *From Liberty to Democracy: The Transformation of American Government.* Ann Arbor: University of Michigan Press.

Knack, Stephen. 1996. "Institutions and the Convergence Hypothesis: The Cross-National Evidence." *Public Choice* 87, pp. 207–228.

Knack, Stephen, and Phillip Keefer. 1995. "Institutions and Economic Performance: Cross-Country Tests Using Alternative Institutional Measures." *Economics and Politics* 7, pp. 207–227.

Last, Jonathan. "Razing New Jersey." 2006. *The Weekly Standard* 11, no. 21 (February 13), accessed at www.weeklystandard.com/Content/Public/Articles/000/000/006/6690pxko.asp, March 21, 2006.

Locke, John. 1967. *Two Treatises on Government.* Cambridge: Cambridge University Press [orig. 1690].

Mercuro, Nicholas, ed. 1992. *Taking Property and Just Compensation: Law and Economics Perspectives of the Takings Issue.* Boston: Kluwer Academic Publishers.

Nowell, Paul. 2006. "Regional Bank to Refuse Loans in Eminent Domain Projects." *Tallahassee Democrat*, January 26, p. E1.

Posner, Richard A. 1972. *Economic Analysis of Law.* Boston: Little, Brown and Company.

Rawls, John. 1971. *A Theory of Justice.* Cambridge, MA: Belknap.

Richardson, Craig J. 2005. "How the Loss of Property Rights Caused Zimbabwe's Collapse." *Cato Institute Economic Development Bulletin* no. 4, November 14.

Soto, Hernando de. 1990. *The Other Path: The Invisible Hand in the Third World.* New York: Harper & Row.

_____. 2000. *The Mystery of Capital: Why Capitalism Triumphs in the West and Fails Everywhere Else.* New York: Basic Books.

# 10

# Arresting Development: Impact Fees in Theory and Practice

*John B. Estill, Benjamin Powell, and Edward P. Stringham*

Development increases the housing stock and makes housing more affordable. But many people argue that developers should be charged fees for negatively impacting existing residents. New development often uses existing (or requires new) infrastructure including roads, sewers, refuse collection, parks, fire, police, and schools, and when governments provide this infrastructure to users for "free" who should pay? Over the past fifty years governments have increasingly charged new development impact fees for imposing costs on communities (Abbott et al., 1993: 51). The modern Pigovian idea is that government can set a fee at the value of the impact to internalize externalities and encourage the economically efficient amount of development.[1] Despite the increasing popularity of development impact fees, several issues make the government's "economically efficient" solution easier said than done.

This paper focuses on traffic impact fees and illustrates a series of difficulties with their use. Contemporary U.S. law suggests that fees be based on a rational nexus of costs and benefits and on rough proportionality of a fee with the external cost imposed by new development. But how are these external costs measured? Can government know the marginal impacts for all homes before they are built? Do all developments have the same marginal impact on infrastructure, and, if not, should they all be charged different fees? Unless government knows the exact marginal impact of each development, they will end up undercharging some and overcharging others making differentiation between "economically efficient" and "economically inefficient" development impossible. In absence of markets with actual prices for these common pool resources, governments will face numerous calculation problems.

Even if governments could know exact marginal impacts, implementation problems arise due to public choice concerns. Existing residents and politicians have incentives to support high fees for several reasons. Proceeds from fees are often used to fund projects used by existing residences rather than just pay for infrastructure that supports new development. If political actors can funnel revenue from impact fees towards their pet programs they might support high fees that have nothing to do with a development's marginal impact. High fees raise the price of development and that can translate into higher prices for its substitute—existing housing—so existing residents have little reason to oppose exorbitant fees on development. Politicians and bureaucrats have an incentive to support high fees, because they can increase their budget and existing residents are their constituents while potential residents are not.

In light of these problems, traffic impact fees are unlikely to internalize externalities in any Pigovian sense. We begin by providing a history of fees and exactions in the United States and California and review the important legal issues surrounding fees and exactions. Next we look at the economics of impact fees, and provide evidence of the level of fees in various California cities. We suggest that the large variation of fees between jurisdictions indicates that at least some cities are miscalculating or misusing traffic impact fees. We conclude by offering some alternatives to impact fees.

## 1. Legal History of Fees and Exactions

Land development often necessitates supporting services and infrastructure. New development usually uses roads, utilities, parks, and schools, as well as police, fire, and waste disposal services. Historically, such improvements were financed with bonds and local property taxes supplemented by state and federal grants along with subdivision dedications and fees (Callies et al., 1). These public expenditures were seen as a spur to private investment (Kolo and Dicker, 197). However, a combination of more complex (and costly) improvements, environmental considerations, a dramatic decline in federal expenditures on local infrastructure in the 1980s (Callies et al., 1), and the property tax revolt epitomized by Proposition 13 in California has led local government to search for other methods of financing needed infrastructure (Ross and Thorpe, 2). Exactions and impact fees have grown increasingly popular with local government as a supplementary financing source. Altshuler and Gomez-Ibanez (1993) find that approximately 60 percent of local governments used impact fees along with in-kind levies by the mid-1980s.

Exactions, the on-site construction of public facilities or dedication of land, had been used for decades (Callies et al., 1). Impact fees, also called exactions, were instituted in the 1920s as a new local financing tool (Kolo and Dicker, 197). Where no appropriate land was available for a traditional exaction, off-site land or a fee-in-lieu could be substituted for a dedication (Kolo and Dicker, 197). Over time, these fees came to include capital costs for on and off-site improvements brought about by new development (Kolo and Dicker, 197). Rooted in the idea that new development should pay its own way, impact fees have been increasingly used to pay for improvements traditionally paid for by property taxes (Abbott et al., 1993: 51). "According to the State Controller's Office, fees and service charges account for almost 20 percent of annual local government revenues" (Abbott et al., 2001: 15). They are generally a one-time charge on new development by local government as a condition of approval for a building permit to pay the development's proportional share of capital improvements (Mathur et al., 1303). Under the law a "fee" is generally defined as a monetary exaction "other than a tax or special assessment" (see California Government Code 66000 for treatment in California). While fees share two characteristics with taxes: they are levied on developers as a monetary charge and they are often assessed on a proportional basis, localities cannot tax without specific legislative authority from the state (Rosenberg, 2–3). This distinction between taxes and fees is important in the evolution of fee implementation. Impact fees, exactions, in-lieu fees, and compulsory dedications are often treated as synonymous since they all are established as conditions precedent to obtaining final development approvals. However, dedications are sometimes treated differently than impact or in-lieu fees. The courts have reviewed these exactions through a series of cases in an attempt to more clearly define their appropriate use and proper legal role.

The legal basis for government intervention in the development process is its police power to protect the public health, safety, and welfare of its citizens (Curtin and Talbert, 1). Quoting United States Supreme Court Justice William O. Douglas in *Berman v. Parker,* "The concept of public welfare is broad and inclusive.... It is within the power of the legislature to determine that the community should be beautiful as well as healthy, spacious as well as clean, well balanced as well as carefully patrolled."[2] While various interventions have spread across the country, cities in Colorado, Florida, and California have taken the lead, particularly with respect to impact fees (Singell and Lillydahl, 82). In several landmark California cases including *First English Evangelical Church v. County of*

*Los Angeles*[3] and *Nollan v. California Coastal Commission*[4] the United States Supreme Court began establishing limitations on the use of police powers for exactions. In California the police power is enumerated in Article XI, Sect. 7 of the Constitution, cities have the power to "make and enforce within limits all local police, sanitary, and other ordinances and regulations not in conflict with general laws" (Curtin and Talbert, 1) and as confirmed in *California Building Industry Association v. Governing Board of the Newhall School District* (Curtin and Talbert, 314).[5] Prior to *First English*, California courts had held that unreasonable land-use regulations denying all beneficial use of property did not require damage award, rather landowners were limited to seeking court invalidation.[6] *First English* overturned this view when the United States Supreme Court held that such a taking required compensation under the Just Compensation Clause of the Fifth Amendment as applied to the states by the Fourteenth Amendment (Curtin and Talbert, 289). This decision imposed a restraint on local governments' use of their police power. Later cases confirmed that a taking consisted of permanently depriving a landowner of all economically viable use of their land; partial and temporary limitations, generally, did not (Curtin and Talbert, 285).[7]

As far back as 1949 in *Ayers v. City Council*[8] California courts had sought a connection between a project's conditions and its impacts when the Californian Supreme Court upheld a street right-of-way dedication abutting a subdivision as a reasonable connection even though its benefits would extend beyond the subdivision's residents (Abbott et al., 2001: 53; Curtin and Talbert, 317). In *Candid Enterprises, Inc. v. Grosmont Union High School District*,[9] the California Supreme Court found that as long as local government is subordinate to state law and limits its powers to its jurisdiction, its police power "is as broad as the police power exercisable by the Legislature itself" (Curtin and Talbert, 1). This power is inherent and needs not be delegated from the state (Curtin and Talbert, 2). The local government must conform to the constitution's due process, and those actions must be, reasonable and non-discriminatory[10] (Curtin and Talbot, 20). The courts established that the necessity and form of regulation encompassed in the police power "is primarily a legislative and not judicial function…" and that the courts may only review such regulations with reasonableness to legislative intent and not by what the court might believe the regulation should be[11] (Curtin and Talbert, 4).

With the courts' confirmation of the validity of the police power of local governments to establish fees and exactions, a series of cases in the 1970s, '80s and '90s set out limitations to that power (Callies et al.,

2). Two cases stand out. First, *Nollan v. California Coastal Commission* established that a rational connection (nexus) must exist between an imposed condition and the development in which the landowner engages. In *Nollan* a landowner proposed to remodel and expand an existing beach house. He requested a permit from the Coastal Commission for the reconstruction. As a condition of the permit the Commission required the landowner dedicate an easement for public use of one-third of the property along the ocean as beach access. The California Court of Appeals upheld the Commission's police power under its duty to protect the coast (Callies et al., 3).

The U. S. Supreme Court reversed the decision. The Commission argued that the easement increased public access to the shore and decreased the psychological barrier to the beach that would be created by continuous development between the street and the sea (Kolo and Dicker, 198). The Court found that the imposed easement provided no relief for this psychological barrier, nor did it remedy any added congestion potentially created by the reconstruction.[12] The Court found that if the Commission had imposed a condition with an essential nexus to the deleterious effects stated, that condition would have been upheld. Since this was not the case, the Commission's condition amounted to a taking, "the lack of nexus between the condition and the original purpose of the building restriction converts that purpose into something other than it was. The purpose then becomes, quite simply, the obtaining of an easement to serve some valid government purpose, but without payment of compensation. Whatever may be the outer limits of 'legitimate state interests' in the takings and land use context, this is not one of them."[13] The Court also implied that the actual conveyance of property might require a closer nexus than the payment of fees, a position later followed by the California Appeals Court in *Blue Jeans Equity W. v. City and County of San Francisco.*[14] However, *Nollan* was sufficient to establish the "rational nexus" condition for exactions. In a second case, from Oregon, *Dolan v. City of Tigard,*[15] the Supreme Court established that development conditions imposed must promote a legal public interest, have a rational connection to the development and, *additionally,* must be reasonably related ("rough proportionality" in the Court's words) to the impact of the proposed development (Callies et al., 5). Of "rough proportionality" the Court said, "No precise mathematical calculation is required, but the city must make some sort of individualized determination that the required dedication is related both in nature and extent to the impact of the proposed development" (Callies et al., 6).

Many land development conditions were struck down for lack of nexus or proportionality[16] (Callies et al., 7). However, because *Nollan* and *Dolan* both dealt primarily with land dedications, it remained unclear how the heightened standards applied to fees in lieu of dedications. The California Supreme Court established its position in *Ehrlich v. City of Culver City*.[17] In the 1970s Ehrlich acquired an undeveloped 2.4 acre parcel and requested a general plan and zoning change for a specific plan to develop a private tennis club. In 1981 due to financial losses he applied to change the land use and construct an office building. Ehrlich did not proceed when the planning commission voted against approval of the application based on the city's need for commercial recreation sites. In 1988 after continuing losses, Ehrlich applied for a general plan, specific plan, and zoning change to build a thirty-unit condominium project valued at $10 million. The application was denied and Ehrlich demolished the facility and donated the athletic equipment to the city. Ehrlich filed suit against the city while entering into negotiations with them for the condominium construction. After a closed-door meeting, the city approved the condominiums conditioned on the payment of fees in the amount of $280,000 for a recreation mitigation fee (based on partial replacement of the lost recreation established by a city study), $33,200 for public art, and $30,000 for in-lieu parkland. Ehrlich protested under Government Code Section 66020–21 and challenged both the recreation and art fees though not the parkland fee (Curtin and Talbert, 323).

The trial court found for Ehrlich, the appeals court reversed. The U.S. Supreme Court remanded to the appeals court in light of *Dolan,* and in 1994 the appeals court in an unpublished decision again upheld the fees. At this point the California Supreme Court agreed to consider the application of *Nollan* and *Dolan* to development fees as opposed to dedications (Curtin and Talbert, 323). The Court found that ad hoc development conditions based on individual negotiations between a developer and a local government posed "an inherent and heightened risk" that the government would use its police powers to impose conditions unrelated to the impacts of development and avoid paying just compensation.[18] The Court established a distinction between legislatively created impact fees on a class of landowners from individual, ad hoc fees. "land use 'bargains' between property owners and regulatory bodies ... where the individual property owner-developer seeks to negotiate approval of a planned development ... the combined *Nollan/Dolan* test quintessentially applies."[19] Additionally, looking at *Blue Jeans* where the court upheld a low-income housing fee on nonresidential development, the Court found that heightened scrutiny was unnecessary where dedicated assessments were established by legislative action on a broad class of properties (Curtin and Talbert, 318). However, dedications *and ad hoc assessments,* must meet the heightened scrutiny test in California (Callies et al., 8), a position also taken by many other states.

In summary all exactions whether dedications or in-lieu fees must meet the test of a legitimate exercise of police power. In the case of dedications, they must meet the additional tests of nexus and rough proportionality whether they are ad hoc or legislatively imposed, though if legislatively imposed on a broad class of property they generally receive less scrutiny. In the case of in-lieu fees that are imposed ad hoc, local government will likely be held to the nexus and proportionality criteria. But, if in-lieu fees are imposed legislatively, they need not be held to the heightened nexus/proportionality test.

Courts throughout the United States have held their own states to varying degrees of strictness in proportionality and nexus tests. An Oregon court overturned a 20,000 square foot dedication established by local ordinance[20] for failure to meet the *Nollan/Dolan* test. Courts have thrown out road improvement fees for lack of proportionality[21] and dedications for lack of written findings establishing nexus and proportionality[22] (Callies et al., 8). Many courts seem to have adopted the *Nollan/Dolan* standard for impact fees and in-lieu fees (Callies et al., 9).[23] The Ohio Supreme Court supported that standard for fees and property exactions in *Home-Builders Ass'n of Dayton & the Miami Valley v. City of Beaverton,*[24] while the Supreme Court of Kansas suggests that impact fees are not subject to the standard in *McCarthy v. City of Leawood*[25] (Rosenberg, 664).

Even where the summarized tests generally establish a reasonable procedure for meeting court scrutiny, there is broad scope for interpretation, and different states have taken different positions, from strict, as in Massachusetts and to very liberal, as in California. Massachusetts has chosen a strict test of "particularized benefit" (Rosenberg, 667). Originally developed in 1983 and most recently established in *Greater Franklin Developers Ass'n v. Town of Franklin,*[26] the court uses a three-part test that includes a charge for services not shared by others, paid by choice (users do not have to utilize the service if they don't pay), and paid only to compensate for the service received. The court found that school impact fees assessed that would benefit others in addition to the plaintiffs were not particularized (1st test) and did not compensate for only the service rendered (3rd test). Therefore they were actually invalid taxes (Rosenberg, 667). The Florida Supreme Court also looked at legislatively imposed school impact fees and held that they could not be imposed on a mobile home park restricted to adults, while the Illinois Supreme Court found that fees must serve a specific rather than county-wide need.[27]

Many states, on the other hand, have taken a more liberal view (Rosenberg, 671). In 1997 the Arizona Supreme Court upheld an impact fee assessed on the basis of future water needs in *Builders Ass'n of Central Arizona v. City of Scottsdale*.[28] New Jersey has used a test based on "fundamental fairness and constitutional doctrine" that holds that rational nexus is not to be construed as mathematical certainty and the mere presence of benefits to others does not necessarily make the fee illegal[29] (Rosenberg, 672).

California's distinction between legislatively imposed and ad hoc fees led to the passage of the Fee Mitigation Act.[30] The Act amended the definition of a fee to include both legislatively imposed fees and ad hoc fees. It clarified that a government entity imposing an impact fee on development projects must: establish the purpose of the fee; establish the use of the fee including public facilities to be financed; show a reasonable nexus between the purpose of the fee and the type of development; show a reasonable relationship between the public facility to be constructed and the type of development; show a reasonable relationship between the specific amount of the fee and the cost of public facilities attributable to the project; account for and spend collected fees only for the purposes intended with provision for the return of unexpended funds (Ross, 3; Curtin and Talbert, 329).

Although the Fee Mitigation Act helped clarify what is required to impose impact fees these fees are still abused. Using California traffic impact fees as an example we will show that many local governments have not taken into account the full effect of the economic difficulties posed. Many commentators consider traffic fees best example of successful impact fees (Rosenberg, 680; Callies et al., 15), but if even the best fees fail to live up to any Pigovian ideal, we might want to start questioning the desirability of development impact fees in general.

## 2. Economics of Traffic Impact Fees

Developers make decisions based on their perceived costs and benefits. In each development they need to provide the efficient level and mix of services to maximize their profits. New development requires infrastructure, and to the extent that these services can be provided within a project, developers have the proper incentive to make an efficient allocation where the benefit of these services matches their cost. Once the cost exceeds the benefit, the developer will provide no more since any further services lower profits.

The catch is that new development may have effects that spill over into surrounding neighborhoods such additional traffic in adjacent neighborhoods. In a zero transaction cost world, where existing residents owned the common pool resources in their neighborhoods a developer could bargain with the individuals and compensate them, again achieving the "efficient" level of services where marginal cost and marginal benefit are equal. In reality, common pool resources are not owned and the transaction costs of bargaining are positive, so the idea is that government should require developers to pay city or county government, an impact fee or exaction so that they compensate the public for the burden the new development places on existing services. Government imposes these exactions on the new development as a condition of approval to build.

According to Pigovian theory, if the exaction exactly matches the costs the new development imposes on the community and the government spends those fees to offset those costs, an economically efficient amount of new development will occur. Although finding the economically efficient level of taxes may be easy to do in a textbook, real world political difficulties may result in governments setting fees at levels significantly above their marginal impact.[31] Governments often use impact fees to raise revenue finance general projects or even to intentionally restrict development. Under these circumstances developers, landowners, and new buyers suffer (Landis et al., 10). Developers respond to high exactions by building less, and prices of the existing building stock increase. There is less developed property for new residents and new and existing businesses causing rents to rise, businesses to close or relocate, and employment to fall (Landis et al., 10). Problems determining the proper level of fees arise in both the calculation and the implementation. Let us look at each problem in turn.

*A. Basic Economics of Impact Fees*

Impact fees increase the price of housing and commercial development. Although legally development impact fees are not considered taxes, their economic effect is the same as a unit tax on new development. Taxes on new construction raise prices for consumers, lower revenue to developers, depress prices for undeveloped land, and decrease the quantity of new construction. Figure 10.1 illustrates the economic effect of an impact fee on new development. The effective supply curve shifts up by the level of the impact fee and that decreases the quantity from Q2 to Q1 and increases price to consumers from P2 to P1.

**Figure 10.1**
**Increased Fees Make Development More Expensive**

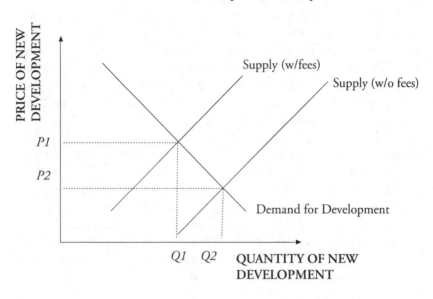

In California the amount of impact fees is considerable. Among eighty-nine communities impact fees account for an average of ten percent of median new home price (Landis et al., 2). Dresch and Sheffrin noted that the fees imposed on single-family dwellings in Contra Costa County, California from 1992 through 1996 were significant, ranging from $20,000 to $30,000 per dwelling and as much as 19 percent of the mean sales price (Dresch and Sheffrin, 74). California's Department of Housing and Development (HCD) found that single-family homebuyers paid an average of $24,325 in development fees for tract homes and $20,327 for in-fill homes, while apartment developers paid $15,531 per new apartment unit (Landis et al., 103). While the HCD reported fees varied significantly across the state (from $4,000 to over $60,000 per single-family dwelling), "Fees were highest relative to housing prices in the State's fastest growing and most affordable communities" (Landis et al., 107).

These communities have relatively low land costs and high levels of development with economies of scale in construction leading to relatively low housing costs. But, they also have little long-term infrastructure planning and financing. They are most dependent on development fees for infrastructure (Landis et al., 107). So, while construction costs are low, fees are high. Many charge the highest fees as a percentage of sales price, more than 15 percent (Landis et al., 87). Fast-growing, affordable communities were more likely to have recently increased fees than slow-growth, expensive ones (Landis et al., 56). HCD noted that among their sample, traffic and transportation fees were the most frequently increased type of capital facility fees (Landis et al., 56) making up 80 percent of exactions (Landis et al., 2). Because fees are normally collected at the start of the project, builders must include fee interest (carrying costs) in their overhead until a house is sold, as well as during any additional processing time, in addition to the actual fee (Mathur et al., 1311).

In addition to making housing less affordable, excessive fees discourage commercial development. A fee acts as a tax on new commercial development just as it does on residential. Imagine a business that is contemplating opening a 100,000 square foot store Salinas California. Under a 2004 proposed fee increase, the store's owner would face a traffic impact fee of between $2,000,000 and $4,800,000 instead of the current fee of $1,112,000[32] and would have to weigh the benefit of being in Salinas against the cost-savings of a nearby lower tax community. Some companies would locate elsewhere leading to less construction and commercial space, a lower tax base, fewer jobs, and higher business costs. There would be a spatial shift of commercial businesses from high fee areas to low fee areas (Landis et al., 9). Where low-fee communities are located beyond the urban limits, the shift will also contribute to urban sprawl.

## B. Problems of Calculating Fees

Although an absence of impact fees would translate into more affordable housing, advocates of impact fees believe that housing imposes negative externalities and should be taxed. According to Pigovian theory, an exaction should be set at the level of impact that new development imposes on existing infrastructure. For traffic impact within the confines of a development project, establishing the proper facilities for ingress and egress is relatively simple. In fact, the simplest way to ensure the efficient cost/benefit nexus of infrastructure within a development is to have the builder finance it himself. However, measuring the impact to surrounding neighborhoods is more problematic. The impact would need to be quantified by measuring traffic usage before and after development, holding other possible causalities constant, and calculating the burden of any increased usage imposed on other citizens.

But holding other causal factors constant is easier said than done. Whether increased traffic is solely from new development or from more intense use in surrounding developments is not always clear. Is the number of drivers in all households on average increasing and are choices of labor and leisure changing, affecting trip generation? Does the new development draw some traffic away from other developments that previously received it? Is the development in-fill or outlying? Any one-size-fits-all or two-tiered system of traffic impact fees will not lead to the Pigovian solution because each individual project will have a differing marginal impact yet be charged the same fee. Thus under such systems some projects that would "pay for themselves" will be unnecessarily discouraged when the fee is higher than the project's marginal impact while some developments with burdens in excess of the fee will be built.

The California Department of Housing and Community Development (HCD) noted that these fees are not an efficient way of paying for capital infrastructure because infrastructure is less expensive when built before it is needed (Landis et al., 5). Exactions based on the next growth increment are necessarily higher than they would be if tied to a realistic and comprehensive general plan established prior to development. HCD finds that the link between traffic impact fees and long-term capital improvement is weak (Landis et al., 2). According to HCD, "Development fees are higher than they should be" (Landis et al., 5).

In theory, the most efficient method of determining the impact of a development is to value its marginal contribution to infrastructure (Landis et al., 16). Suppose an area is undeveloped, but has a general plan to accommodate 1,000 homes prepared by its jurisdiction. With a long-term capital improvement plan funded and in place, each new development could pay its incremental (marginal) share of the necessary improvements until the area was built out. However, in California where such funding is generally lacking and some development has already taken place, estimating marginal costs is complicated. Most fee determinations are made on an average cost basis (Landis et al., 102). Average cost pricing is problematic on two counts. First, it is difficult to separate the impact of new development from improving conditions of existing development. Second, if the average cost is calculated based on the total improvement cost divided by the current population rather than total developed population, new development pays a disproportionate share. While the California Supreme Court considers this practice illegal, HCD found, "it is implicit to some degree whenever fees are set on the basis of average cost" (Landis et al., 17).

The calculation of appropriate exactions presents many difficulties. The government must be able to know the marginal impact that a development's drivers will have on the roads. The impact of any project is individual and changes over time so reasonable measurement is extremely difficult. It puts government in a position akin to central planners attempting to measure marginal costs or marginal benefits of different actions in the absence of prices. Government can attempt to create a formula where it assumes that a certain type of development generates so many trips but depending on where those developments are located the marginal impact will differ. For example, the marginal impact of a development in a part of town where there are plenty of empty roads will be much less than the marginal impact of a development where there is congestion or lack of existing roads. To truly charge fees at the level of the marginal impact, the government would need to have a different fee for each resident of each development based on how much, when, and where they drive. This is not the current practice.

As a substitute to measuring marginal impact, many governments turn to average cost pricing. In many cases, the government decides how much it wants to spend on road improvements, it subtracts the dollar amount that can be financed through other means, and then divides the remaining costs between all proposed development.[33] This method is mathematically easier to calculate but extremely flawed. Why should developers in one part of town have to pay for the construction of a road in a separate part of town where their customers will not drive? Despite the legal requirement that fees have to be proportional with impact, in practice they are not.

## C. Political Problems of Implementing Fees

Public choice economics teaches us that government officials, like ordinary citizens, are influenced by incentives, so in order to fully understand the politics of exactions, one must examine the incentives of those who implement them. These include politicians who propose them, residents who vote for them, and bureaucrats who apply them.

First let us consider the incentives faced by a politician seeking to get elected. One potentially perverse incentive is that politicians must cater to current residents because future residents do not vote in current elections. That means that politicians may focus on short-run thinking that benefits current residents at the expense of future residents or those who never get a chance to move in. This can translate into incentives to engage in "fiscal zoning" to restrict residential development (Landis et al., 9, 27) and to discourage some, or even all, types of growth. Implementing overly high exactions is one way to accomplish these goals. This is not good for affordability but it is good politics because it can benefit the current electorate at the expense of future residents.[34]

Current residents can benefit from high impact fees in several ways. First, they can act to limit newcomers to their community who may be perceived as service intensive (e.g., high density or low-cost housing) through exclusionary zoning. Second, they can have new development foot the bill for infrastructure upgrades that benefit primarily existing residents (Dresch and Sheffrin, 21). Third, while both of these policies will decrease housing affordability, voters who already own their home may not care. Existing homes are a close substitute for new homes, and as fees drive up the cost of new homes, existing home values increase.

Bureaucrats have incentives to support higher fees. Increased fees give bureaucrats larger budgets and also more authority. For example, as the local planning director becomes more important he might be able to demand a higher salary and benefit from having a larger planning staff, increasing the reach of his department, his influence, and his future job opportunities. In addition if bureaucrats have authority to waive fees they are in a position to exact resources from builders in other ways.

Thus, politicians, existing residents, and bureaucrats can find their incentives aligned to raise fees excessively. The economic analysis of politics gives us theoretic reasons to believe local governments' impact fees are not set based on some Pigovian model. We can look for additional evidence by examining the variation in fees among jurisdictions.

Variation in fees, in and of itself, is not flawed since new development may have different impacts in different communities. If fees are set according to the Pigovian criteria, cities with similar economic and demographic characteristics should have similar fee structures validated by comprehensive nexus studies. Fees should vary according to differences in city population, growth, age, density, income, and development activity. However, if politics is driving fee structures in California cites, fees should vary greatly with no obvious relationship with the above characteristics. In fact, fees vary widely across California. Total development fees vary from 2 percent to 20 percent of new housing prices, which translates from $11,176 to $59,703 for single-family tract homes (Landis et al., 2001: 103–104). Capital facility fees, the major portion of which are traffic fees, make up 80 percent of housing fees and 86 percent of apartment fees (Landis et al., 2). Of all fees, traffic fees varied the most between jurisdictions (Landis et al., 22), and they were the most frequently increased capital facilities fees (Landis et al., 56). Figure 10.2 illustrates the level of traffic impact fee by Californian city. Is the actual marginal traffic impact of an additional house zero dollars in Santa Barbara and $7,000 in Berkeley? It's possible but unlikely.

Because California courts have firmly upheld the nexus of development fees and infrastructure costs (albeit in a more distant sense for legislative enactments), fees should vary in a predictable way. The California Department of Housing and Community Development states, "If the Fee Mitigation Act is working as intended—that is, if there truly is a nexus

**Figure 10.2**
**1999 Residential Traffic Impact Fees by California Jurisdiction**

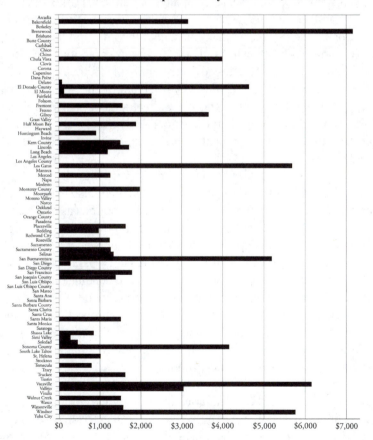

Source: Data collected from Landis et al. at Appendix B

between development fees and capital facilities costs—then development fees should vary in ways both recognizable and explainable" (Landis et al., 59). But they do not.

The California Department of Housing and Community Development surveyed impact fees in 89 communities in California. They found some charged a multitude of fees and some a consolidated fee (Landis et al., 62). Some communities lumped fees together without explanation leaving both staff and developers without a reliable way to estimate project fees (Landis et al., 7). The Department of Housing and Community Development used regression models to try to determine what caused this variation. They controlled for type of jurisdiction (city or county), population, population change, housing supply ratio,[35] city age, gross density, per capita net expenditure and median household income. They were only able to explain 48 percent of the variation in traffic fees between cities (Landis et al., 79). Only three factors were significant and they were positive: city age, median household income, and housing supply ratio (Landis et al., 80). They ran nine different regressions, one for each type of impact fee a city charged (i.e., planning fees, traffic, school, etc.) and were able to explain as little as 4 percent of the variation in a fee to as much as 48 percent of the variation (Landis et al., 79). When all of the impact fees cities charged were added together their model was only able to explain 24 percent of the variation in fees between cities (Landis et al., 79).

The regressions clearly show that these variables provided a poor explanation of fee variation (Landis et al., 78). Fees also varied inconsistently by region and, generally as much within regions as between them (Landis et al., 103). Fees did not substitute for public debt as might be expected if they cover capital infrastructure (Landis et al., 86). The large variation in fees unaccounted for by explanatory parameters is strong evidence that impact fees are set by politicians to benefit current residents and are not set to encourage economically efficient development, as the law requires. If one believes that the fees are set proportional to impact, we must conclude that the marginal impact on traffic of an additional residence is zero in Santa Monica, a few hundred dollars in San Diego, and more than $10,000 in Brentwood.

The Fee Mitigation Act requires the reasonable connection between fees and actual impact. Communities are supposed to commission studies establishing this nexus. Yet twenty of eighty-nine jurisdictions surveyed could *not produce even one* nexus study. Few nexus studies were comprehensive and most were passed simply as city council findings. They were generally two to five years old and cities had few resources to up-date them. Seventeen had general studies, nine had specific traffic studies, and thirty had a nexus study for at least one category of fee (Landis et al., 52–54). Where nexus studies existed, they usually employed average cost pricing and were poorly linked to capital spending (Landis et al., 51).

Impact fees in California are not set according to comprehensive studies that match the marginal cost of development to the fee charged. The incentives of politicians, current residents, and local bureaucrats are aligned to impose high fees rather than any type of Pigovian fee. The fee setting process in California is ad hoc and political. When combined with the difficulties of calculating proper fees (if jurisdictions were so minded) and the inefficiencies of their collection, traffic impact fees are a flawed method of providing infrastructure. In the following section we will discuss some alternative methods of infrastructure provision that could avoid these problems.

### 3. Alternatives to Impact Fees

Fees are far from some Pigovian ideal. Calculating each individual project's specific impact is easier said than done and using any single or multi-tier average fee will discourage some developments that would be economically efficient. But what about the fact that development might impact a neighbor's subjective well being in both positive and negative ways? We have seen that impact fees are unlikely to successfully internalize any externalities, but are these extremely problematic impact fees the only option available? Luckily, alternatives to impact fees exist. Simply changing the way roads are provided would allow developers and others to internalize these costs. If all costs could be internalized through road provision reforms there would be no spillover costs and hence no need for inefficient impact fees. Let us consider some market solutions.

*A. Traffic Alternatives*

New development traffic costs spill over onto existing residents and city budgets in three ways. Most obviously, new outlying development requires new local roads to be constructed within the development and roads to connect it to the existing traffic grid. When cities are responsible for constructing and/or maintaining these roads existing taxpayers bear some of the burden of new development if new residents do not pay their share. New development also brings in more residents whose travel crowds major highways and thoroughfares. Often additional highway lanes or new entrances are needed to offset this burden. Taxpayers again bear the cost of construction. Finally, the community's increased population also burdens the existing local traffic grid. This imposes costs on local residents both through increased delays and gridlock, and through government expenditures to finance road widening and other traffic control measures. But is the problem inherent to the market or is the problem due to the way government provides these common pool resources?[36] If government simply turned over the provision of roads to the private sector (as proposed by the numerous authors in Roth [2006]) then the problem of externalities would not arise. Let us consider some potential solutions that could arise in the market:

*Local and Connecting Roads.* Local roads within a new development and those roads needed to connect the development to the existing traffic grid are the easiest to envision being provided without impact fees. If local governments do not finance or construct the roads within a development existing residents do not have to foot the bill. The potential builder wishing to construct a new development would have to bear the cost of installing the roads himself in order to complete his project. This is already common with many developments in California and elsewhere in the United States (Benson, 2006: 39). Because a developer can only sell homes if they are accessible to their residents, the developer has an incentive to install any necessary roads. Since the developer benefits from the roads and bears the costs if they are not built, developers will be naturally led to construct only those projects where the cost of development is less than the expected consumer value once the project is complete. All costs and benefits of the local and connecting roads are borne by the individual developer so that any local costs are internalized. And perhaps most importantly, this would bring the design and placement of the roads into the realm of economic calculation, which as Ludwig von Mises (201–232) has discussed, is so important. With private provision, the developer will want to design the road system in a way that maximizes the final value of the new development. With government provision, in contrast, the profit and loss system is absent, so governments have little information or incentive to maximize the value of a specific tract.

In addition to construction costs, road maintenance could also be separated so no costs spill over on the existing community. After the development is completed the beneficiaries of the local and connecting roads will be the residents of the development. Many neighborhoods already have homeowners (or street owners) associations to govern collecting fees and paying for maintenance of the streets. (See chapter 14 for a discussion of neighborhood associations.) Essentially, purchasing a home can be bundled with purchasing a fractional share of its neighborhood and connecting roads. When structured this way existing local residents would bear neither the immediate nor future infrastructure costs of servicing the new development. All costs of local and connecting roads would be internalized to the new development so there would be no need for impact fees to finance them.

There is already much evidence that development in the United States can provide its own local roads as private or club goods. Today more than 55 million people, about 18 percent of the U.S. population, live in private neighborhood associations and more than half of all new housing was built in neighborhood associations between 1980 and 2000 (see Nelson, chapter 14). In short, there is little theoretic or empirical justification for governments to fund the construction and maintenance of local and connecting roads in new development through the use of traffic impact fees.

*Highways and Thoroughfares.* Highways and thoroughfares cannot be efficiently financed by only new development (if developments are on a small scale) because existing residents also benefit from the construction and expansion. If new development bore the full burden of constructing or expanding these roads, development would be inefficiently discouraged. To have efficient highway development those who benefit from the highway, i.e., drive on it, must be the ones who pay for it. Currently most highways are funded through tax dollars not through direct usage charges.[37] Thus highways are often overcrowded and underprovided. New development often compounds this problem by adding more drivers to the highways. Because of the difficulties in calculating and implementing impact fees on new development, whenever highways can be provided by the private sector economic efficiency will be enhanced.

Private construction and maintenance of highways is less common today but many successful modern and historical examples of private provision exist. Klein (76–101) documents how many early American turnpikes were constructed and financed privately. Between 1794 and 1840 3,750 miles of New England private turnpikes were built and operated by 238 turnpike groups. New York had over 4,000 miles of private turnpikes by 1821. Similarly Pennsylvania had about 2,400 miles in 1832 while Maryland had 300 miles of private roads in 1830 and New Jersey companies provided about 550 miles of private turnpikes in 1821 (Klein, 84). Overall, relative to the size of the economy colonial turnpikes in the early U.S. were larger than the post-World War II interstate system (Gunderson, 192).

SR91 in southern California is the best-known modern U.S. example of a privately constructed and operated highway.[38] In 1995 $134 million dollars of private capital was spent to construct a four-lane private toll highway adjacent to an existing non-toll government highway in Orange County just east of Anaheim (Sullivan). The road is approximately 10 miles long and charges a fixed toll that varies between $1.00 and $5.50 depending on the time of day (Sullivan, 191). The road generates annual revenue of approximately $29 million and has turned a profit every year since 1998 (Sullivan, 197). In addition to shorter commute times drivers report that the private toll lanes are safer than the adjacent freeway (Sullivan, 209). The toll way also manages to avoid the cost and delay of tollbooths by using 100 percent electronic toll monitoring that allows drivers to continuously maintain highway speed.

Orange County has several highways that, although not completely private, follow the SR91 model comprising 51 miles of congestion relieving toll roads operated by TCA, a public/private transportation partnership (Orange County's Toll Roads). Chicago recently joined in the move to privatization when it leased the Chicago Skyway to a private Spanish/Australian investor group for 99 years for $1.83 billion (*Toll Roadnews*, 1). Growing interest in toll roads spurred the Bush administration to propose a new $100 million "Open Roads Financing Pilot Program" to explore the expanded use of tolls (Bauer, 1).

Privatization provides another advantage by allowing governments to reduce their borrowing needs or use their scarce revenue on in other ways. Dana R. Levenson, City of Chicago chief financial officer is quoted, "This transaction, which is the first of its kind in the nation, fulfills Mayor (Richard) Daley's continued commitment to pursue innovative financing techniques, and has provided Chicago taxpayers with an unprecedented single up-front payment of $1.83 billion that we will use to invest in our people and protect Chicago's taxpayers both today and in the future" (*Toll Roadnews,* 1). Nevada is currently investigating toll roads to help ease a $3.8 billion shortfall in Nevada's highway budget between now and 2015 (Riley, 1). This solution is becoming increasingly necessary as gas tax revenues shrink with more fuel-efficient vehicles at the same time the aging highway system requires more maintenance (Orange County's Toll Roads, 4). Indiana and New Jersey are currently studying the privatization of state-owned facilities (Orange County's Toll Roads, 4).

Toll roads also offer an additional potential advantage: congestion pricing. Many businesses already use congestion pricing including movie theaters that charge a low price on a midweek afternoon when the additional cost of filling an empty seat is close to zero and a higher price on weekend evenings when demand is high and the opportunity cost of the seat is driven up by the number of people willing to occupy it (Flamm and Rosston, 2). Traffic congestion pricing is similar. While the marginal cost of traffic impacts from development is difficult to measure, the marginal cost of congestion is simple using existing road sensor technology and FasTrac electronic tolling. SR91 in Orange County uses a variable-hour pricing system with price fluctuations tied to historical traffic conditions.[39] Although the argument has been made that tolling unfairly disadvantages the poor, a study of Orange's SR91 showed that the toll road was not used entirely by the wealthy. "The ability to save time and reduce uncertainty confers substantial benefits to all drivers, including service professionals who can make more service calls and parents of any income group rushing to avoid charges for child care" (Flamm and Rosston, 3). Not only does congestion pricing reduce demand at peak travel periods, where it generates profits, it provides the incentive to build more roads, further lowering the costs of congestion. Private tolling provides both a demand and supply solution. It is a better method of financing and operating new highways than charging new development impact fees.

*Existing Local Traffic Grid.* The inefficiencies of development impact fees would shrink significantly if new developments had to pay for their own local and connecting roads and highways were privately provided and financed. The only traffic impact that would remain is increased congestion on existing local roads. Here, too, each development has a different marginal impact so fees are not going to provide the Pigovian solution, though the total "economic inefficiency" would be smaller than when fees are used to cover all types of road construction. But even here private alternatives could eliminate the alleged need for impact fees.

One could imagine numerous different ways of privatizing existing roads but let us consider one. Existing local roads could simply be turned over to local residents who live on them. New street owners associations could be formed to establish rules, limit access, and to finance their maintenance.[40] Streets with many commercial businesses would likely find it advantageous to encourage usage so that the businesses could attract customers (think of free streets around shopping malls), while residential streets might try to limit access to only residents and guests (think of the gated community with a single entrance). The individual decisions could be left up to each association. Under this situation, residents would be able to limit the impact of new development to minimize spillover costs.

Reforming local ownership by deeding back existing streets to citizens is the most radical change necessary to eliminate the traffic impact of new development. However, it is not without precedent in the United States. In the 1970s and 1980s the city of St. Louis deeded back a number of its existing streets to current residents to govern through street owners associations. The process began in 1970 when the Westminster Place area of St. Louis petitioned the city to deed the streets back to the residents because they were unhappy with the approximately 6,000 cars a day that were using the area as a short-cut around major boulevards with traffic lights (Gage, 18–20). The street owners association was given responsibility for street, sewer, and streetlight maintenance, garbage pickup, and the right to limit through traffic and install speed bumps (Benson, 2006: 4). The success of private street associations led to their spread in St. Louis. The city had over 427 private street associations by 1982 (Parks and Oakerson, 191) and in two municipalities more than 50 percent of the street mileage was privately provided (Foldavary, 191). Although the privatization of the existing street grid is more complicated than developers financing their own local and connecting roads, and more complicated than privatizing highways, the St. Louis case shows that it is an option.

If communities: (1) simply had developers build their own local and connecting roads, (2) used toll roads to privatize highways and thoroughfares, and (3) deeded the existing traffic grid back to local residents, then local development no longer creates any spillover costs on local communities. The alleged need for traffic impact fees would no longer exist.

## B. Privatization of Other Impacts

In addition to traffic impact fees, government also often charges development impact fees for water provision, sewers, storm systems, parks, schools, refuse collection, and police and fire services. These goods are often considered public goods because their provision has spillover effects on the community. But attempting to charge developers the marginal impact that their developments cost the community faces the same calculation problems as traffic impact fees. Yet an important alternative to government exactions for these impacts exists. Here too, advocates of impact fees usually overlook the simplest way of eliminating this problem: private provision.

A large literature in economics demonstrates that many of these "public goods" traditionally associated with local governments can be provided through the market.[41] Why would private enterprise have an incentive to provide positive public goods or minimize negative externalities? Private parties will do so if they can internalize those benefits. Harold Demsetz described how this can be done:

> The enclosing of land into a single ownership entity which often undertakes to provide services usually provided by the government from tax revenue, such as streets, sidewalks, refuse collection, and even police protection, allows the owner to exclude those who refuse to pay rentals which cover the cost of these services (Demsetz, 1964).

Market arrangements can take many forms from contractual homeowners associations with multiple parties to multi-tenant income properties with a single owner (MacCallum, 2002).

Consider a proprietary community such as Disney World or Disney's privately planned city, Celebration. These communities are essentially private cities that internalize the production of local public goods (Beito, Gordon, and Tabarrok, 2002). Disney provides private security, sanitation, commercial, recreational, and residential goods to residents and visitors over a 45 square-mile area.[42]

One important difference between private entities such as Disney and public government is that private entities are motivated and disciplined by the profit mechanism. An advantage of the profit motive is that it aligns the incentives of proprietors with the incentives of their customers, because the proprietors can only make money if their customers are satisfied.

Disney, for example, has an incentive to calculate and provide the optimal amount of local public goods because they want to maximize the value of their land. If they have refuse, crime, or sewer problems, they will suffer losses. The incentives for local governments, on the other hand, are much less clear given the absence of prices, profits, and losses.[43] If government officials make bad decisions they may need to worry about being fired or being voted out of office, but the feedback mechanism is much less direct (Mitchell and Simmons).

How do private parties get compensated for providing local public goods? Even though there might not be explicit prices for goods like roads, bundling them with goods that must be purchased such as housing enables the private party to recoup his or her investment when the price of the private good increases. A home with a road next to it, of course, is worth more than a home with no road at all, so if providing a road makes sense then the developer will have an incentive to provide it. As economist Tyler Cowen points out:

> Shopping malls and condominiums are other examples of the use of tying arrangements for public goods supply. In the case of shopping malls, public goods such as streets and security are paid for through the provision of private goods such as shoes, clothing, and books (Cowen, 10).

They essentially tie the provision of public goods that have no price with the provision of private goods that have an explicit price, and as long as there is a competitive market in housing there will be an efficient provision of housing and the accompanying public goods. The advantages of such arrangements are further explored in the literature on private communities by authors including MacCallum (1970, 1997, 2002); Foldvary; and Deng, Gordon, and Richardson.

Some might wonder whether privately produced public goods would work on a large scale. Although great weight is often attached to the importance of spillover effects for local government services (Edwards, 80–96), Cowen argues that "Most real-world public goods, however, are local," rather than, "national or global, which implies there is only one community and that it has a fixed membership" (Cowen, 14). Tom Means and Stephen Mehay test such a hypothesis econometrically and conclude that, "most local government services do not exhibit a significant degree of publicness" (Means and Mehay, 626). Given that the externalities, spillover, or neighborhood effects of these public goods are very local, it is not surprising to see so many private communities providing them on their own. Foldvary, and Beito, Gordon, and Tabarrok provide the most comprehensive discussions of how private communities can provide local public goods. Places like Lake Havasu City, Arizona and Irvine Ranch, California have been entirely created with private funds (Beito, Gordon, and Tabarrok, 270). As of 1998 there were about 205,000 neighborhood associations in the United States housing nearly forty-two million residents providing a multitude of services including garbage collection, street maintenance, snow removal, gardening, and maintenance of common areas and recreational facilities (Beito, Gordon, and Tabarrok, 310–311).

These private associations are not all small condominium associations or entertainment complexes such as Disney World. Some are quite large permanent residential and commercial areas that provide a wide range of public goods for which many politically governed jurisdictions charge impact fees. Ford's Colony near Williamsburg, Virginia is a private 2,500-acre community of single-family houses, town homes, and condominiums that owns all of its own streets and operates a golf course (Foldvary, 188). Sea Ranch, California, is a private community with more than 10,000 residents (Arne, 103). It provides community goods such as roads, sewers, electricity, fire protection, security patrols, hiking trails, golf, tennis, swimming, and a private airstrip (Arne, 103). Although some cities charge impact fees for parks, Arne notes, "Sea

Ranch is a park; its commissioners merely put the roads and trails in to let people enjoy nature's wonders. These entrepreneur-mandated improvements, coupled with extensive rules of preservations, took the place of city park commissions and charitable donors" (Arne, 118). Reston, Virginia, is a mixed-use, privately planned, and constructed community where more than 40,000 people reside and 22,000 people work, and it remains unincorporated in Fairfax County despite its size (Boudreaux and Holcombe, 297). It has a mix of single-family detached homes, apartments, commercial, and light-industrial businesses as well as schools, lakes, trails, and golf courses (Boudreaux and Holcombe, 297). Reston has 1045 acres of open space that includes woodland, trails, a park with horse and jogging trails, four lakes, ponds, gardens, two golf courses, sports fields and tennis courts, child playgrounds, 16 swimming pools, and lakes for fishing and boating (Foldvary, 179). Overall, there are 20 acres of recreational facilities and parks per 1,000 residents of Reston (Foldvary, 180). This exceeds the recommended 9.7 acres established by the National Recreation Association (Foldvary, 180).

The justification for impact fees is that development entails costs that spill over onto existing residents. Yet these costs exist only because of the way roads, sewers, refuse collection, etc. are currently financed with tax dollars. If, however, all goods were instead privately provided, impact fees would not be needed in the first place. Although impact fees are charged for numerous "public goods," if one looks around one can find that nearly all of these services are provided through the market in various places.[44] Through private provision the calculation and implementation problems are avoided. The use of government impact fees to pay for provision of "public" goods and services is not as necessary as many people presume and we would do well to minimize the inefficiencies they create by privatizing as many of these goods as possible.

## 4. Conclusion

Development fees are not as close to the ideal corrective devise as many people assume. One could imagine impact fees being set according to the marginal impact development has on a community, but despite the legal requirement in places like California that impact fees are supposed to approximate marginal impact, in practice they do not. Each individual development has a different impact. For there to be a true nexus between a fee and development's marginal impact, each development would have to be individually evaluated for a unique charge. Governments are unable to calculate specific, or even average marginal impacts of developments, so they assess fees in numerous questionable ways. Development impact fees vary greatly between jurisdictions with many imposing fees that are difficult to justify. Many governments simply come up with a wish list of public projects and then they try to get them financed by developers. In these cases, the impact fees are nothing more than a general tax on development. Eliminating impact fees will encourage development and make real estate more affordable.

The elimination of development impact fees need not burden existing residents with any spill over costs of new development. Roads and other "public goods" which new developments are charged impact fees for have been privately provided. Reforms should move these goods back to the private sector while simultaneously eliminating impact fees so that a more efficient level, mix, and dispersion of development can occur.

## Notes

1.  Pigovian taxes are used to correct externalities and are set at a rate that equals the spillover cost. See Frank in *Macroconomics and Behavior* at 640–644 for a discussion of Pigovian taxes. The theory is government can measure the marginal externalities and set fees at exactly that level.
2.  See *Berman v. Parker,* 348 U.S. 26 (1954).
3.  See *First English Evangelical Church v. County of Los Angeles,* 482 U.S. 304 (1987).
4.  See *Nollan v. California Coastal Commission,* 483 YU.S. 825 (1987).
5.  See *California Building Industry Association v. Governing Board of the Newhall School District,* 206 Cal. App. 3d 212 (1988).
6.  See *Agins v. City of Tiburon,* 24 Cal. 3d 266 (1979).
7.  See Curtin in *California Land Use and Planning Law* at Chapter 12 "Takings" for a full discussion.
8.  See *Ayres v. City Council,* 34 Cal. 2nd 31 (1949).
9.  See *Candid Enterprises, Inc. v. Grosmont Union High School District,* 39 Cal. 3d 878, 885 (1985).
10. See *G & D Holland Construction C. v. City of Marysville,* 12 Cal. App. 3d 989 (1970).
11. See *Consolidated Rock Products Co. v. City of Los Angeles,* 57 Cal. 2d 515, 522 (1962).
12. "It is quite impossible to understand that people already on the public beaches be able to walk across the Nollans' property reduces any obstacles to viewing the beach created by the new house. It is impossible to understand how it lowers any "psychological barrier" to using public beaches, or how it helps remedy any additional congestion on them caused by construction of the Nollans' new house. We therefore find that the Commission's imposition of the permit condition cannot be treated as an exercise of its land use power for any of these purposes." *Nollan v. California Coastal* at 838–839.
13. Id. at 836.
14. See *Blue Jeans Equity W. v. City and County of San Francisco,* 3 Cal. App. 4th 164 (1992). The court upheld a transit impact fee as a regulatory taking versus a pos-

sessory taking and therefore fell sort of strict scrutiny. For a thorough discussion see Curtin 318–319.

15. See *Dolan v. City of Tigard,* 114 S. Ct. 2309 (1994).
16. Both Callies (6–10) and Rosenberg offer additional analysis of different states' implementation of these rules.
17. See *Ehrlich v. City of Culver City,* 12 Cal. 4th 854 (1996).
18. Id. at 869.
19. Id. at 868.
20. See *Shultz v. City of Grants Pass,* 884 P.2d 569 (Or. 1994).
21. See *Cobb v. Snohomish County,* 829 P.2d 169 (Wash. Ct. App. 1991).
22. See *Dellinger v. City of Charlotte,* 441 S.E. 2nd 626 (N.C.1994).
23. See *Castle Homes & Devt, Inc. v. City of Brier,* 882 P.2d 1172 (Wash. 1994) and *Lancaster Redevelopment Agency v. Dibley,* 25 Cal. Rptr. 2d 593 (1993). Rosenberg cites.
24. See *Home-Builders Ass'n of Dayton & the Miami Valley v. City of Beaverton,* 729 N.E.2d 349, 356 (Ohio 2000).
25. See *McCarthy v. City of Leawood,* 894 P.2d 836, 845 (Kan. 1995).
26. See *Greater Franklin Developers Ass'n v. Town of Franklin,* 730 N.E.2d 900, 902 (Mass. App. Ct. 2000).
27. See *Volusia County v. Aberdeen at Ormond Beach, L.P.,* 760 So. 2d 126, 128 (Fla. 2000) and *Northern Illinois Home Builders Ass'n v. County of Du Page,* N.E.2d 384, 389–90 (Ill. 1995).
28. See *Builders Ass'n of Central Arizona v. City of Scottsdale,* 930 P.2d 993, 997, 998 (Ariz. 1997).
29. See *F & W Assocs. v. County of Somerset,* 648 A.2d 482, 487 (N.J. Super. Ct. App. Div. 1994).
30. Assembly Bill 1600 took effect in 1989.
31. California's Department of Housing and Development (HCD) reports, "California development fees are extremely high. Single-family homebuilders in California in 1999 paid an average of $24,325 per unit in residential development fees, based on the results of a sample of 89 cities and counties. Owners of new infill homes paid an average of $20,327 per unit. Apartment developers paid an average of $15,531 per new apartment unit." *Id.,* at 1.
32. Two alternative fee increase proposals were made and eventually voted down by the Salinas City Council that would have made that city one of the highest traffic fee cities in the state. See Kasavan.
33. Powell and Stringham encountered the City of Salinas attempting to use this method with a proposed impact fee increase in 2004. See Kasavan.
34. Of course, owners of raw undeveloped land are also harmed but they are often not residents of the community where the land is owned and even if they are they only get one vote compared to the many votes of the owners of homes throughout the community.
35. The housing supply ratio was computed by 1994–96 residential permit activity by the number of 1990 housing units (Landis, 47).
36. See Bruce Benson (1994) "Are Public Goods Really Common Pools" for a discussion of this.
37. Gasoline taxes are an inefficient method of financing roads because they do not distinguish who drives on which roads and at what times. Different roads have different demands and levels of congestion and to be operated efficiently should have different prices to reflect that. Gasoline taxes fail to do this.
38. The California Private Transportation Company eventually sold the SR 91 franchise to Orange County in 2003 for $207.5 million.

39.    Many other countries are experimenting with similar pricing schemes ranging from simple downtown daily driving fees practiced in London and Singapore to area, facility, or distance-based programs in Norway, Hong Kong, the Netherlands, Italy, and France, to San Diego that uses real-time congestion data to change tolls up to every six minutes with electronic notification to drivers (Flamm and Rosston, 3).

40.    Although charging tolls is a possibility, the transaction costs of this are likely too high at present. In the future the use of electronic tolls which charge drivers via satellite or overhead monitor may overcome transaction costs allowing these roads to operate more like modern toll-financed private highways.

41.    See the following: MacCallum, 1970; MacCallum, 1997, 2876–302; MacCallum, 2002, 371–400; Foldvary, 1994; Deng, Gordon, and Richardson, 2002; Cowen, 1988, 1–26; and Cowen and Crampton, eds., 2002.

42.    See Foldvary in *Public Goods and Private Communities* at 114–133 for a discussion of the community goods Disney provides.

43.    See von Mises in *Human Action* at Chapter XVI and Hayek in *Individualism and Economic Order* for well-developed discussions of prices. See also Schumpeter in *Capitalism, Socialism, and Democracy* at 81–86 for an explanation of creative destruction with profit and losses.

44.    Many historic examples of privately provided community goods in industrial areas can be found in Arne's "Entrepreneurial City Planning." Examples of private schooling that educated 90 percent of the population can be found in Tooley's "Education in the Voluntary City." Private provision of police can be found in Davies' "Private Provision of Police During the Eighteenth and Nineteenth Centuries."

# References

Abbott, William, Peter Detweiler, M. Thomas Jacobson, Margaret Sohagi, Harriet Steiner. 2001. *Exactions and Impact Fees in California.* Pt. Arena, CA: Solano Press Books.

Abbott, William, Marian Moe, Marilee Hanson. 1993. *Public Needs and Private Dollars.* Pt. Arena, CA: Solano Press Books.

Altshuler, Alan A. and Gomez-Ibanez, Jose A. 1993. *Regulation for Revenue: The Political Economy of Land Use Exactions.* Washington, D.C.: The Brookings Institute.

Arne, Robert. 2002. Entrepreneurial City Planning. In *The Voluntary City,* eds. David Beito, Peter Gordon, and Alexander Tabarrok. Ann Abor, MI: The Independent Institute and University of Michigan Press.

Bauer, David, Editor, Washington Update, *American Road and Transportation Builders Association,* Feb. 13, 2006, No. 06–02.

Beito, David, Peter Gordon, and Alexander Tabarrok, eds. 2002. *The Voluntary City.* Ann Abor, MI: The Independent Institute and University of Michigan Press.

Benson, Bruce 1994. "Are Public Goods Really Common Pools: Considerations of the Evolution of Policing and Highways in England," *Economic Inquiry*, Vol. 32, No. 2, pp. 249–271.

Benson, Bruce 1995. *To Serve and Protect.* New York, NY: New York University Press, for The Independent Institute.

Benson, Bruce. 2006. *Are Roads Public Goods, Club Goods Private Goods or Common Pools?,* Working Paper. Tallahassee, Florida: Florida State University: 39.

Boudreaux, Donald and Randall Holcombe. 2002. Contractual Governments in Practice and Theory. In *The Voluntary City,* eds. David Beito, Peter Gordon, and Alexander Tabarrok. Ann Arbor, MI: The Independent Institute and University of Michigan Press.

California Government Code. 2005. Section 66000–66008 and 66016–66018.5. Sacramento, California: WAIS Document Retrieval. A:\Wais Document Retreival.htm (accessed July 1, 2005).

Callies, David L., Benjamin A. Kudo, and William S. Richardson. 1998. *Exactions, Impact Fees and Other Land Development Conditions.* Proceedings of the 1998 National Planning Conference. AICP Press available at www.asu.edu/caed/proceedings98/Callies/callies2.html.

Cowen, Tyler. 1988. Public Goods and Externalities: Old and New Perspectives. In *The Theory of Market Failure,* ed. Tyler Cowen, 1–26. Fairfax, VA: George Mason University Press.

Cowen, Tyler and Eric Crampton, eds. 2002. *Market Failure or Success: The New Debate.* Oakland, CA: Edward Elgar Publishing and the Independent Institute.

Curtin, Daniel J. Jr. and Cecily T. Talbert. 2005. *California Land Use and Planning Law.* Pt. Arena, CA: Solano Press Books.

Davies, Stephen. 2002. The Private Provision of Police During the Eighteenth and Nineteenth Centuries. In *The Voluntary City,* eds. David Beito, Peter Gordon, and Alexander Tabarrok. Ann Abor, MI: The Independent Institute and University of Michigan Press.

Demsetz, Harold. 1964. The Exchange and Enforcement of Property Rights, *Journal of Law and Economics* 7: 293–306.

Deng, Fredrick, Peter Gordon, and Harry Richardson. 2002. *Private Communities, Market Institutions, and Planning,* working paper, University of Southern California.

Dresch, Marla and Steven M. Sheffrin. 1997. *Who pays for development fees and exactions?* San Francisco, CA: Policy Institute of California.

Edwards, John H.Y. 1990. Congestion Function Specification and the Publicness of Local Goods. *Journal of Urban Economics,* January 1990: 80–96.

Ekeland, Robert B. Jr. and Robert D. Tollison. 2000. *Microeconomics: Private Markets and Public Choice.* (6th ed.). Menlo Park, CA: Addison Wesley Longman, Inc.

Flamm, Bradley and Gregory Rosston. 2005. *Traffic congestion, congestion pricing, and the price of using California's freeways.* Stanford Institute for Economic Policy Research Policy Brief. Stanford, CA. http://SIEPR.stanford.edu.

Foldvary, Fred. 1994. *Public Goods and Private Communities.* Aldershot, UK: Edward Elgar Publishing.

Frank, Robert. 2003. *Microeconomics and Behavior.* New York, NY: McGraw-Hill Irwin.

Gage, Theodore J. 1981. "Getting Street-Wise in St. Louis." *Reason.* 13: 18–20.

Gunderson, Gary. 1989. Privatization and the 19th-Centruy Turnpike. *Cato Journal,* 9(1): 192.

Hayek, Friedrich A. 1948. *Individualism and Economic Order.* Chicago, IL: The University of Chicago Press.

Kasavan, Peter. 2004. Traffic impact fee boost tempered a bit. *Californian* (Salinas, CA), April 20.

Klein, Daniel. 2002. The Voluntary Provision of Public Goods? The Turnpike Companies of Early America. In *The Voluntary City,* eds. David Betio, Peter Gordon, and Alexander Tabarrok. Ann Abor, MI: The Independent Institute and University of Michigan Press.

Kolo, Jerry and Todd J. Dicker. 1993. Practical issues in adopting local impact fees. *State and Local Government Review,* Fall 1993, 25, No. 3: 197—206. http://www.redcoop.org/Downloads/KoloDicker.pdf.

Landis, John, Michael Larice, Deva Dawson, and Lan Deng. 2001. *Pay to play: residential development fees in California cities and counties, 1999.* Institute of Urban and Regional Development for California Department of Housing and Community Development. Sacramento, CA.

MacCallum, Spencer. 1970. *The Art of Community.* Menlo Park, CA: Institute for Humane Studies.

MacCallum, Spencer. 1997. The Quickening of Social Evolution: Perspectives on Proprietary (Entrepreneurial) Communities, *The Independent Review* 2: 287–302.

MacCallum, Spencer. 2002. The Case for Land Lease versus Subdivision. In *The Voluntary City,* eds. David Beito, Peter Gordon, and Alexander Tabarrok, 371–400. Ann Arbor, Michigan: The Independent Institute and University of Michigan Press.

Mathur, Shishir, Paul Waddell, Hilda Blanco. 2004. The effect of impact fees on the price of new single-family housing. *Urban Studies,* June 2004, 41 (7): 1303–1312.

Means, Tom S. and Stephan L. Mehay. 1995. Estimating the publicness of local government services: Alternative congestion function specifications. *Southern Economic Journal,* v.61, n.2: 614–627.

Mises, Ludwig von. 1998. *Human Action: A Treatise on Economics,* Scholar's ed. Auburn, AL: The Ludwig Von Mises Institute.

Mitchell, William and Randy Simmons. 1994. *Beyond Politics.* San Francisco CA: Westview Press, for The Independent Institute.

National Association of Home Builders. 2005. *Consumer guide to understanding impact fees.* Washington, DC. http://www.nahb.org/generic.aspx?genericContentID=3792 (accessed 6/11/06).

Orange County's Toll Roads: A Model for California. http://www.thetollroads.com/home/about_history.htm (accessed 3/7/06).

Parks, Roger B. and Ronald J. Oakerson. 1988 *Metropolitan Organization: The St. Louis Case.* Washington, DC: United States Advisory Commission on Intergovernmental Relations.

Riley, Brendan. 2006. Nevada task force eyes toll roads to resolve shortfall, *Construction Equipment Guide,* Feb. 4, Vol. 2, No.3.

Rosen, Harvey S. 2002. *Public Finance.* 6th ed. San Francisco, CA: McGraw-Hill Irwin.

Rosenberg, Nick. 2003. Development Impact fees: Is limited cost internalization actually smart growth? *Boston College Environmental Affairs Law Review* 2003.

Ross, Dennis H. and Scott Ian Thorpe. 1991. Impact Fees: Practical Guide for Calculation and Implementation. *Journal of Urban Planning and Development,* September 1992. www.revenuecost.com/imp_fees.httml.

Roth, Gabriel. 1996. *Roads in a Market Economy.* Aldershot. UK: Avebury Technical.

Roth, Gabriel, ed. 2006. *Street Smart.* New Brunswick, NJ: Independent Institute and Transaction Publishers.

Schumpeter, Joseph A. 1950. *Capitalism, socialism and Democracy,* 3rd ed. New York, NY: Harper & Row.

Singell, Larry D. and Jane H. Lillydahl. 1990. An Empirical Examination of the Effect of Impact Fees on the Housing Market. *Land Economics,* Vol. 66. No. 1, February 1990: 82–92.

Sulliv, Edward. 2006. Hot lanes in southern California. In *Street Smart,* ed. Gabriel Roth. New Brunswick, NJ: Independent Institute and Transaction Publishers.

*TollRoadnews.* 2005. Chicago Skyway handed over to Cintr-Macquarie after wiring $1830M. Jan. 24. http://www.tollroadnews.com/cgi-bin/a.cgi (accessed January 17, 2006).

Tooley, James. 2002. Education in the Voluntary City. In *The Voluntary City,* eds. David Beito, Peter Gordon, and Alexander Tabarrok. Ann Abor, MI: The Independent Institute and University of Michigan Press.

Tullock, Gordon, Arthur Seldon, and Gordon Brady. 2002. *Government Failure.* Washington D.C.: Cato Institute.

# 11

# The Economics of Housing Bubbles

*Mark Thornton[1]*

Nothing better illustrates government failure and the housing crisis than the housing bubble. Government policies make homes increasingly expensive and beyond the economic reach of first-time homebuyers. Then, as interest rates rise and housing prices fall, many homebuyers find themselves with bad investments that they can no longer afford. What started as a government effort to improve the prospects for homeownership through a policy of "easy money" ends up having unintended consequences that will leave many Americans economically scarred for the rest of their lives.[2]

When an economic bubble pops many people suffer economic harm. In the case of a housing bubble, this includes homeowners, particularly new homeowners who buy homes during the peak phase of the housing bubble. However, the harm also spreads to labor because of unemployment, and creates a loss of value to owners of capital, particularly in housing-related industries. At the individual level many people are forced into bankruptcy. On the macroeconomic level the bursting of the housing bubble can send the overall economy into recession or depression. Housing bubbles concentrate their impact in the home building, materials and furnishings, real estate sales, and mortgage businesses.

On top of all that, people suffer psychological consequences as well. Before the bubble bursts, the people most involved in the bubble are confident, jubilant, and self-assured by their apparently successful decision-making. When the bubble bursts they lose confidence, go into despair and lose confidence in their decision-making. In fact, they lose confidence in the "system," which means they lose confidence in capitalism and become susceptible to new political "reforms" that offer structure and security in exchange for some of their autonomy and freedoms.

The reason economic crises create fear and subversion of liberty is that people do not generally understand what caused the bust or economic crisis and generally do not even know that there was a bubble in the first place. In fact, as the bubble is bursting many people will deny that there is a problem and believe that the whole situation will quickly return to what they consider normal. The average citizen thinks very little about what makes the economy work, but simply accepts the system for what it is, and tries to make the most of it.

The purpose of this chapter is to show how the "system" works, why it generates bubbles, why they eventually burst, and the macroeconomic effects of bubbles. Here we apply the economic understanding of bubbles derived from the Austrian business cycle theory (ABC theory)[3] to the current case of the housing bubble and show that this aspect of the housing crisis is the result of government failure—the inevitable failure of a government bureaucracy (i.e., the Federal Reserve Bank) to manage the money supply and interest rates in an economically rational manner.[4] However, the same reasoning can be applied to historical bubbles, from the Tulip mania in seventeenth-century Holland (see French, 2006) to the dot.com tech bubble of the late 1990s (see Callahan and Garrison 2003), and to future bubbles.

## 1. What Causes Housing Bubbles?

There are three basic views of bubbles that are held by economists and the general public. The dominant view among the general public and modern mainstream economists, including the Chicago school and proponents of Supply-Side economics, is to deny the existence of bubbles and to declare that what is thought to be "bubbles" is really the result of "real" factors. The second view, which is espoused by Keynesians and by proponents of Behavioral Finance, is that bubbles exist because of psychological factors such as those captured by the phrase "irrational exuberance." The third view is that of the Austrian school, which sees bubbles as consisting of real and psychological changes caused by manipulations of monetary policy. This view has the advantages of being forward looking and identifying an economic cause of bubbles. By identifying an economic cause it also directs us to policy choices that would prevent future bubbles.

Most people agree with the majority of economists, that there is no such thing as a housing bubble—housing prices, they say, "never go down." Supply Siders and Chicago school economists seem to view the declaration of a bubble as an affront to *Homo economicus*—rationally economic man—because they view it as an assertion of some psychological flaw in people that requires government intervention.[5] They note that if there were a rational cause or causes of housing bubbles, or any type of bubble for that matter, then even if only some people believed it was a bubble, they could profit by selling homes at inflated prices and deflate the bubble long before it ever became over-inflated and burst. Furthermore, if housing bubbles had irrational foundations, then certainly a rational economic man could profit enormously by shedding light on the erroneous psychological motivations that were causing the bubble.[6]

Although there is much diversity in this camp, it is well illustrated by two economists from the Federal Reserve Bank of New York who recently examined concerns about the existence of a speculative bubble in the U.S. housing market. While McCarthy and Peach (2004: 2) did find that a housing bubble could have a severe impact on the economy—if it existed and were to burst—they ultimately concluded that such fears were unfounded:

> Our main conclusion is that the most widely cited evidence of a bubble is not persuasive because it fails to account for developments in the housing market over the past decade. In particular, significant declines in nominal mortgage interest rates and demographic forces have supported housing demand, home construction, and home values during this period (2004: 2).

Furthermore they find "no basis for concern" for any severe drop in housing prices. In the past when the United States has gone into recession or has experienced periods of high nominal interest rates, they found that any price declines have been "moderate" and that significant declines can only happen regionally so that they would not have "devastating effects on the national economy."

This is essentially the view of Alan Greenspan (former chairman of the Federal Reserve Bank, or Fed for short) and Ben Bernanke (current chairman of the Fed). In particular, Greenspan was aware of the possibility of a housing bubble, but he offered many reasons to suggest that it did not exist, and that if it did exist it would not be a major problem. The chairman is usually difficult to interpret and at times so incomprehensible as to be almost misleading that his testimony before Congress has been labeled "Greenspam" (Thornton, 2004b). However, on the topic of the housing bubble he is clear and direct and worth quoting at length.

> The ongoing strength in the housing market has raised concerns about the possible emergence of a bubble in home prices. However, the analogy often made to the building and bursting of a stock price bubble is imperfect. First, unlike in the stock market, sales in the real estate market incur substantial transactions costs and, when

most homes are sold, the seller must physically move out. Doing so often entails significant financial and emotional costs and is an obvious impediment to stimulating a bubble through speculative trading in homes. Thus, while stock market turnover is more than 100 percent annually, the turnover of home ownership is less than 10 percent annually—scarcely tinder for speculative conflagration. Second, arbitrage opportunities are much more limited in housing markets than in securities markets. A home in Portland, Oregon is not a close substitute for a home in Portland, Maine, and the "national" housing market is better understood as a collection of small, local housing markets. Even if a bubble were to develop in a local market, it would not necessarily have implications for the nation as a whole (2002).

As the bubble was reaching its peak Greenspan (2005b) did admit that there was some "apparent froth" in some local housing markets, but overall he found that conditions in the housing market were "encouraging." In his first speech after leaving office Greenspan said that the "extraordinary boom" in the housing market was over, but that there was no danger and that home prices would not decrease (Bruno, 2006). The new Fed chairman, Ben Bernanke (2006b), has admitted to the possibility of "slower growth in house prices," but confidently declared that if this did happen he would just lower interest rates. Bernanke (2006a) also believes that the mortgage market is more stable than in the past. Bernanke noted in particular that:

> Our examiners tell us that lending standards are generally sound and are not comparable to the standards that contributed to broad problems in the banking industry two decades ago. In particular, real estate appraisal practices have improved (2006a).

A second view of housing bubbles and bubbles in general is that they exist, but that they are fundamentally caused by psychological factors. Many people and many important economists subscribe to this view of bubbles, including Keynesian economists and proponents of Behavioral Finance, such as Robert Shiller. From this perspective the business cycle is seen as the ebb and flow of mass consciousness and emotions. Real factors may play a role, but the important causal factors for deviations in the business cycle are psychological. Booms develop because people become confident and then overconfident in the economy. Investors likewise are confident and increase their tolerance for taking risk. Rising profits and asset prices lead to "speculative" behavior where economic decisions are no longer based on old rules and procedures, but on the bravery instilled by a "new era."[7] As the investment mania sets in the bubble expands. Then, for whatever reason, people begin to lose faith and new investments are exposed as disappointing. Economic reports and statistics turn sour, and stories of scandal begin to appear in the press.[8] Many investors remain determined that this turn of events is only temporary, but results grow worse, prices continue to fall, and investment projects are postponed, halted or cancelled. The mood of the market is one of gloom or even doom. The economy enters a *depression.*

Representing the Behavioral Finance camp is Professor Robert Shiller of Yale University, who is the author of *Irrational Exuberance,* the first edition of which correctly predicted the stock market bubble; the second edition predicts the housing bubble, whose "ultimate causes are mostly psychological." Like the Keynesians to follow, Shiller (2004) does not deny the existence of real factors; he simply downplays them in order to emphasize psychological factors. With the case of the housing bubble he finds three important factors. First, the increased risk and chaos in the world since the technology bubble and the terrorist attacks of 9/11 have caused a flight of investment into quality and safety—your own home. Second, the explosive growth in global communications has increased the glamour appeal of living in one of the world's leading cities such as Paris, London, New York, and San Francisco. The third psychological factor is "the speculative contagion that underlies any bubble." Here one higher price begets another and higher prices in one city lead to higher prices in another city, and the process of higher prices simply builds on itself. Shiller declared that the first two factors will remain in effect, but the third factor cannot last forever. Once prices begin to drop the contagion works in the downward direction and can last for years before the process is reversed again.

Representing the Keynesian camp is Paul Krugman, who is an economics professor at Princeton University and a writer for the *New York Times.* Krugman did not predict a housing bubble, but he did finally realize that we were in one and that it presented a big problem for the U.S. economy. Commenting on the hectic pace of housing construction and the "absurd" housing prices Krugman (2005a) drew parallels to previous investment manias:

> In parts of the country there's a *speculative fever* among people who shouldn't be speculators that seem all too familiar from past bubbles—the shoeshine boys with stock tips in the 1920's, the beer-and-pizza joints showing CNBC, not ESPN, on the TV sets in the 1990s (2005a).

It is also correct to connect the phenomenon of day traders of technology stocks in the late 1990s to the house flippers of the recent housing bubble. The real question is: what causes this irrational behavior? Krugman (2005b) suggested that, with the housing bubble, the bubble builds on expectations of capital gains.

> So when people become willing to spend more on houses, say because of a fall in mortgage rates, some houses get built, but the prices of existing houses also go up. And

if people think prices will continue to rise, they become willing to spend even more, driving prices still higher, and so on … prices will keep rising rapidly, generating big capital gains. That's pretty much the definition of a bubble (2005b).

Notice that Krugman places his emphasis on a supposedly unfounded change in taste or demand—"when people become willing to spend more on houses," but that the actual cause of the change in the demand for housing—"say because of a fall in mortgage rates"—is downplayed, as if anything might have ignited the bubble. The more Krugman tries to provide an *economic* rationale for the bubble the more he sounds like the Austrian economists who dominate the third and final view of the housing bubble.[9] In fact, Krugman (2005a) cites fellow Keynesian Paul McCulley, who did correctly predict the housing bubble and did so in the manner typical of Austrian economists, where interest rate cuts lead to higher home prices, a construction boom, and higher consumer spending all based on increased debt—and he explicitly placed the blame for the bubble on the Fed. The problem for Keynesians like Krugman and McCulley is that their cures—discretionary monetary and fiscal policy—usually make matters worse. (See Gallaway and Vedder, 2000.) Even if they could be made to work perfectly it would create a conundrum for Keynesian economists because a highly stabilized economy desensitizes investors to risk and makes them "irrationally exuberant" and thus creates the prerequisite for bubbles. Even Alan Greenspan (2005a) has warned, in his own convoluted way, that "history has not dealt kindly with the aftermath of protracted periods of low risk premiums."

As you can see, the first view wishes to dismiss psychological reasons for bubbles to focus only on real factors while the second view wishes to downplay real factors in order to emphasize psychological causes. The third view believes that there are changes in both real factors and market psychology during bubbles and that both are driven by the cause of the business cycle—policy manipulations by the Federal Reserve. This view of bubbles is based on the Austrian business cycle theory (hereafter ABC theory). This is a minority view held by Austrian school economists and some "fellow travelers" of the school.[10]

According to the ABC theory, if the Fed does not pursue a loose monetary policy then bubbles like the technology stock bubble of the late 1990s or the one in housing that we are now experiencing would not develop. If the Fed does follow a loose monetary policy, then a bubble can develop somewhere in the economy, whether it be in tulip bulbs, stocks, or real estate. If the new money is directed toward housing, a bubble will develop in housing. Austrian economists further emphasize that the additional resources allocated to housing are resources that are not available elsewhere in an economy, so that while more resources than normal are allocated to housing construction, fewer resources are available to other areas of the economy such as manufacturing, which will experience higher costs for its inputs such as labor and materials and will produce a proportionately smaller output. It is this mismatching of resources across industries and sectors that has to be resolved—painfully—in the inevitable bust or correction.

In a real estate bubble the price of existing homes rises. The bubble also fuels the construction of new homes so that the wages of construction workers rises and labor reallocates itself into construction and related industries. The bubble also increases the price of construction materials and land. Construction and construction-related industries is also where the most unemployment occurs and where the biggest price and wage declines occur in the inevitable bust.

A unique feature of the Austrian approach is that it does not see a need for prices to increase uniformly across markets, or for prices to increase to extreme levels in all markets. Many doubters of the housing bubble point to the smaller price increases in the center of the country compared to coastal regions, but price is only one dimension of bubbles—quantity can also increase beyond sustainable levels. In fact, one could conceptualize a bubble where prices stayed the same and all the bubble adjustment occurred only in the quantity dimension. If we doubled the number of houses and prices barely budged, we would be left with too many houses for the population and all the labor and materials that went into the production of those goods (i.e., houses) would be tied up and unavailable to serve more urgent needs after the bursting of the bubble revealed that the superfluous houses were bad investments.

Among the Austrians who identified the housing bubble is economist Frank Shostak (2003) who defined a bubble as any activity that "springs up" from loose monetary policies. "In other words, in the absence of monetary pumping these activities would not emerge." As a result of this pumping, a misallocation of resources develops whereby non-productive activities increase relative to productive activities—something that seems to clearly characterize the U.S. economy since he wrote in early 2003:

> The magnitude of the housing price bubble is depicted ... in terms of the median price of new houses in relation to the historical trend between 1963 and 1979. In this regard the median price stood at 73% above the trend in December 2002 (2003).

The only "problem" with his warning is that it came too soon. A year later Shostak (2004) warned that there "is a strong likelihood that the U.S. housing market bubble has already reached dangerous dimensions." While early warning maybe a problem for investors in home building stocks, the problems of predicting the timing and magnitude of bubbles and business cycles affects all forecasters, and Shostak's warning was primarily for the purpose of judging public policy. In effect he was noting that policymakers have made a mistake that they should correct immediately and not make the situation in the housing market any worse.

Also from the Austrian camp is banker Christopher Meyer (2003), who noted that there is always a bubble in the making in a world of fractional reserve banking and fiat currency, and that housing has often been impacted by bubble conditions in the United States and elsewhere. In the summer of 2003 he identified the current housing bubble:

> The strong housing market has all the makings of being the next bubble—in particular high leverage and unsustainable price increases. While the larger economy seems to sputter along, the housing market continues to run a hot race. Low interest rates have propelled refinancing, freeing up $100 billion last year alone, according to the Wall Street Journal. Not surprisingly, the low interest rates have increased buying power and supported housing prices (2003).

In early 2004 I pointed out the on-going housing bubble to investors and specifically said that it might not be a good idea to increase your mortgage: "it might not be a good time for you to obtain a home equity loan to invest in hot tech stocks. We are going through a housing bubble" (2004b). I followed this up later that year (Thornton, 2004c) with a more detailed examination of the housing bubble and found:

> Signs of a "new era" in housing are everywhere. Housing construction is taking place at record rates. New records for real estate prices are being set across the country, especially on the east and west coasts. Booming home prices and record low interest rates are allowing homeowners to refinance their mortgages, "extract equity" to increase their spending, and lower their monthly payment! As one loan officer explained to me: "It's almost too good to be true." In fact, it is too good to be true (Thornton, 2004c).

The problem with the "new era" diagnosis is that it ignores the historical fact that the housing market, and the construction of structures in general, has experienced regular cycles of boom and bust, with prices rising and falling for residential, commercial, industrial, and agricultural real estate. Likewise, occupancy and lease rates, new construction, and the fate of construction firms and land speculators point us to the history of real estate bubbles. In fact, statistically, housing starts are a leading indicator of the business cycle and home construction is procyclical (i.e., home construction is positively related to changes in the overall economy, but more volatile). The Skyscraper Indicator even shows that historically the building of a record-setting high skyscraper foreshadows severe negative changes in the economy (see Thornton, 2005a).

## 2. What Goes Up

The ABC theory demonstrates that monetary inflation has different effects depending on who receives the new money first and how it is spent. Is the new money introduced into the economy in the areas of banking and investment, consumer loans, or directly to a group of consumers or producers? Do the people who receive the money want to save it or spend it? If they save it interest rates will go down, and if they spend it interest rates will go up as entrepreneurs borrow money in order to increase production. If the money is spent, it depends on who is spending it. The economy will experience different changes if the money is given to welfare recipients instead of military generals. If the money is saved, the economy will experience different changes if it is invested in stocks, rather than housing. The point here is that monetary inflation can cause bubbles and booms in the areas of the economy where it is first introduced. This foundation of the ABC theory comes down to us from Richard Cantillon (1755), the founder of economic theory, who wrote in the aftermath of the Mississippi Bubble (circa 1730). Tracking the flow of monetary inflation through the economy is very difficult and most mainstream economists just assume away the problem and declare that money is neutral on the economy.

By the end of the eighteenth century, the world had converted from free banking to central banking, with the United States being the last major nation to establish a central bank in 1913. In the first treatise on monetary theory in the modern era, Ludwig von Mises (1912) produced the ABC theory. With central banks established for the purpose of producing monetary inflation, Mises could now establish a general theory of business cycles rather than the case-by-case basis of Cantillon. By integrating the contributions of Carl Menger, Eugen von Böhm-Bawerk, and Knut Wicksell he was able to show that when the central bank (e.g., the Fed) increases the supply of money, it causes the market rate of interest to fall below the natural rate of interest that would have existed in the absence of Fed intervention. This would cause investors to borrow more money, to expand their investments, and to undertake riskier projects and more roundabout production processes.[11] As these borrowers compete for assets, resources, and goods, price inflation inevitably occurs and the rate of interest will increase. This in turn will negatively affect the economy and some of the riskier and more roundabout investment projects will be discovered to be bad investments. Bankruptcies can also impact previously existing investments and production processes that are caught in the wake of the bust. Mises's student F.A. Hayek expanded the ABC theory to include capital theory and its integration into the structure of production.

According to the ABC theory, when a central bank makes loans or purchases government bonds from banks it is injecting bank reserves into the economy. Banks now have excess reserves which they can lend, but the existence of excess loanable funds means that banks must reduce the interest rate they charge, reduce the credit quality requirements of borrowers, or both. The result is a greater quantity of borrowing and investing, particularly in projects that "pay off" over a long period of time. Lower interest rates also discourage savings because the return from savings is lower. In this manner the Federal Reserve drives the market rate of interest below the natural rate of interest that would have existed in the absence of Federal Reserve intervention.

Ever since the Depository Institutions Deregulation and Monetary Control Act of 1980 and Paul Volcker's (chairman of the Fed from 1979 to 1987) war on inflation of the early 1980s, interest rates have been on a downward path. This culminated in the large reductions in the Federal Funds rate that followed in the aftermath of the 9/11 terrorists attack in 2001. Under Greenspan the rate was reduced from 6.5 percent in November of 2000 to 1 percent in July of 2003. The Federal Funds rate remained at 1 percent until June of 2004, coinciding with the launching of the final phase of the housing bubble.[12] At this low level, interest rates were actually negative when price inflation is taken into account.

Figure 11.1 depicts the history of the Federal Funds rate, which is the rate that banks can borrow from other banks in order to meet their reserve requirements imposed by the Fed. The Fed "targets" this short-term rate and injects reserves into this market by purchasing government bonds from banks, thereby freeing up reserves in the banking system. This essentially is the engine of inflation because the Fed simply makes a bookkeeping entry in the bank's account with the Federal Reserve—modern inflation is essentially an electronic bookkeeping entry. In Figure 11.1 the shaded areas represent periods that are considered to have been recessions in the economy. As you can see, the low rates of the 1960s resulted in no recession and a booming economy, but those low rates also caused

**Figure 11.1**
**Effective Federal Funds Rate (Percent)**

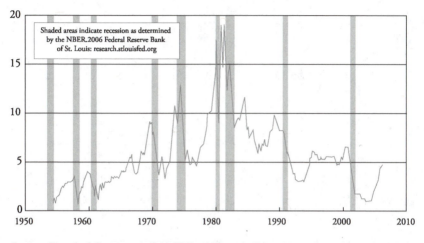

Shaded areas indicate recession as determined by the NBER.2006 Federal Reserve Bank of St. Louis: research.stlouisfed.org

*Source:* Board of Governors of the Federal Reserve System.

the stagflation of the 1970s, where both price inflation and unemployment were very high. This culminated in Volcker's war on inflation of the early 1980s. By greatly reducing expectation of price inflation and deregulating the banking system, the Fed has been able to reduce interest rates and ignite a giant boom in financial and asset markets throughout the 1980s and 1990s, as well as the housing bubble of the early 2000s when rates were pushed below their natural levels and when real rates were negative, when adjusted for inflation.

When banks have access to bank reserves from the Fed at low rates they can offer their customers lower rates on loans. Figure 11.2 shows the impact of changes in the Federal Funds rate on mortgage rates; increasing during the 1970s and peaking during Volcker's war on inflation at 18 percent, and then generally declining throughout the 1980s and 1990s and then reaching historical lows during the early 2000s. During the housing bubble interest rates on 30-year conventional mortgages were at their lowest levels ever during the post-gold standard era. When interest rates fall, asset prices and real estate prices tend to rise, and vice versa.

Naturally, lower rates for home mortgages have stimulated borrowing for real estate purposes. Figure 11.3 shows that the amount of real estate loans at commercial banks first exceeded $1 trillion in November 1994. In quick succession they then exceeded $2 trillion in November of 2002 and $3 trillion in May of 2006. In addition to the Fed, there are other factors

**Figure 11.2**
**30-year Conventional Mortgage Rate (Percent)**

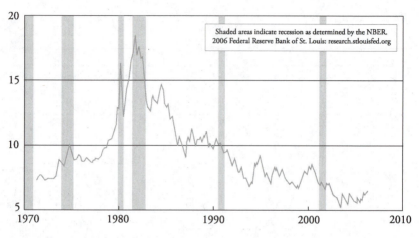

*Source:* Board of Governors of the Federal Reserve System.

that helped direct all this new credit money into real estate. First, in 1997 homeowners were given a $250,000 exemption ($500,000 for couples) for capital gains that resulted from the sale of their house, adding greatly to the tax benefits of homeownership. This tax break could be said to have lit the fuse of the housing bubble. Second, government-sponsored credit corporations such as Fannie Mae and Freddie Mac, who can acquire capital at a subsidized rate because of the implicit assumption that the federal government will bail them out, began to collateralize home mortgage debt on a grand scale so that lenders could quickly and easily resell the loans they make. These government-sponsored agencies have helped stimulate the flow of credit to riskier borrowers who might not otherwise have access to credit, and have therefore helped to lower the credit standards of lending institutions. The problem with these institutions is so large that even Alan Greenspan has publicly scolded them (Hays, 2005). In truth, the original problem lies with Alan, not Fannie or Freddie.

The artificially low rates generated by the Fed also have the effect of discouraging people from saving money and encourages them to borrow more for consumption and speculation. The impact of monetary pumping by the Fed has driven down the personal savings rate (as depicted in Figure 11.4) throughout the 1980s and 1990s, and during the early 2000s it has driven the rate to zero—and even below—which means that on average people are spending more than they earn. Contributing to the

**Figure 11.3**
**Real Estate Loans at All Commercial Banks (Billions of Dollars)**

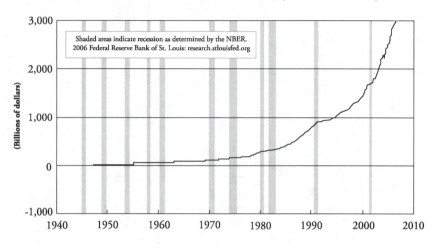

Shaded areas indicate recession as determined by the NBER.
2006 Federal Reserve Bank of St. Louis: research.stlouisfed.org

Source: Board of Governors of the Federal Reserve System.

problem of the low personal savings rate are the artificially inflated asset and real estate prices which naturally make people feel wealthier and allow them to "cash out" equity from their homes when they refinance their home mortgages. During the housing bubble many Americans have used their homes as a kind of giant ATM to withdraw cash from the equity in their homes. Others have used the "magic checkbook" from second mortgages to spend the equity they have in their homes (Lloyd, 2006).

At this point one should be wondering—how can borrowing be going up and savings going down? One answer to the question is that America is borrowing money from overseas in the form of the trade deficit, but the main answer is monetary pumping by the Fed. By artificially lowering rates via increases in the money supply the Fed has created a giant gap between borrowing and saving. In Figure 11.5, the U.S. money supply is given from 1959 to 2006 as measured by MZM (money of zero maturity).[13] During the period from January 1959 to August 1971 (11.7 years), when Nixon took the United States off the gold standard, the money supply grew by 82.2 percent for an average annual growth rate of 5.26 percent. Between August of 1971 and 1984, when complete decontrol was established in 1984 from the Depository Institutions Deregulation and Monetary Control Act of 1980 (13 years), the money supply increased by 180.4 percent for an average annual growth rate of 8.25 percent. Since 1984 (16.6 years) the money supply as measured by

**Figure 11.4**
**Personal Savings Rate (Percent)**

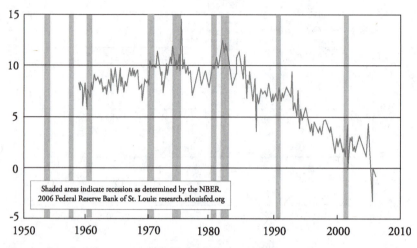

Shaded areas indicate recession as determined by the NBER.
2006 Federal Reserve Bank of St. Louis: research.stlouisfed.org

*Source:* Board of Governors of the Federal Reserve System.

MZM has grown by 390.1 percent, or an average annual growth rate of 10 percent. It would seem that all this new money first went into the New York Stock Exchange, especially during the 1980s, then the NASDAQ stock market during the late 1990s, and finally into the housing market since the dot.com bust in 2000. ◦

A large part of the increase in the money supply found its way into the market for home mortgages. Since the recession of 2001 the increase in mortgage debt is about equal to the increase in MZM. This one stylized fact probably best illustrates the housing bubble and its cause. Another measure of the housing bubble is the amount of real private residential fixed investment as presented in Figure 11.6. Investment in housing was low during the Great Depression and World War II, but beginning in the mid-1940s investment in housing (adjusted for price inflation) has shown a positive trend, which is based on economic and population growth over that same period. Superimposed on the graph are upper and lower channel lines based on the period from the 1920s to the mid-1990s. This channel allows us to illustrate the normal booms and busts that occurred in the housing market. A dot-and-dash trend line is drawn over the basic trend in housing investment. This shows us that the cycle in housing investment was less severe before we went off the gold standard, more severe on the fiat standard, and even more severe after monetary deregulation in 1980. Most noteworthy is that investment in housing hit a boom high during the

**Figure 11.5**
**MZM Money Stock (Billions of Dollars)**

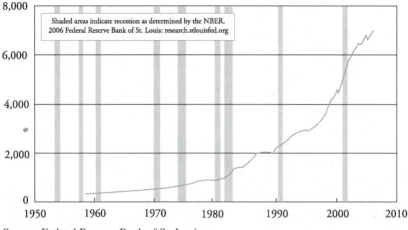

Shaded areas indicate recession as determined by the NBER.
2006 Federal Reserve Bank of St. Louis: research.stlouisfed.org

Source: Federal Reserve Bank of St. Louis.

dot.com bubble of the late 1990s and then "jumped the tracks" during the recession of 2001, when historically it would have retreated back toward recessionary levels. It therefore seems clear that in terms of *investment value* there has been a housing bubble since at least the recession of 2001.

The ABC theory does not rely on measuring the cycle or bubble, but such empirical measures do often help illustrate the approach. The next such measure is the number of homes built. Figure 11.7 presents the number of privately owned housing starts (apartments and other multi-unit structures are not included here). Notice that sharp downturns in the number of housing starts often coincides with the beginnings of recessions (shaded in gray) and that the sharper the drop the longer the recession. For example, in the late 1970s the number of housing starts fell from an annual rate of over 1.5 million to a rate of barely a half a million in the early 1980s, which was a severe recession. Since the recession of 1991 the trend in new housing starts has been steeply upward and there was no noticeable downturn in housing starts during the recession of 2001—the only recession on record where that did not occur. Instead housing starts continued to increase and have set several new records over the last few years. In terms of this *quantity dimension* the United States has been in a housing bubble since the early 2000s.

The final dimension of the housing bubble presented here is the price of houses. Doubters of the housing bubble claim that housing prices are rising on the east and west coasts, but are not rising by bubble propor-

**Figure 11.6**
**Real Private Residential Fixed Investment (Billions of Chained 2000 Dollars)**

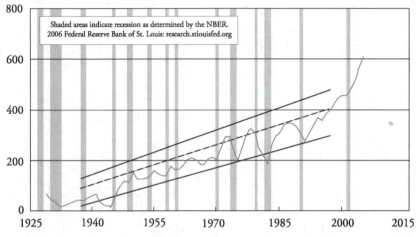

Source: U.S. Department of Commerce: Bureau of Economic Advisors.

tions in much of the center of the country. Of course housing prices have increased faster in the West and Northeast compared to the Midwest and South, but ABC theorists would be shocked if home prices were rising uniformly across the country. After all, the whole theory is based on changing relative prices, not uniform increases or decreases in a price level. There are microeconomic and public policy reasons why home prices rise more dramatically and are always at a higher level in, for example, California than they are in Alabama. These issues are explored in many of the other contributions to this book. However, the same could be said about stock prices during the technology bubble—rare stocks in tight supply (e.g., dot.coms) did much better than widely held stocks (e.g., stocks in the DJIA). The same was true of tulip bulbs during the Tulip Mania that happened in seventeenth-century Holland—rare species were affected more by monetary conditions than ordinary species, but they all went up in price (see French, 2006).

The ABC theory expects prices in general to rise, but not to rise uniformly. The extent of the rise depends on both where the money is being injected and the flexibility of the supply side of the markets where the injections are taking place. However, if we consider the national price index for the typical 1996 one-family house between 1998 and 2005 we find that prices have increased by 45 percent, which is 1.25 times larger than the increase in the Consumer Price Index. According to the

**Figure 11.7**
**Privately Owned Housing Starts: 1-Unit Structures (Thousands of Units)**

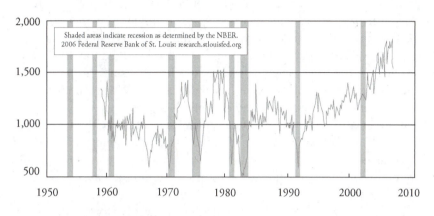

Source: U.S. Department of Commerce: Census Bureau.

Bureau of the Census, the price of the average house, as opposed to the "typical" house, has been increasing even faster, which indicates that people are buying bigger more expensive homes as well. The price dimension—while muted somewhat by the economy's ability to produce greater quantities of housing—still indicates a large increase in the real price of housing. We should also remember that new housing is generally is built on lower-priced land, that house-building technology has reduced building costs, and that the large influx of labor from Mexico has also helped hold down labor costs.

### 3. Must Come Down

The ABC theory shows that government failure is responsible for starting the housing bubble in the first place. The monetary policies of the Fed have caused resources to be allocated in an ultimately unsustainable fashion. In a housing bubble too many houses are built, houses of the wrong sort are built, and houses are built in the wrong locations based on the underlying fundamentals of the economy and people's real desires for housing not artificially stimulated by monetary inflation by the Fed. While most people are very happy during boom times, the Austrian economists view the boom as the real problem because this is where resources are misallocated. This is also when people become financially overextended and engage in excessive luxury spending (Kostigen, 2006). Inflationary periods tend to be when the rich get richer and the poor get poorer.

The bubble must come to an end because it is based on an irrational allocation of resources caused by the Fed's misleading interest rate policy. Money that is tied up in an asset bubble initially prevents monetary inflation from being revealed as price inflation as measured by the Consumer Price Index. However, if the monetary pumping is used to purchase assets like stocks, bonds, or real estate then the inflation is revealed in the price of those assets, which will rise even though the underlying earnings of the assets has not improved. When money begins to leak out of asset bubbles into consumption, then the price of goods that are used to construct the Consumer Price Index (CPI) will begin to rise. The asset bubble is popped or deflated when interest rates rise. This can occur when either the market raises rates due to rising inflation premiums on loans or when the Fed tries to curtail increases in the CPI by preemptively raising rates.

The bursting of the bubble reveals the cluster of errors in the housing market and related industries and begins the process of reallocating resources to their best uses by changes in prices, buying and selling, relocation, bankruptcy, and unemployment. The macroeconomic effect of deflating the bubble is that it causes the economy to go into recession or depression. However, the effects of the bubble will also be concentrated as it is deflated. Notice in Figure 11.8 that the bubble (as described by employment in the construction industry) began in 1997 when it rose above the level of the channel, which dates back to the end of World War II. Notice too that the trend in construction employment has always been negative during recessionary periods—even the recession of 2001—and that the negative trends often begin prior to and extend beyond the periods identified as recession. Because the trends in construction employment have been so strong for so long during the housing bubble, it would not be surprising that the negative impact of the bubble would take on a similar, but negative effect on construction employment and spending, and that these effects would spread beyond to the construction materials industry, mortgage lending, real estate sales, furniture, appliances, and household goods items.

Another natural concern about the bursting of the housing bubble is the indebtedness of the average American. As we previously have shown, the personal savings rate of Americans has been declining for many years, in part due to the fact that Americans have felt wealthier due to the rising price of their real estate properties. This is then coupled with the rising debt of the average American household. As shown in Figure 11.9, total household debt was less than $500 billion when the United States went

**Figure 11.8**
**All Employees: Construction (Thousands)**

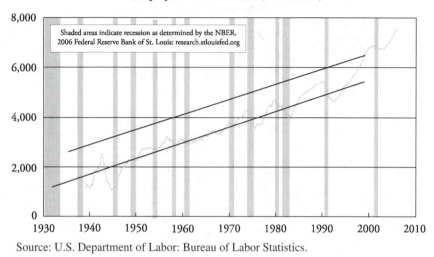

Shaded areas indicate recession as determined by the NBER.
2006 Federal Reserve Bank of St. Louis: research.stlouisfed.org

Source: U.S. Department of Labor: Bureau of Labor Statistics.

off the gold standard in 1971, first exceeded $5 trillion in 1996 and $10 trillion in 2004. In October of 2005, the last reported period, total debt exceeded $11.5 trillion. Certainly these figures should be adjusted for inflation, population, and economic growth, but that does not reverse the fact that many Americans have taken on a large amount of debt and have not set aside a similar amount of saving to offset this debt or to insulate themselves from periods of economic distress.

As the economy goes into recession and unemployment increases, homeowners with large mortgages will have a difficult time making their monthly payments and may face the possibility of bankruptcy. This "squeeze" will be compounded by the fact that many homeowners have taken equity out of their homes in recent years, increasing the size of their mortgage. Further difficulties are presented by the fact that a large percentage of borrowers have taken out variable-rate mortgages rather than fixed rate mortgages, which means that their monthly payment will rise substantially when interest rates increase. With some variable rate mortgages the monthly payment stays the same, but then the principal on the loan increases when rates rise, which could place these borrowers "upside down" on the homes—which means the mortgage would be much larger than the value of the home. Lenders have also been providing mortgage loans based on much smaller down payments (in percentage terms) with some lenders even providing loans that exceed 100 percent

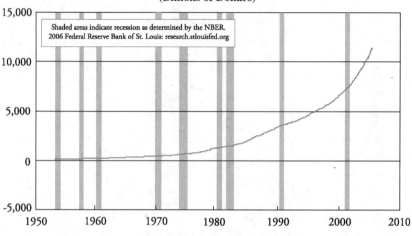

Figure 11.9
Household Sector: Liabilities: Household Credits Market Debt Outstanding
(Billions of Dollars)

Source: Board of Goverors of the Federal Reserve System.

of the price of the house. All of this points to the likelihood of a large number of foreclosures and bankruptcies. This in turn points our attention to the stability of the banking and mortgage lending industries and the likelihood of a taxpayer bailout of banks and government-sponsored institutions like Freddie Mac that buy mortgage loans from lenders.

## 4. Summary and Conclusions

There are three views of the housing bubble. The mainstream view does not believe in bubbles and attributes such changes in the economy to real factors such as technology shocks, and believes there is nothing the government can do to solve such real problems. The Keynesian view is that bubbles exist because of psychological instabilities in the economy, not real factors, and that countercyclical policies of the government should be used to tame the business cycle. The Austrian business cycle (i.e., ABC) theory incorporates real and psychological changes into a view where bubbles are caused by the policy manipulation of the Federal Reserve.

The housing bubble that began in the late 1990s is a classic example of government failure as applied to the housing crisis. Inflation of the money supply that accompanied the Fed's cheap credit policy led to a borrowing and building binge of an unprecedented scale. The number of new homes built, the price of new and existing homes, and the to- tal amount of real estate investment all indicate that the Fed's policy, combined with a favorable tax policy and taxpayer-subsidized lending practices, created the housing bubble.

The bubble is not just a bunch of hot air. Real resources are involved, which have been misdirected during the bubble and which will have to make painful adjustments in the aftermath of the bubble. This will involve unemployment, foreclosure, and bankruptcy for many people, especially those in the construction and construction-related industries. The macro economy will be sent into a recession or depression, which could be of a lengthy duration because of the slowness of the housing market as compared to the stock market, which can process very large changes in value within the period of one market day.

The lesson of the housing bubble is that what at first appeared to be the government trying to help improve homeownership for Americans has been a giant government failure and will have the unintended effect of economically scaring many homeowners, particularly those who bought houses at the peak of the bubble. Others have been fooled into extracting equity from their homes, increasing their mortgages and taking loans, such as variable-rate loans, which they believed were necessary to qualify to buy houses at inflated prices.   Similar trends in housing have occurred in countries around the world as many of the world's central banks have been engaged in monetary pumping that has been injected into their housing sectors.

The policy lesson of the housing bubble, as provided by the ABC theory, is that the Fed is responsible for the housing bubble as well as the normal booms and busts in the economy, and that as long as it retains its authority to set what are in effect price controls on interests rates, such bubbles will periodically appear in the economy. Federal policy toward housing should be guided by the principles neutrality, laissez faire, and do no harm.[14]

## 5. Postscript (08/08/08)

The housing and financial crisis discussed in this chapter is now well underway and we may well have entered the worst global economic crisis of this generation. The question of how economic policy will address these problems has also been revealed in that the Federal Reserve and the U.S. Treasury have initiated aggressive and unprecedented policy responses. Under the cover of preventing a financial market meltdown, these policy responses are really attempts to bailout the owners of large financial business. They will do little to help the housing market and will increase the overall economic harm of the housing bubble.

Will policy responses continue to be aggressive and unprecedented in the direction of greater government centralization and power as the economic crisis worsens? The importance of this question goes beyond any measure of economic harm because it can result in fundamental changes in society. It could of course result in correct economic reforms such as the abolition of the Federal Reserve, the restoration of the gold standard, and the abandonment of Federal government subsidies to housing, but as I wrote in the initial draft of this chapter (06/06/06):

> On top of all that, people suffer psychological consequences as well. The people most involved in the bubble are confident, jubilant, and self-assured by their apparently successful decision making. When the bubble bursts they lose confidence, go into despair and lose confidence in their decision making. In fact, they lose confidence in the "system," which means they lose confidence in capitalism and become susceptible to new political "reforms" that offer structure and security in exchange for some of their autonomy and freedoms.
>
> In this manner, great nations of people have given away their liberties in exchange for security. The Russians submitted to Communism and the Germans submitted to National Socialism because of economic chaos. In 20th century America, economic crises—and fear more generally—provided the justification for the adoption of "reforms" such as a central bank (i.e. the Federal Reserve), the New Deal, the Cold War, and even fiat money during the economic crisis of the early 1970s.[15] Fear of terrorism after 9/11 resulted in a massive transfer of power to government at the expense of individual liberty.[16] Submission of liberty and individual autonomy in exchange for security and the "greater good" is now often referred to as choosing the dark side.[17]

The reason economic crises create fear and submission of liberty is that people do not generally know what caused the bust or economic crisis and generally do not even know that there was even a bubble in the first place. In fact, as the bubble is bursting many people will deny that there is a problem and believe that the whole situation will quickly return to what they consider normal. The average citizen thinks very little about what makes the economy work, but simply accepts the system for what it is, and tries to make the most of it.

Increased government intervention in housing markets and the virtual socialization of the Government-Sponsored Entities (GSEs such as Fannie Mae), and the risk of mortgage-backed securities indicates that this dangerous trend will continue.

## Notes

1.    The author would like to thank Robert Blumen, Kevin Duffy, Robert Ekelund, Mike Pollaro, Jeff Scot, Jeffrey Tucker, Doug Wakefield, Paul Wicks and the editors of the book for their commentary and assistance. All error remains my responsibility.
2.    An easy money policy involves the central bank—the Fed—setting low interest rates and expanding the money supply so that it is easier to get credit (i.e., loans)

and it also involves government-sponsored credit organizations like Fannie Mae and Freddie Mac who make getting home mortgages easier.

3.    The Austrian school of economics is based on the writings of Carl Menger. It was members of the German historical school who coined the term to derisively describe Menger and his students. Ludwig von Mises and F. A. Hayek developed the Austrian business cycle theory, which rests on the foundation laid by Richard Cantillon in his 1730 book (See Thornton, forthcoming). Interestingly, former Fed chairman Alan Greenspan attended Ludwig von Mises's New York seminar and is thought to have been influenced by it, although as Fed chairman he has distanced himself from the Misesian approach.

4.    An important justification for stressing the ABC theory is the success of its practitioners in correctly predicting previous bubbles. See for example Thornton (2004d).

5.    *Homo Economicus* is the model of the rational economic person that economists use to build their models and theories about the economy. This assumption asserts that people are rational and will always attempt to maximize their utility. This is a source of contention and misunderstanding among economists and between economists and other social scientists.

6.    In the latest restatement of the Austrian business cycle theory by Hülsmann (1998).

7.    All of our actions involve some speculation about the future. Here "speculative" behavior refers to actions that involve great risks that are unwarranted based on the normal or known fundamentals of the economy. For example, betting on a round of golf with your friend involves some speculation and uncertainty, but past experience provides some guidance to the risks you are taking. Here, betting on a round of golf with Tiger Woods would be "speculative."

8.    It is a common misconception that corporate scandal is the source of bubbles and that it was companies like Enron and WorldCom that tricked investors during the late 1990s to bid up the stock markets to such high levels. It is true that scandal is a common feature of bubbles, but scandal could never account for more than a small percentage of bubbles and in reality scandal is caused by the same source as the bubble itself—the existence of cheap and abundant credit which must be allocated to increasingly risky and suspect investments.

9.    Another possible example of this is Baker and Rosnick (2005) who demonstrate the case for a housing bubble and do so in a manner similar to Austrian economists. Even though they date the beginning of the bubble to 1997 they ignore the real factor that tax law changes in that year were a catalyst to housing and higher housing prices.

10.    A fellow traveler is someone who sympathizes with or supports various tenets of the Austrian school without being an acknowledged member or embracing all aspects of Austrian economics.

11.    More roundabout production processes are production processes that use advanced technology and require more time to complete, but are more productive. An example of a direct production process would be a dairy farmer who produces milk, processes it and sells it to people in the vicinity of his farm. A more roundabout technique would be dairy farmers who sell their milk to a central processing facility (with advanced technology) of a national company with headquarters in a different state and who in turn sell to wholesalers and retailers all over the region.

12.    The Philadelphia Housing Sector stock index apparently peaked at the end of August 2005.

13.    MZM is a relatively new measure of the money supply and one that is close to the Austrian school definition of money, which is that "money" is immediately

redeemable at par. MZM includes currency, demand deposits (checking accounts), traveler's checks, savings deposits, and deposits in money market mutual funds.

14.   For recent statements concerning Austrian recommendations for reform regarding the money and the business cycles see Herbener (2002) and Cochran (2004).

15.   Higgs (1987) shows how crisis (such as war or depression) lead to large increases in the size of government that were only partially offset by cutbacks after the crisis was over. On the final page of the book Higgs correctly predicted that future crises would include terrorism in addition to war and depression.

16.   Higgs (2005, p. 4) correctly predicted (in the days immediately after 9/11) that among other things that government would greatly expand its power "particularly surveillance of ordinary citizens."

17.   A crisis is a crossroad or turning point where the decision maker can make the correct or incorrect choice. The wrong, fear driven choice is now often referred to as choosing the "dark side" a la *Star Wars* movies. See Thornton (2005).

# References

Baker, Dean and David Rosnick. 2005. Will a Bursting Bubble Trouble Bernanke? Evidence for a Housing Bubble. Washington, DC.: Center for Economic and Policy Research, November. Available at: http://www.cepr.net/publications/housing_bubble_2005_11.pdf

Bernanke, Ben S. 2006a. Speech to the Independent Community Bankers of America National Convention and Techworld, Las Vegas, Nevada, March 8. Available at: http://www.federalreserve.gov/BoardDocs/Speeches/2006/20060308/default.htm.

Bernanke, Ben S. 2006b. Reflections on the Yield Curve and Monetary Policy. Remarks before the Economic Club of New York, March 20. Available at: http://www.federalreserve.gov/boarddocs/speeches/2006/20060320/default.htm.

Bruno, Joe B. 2006. Former Fed Chair Says Housing Boom Over. Associated Press, May 19. Available at: http://biz.yahoo.com/ap/060519/greenspan_speech.html?.v=2.

Bureau of the Census. Price Indexes of New One-Family Houses Sold. Available at: http://www.census.gov/const/price_sold.pdf.

Callahan, Gene and Roger W. Garrison. 2003. Does the Austrian Theory of the Business Cycle explain the Dot.com Boom and Bust? *Quarterly Journal of Austrian Economics.* 6 (summer): 67–98.

Cantillon, Richard. 1755 [1931]. *Essai sur la Nature du Commerce en Général.* Edited with an English translation by Henry Higgs, London: Frank Cass and Company.

Cochran, John P. 2004. Capital, Monetary Calculation, and the Trade Cycle: The Importance of Sound Money. *Quarterly Journal of Austrian Economics.* 7 (spring): 17–25.

French, Doug. 2006. The Dutch Monetary Environment during Tulipmania. *Quarterly Journal of Austrian Economics.* 9 (spring): 3–14.

Gallaway, Lowell and Richard Vedder. 2000. The Fraud of Macroeconomic Stabilization Policy. *Quarterly Journal of Austrian Economics.* 3 (fall): 19–33.

Greenspan, Alan. 2002. Monetary Policy and the Economic Outlook. Testimony before the Joint Economic Committee of the U.S. Congress, April 17. Available at: http://www.federalreserve.gov/boarddocs/testimony/2002/20020417/default.htm.

Greenspan, Alan. 2005a. Reflections on Central Banking. Speech given at a symposium sponsored by the Federal Reserve Bank of Kansas City, Jackson Hole, Wyoming August 26. Available at: http://www.federalreserve.gov/Boarddocs/Speeches/2005/20050826/default.htm.

Greenspan, Alan. 2005b. Mortgage Banking. Speech to the American Bankers Association Annual Convention, Palm Desert, California (via satellite), September 26. Available at: http://www.federalreserve.gov/BOARDDOCS/SPEECHES/2005/200509262/default.htm.

Hays, Kathleen. 2005. Greenspan steps up criticism of Fannie: Fed chief says company and Freddie Mac have exploited their relationship with the Treasury. *CNN.com,* May 19. Available at: http://money.cnn.com/2005/05/19/news/economy/greenspan_fannie/.

Herbener, Jeffrey M. 2002. After the Age of Inflation: Austrian Proposals for Monetary Reform. *Quarterly Journal of Austrian Economics.* 5 (winter): 5–19.

Higgs, Robert. 1987. *Crisis and Leviathan: Critical Episodes in the Growth of American Government.* New York: Oxford University Press.

Higgs, Robert. 2005. *Resurgence of the Warfare State: The Crisis Since 9/11.* Oakland, Calif: The Independent Institute.

Holcombe, Randall G. 1995. *Public Policy and the Quality of Life: Market Incentives versus Government Planning.* Westport, Conn: Greenwood Press.

Hülsmann, Jörg Guido. 1998. Toward a General Theory of Error Cycles. *Quarterly Review of Austrian Economics.* 4 (winter): 1–23.

Kostigen, Thomas. 2006. Skewed views: If the rich are doing so well, how much worse off are the rest of us? *MarketWatch,* May 23. Available at: http://www.marketwatch.com/News/Story/Story.aspx?guid=%7B3003D864–9DF1–4829–8DB3–01E56C3A0F70%7D&siteid=google.

Krugman, Paul, 2005a. Running out of Bubbles. *New York Times.* May 27. Available at: http://www.nytimes.com/2005/05/27/opinion/27krugman.html?ex=1274846400&en=ee73a0d5d3c35710&ei=5088&partner=rssnyt&emc=rss.

Krugman, Paul. 2005b. That Hissing Sound. *New York Times,* August 8. Available at: http://www.nytimes.com/2005/08/08/opinion/08krugman.html?ex=1281153600&en=7125767d2baf3fae&ei=5088&partner=rssnyt&emc=rss.

Lloyd, Carol. 2006. Home Sweet Cash Cow: How our houses are financing our lives. *SFGate.com,* March 10. Available at: http://www.sfgate.com/cgi-bin/article.cgi?file=/gate/archive/2006/03/10/carollloyd.DTL.

McCarthy, Jonathan and Richard W. Peach. 2004. Are Home Prices the Next "Bubble"? *FRBNY Economic Policy Review* (December): 1–17.

Meyer, Christopher. 2003. The Housing Bubble. *The Free Market* (August). Available at: http://www.mises.org/freemarket_detail.asp?control=450.

Mises, Ludwig von. 1912 [1981]. *The Theory of Money and Credit.* Indianapolis, Ind.: Liberty Classics.

Shiller, Robert J. 2000. *Irrational Exuberance.* Princeton, N.J.: Princeton University Press.

Shiller, Robert J. 2004. Are Housing Prices a House of Cards? Project-Syndicate.org, September. Available at: http://www.project-syndicate.org/commentary/shiller17.

Shiller, Robert J. 2005. *Irrational Exuberance.* 2nd Edition. Princeton, N.J.: Princeton University Press.

Shostak, Frank. 2003. Housing Bubble: Myth or Reality? *Mises Daily Article* (on line), March 04. Available at: http://www.Mises.org/story/1177.

Shostak, Frank. 2004. Who Made the Fannie and Freddie Threat?" *Mises Daily Article* (on line), March 05. Available at: http://www.Mises.org/story/1463.

Thornton, Mark. 2004a. Bull Market? *LewRockwell.com,* February 9. Available at: http://www.lewrockwell.com/thornton/thornton11.html.

Thornton, Mark. 2004b. Greenspam. *LewRockwell.com,* February 16. Available at: http://www.LewRockwell.com/thornton/thornton13.html.

Thornton, Mark. 2004c. Housing: Too Good to be True. *Mises Daily Article* (on line), June 04. Available at: http://www.Mises.org/story/1533.

Thornton, Mark. 2004d. Who Predicted the Bubble? Who Predicted the Crash? *The Independent Review.* 9 (summer): 5–30.

Thornton, Mark. 2005a. Skyscrapers and Business Cycles. *Quarterly Journal of Austrian Economics.* 8 (spring): 51–74.

Thornton, Mark. 2005b. What is the "Dark Side" and Why Do Some People Choose It? *Mises Daily Articles* (on-line), May 13. Available at: http://www.mises.org/articles. asp.

Thornton, Mark. 2006. Cantillon on the Cause of the Business Cycle. *Quarterly Journal of Austrian Economics* 9 (3): 45–60.

# 12

# Fannie Mae, Freddie Mac, and Housing: Good Intentions Gone Awry

*Lawrence J. White*

The Federal National Mortgage Association (Fannie Mae) and the Federal Home Loan Mortgage Corporation (Freddie Mac) are the two dominant entities in the secondary market for residential mortgages in the United States. They are also special organizations, in many ways, and their dominance and large size owe much to their specialness.

This chapter will discuss and describe these two companies and their special status in the U.S. residential mortgage market, with the recommendation that their special status be terminated—i.e., that they be truly privatized. We also recommend a set of additional reform measures that would improve the efficiency of housing construction and consumption in the U.S. economy. Along the way, we will address a number of major issues that concern housing and its special place in the political landscape of America and we add an August 2008 postscript.[1]

## 1. Fannie and Freddie: The Basics

### A. *What They Do*

As of year-end 2004, Fannie Mae ($989 billion in assets) and Freddie Mac ($795 billion in assets) were the fourth and sixth largest companies in the United States, respectively, when ranked by assets.[2] In addition, these two companies are the largest issuers of residential mortgage-backed securities (MBS): Fannie Mae had $1,598 billion in MBS outstanding as of year-end 2005; Freddie Mac's outstanding MBS totaled $974 billion.

These two large companies focus all of their business activity on the residential mortgage market. In that market, they do primarily two things:

(1)    Fannie Mae and Freddie Mac create and issue MBS, by swapping their newly created MBS for the residential mortgages that have been originated by commercial banks, savings institutions, and mortgage banks.[3] In essence, the MBS represent pass-through claims on pools of underlying residential mortgages. The holders of the MBS get the (passed-through) interest and principal payments of the mortgage borrowers, less a "guarantee fee" charged by Fannie Mae and Freddie Mac.[4] The guarantees of the two companies protect the MBS holders against losses due to "credit risk" (i.e., against the possibility that the borrower fails to repay her mortgage loan).[5] The mortgage originators can sell their swapped MBS into the secondary market for these securities or hold the MBS as relatively liquid assets in their portfolios.

(2)    Fannie Mae and Freddie Mac buy their own MBS in the secondary market (as well as buying some "whole loan" mortgages directly from originators) and hold these mortgages[6] in their portfolios as assets. These assets have been funded largely (97 percent) by debt issued by the two companies and to a much lesser extent (3 percent) by equity.

## B. Who They Are

Fannie Mae was created in 1938, under the auspices of the National Housing Act of 1934. Until 1968, Fannie Mae was formally part of the federal government, issuing debt and purchasing and holding in portfolio residential government-insured[7] mortgages that it purchased from mortgage bank originators. In 1968, Fannie Mae was converted into a private corporation, with publicly traded shares listed on the New York Stock Exchange (NYSE), although it retained a unique federal charter with attributes that will be discussed below.[8]

Freddie Mac was created by act of Congress in 1970 to support mortgage markets by securitizing (i.e., issuing MBS) that were originated by savings and loan associations (S&Ls).[9] During the 1970s and 1980s, Freddie Mac was technically a private company, with its shares held by the 12 Federal Home Loan Banks (FHLBs) and by the S&Ls that were members of the FHLB system. In 1989 Freddie Mac was converted into a publicly traded company, with shares listed on the NYSE and with the same special features (to be discussed below) as apply to Fannie Mae.[10]

Table 12.1 shows the major size dimensions of the two companies over the period 1971—2005. Especially noteworthy is the rapid growth of both companies between 1990 and 2000 and between 2000 and 2003. The reasons for that growth will be addressed below.

## C. Their Special Features

As was mentioned above, Fannie Mae and Freddie Mac are publicly traded companies, whose shares trade on the NYSE. They are, however,

**Table 12.1**
**Fannie Mae and Freddie Mac Assets and Mortgage**
**Backed Securities, and the Residential Mortgage Market**
**(in billions of dollars)**

| Year | Fannie Mae | | | Freddie Mac | | | |
|------|------------|---|---|-------------|---|---|---|
| | Total Assets | Retained Mortgage portfolio[a] | Mortgage-Backed securities outstanding[b] | Total Assets | Retained Mortgage portfolio[a] | Mortgage-Backed securities outstanding[b] | Total non-farm, residential mortgages |
| 1971 | $19 | $18 | $0 | $1 | $1 | $0.1 | $388 |
| 1975 | 32 | 31 | 0 | 6 | 5 | 2 | 575 |
| 1980 | 58 | 56 | 0 | 6 | 5 | 17 | 1,100 |
| 1985 | 99 | 94 | 55 | 17 | 14 | 100 | 1,724 |
| 1990 | 133 | 114 | 288 | 41 | 22 | 316 | 2,903 |
| 1995 | 317 | 253 | 513 | 137 | 108 | 459 | 3,727 |
| 2000 | 675 | 608 | 707 | 459 | 386 | 576 | 5,581 |
| 2001 | 800 | 707 | 859 | 641 | 504 | 653 | 6,019 |
| 2002 | 888 | 801 | 1,030 | 752 | 590 | 730 | 6,731 |
| 2003 | 1,010 | 902 | 1,300 | 803 | 661 | 752 | 7,581 |
| 2004 | 989 | 905 | 1,403 | 795 | 665 | 852 | 8,642 |
| 2005 | n.a. | 727 | 1,598 | 806 | 710 | 974 | 9,851 |

Note: Includes single- and multi-family mortgages.
[a] Includes repurchased mortgage-backed securities.
[b] Excludes mortgage-backed securities that are held in the company's own portfolio.
Sources: Federal Reserve; OFHEO; Fannie Mae; Freddie Mac

different from any other publicly traded company in the United States, in a number of important ways:

- The corporate charter of each company is based on an act of Congress, rather than being granted by the corporation department of one of the 50 states;
- The president of the United States can appoint 5 of each company's 18 board members;[11]
- Neither company pays any state or local income taxes;
- The U.S. Treasury is authorized to purchase up to $2.25 billion of each company's securities;[12]
- The two companies' securities are "government securities" under the Securities Exchange Act of 1934;
- The two companies are not required to register their securities with the Securities and Exchange Commission (SEC);[13] they are exempt from SEC fees;

- The two companies' securities can be purchased in unlimited quantities by banks and saving institutions;[14]
- The two companies' securities can be purchased by the Federal Reserve for open-market operations;
- The two companies can use the Federal Reserve as their fiscal agent; and
- The insolvency of either company must be resolved by the Congress, rather than by a regulator or by a bankruptcy court.

Virtually all of the above-listed features would be considered as advantages for the two companies. They are also subject to substantial limitations:

- The two companies are allowed to engage only in residential mortgage finance;
- The two companies cannot originate mortgages;
- The mortgages that the two companies can buy or securitize are subject to a maximum value (usually described as the "conforming loan limit"); for 2006 that ceiling is $417,000;[15]
- The two companies are subject to "mission" regulation by HUD, which sets targets for "affordable housing" mortgages that the companies should purchase or securitize;
- The two companies are subject to "safety-and-soundness" regulation by the Office of Federal Housing Enterprise Oversight (OFHEO),[16] which aims to keep them adequately capitalized and operating in a safe-and-sound manner (and thus to avoid their becoming insolvent);[17] and
- The U.S. Treasury must approve all debt issuances by the two companies.[18]

## D. The Consequences

The two companies clearly have a special and extensive involvement with the federal government;[19] it is no accident that the two companies are often described as "government-sponsored enterprises" (GSEs). As a consequence, the financial markets treat them in a special way: The two companies are able to borrow on more favorable terms (i.e., at lower interest rates) than their financial status would otherwise justify. Typically, the two companies can borrow at rates that are better than those that apply to a AAA-rated company (though not quite as good as the rates that apply to U.S. Treasury debt), even though the two companies' stand-alone (i.e., absent their special position) financial ratings would be about AA- or less. For their straight debt, this translates into about a 35–40 basis point advantage;[20] similarly, for their MBS, they enjoy about a 30 basis point advantage.

In essence, their special status has convinced the financial markets that, in the event that either company were to be in financial difficulty and could not honor its obligations, the federal government would very likely step in and "bail out" the company (and thus bail out the company's creditors).[21] This apparent belief by the financial markets has come to be described as the markets' belief in an "implicit guarantee" by the federal government—which is remarkable, since the legislative acts creating the two companies, as well as every one of their securities, carries explicit language that states that the two companies' securities are not the obligations of the U.S. Government. Counteracting this language, however, is the historical experience: In the late 1980s the Federal Government did provide a bailout for the Farm Credit System (which enjoyed similar special GSE benefits and relationships with the federal government); and in the late 1970s and early 1980s, though Fannie Mae was insolvent on a market-value basis, the federal government exercised forbearance and did not move to close or liquidate the company. Also, government officials—even in the otherwise GSE-hostile Bush administration—have not explicitly repudiated the "implicit guarantee." Instead, they have tiptoed around the subject, reminding the public that there is no explicit guarantee but *not* also stating that they would never consider a bailout.

To the extent that the financial markets are correct in their judgment, U.S. taxpayers are at risk in the event of financial difficulties at either company.[22] This at-risk posture is a clear justification for OFHEO's safety-and-soundness regulation and highlights its importance.[23]

In turn, the two companies' activities in the secondary market for residential mortgages cause conforming mortgage loans to be about 20–25 basis points less than "jumbo" mortgages that are larger than the conforming loan limit. This reduction in the cost of mortgage borrowing (for conforming loans) is, of course, the primary reason for the two companies' creation by the Congress and the Congress's continuing support for them.[24]

In addition, the two companies' presence in the secondary mortgage market may well be a stabilizing influence. Historically, the two companies were able to bring greater uniformity and unification to what otherwise would have regionally fragmented mortgage markets, since during most of the twentieth century regulatory restrictions on interstate branching by banks and S&Ls were present and prevented these institutions from bringing this unification. The two companies were also stabilizing influences in the mortgage markets immediately after the stock market free-fall of October 1987, the nervousness that accompanied the demise of Long Term Capital Management in September 1998, and the market distress that followed September 11, 2001. In addition, the two companies' size and importance in the secondary mortgage market may have caused them to be focal points for the standardization of mortgage origination and processing and for the transmission of technological advances in these areas. Finally, it is clear that (along with Ginnie Mae) Freddie Mac in the 1970s and then Fannie Mae also in the 1980s were important in the development of the secondary mortgage market and of mortgage securitization as an alternative mechanism for the financing of residential mortgages.

### E. Why Did They Grow So Fast?

The growth of the two companies between 1990 and 2000 and between 2000 and 2003—in terms of both their portfolios sizes and their stocks of outstanding MBS—was truly breathtaking and warrants some further explanation.

There is little question that part of this growth was due to the blossoming of a new and efficient technology for financing residential mortgages: mortgage securitization. But there was more going on as well. Partly, the securitization process was aided by the capital requirements that applied to banks and S&Ls in their holdings of residential mortgages and MBS. For holding "whole loan" residential mortgages, the depository institutions were required to maintain 4 percent capital; for holding MBS, they were required to maintain only 1.6 percent capital.[25] Though holding the GSEs' MBS meant that the depository institution also had to give up 20 basis points of yield (as payment to the GSEs for the latter's guarantees), the substantially reduced capital requirement usually more-than-compensated for the slightly reduced yield. Also, the MBS had a further advantage in being a more liquid and transactable asset than the equivalent pool of whole loan residential mortgages.

In addition, Fannie Mae and Freddie Mac were required to maintain only 2.5 percent capital (as compared with the depositories' 4 percent requirement) for holding mortgages in their own portfolios, and they could float debt with the 35–40 basis-point borrowing advantage discussed above, which gave them an advantage in acquiring mortgages and MBS for their own portfolios.

Finally, in 1989 Freddie Mac became a publicly traded company, and its senior management clearly saw rapid expansion, using high leverage (97 percent debt) and a favorable borrowing rate, as an excellent way to achieve rapid earnings growth for its shareholders. The senior management of Fannie Mae, after being traumatized by the high interest rates of the late 1970s and early 1980s, which meant that the market value of the company's mortgage portfolio shrunk below the value of its outstanding debt obligations, finally established a more solid financial foundation for the company and, like Freddie Mac, saw rapid, leveraged growth as the way to earn high and growing returns for the company's shareholders.

*F. Recent Events*

In early 2003, Freddie Mac's new external auditor (PriceWaterhouse-Coopers)[26] raised substantial questions about the company's accounting practices. These questions eventually led to the removal of the company's senior management and an agreement with OFHEO to maintain higher levels of capital than had previously been necessary, which effectively brought the company's rapid growth to a halt.

The accounting scandal at Freddie Mac clearly took OFHEO by surprise. The senior management of the agency then decided that a closer look at Fannie Mae's accounting was warranted, which led to the agency's determination in September 2004 that Fannie Mae's accounting too was seriously flawed. The company appealed this decision to the Securities and Exchange Commission, which sided with OFHEO. In early 2005 the senior management of the company was removed, and it too agreed to higher capital levels, which necessitated slower growth and actual shrinkage of assets.

In an important sense, the accounting scandals at the two companies were "sideshows" with respect to the important policy and regulatory issues that are the subject of this chapter. But the scandals did embarrass the two companies' political allies and provided the companies' critics with the opportunity to be able to say, in essence, "Look, things can go wrong at these two companies, and the next time the mistakes may be at the taxpayers' expense." Also, in both cases, OFHEO negotiated agreements that required the companies to maintain higher levels of capital, which slowed the companies' growth.[27]

## 2. The Major Issues

*A. Housing and Homeownership*

The special position of Fannie Mae and Freddie Mac is not an incidental or accidental feature of government policy. Instead, the two companies' GSE status can be understood as part of a larger mosaic of efforts by governments at all levels in the United States to encourage housing consumption and homeownership. This wide range of government policies, past and present, has included:

- Tax advantages: the exclusion of the implicit income from housing by owner-occupiers for income tax purposes while allowing the deduction of mortgage interest and local real estate taxes; the partial exemption of owner-occupied houses from capital gains taxes; accelerated depreciation on rental housing; and special tax credits, exemptions, and deductions;
- Rent subsidization programs;
- Subsidization of home down payments;
- Direct government provision of rental housing ("public housing");
- Mortgage insurance provided by FHA and VA;
- Securitization of FHA- and VA-insured mortgages by Ginnie Mae;
- Securitization of conforming mortgages by Fannie Mae and Freddie Mac;
- Purchases of conforming mortgages for portfolio holdings by Fannie Mae and Freddie Mac;
- Separate depository charters for S&Ls, with mandates to invest in residential mortgages;
- Favorable funding for savings institutions and other depositories that provide substantial residential mortgage lending through membership in the Federal Home Loan Bank (FHLB) system (another GSE); and
- Federal deposit insurance for savings institutions and other depositories whose portfolios contain some residential mortgages.

"Too much is never enough" seems to be a fitting description for government policies toward housing.

The motives and goals for this broad array of policies are also broad and varied. Partly, housing can be a component of direct in-kind redistribution of income toward lower-income households (although this motive cannot justify the various income tax exclusions, exemptions, and deductions, which benefit primarily higher income households). Partly, enhanced sales revenues and employment for the residential construction industry (i.e., the home builders and their employees) and their complementary industry allies (e.g., real estate brokers, mortgage lenders, mortgage brokers, building materials suppliers, etc.) provide a powerful political base. And, partly, encouraging homeownership is seen as an important social/political goal (although policies that encourage rental housing would seem to be in conflict with that goal).

It is this last motive—encouraging homeownership—that is most closely associated with Fannie Mae and Freddie Mac[28] (as well as with the income tax deduction for owner-occupiers' mortgage interest and local real estate taxes and their partial exemption from capital gains taxes) and is thus worth addressing.

There are good theoretical arguments to support the idea that encouraging homeownership is a worthwhile goal. In principle, an owner-occupier can internalize the potential conflicts that can arise (because of asymmetric information problems) between tenant and landlord. Further, and more important from a social perspective, an owner-occupier household is more likely to become community-minded. Over the past decade a small but important empirical literature has developed that provides evidence-based support for these logical but previously unsupported arguments. In addition, homeownership has often provided a means for households to amass wealth: through the forced saving that occurs through the repayment of principal on a mortgage, and through the post-World War II phenomenon of generally rising home prices.

One should hasten to add that homeownership is not, and should not be, for everyone. A house is a large, relatively illiquid asset. The transactions costs of buying and selling are large. As a consequence, homeownership can impede labor force mobility when the best employment opportunity for an individual would necessitate moving (and incurring those large transaction costs). Also, house prices do not always rise in all periods in all geographic areas. Finally, some households may not have the steady income and/or the budgetary habits and discipline to be able to make the regular periodic mortgage payments that are required of homeowners.

Nevertheless, there clearly are net positive aspects to homeownership that extend beyond just the private gains to the home-owning household that could justify some social encouragement.

The logical implication of this line of argument is that social policy should focus on providing help at the margin—a monetary "nudge" that would push low- and moderate-income households that are on the cusp of a decision as to whether to stay as renters or to become homeowners to take the latter course of action. This nudge could take the form of assistance with a down payment or with monthly mortgage payments, or both. In essence, social policy should operate in a focused manner in the area that matters.

Though there are such focused programs,[29] the major forms of government assistance for housing mentioned above operate instead on a broad-swath basis—largely encouraging households who would likely buy anyway to buy a larger, better-appointed house on a larger lot (or to buy a second home). Since it is the act of being an owner-occupier that likely creates the positive externalities for a community, while the extent or amount of ownership would likely provide (at best) only secondary social benefits, such programs are extremely wasteful in terms of actually achieving the stated goal of encouraging more widespread homeownership.[30] Indeed, research over the past few decades has indicated that too much of the capital stock of the United States has been devoted to housing, at the expense of investments in physical industrial capital and human capital, with aggregate U.S. income suffering as a consequence. And since the tax-based incentives operate through deductions and exemptions (rather than tax credits), which are worth more to upper-income households with higher marginal tax rates, it is clearly not the low- and moderate-income households who are the major beneficiaries of these programs.

The Fannie Mae and Freddie Mac structure is in this broad-brush tradition, rather than being tightly focused. Recall that the conforming loan limit for 2006 is $417,000. This size mortgage, plus a 20 percent down payment, would allow a buyer to purchase a $521,000 home. Except for the "hot" real estate markets along the Atlantic and Pacific coasts, a $521,000 house would be considerably above average in most American communities.

This last point can be made more specific by using slightly historical data. In 2004 the conforming loan limit for Fannie Mae and Freddie Mac was $333,700, which would support the purchase of a $417,000 house. In that year the median price of a new home that was sold in the United States was only $221,000; the median price of an existing home that was sold was $184,000. Thus, the housing that can be bought through a Fannie Mae or Freddie Mac mortgage far exceeds what is likely to be bought by a first-time low- or moderate-income household homebuyer.

Of course, the two companies do also cater to low- and moderate-income households. HUD has set targets for their efforts with respect to "affordable housing," and the two companies have met those targets.[31] But the bulk of their mortgage purchases are not focused on the group that ought to be the target of ownership-encouraging activities. Indeed, when HUD in 2004 decided to ratchet-up these targets, a major support for this ratcheting was HUD's findings that the two companies' mortgage purchases of loans for low- and moderate-income households and for first-time buyers were below (on a percentage basis) those of all lenders for comparable residential mortgages. Consistent with this, it appears that the activities of the two companies have had little or no effect on the rate of homeownership in the United States.

In sum, the aggregate of housing policies in the United States have encouraged this country to over-invest in housing at the expense of other goods and services. The programs involving Fannie Mae and Freddie Mac have contributed to this over-investment in housing, while also not doing an especially good job of focusing on the low- and moderate-income first-time homebuyer where the social argument for encouraging homeownership is the strongest.

## B. Safety-and-Soundness Regulation

To the extent that the financial markets are correct in their belief in the "implicit guarantee" by the federal government of the two companies' debt issuances—i.e., that in the event that either company experienced financial difficulties and could not honor its obligations, the federal government would "bail out" the company (or, really, the company's creditors)—then the creditors will not monitor the companies as carefully as if the creditors believed that they would be fully exposed to any losses. In turn, this reduced monitoring would encourage the companies' managements to undertake riskier activities (than if they were more closely monitored), since the companies' owners would benefit from the "upside" of risky outcomes, while (because of the protections of limited liability) being buffered from the full consequences of the "downside" losses. The creditors' implicit guarantor—the federal government—is thus exposed to potential losses from such "moral hazard" behavior.

This problem of creditors exposed to moral hazard behavior by corporate managers is a general problem in a limited liability context. For most companies, lenders long ago came to understand this problem and learned how to protect themselves—e.g., through limitations on managements' actions that are embodied in bond covenants and banks' lending agreements, as well through direct monitoring arrangements. For banks and other depository institutions, where the creditors (i.e., depositors) are considered to be less able to protect themselves and the adverse consequences of the institution's insolvency are likely to be substantial, the states and the federal government have long understood that safety-and-soundness regulation[32] ought to be the public sector's counterpart to those private lenders' monitoring arrangements. Similar arguments underlie the states' safety-and-soundness regulation of insurance companies.

The federal government's exposure to potential losses from excessive risk-taking by Fannie Mae and Freddie Mac would logically call for a formal regime of safety-and-soundness regulation that would apply to the two companies. Only in 1992, however, did the Congress come to this realization, by enacting the Federal Housing Enterprises Financial Safety and Soundness Act. That Act created the Office of Federal Housing Enterprise Oversight (OFHEO), lodged in HUD, as the safety-and-soundness regulator of the two GSEs and instructed the agency to develop a set of forward-looking risk-based capital requirements that would apply to them. The agency required ten years before it was able to issue a final set of risk-based capital rules. That delay, plus Fannie Mae's revelation of a large exposure to interest-rate risk in 2002 and Freddie Mac's revelation in 2003 of an accounting scandal that required large revisions in its statements of recent years' income and balance sheet values,[33] reinforced a general perception that OFHEO was a weak and less than fully effective financial regulator. Though the agency gained a great deal of credibility through its vigorous investigation of Fannie Mae's accounting and the revelation in 2004 that the company too had manipulated its income statements and balance sheet values,[34] it has nevertheless been clear that the agency requires strengthening.

Some of the proposals that have been actively considered include:

- Moving the agency out of HUD (where the culture is focused on housing, and safety and soundness is a secondary consideration) and into the Treasury (where the culture is more focused on safety and soundness);
- Moving the agency out of the executive branch entirely and establishing it as a freestanding "independent" regulatory body, where it would be less susceptible to direct White House influence;
- Bringing the FHLBs, which are also GSEs and are currently regulated by a separate (and frequently criticized) agency—the FHFB—under the aegis of whatever agency emerges from the legislation;
- Strengthening the agency's ability to levy fees on Fannie Mae and Freddie Mac and thereby allowing it to fund itself in a way that would put it less at the mercy of the political vagaries of Congressional budgetary appropriations;
- Giving the agency full authority to revise the minimum capital requirements that the two companies must meet;
- Giving the agency a role in the setting of the social targets that the two companies must meet; and
- Giving the agency the power to appoint a receiver that could liquidate or otherwise dispose of either company's assets in the event that the company was unlikely to meet its minimum capital requirements and thus was perilously close to insolvency.

Though these proposals have been actively considered by the Congress for well over two years, and the two companies' formidable lobbying powers (that would oppose stronger regulatory restrictions) were thought to be considerably weakened by the accounting scandals that engulfed first the one company and then the other, and the Bush administration has made regulatory reform a high priority, no legislation had been passed as of the summer of 2006.

## C. Systemic Risk

As the two companies have grown substantially larger, concerns about the consequences of their size for systemic risk have increasingly been voiced, accompanied by proposals that would impose severe limits on the sizes of the two companies' mortgage portfolios. Systemic risk refers to the "system" effect that a financial failure of either company could have on mortgage markets generally or on financial institutions specifically. In an important sense, this is an adjunct to the safety-and-soundness issue, since how strongly one feels about the systemic risk issue should logically be linked to how one feels about the strength of the safety-and-soundness regulatory system.

The two companies are exposed primarily to two kinds of risk: credit risk, which is the risk that the underlying mortgage holder defaults on her mortgage (and the repossessed home is worth less than the value of the mortgage); and market risk, which is primarily the risk that interest rates change after the company has invested in a mortgage at a fixed interest rate. Credit risk applies to all of the mortgages associated with the two companies—those that they hold in portfolio and those that they securitize, since they offer guarantees to the holders of the latter. Market risk applies only to the mortgages that the two companies hold in their portfolios, since the holders of the MBS are holding a pass-through instrument and thus are the ones who are exposed to the interest rate risk on the underlying mortgages.

Credit risk is generally considered to be the lesser of the risks facing the two companies.[35] For the sixty years following the end of World War II, American housing markets have generally been strong, and housing prices have generally moved upward. The two companies' portfolio holdings and MBS are a large and nationally diversified stock and thus are unlikely to be seriously affected by scattered localized downturns. Further, the underwriting criteria used by mortgage originators—primarily adequate household income and a good credit history, supported by an appraisal on the house—are a good initial screen to protect the lender (or guarantor) against default. Also, the initial down payment of (typically) 20 percent, or mortgage insurance provided by a third party if the down payment is less than 20 percent, provides an initial buffer of protection.

Consistent with this optimistic picture, the credit losses by the two companies over the years 1987–2005 averaged less than 5 basis points (i.e., less than 0.05%) annually on their total exposure; for the years 1999–2005, their credit losses averaged only 1 basis point annually. Of course, if the U.S. economy were to experience the upheavals and collapse of housing prices and household incomes that occurred during the Great Depression, credit losses would be considerably higher. Still, credit losses are not where the concerns have been focused.

Instead, attention has centered on the two companies' market risk, which is exacerbated by the fact that the long-term fixed-rate mortgages that they hold can all be pre-paid by the borrowers with no penalties. The holder of a long-term fixed-rate debt instrument generally experiences a capital loss when interest rates rise but experiences a capital gain when interest rates fall. Pre-payable mortgages, however, are more likely to be pre-paid and refinanced (at the newly lower interest rates) when interest rates decline, so that the holder of the mortgage (or MBS) is less likely to experience a capital gain.

The two companies each have over $700 billion in residential mortgages in their portfolios, largely in the form of long-term fixed-rate mortgages that can be prepaid by the borrower at any time without a prepayment penalty. To some extent the companies offset this risk by issuing callable debt (so that, as mortgages prepay, the companies can call in the debt that has funded the mortgages). In addition, they use derivative instruments, such as interest-rate swaps and options on swaps, to construct obligations that largely match the profile of their mortgage assets.

The fear of critics is that this hedging process might go awry—because of sloppiness or cutting corners or counterparty failures. In that event, there surely would be effects on the mortgage and debt markets, because of the sheer size of the companies' portfolios and because even the holders of their MBS could become nervous. The size of the impact would depend on the extent of the apparent losses, on whether there would be a "contagion" effect that would affect the other company even if only one of the two initially experienced difficulties, and on how quickly the other major "players" in the mortgage markets could expand to take up the slack.[36] Because there never has been such an event, it is difficult to estimate how serious the effects on the residential markets would be.

## D. Efficiencies and Inefficiencies

Are the two companies efficient organizations for doing what they do? In an important sense, there is no "market test" for finding out the answer to this question. The Congress chartered only the two companies with their specific characteristics and special privileges. The ability of competitive processes to winnow inefficient firms from the marketplace is thereby inhibited. Though the FHLB system—another GSE—has entered the secondary residential mortgage market within the last decade, recent expansion by the FHLBs has been inhibited by capital limitations and some accounting difficulties of their own.

Further, the two companies are not required periodically to rebid for their franchises against potential replacements. In essence, they have been "grandfathered" indefinitely with respect to their special charters. Also, the market for corporate control cannot operate effectively: Their limited charters make them immune to takeover by any other firm, and their large size and special GSE status make them virtually immune to a "hostile" takeover by an outside investor group. Major accounting scandals and OFHEO pressure were required to remove the two companies' senior managements in the past few years.

As a related matter, any time that the two companies have attempted to expand either "horizontally" (e.g., into "subprime lending") or "vertically" (e.g., into providing underwriting software to mortgage originators)—or have contemplated such expansions—rivals have cried "foul" and complained that the companies' expansions were possible only because of their special borrowing advantages and not because of inherent synergies or efficiencies. Without a "clean" market test, there is no easy way to resolve such questions.

### 3. What Is to Be Done?

## A. First-Best

If there ever was a good social reason for the special GSE status of Fannie Mae and Freddie Mac—arguably, they helped unify local and regional mortgage markets at a time when banks and S&Ls could not due to regulatory barriers, and their special GSE status may well have helped the worthwhile technology of mortgage securitization gain traction in the financial markets—that time has since passed. Sunk benefits are sunk! Securitization is now a well-established technology that other financial institutions handle routinely. And mortgage markets are now integrated because of the active secondary market (which would survive in the absence of the two companies' special status) and because depository institutions can now branch nationwide.

As has been argued above, the two companies are primarily a part of the broad-brush American policies that encourage over-consumption of housing at the expense of alternative uses of the resources, and they are not especially good in the area where their social value would be the highest: encouraging low- and moderate-income households who are on the cusp to become first-time homebuyers. Accompanying the two companies' GSE status has been the financial markets' belief that, in the event that either company experienced financial difficulties, the federal government would very likely bail out the company's creditors, thus exposing the government and ultimately the nation's taxpayers to a substantial contingent liability.

Though the idea of enlisting the private sector and its efficiencies for the pursuit of social goals has attractive aspects, there are rarely free lunches to be enjoyed. In this case, too much housing has been encouraged, and the shareholders of the two companies have enjoyed substantial gains while taxpayers have been exposed to the risks of a sizable contingent liability. This policy of "privatizing the gains, socializing the losses" is not an attractive one.

Accordingly, the first-best policy would be to privatize them fully. This would mean that the Congress should enact legislation that would eliminate all of the special features that were outlined in Section II, and the two companies would be told to seek a state corporate charter (probably from Delaware), just like any other corporation.[37] In essence, their past and present senior managements would be (literally and figuratively) publicly patted on the back for a job well done in bringing about securitization and the national integration of residential mortgage markets (but not for the accounting scandals) and then pointed toward the office of the secretary of state in Dover, Delaware, to seek a corporate charter.

At the Congressional hearings on this legislation (and on all other opportunities), the secretary of the treasury should loudly proclaim that henceforth (following enactment) the two companies will be treated just like any other private-sector company, with no special treatment from the Treasury, and that the bankruptcy laws should apply in the event that they experience financial difficulties. At the official signing of the legislation, the president should repeat this message.[38]

Note that this true privatization does not mean the demise or disappearance of the two companies. They appear to be generally good at what they do (notwithstanding their accounting failures); but they should be doing it in a context where their owners and creditors bear the full risks of the companies' actions, rather than the taxpayers bearing those risks, and where they will be subject to a full market test to see how well they really do. The companies would begin their fully private experience at their current sizes, which (arguably) would give them some advantages. But without their special status, their borrowing costs should rise to be commensurate with their stand-alone status (i.e., AA-), and/or they will raise more (costly) capital so as to improve their financial status and keep their borrowing costs low and/or make other adjustments in their financial structure and activities. Over time their presence in the residential mortgage markets would shrink somewhat (as a consequence of their higher borrowing costs); but freed from the restraints that currently confine them to the secondary mortgage market, they might well apply their expertise to related markets, such as consumer lending, mortgage insurance, or even mortgage origination.

As a further consequence, interest rates on residential mortgages (below the conforming loan limit) would rise by approximately 20–25 basis points. This is well within the range of annual variations in mortgage interest rates and would be easily accommodated. Grass would not grow in the streets of America; and grass would continue to grow in most backyards in America. Ironically, since much of what the 20–25 basis point reduction in mortgage interest rates does is to encourage excessive investment in and consumption of housing, this price increase would represent a net improvement in the use of the American economy's resources.

As a more focused and efficient way of encouraging homeownership Congress should enact legislation that would expand on the American Dream Downpayment Act of 2003 in place of the special status of Fannie Mae and Freddie Mac. More funds could be made available for down payment assistance for low- and moderate-income first-time homebuyers, and assistance for monthly payments could also become part of the program. Not only would an expansion of this program better serve the social goal of encouraging homeownership in the United States, but this would be in the form of an explicit on-budget program (rather than the implicit off-budget contingent liability approach that the GSE route represents)—always a better way for government to operate.

Further, as a way to reduce the costs of building and buying housing, more attention should be given to other government policies that restrict supply and elevate costs. Prime candidates at the national level would be: 1) eliminating restrictions on the import of lumber from Canada; 2) eliminating restrictions on the import of cement from Mexico; 3) reforming the Real Estate Settlements Practices Act of 1974 in ways that would allow more competition and efficiencies and yield lower charges for closing costs on home purchases; and 4) allowing banks and other depositories to enter real estate brokerage, so as further to reduce the transactions costs on home purchases. At the state and local level, prime candidates would be: 1) repealing state policies that restrict competition in real estate brokerage; 2) repealing state policies that prevent lenders from charging fees for mortgage prepayments;[39] 3) eliminating inefficient local building codes that raise the cost of building local housing by more than safety or similar considerations warrant; and 4) repealing local large-lot zoning measures that restrict the availability of land for lower-cost, higher-density housing in areas where land would otherwise be inexpensive.

## B. Second-Best

The true privatization of Fannie Mae and Freddie Mac is probably a quixotic dream in the current political environment. The political attractiveness of an arrangement that reduces housing costs with no apparent on-budget consequences is understandable. Indeed, it is remarkable that, despite the accounting scandals that beset the two companies and their apparent consequent political weakening, there has been no regulatory reform legislation that has been enacted as of the summer of 2006.

Accordingly, consideration of second-best measures is worthwhile:

First, even in the absence of the privatization of the two companies, an expansion of on-budget programs to help low- and moderate-income first-time homebuyers would be worthwhile, as would all of the efforts to decrease the artificially raised costs of building and buying housing that were described above.

Second, the secretary of the treasury should proclaim loudly, at frequent intervals, that it is the policy of the federal government to adhere to what is explicitly stated on the two companies' securities: that these are not the obligations of the U.S. Government and that the government has no intention of ever "bailing out" the two companies or their creditors.

Third, the two companies' residential mortgage purchases should be restricted to mortgages on single-family homes. Their purchases of mortgages on multi-family (rental) housing do nothing to encourage homeownership and may even discourage it.

Fourth, in addition to keeping and possibly even increasing the pressures of HUD's "mission" regulation to keep the GSEs focused on affordable housing,[40] the "conforming loan" ceiling should be frozen at its current level until the median sales price of housing (or, really, 80 percent of the median sales price) catches up to that level. Even better would be a steady rollback toward the median. Any narrowing of the gap between the conforming loan limit and the median price of housing would more directly focus the two companies on the segment of the housing market where their social value would be the greatest. It would also have the beneficial effect of limiting the two companies' growth and portfolio sizes and thereby easing potential systemic risks.[41]

Fifth, banking regulators should repeal the special exemption from the "loans to one borrower" rules that applies to banks' and S&Ls' holdings of the two companies' debt.

Sixth, the safety-and-soundness regulatory regime that applies to the GSEs should be strengthened. OFHEO (or a successor agency) should be moved from HUD into the Treasury.[42] The agency should be granted explicit receivership powers and the ability independently to set risk-based capital requirements, as well as having a say in the development of any social goals.

## 4. Conclusion

Housing is too important to be left to the gentle mercies of Fannie Mae and Freddie Mac in their current GSE form. There are far better ways to pursue the social goal of encouraging homeownership in America. Truly privatizing the two companies, as well as pursuing a range of sensible reforms, would better encourage homeownership in ways that would improve the efficiency of the U.S. economy and increase social welfare and equity. There is no better time to start this effort than the present.

## 5. Postscript (8/26/08)

The chickens have come home to roost. As this postscript is written in late August 2008, both Fannie Mae and Freddie Mac are in seriously weakened financial condition. They both ran losses during calendar year 2007 and for the first two quarters of 2008, and there is substantial speculation in the financial press that a federal bailout of both companies is imminent.

The causes of the two companies' difficulties are somewhat different than had been predicted earlier; but the ultimate cause—inadequate capital to cover the risks to which they were exposed—is fundamental. Most critical commentary in the earlier part of this decade warned against the interest rate risks to which the two companies were potentially exposed and expressed fears that their hedging against these risks was inadequate.

But it was not interest rate risks but instead credit risks—mounting defaults by homebuyers, as a consequence of the bursting of the housing bubble that engulfed the U.S. economy earlier in the decade—that have caused financial difficulties for the two companies. Although neither company was involved in the subprime lending activities that were the first indicators of the bursting of the bubble, even the higher quality residential mortgage loans that the two companies typically securitize or retain have been subject to substantially higher rates of borrower defaults as a consequence of the declines in housing prices, especially the sizable declines in previously "hot" housing areas, such as California, Las Vegas, and Florida. These defaults expose the two companies to losses on both the securitized mortgages (on which the two companies provided guarantees to investors) and on the loans that they retained in their own portfolios.[43]

Until the spring of 2008 both Fannie Mae and Freddie Mac were expected to be part of the general solution to the difficulties in the housing market. The economic stimulus legislation that was enacted in February 2008 increased the conforming loan limit to $729,750 in expensive housing areas (from the $417,000 level that would otherwise have prevailed), in the hopes that expanded GSE purchase of mortgage loans would help stabilize these markets. But the revelation of the continued weakened financial condition of the two companies later in the spring of 2008 led to the inclusion of specific "bailout" provisions in the Housing and Economic Recovery Act of 2008, which was enacted in July 2008. In addition to replacing OFHEO with a new agency (the Federal Housing Finance Authority (FHFA) that has stronger powers to set capital requirements for the GSEs and has receivership powers, the legislation authorizes the U.S. Treasury to invest unlimited funds directly in the two companies, which thus makes more explicit the formerly "implicit" guarantee for the two companies' debt.[44] Despite the legislation, however, the two companies have continued to experience far greater difficulties in the debt markets—with far wider spreads between GSE debt and treasury debt than had been true previously—than had previously been the case.

If Treasury funds actually are injected into either or both companies, the fate of their shareholder owners remains uncertain. Although good policy would call for the owners to be washed away in such circumstances (and thus only the companies' creditors would be protected and, arguably, "bailed out"), the legislation does not require this outcome, and the Treasury has been (understandably) silent on this matter.

In sum, the ambiguous nature of the two companies remains. And, at this writing, the outcomes for the two companies remain cloudy and ambiguous as well.

## Notes

1.  This chapter draws heavily on White (1991, 2003, 2004, 2005, 2006) and Frame and White (2004, 2005, 2006); more extensive support and references for many of the points advanced in this chapter can be found in those publications.
2.  Citigroup, Bank of America, and JPMorgan Chase were the first three; and AIG was fifth. Asset data for Fannie Mae for 2005 are not currently available, because of the company's accounting difficulties that are described in the text below.
3.  Mortgage banks are originators of residential mortgages that typically sell the mortgages quickly into the secondary market rather than holding them in portfolio.
4.  In recent years the guarantee fees have been approximately 20 basis points (i.e., 0.20 percent) on the unpaid balance of the underlying pool of mortgages.
5.  It is important to note that the MBS holder remains exposed to "market risk"— largely the risk that interest rates will change, which will affect the value of the MBS in ways that will be discussed later in this chapter.
6.  When Fannie Mae and Freddie Mac buy back their MBS from the secondary market, they are effectively just holding the underlying mortgages, since their guarantee is then meaningless for themselves.
7.  Insured by the Federal Housing Authority (FHA), which was also created by the National Housing Act of 1934. After the Second World War, residential mortgages insured by the Veterans Administration (VA—now, the Department of Veterans Affairs) also became eligible for purchase by Fannie Mae.
8.  Apparently, a major motive in this conversion to a private corporation was to remove Fannie Mae's debt from the national debt total. Fannie Mae was replaced within the federal government by the Government National Mortgage Administration (Ginnie Mae), an agency within the U.S. Department of Housing and Urban Development (HUD) that guarantees MBS that have as their underlying assets residential mortgages that are insured by the FHA or the VA.
9.  Ginnie Mae was the first issuer of MBS, in 1970. Freddie Mac was a fast second, with its first issuance in 1971. Fannie Mae's first MBS were issued in 1981.
10. A major motivation for the conversion of Freddie Mac to a publicly traded company was the hope that wider holding of the company's shares would enhance the value of the shares then held by the ailing S&L industry and thus strengthen the balance sheets of the latter.
11. For the past few years the Bush administration has refrained from making these appointments, as a way of separating itself from the two companies.
12. This is often described as the two companies' each having a line of credit of $2.25 billion with the Treasury.
13. Both companies have voluntarily pledged to do so. Fannie Mae has made good on its promise (before its accounting difficulties of 2004 caused great delays in the revelation of standard accounting information); Freddie Mac was enveloped in an accounting scandal in 2003 before it could follow through but is still committed to doing so eventually.
14. Their securities are thus exempt from the "loans to one borrower" limitations that apply to all other loans and securities held by depository institutions.
15. The conforming loan limit is linked to an index of housing prices that is com-

piled by the Federal Housing Finance Board (FHFB). The value indicated in the text applies only to a mortgage on a single-unit residence; higher limits apply to mortgages on two-unit, three-unit, and four-unit dwellings and to mortgages for multifamily housing. Limits are 50 percent higher for Hawaii, Alaska, and the Virgin Islands.

16. OFHEO is an independent regulatory agency that is structurally located within HUD.

17. Safety-and-soundness regulation has been practiced with respect to banks and other depository institutions for over two centuries. It was first instituted formally for Fannie Mae and Freddie Mac in 1992.

18. Until 2006, the Treasury had routinely approved all of the two companies' debt issuances. In mid-2006, the Bush administration announced that it was exploring the possibility of using its potential disapproval power as a means of limiting the sizes of the two companies' mortgage portfolios, since those portfolios are funded almost entirely through debt issuances.

19. As one reflection but also a reinforcement of this specialness, financial publications that report the prices and interest returns on the two companies' debt usually list them in a special box that is separate from listings of standard corporate debt. *The Wall Street Journal*, for example, lists their debt daily in a separate box that is labeled "Government Agency & Similar Issues."

20. This differential varies over time, with financial conditions, and with the nature of the specific debt instrument being considered.

21. Since the two companies cannot borrow on terms that are quite as favorable as those enjoyed by the U.S. Treasury, the phrase "very likely" rather than "definitely" seems appropriate.

22. A rough measure of that exposure can be calculated by multiplying the borrowing advantages of the two companies (35–40 basis points on straight debt, 30 basis points on MBS) by the aggregate stocks of outstanding debt of the two companies. As of year-end 2005, this annualized aggregate exposure was around $13–14 billion. The present discounted value of these annual flows—the contingent liability to taxpayers—would be around $200 billion.

23. An ironic consequence is that any strengthening of OFHEO's safety-and-soundness powers may well strengthen the financial markets' belief in an implicit guarantee.

24. As of 2003, this passed-through benefit was estimated to be worth approximately $13.4 billion to homeowners.

25. The 1.6% capital requirement applies to all GSE MBS and to any "private label" MBS (i.e., issued by companies other that the GSEs) that is rated AA or better.

26. Freddie Mac's previous auditor had been Arthur Andersen. With Andersen's post-Enron indictment and demise, the company switched to PWC. It is often the case that a new auditor looks harder at some things than did the former auditor.

27. And, more specifically, in May 2006 OFHEO negotiated an agreement with Fannie Mae whereby the latter agreed to freeze its portfolio size at $727 billion for an indefinite period.

28. Although both companies also buy and securitize mortgages on multi-family rental housing.

29. The FHA and VA mortgage programs have limits that are 50–60 percent of the conforming loan limits for Fannie Mae and Freddie Mac, and thus these former programs tend to serve lower income households. Also, at the end of 2003 the Congress enacted the American Dream Downpayment Act, which authorized $200 million annually to help low- and moderate-income homebuyers. This latter amount is only a small fraction, however, of the annual benefits that accrue mostly

to upper-income homeowners through the various tax advantages of home owning, as well as through the activities of Fannie Mae and Freddie Mac.

30. And, of course, programs that encourage the expansion of the supply of rental housing may actually discourage the spread of homeownership.

31. It is worth noting that the two companies get credit toward meeting those targets by purchasing mortgages on affordable rental housing—which, of course, does nothing to encourage homeownership and may even discourage it.

32. This is a shorthand phrase that describes regulatory efforts to maintain the solvency of financial institutions through minimum capital (net worth) requirements, limitations on risky activities, and managerial competence requirements.

33. The scandal led to the departure of the senior management of the company.

34. This scandal too led to the departure of the company's senior management.

35. Consistent with this argument, the size limits that have been proposed for the two companies have applied only to their holdings of mortgage assets and not to their MBS issuances.

36. Although banks and S&Ls are relatively large holders of the two companies' securities, it does not appear that a financial crisis by either company would cause a serious cascade of depository insolvencies.

37. The same treatment should apply to the FHLB system.

38. Lest anyone think that this true privatization would cause an overnight crisis in the financial markets, it is worth emphasizing that any such effort would likely require years in going from initial consideration (e.g., a presidential task force formation and then subsequent recommendation, congressional hearings, etc.) through eventual congressional passage and final signing. The financial markets would have plenty of time gradually to adjust their beliefs as to the likelihood that this idea would be converted into reality.

39. Requiring that lenders allow all mortgage borrowers to have the free option of prepaying their mortgage means that the interest rate risk borne by lenders is increased. To compensate for that risk, lenders raise the interest rates on all such mortgages. If lenders could explicitly price the prepayment option, mortgage interest rates would generally be lower, and only those who prepaid would bear the cost.

40. Except that, consistent with the previous point, the GSEs' purchases of mortgages on multi-family (i.e., rental) housing ought not to be included.

41. Freezing or decreasing the conforming loan limit would be a superior means of limiting the GSEs' mortgage portfolios, as compared with a simple limit on their portfolio sizes. The latter would create an incentive for them to concentrate more on the higher end of the mortgage market, where they could earn higher profits per dollar of their (limited-size) portfolios.

42. Keeping the agency within the executive branch rather than moving it to a wholly independent status is worthwhile, because an executive-branch location focuses political responsibility and accountability.

43. Also, the private mortgage insurers, on which Fannie and Freddie relied when making mortgage loans with down payments of less than 20 percent, are also in weakened financial shape and may not be able to honor their obligations to the GSEs. This is another potential source of loss for the GSEs in the event that such borrowers default.

44. The bulk of the Act is aimed at dealing with the subprime mortgage lending debacle. With respect to the GSEs, the legislation also sets the conforming loan limit at a maximum of $625,000 for high-price areas for 2009, and it abolishes the former regulator of the Federal Home Loan Bank (FHLB) system and brings the FHLBs under the aegis of the FHFA.

# References

Frame, W. Scott and Lawrence J. White. 2004. Regulating Housing GSEs: Thoughts on Institutional Structure and Authorities. Federal Reserve Bank of Atlanta *Economic Review* 89 (second quarter): 87–102.

Frame, W. Scott and Lawrence J. White. 2005. Fussing and Fuming over Fannie and Freddie: How Much Smoke, How Much Fire? *Journal of Economic Perspectives* 19 (spring): 159–184.

Frame, W. Scott and Lawrence J. White. 2007. Charter Value, Risk-Taking Incentives, and Emerging Competition for Fannie Mae and Freddie Mac. *Journal of Money, Credit, and Banking* 39 (February): 83-103.

White, Lawrence J. 1991. *The S&L Debacle: Public Policy Lessons for Bank and Thrift Regulation.* New York: Oxford University Press.

White, Lawrence J. 2003. Focusing on Fannie and Freddie: The Dilemmas of Reforming Housing Finance. *Journal of Financial Services Research* 23 (February): 43–58.

White, Lawrence J. 2004. Fannie Mae, Freddie Mac, and Housing Finance: Why True Privatization is Good Public Policy. *Policy Analysis,* No. 528. Washington, D.C.: Cato Institute (October 7).

White, Lawrence J. 2005. On Truly Privatizing Fannie Mae and Freddie Mac: Why It's Important, and How to Do It. *Housing Finance International* 20 (December): 13–19.

White, Lawrence J. 2006. The Residential Real Estate Brokerage Industry: What Would More Vigorous Competition Look Like? *Real Estate Law Journal* 34 (Summer): 22–42.

# 13

# Anatomy of a Train Wreck: Causes of the Mortgage Meltdown

*Stan J. Liebowitz*

The mortgage meltdown has been the largest economic story, perhaps the largest story of any kind, since mid-2007. In the coming years, many books will be written about how and why the mortgage mess came about.

The basic outlines of the event are uncontroversial and fairly easy to state. Through the early years of the twenty-first century, the housing market experienced a pricing boom of almost unprecedented scale. That came to an abrupt end in the second quarter of 2006 at which time a steep decline in home prices began. Not coincidentally, in the third quarter of 2006, mortgage defaults began to rise to what would be, in modern times, unprecedented levels, although it was not until mid-2007 that the mortgage stories began to make front page news because the financial system, which had invested heavily in securitized mortgages, began to experience signs of possible collapse. The stock market swooned, GDP growth groaned to a halt, and politicians stepped in to propose various "fixes" to the problem.

The financial difficulties are continuing through the summer of 2008 as this chapter is being written. Drastic actions taken by the Federal Reserve in the spring of 2008, including the Fed bartered fire sale of Bear Stearns to JPMorgan Chase, the Fed's willingness to open its discount window to investment banks, and its acceptance of new types of securities as collateral, are all indicative of a massive effort to preempt a possible financial calamity. More recently, the political classes, led by the Treasury, have agreed that they would bail out Fannie Mae and Freddie Mac if necessary. Finally, Congress and the president have enacted legislation to put a potential bailout of those two organizations in statutory language, allowing the now saved Fannie Mae and Freddie Mac to act as "saviors," a strange position for two essentially bankrupt organization that wholeheartedly helped engineer the financial calamity they are now supposed to fix.

As we will see, a record breaking level of mortgage foreclosures occurred when the economy was still robust and before housing prices had fallen very far. These increased foreclosures occurred at the same time and with virtually the same intensity for both the prime and the subprime mortgage markets, although this has not been commonly understood. The very steep home price decline that followed has greatly exacerbated the foreclosure problems.

The increase in foreclosures caught the banking and finance industries by surprise and greatly lowered the value of securities based on these mortgages. The declining value of these securities, in turn, decimated the mortgage specialists such as Countrywide and IndyMac, badly damaged major finance and banking firms such as Citicorp and Merrill Lynch, and brought the behemoth Government Sponsored Enterprises (GSEs) Fannie Mae and Freddie Mac to the brink of bankruptcy.

The point of this chapter is to help provide some understanding of how it is that the mortgage market melted down so badly. A seismic economic fracture, such as this one, does not have but a single cause. Nevertheless, a precondition for the market to self-destruct due to a record level of mortgage foreclosures is that a great many mortgage recipients must have been unable or unwilling to continue to pay their mortgages.

How did this come about? Why were there so many defaults when the economy was not particularly weak? Why were the securities based upon these mortgages not considered anywhere as risky as they actually turned out to be?

It is the thesis of this chapter that this large increase in defaults had been a potential problem waiting to happen for some time. The reason is that mortgage underwriting standards had been under attack by virtually every branch of the government since the early 1990s. The government had been attempting to increase homeownership in the United States, which had been stagnant for several decades. In particular, the government had tried to increase homeownership among poor and minority Americans. Although a seemingly noble goal, the tool chosen to achieve this goal was one that endangered the entire mortgage enterprise: intentional weakening of the traditional mortgage lending standards.

After the government succeeded in weakening underwriting standards, mortgages seemed to require virtually no down payment, which is the main key to the problem, but also few restrictions on the size of monthly payments relative to income, little examination of credit scores, little examination of employment history, and so forth. This was exactly the government's goal.

The weakening of mortgage lending standards did succeed in increasing homeownership (discussed in more detail below). As homeownership rates increased there was self-congratulation all around. The community of regulators, academic specialists, and housing activists all reveled in the increase in homeownership and the increase in wealth brought about by homeownership. The decline in mortgage underwriting standards was universally praised as an "innovation" in mortgage lending.

The increase in homeownership increased the price of housing, helping to create a housing bubble. The bubble brought in a large number of speculators in the form of individuals owning one or two houses in the hope of quickly reselling them at a profit. Estimates are that one quarter of all home sales were speculative sales of this nature.

Speculators wanted mortgages with the smallest down payment and the lowest interest rate. These would be adjustable rate mortgages, option ARMs, and so forth. Once housing prices stopped rising, these speculators tried to get out from under their investments made largely with other people's money, which is why foreclosures increased mainly for adjustable rate mortgages and not fixed rate, regardless of whether mortgages were prime or subprime. The rest, as they say, is history.

In good times, strict underwriting standards seem unnecessary. But like levees against a flood, they serve a useful purpose. When markets turn sour, these standards help ensure that homeowners will not bail out of homes at the first sign of price declines, that they will have the financial wherewithal to survive economic downturns, and that even if homeowners can't make their payments, mortgage owners will be covered by the equity remaining in the home. Removing these protections greatly increased the risk in this market when a storm did approach.

Unfortunately, it seems likely that our governing bodies have learned little or nothing from this series of events. If the proper lessons are not learned we are likely to have a reprise sometime in the future.

## 1. The Birth of "Flexible Underwriting Standards"

After the warm and fuzzy glow of "flexible underwriting standards" has worn off, we may discover that they are nothing more than standards that led to bad loans. Certainly, a careful investigation of these underwriting standards is in order. If the "traditional" bank lending processes were rational, we are likely to find, with the adoption of flexible underwriting standards, that we are merely encouraging banks to make unsound loans. If this is the case, current policy will not have helped its intended beneficiaries if in future years they are dispossessed from their homes due to an inability to make their mortgage payments. It will be ironic and unfortunate if minority applicants wind up paying a very heavy price for a misguided policy based on badly mangled data (Day and Liebowitz, 1998).

Home mortgages have been a political piñata for many decades. All politicians at all times seem to be in favor of homeownership. What could be more apple pie than owning a home? Indeed, there can be many positive effects on behavior brought about by homeownership.

But homeownership wouldn't seem to require much help from the federal government. If you let builders build, developers develop, and lenders lend you will soon have people living in private homes, assuming that local governments adequately perform their function of enforcing private contracts. This view is verified by that fact that at the turn of the twentieth century, before the federal government became involved in the housing industry, homeownership in the United States, according to the Census, stood at 47 percent (compared to 66 percent in 2000). That was before the enormous wealth increase of the twentieth century and before mortgage deductibility was enacted as a form of homeownership subsidy, both factors that would be expected to increase the ownership of homes. Clearly, homeownership rates would have increased even without flexible underwriting policies.

Nevertheless, during the great depression of the 1930s, homebuilding, like many other industries, experienced a profound decline. Mortgages were generally of a short duration, often only a year or two. Because banks were cashed strapped and nervous about being paid, when a mortgage came due, instead of offering to refinance it, the banks often asked for payment in full. It was difficult or impossible for homeowners, even those with the financial ability to handle a mortgage, to pay the full amount of the mortgage all at once.

To help alleviate such problems, the federal government in 1934 created the Federal Housing Administration, which guaranteed mortgages against default, thus removing the risk from the bank. This was the first major intrusion in the mortgage market. In 1938 Fannie Mae was created to purchase FHA mortgages. Its purpose was later widened and it now purchases and repackages a large share of all private mortgages in the country. In more recent decades, FHA mortgages have generally been used by lower-income homebuyers since there have been income and mortgage size limitations built into the program.

The government became heavily involved in the mortgage market in a new way after concerns about mortgage discrimination arose in the 1970s. The government passed the Community Reinvestment Act (CRA) in 1977, requiring banks to conduct business across the entirety of geographic areas in which they operated, thus preventing them from doing business in a suburb, say, while neglecting a downtown area. Congress also passed the Home Mortgage Disclosure Act in 1975 (HMDA), which required that mortgage lenders provide detailed information about mortgage applications. Every year banks receive a score on their CRA compliance just as they received a score on their financial viability and banks strive to do well on both parts of their examination.

In 1991 the HMDA data was expanded, allowing for comparison of rejection rates by race. Various news organizations started publicizing simple examinations of HMDA data showing that minorities were denied home mortgages at a rate far higher than that for whites. It was and still is common for newspapers in large cities, shortly after the yearly HMDA data are made public, to do exposés examining the differences by race in rejection rates on mortgage applications. There are even turnkey kits for newspaper reporters aspiring to demonstrate such results. Although such comparisons are completely unable to distinguish between the possibility of discrimination or differences in credit worthiness as explanations and are therefore fairly meaningless, these results were and are trumpeted far and wide in the media.

The last defense of banks trying to defend themselves against charges of engaging in biased mortgage lending appeared to fall when the Boston Fed conducted an apparently careful statistical analysis in 1992 purporting to demonstrate that even after controlling for important variables associated with creditworthiness, minorities were found to be denied mortgages at higher rates than whites.

In fact, the study was based on horribly mangled data that the authors of the study apparently never bothered to examine. Every later article of which I am aware accepted that the data were badly mangled, even those authored by individuals who ultimately agreed with the conclusions of the Boston Fed study. The authors of the Boston Fed study, however, stuck to their guns even in the face of overwhelming evidence that the data used in their study was riddled with errors. Ex post, this was a wise decision for them, even if a less than honorable one.

The winds were behind the sails of the study.[1] Most politicians jumped to support the study. "This study is definitive," and "it changes the landscape" said a spokeswoman for the Office of the Comptroller of the Currency. "This comports completely with common sense" and "I don't think you need a lot more studies like this," said Richard F. Syron, president of the Boston Fed (and now head of Freddie Mac). One of the study's authors, Alicia Munnell said, without any apparent concern for academic modesty "the study eliminates all the other possible factors that could be influencing [mortgage] decisions."[2] When quotes like these are made by important functionaries, you know that the fix is in and that scientific enquiry is out.

My colleague, Ted Day, and I only decided to investigate the Boston Fed study because we knew that no single study, particularly the first study, should ever be considered definitive and that something smelled funny about the whole endeavor. Nevertheless, we were shocked at the poor quality of the data created by the Boston Fed. The Boston Fed collected data on approximately 3000 mortgages. Data problems were obvious to anyone who bothered to examine the numbers. A quick summary of the data problems: a) the loan data created by the Boston Fed had information which implied, if it were to be believed, that hundreds of loans had interest rates that were much too high or much too low (about fifty loans had negative interest rates according to the data); b) over 500 applications could not be matched to the original HMDA data upon which the Boston Fed data was supposedly based; c) 44 loans were supposedly rejected by the lender but then sold in the secondary market which, of course, is impossible; d) two separate measures of income differed by more than 50 percent for over 50 observations; e) over 500 loans that should have needed mortgage insurance to be approved were approved even though there was no record of mortgage insurance; e) several mortgages were supposedly approved to individuals with net worth in the negative millions of dollars.

When we attempted to conduct the statistical analysis removing the impact of these obvious data errors we found that the evidence of discrimination vanished. Without discrimination there would be no reason to try to "fix" the mortgage market.

Nevertheless, our work largely evaporated down the memory hole as government regulators got busy putting the results of the Boston Fed study to use in creating policy. That policy, simply put, was to weaken underwriting standards. What happened next is nicely summed up in an enthusiastic Fannie Mae report authored by some leading academics (Listokin et al., 2002):

> Attempts to eliminate discrimination involve strengthened enforcement of existing laws.... There have also been efforts *to expand the availability of more affordable*

*and flexible mortgages.* The Community Reinvestment Act (CRA) provides a major incentive.... Fannie Mae and Freddie Mac ... have also been called upon to broaden access to mortgage credit and homeownership. The 1992 Federal Housing Enterprises Financial Safety and Soundness Act (FHEFSSA) mandated that the GSEs increase their acquisition of primary-market loans made to lower income borrowers.... Spurred in part by the FHEFSSA mandate, Fannie Mae announced a trillion-dollar commitment.

The result has been a wider variety of innovative mortgage products. The GSEs have introduced a *new generation of affordable, flexible, and targeted mortgages, thereby fundamentally altering the terms upon which mortgage credit was offered in the United States from the 1960s through the 1980s.* Moreover, these secondary-market innovations have proceeded in tandem with shifts in the primary markets: depository institutions, spurred by the threat of CRA challenges and the lure of significant profit potential in underserved markets, have pioneered flexible mortgage products. For years, depositories held these products in portfolios when their underwriting guidelines exceeded benchmarks set by the GSEs. Current shifts in government policy, GSE acquisition criteria, and the primary market have fostered greater integration of capital and lending markets.

These changes in lending herald what we refer to as *mortgage innovation* [emphasis added].

One man's innovation can be another man's poison, in this case a poison that infected the entire industry. What you will not find, if you read the housing literature from 1990 until 2006, is any fear that perhaps these weaker lender standards that *every government agency* involved with housing tried to advance, that congress tried to advance, that the presidency tried to advance, that the GSEs tried to advance, and with which the penitent banks initially went along and eventually enthusiastically supported, might lead to high defaults, particularly if housing prices should stop rising.

## 2. Relaxed Lending Standards—Everyone's Doin' It

Within a few months of the appearance of the Boston Fed study a new manual appeared from the Boston Fed. It was in the nature of a "Non-Discriminatory Mortgage Lending for Dummies" booklet.[3] The president of the Boston Fed wrote in the foreword:

The Federal Reserve Bank of Boston wants to be helpful to lenders as they work to close the mortgage gap [higher rejection rate for minorities]. For this publication, we have gathered recommendations on "best practice" from lending institutions and consumer groups. With their help, we have developed a comprehensive program for

lenders who seek to ensure that all loan applicants are treated fairly and to expand
their markets to reach a more diverse customer base.

Early in the document the Fed gracefully reminds its readers of a few
possible consequences of not paying attention:

> *Did You Know?* Failure to comply with the Equal Credit Opportunity Act or Regula-
> tion B can subject a financial institution to civil liability for actual and punitive dam-
> ages in individual or class actions. Liability for punitive damages can be as much as
> $10,000 in individual actions and the lesser of $500,000 or 1 percent of the creditor's
> net worth in class actions.

The part of this document that is of greatest interest to us is the section
on *underwriting standards*. This is where we find the seeds of today's
mortgage meltdown. It starts out:

> Even the most determined lending institution will have difficulty cultivating business
> from minority customers if its underwriting standards contain arbitrary or unreason-
> able measures of creditworthiness.

You might think that it would be difficult for a bank to cultivate business with *any* mortgage applicants, or merely to stay in business, if it
had arbitrary and unreasonable measures of creditworthiness. But then
you would be failing to understand the doublespeak that is actually the
point of this quote. What the quote is really saying is that if a bank's
underwriting standards do not allow a sufficiently high percentage of
minority mortgage approvals, they must be arbitrary or unreasonable.
"Unreasonable and arbitrary" include the standards that prevailed in the
several decades prior to the 1990s.

The document continues:

> Management should be directed to review existing underwriting standards and prac-
> tices to ensure that they are valid predictors of risk. Special care should be taken to
> ensure that standards are appropriate to the economic culture of urban, lower–income,
> and nontraditional consumers.

You might have thought that financial standards that indicate a high
probability of success in making mortgage payments, such as steady
employment, a record of savings, and keeping the loan payment small
relative to income, might have been prudent standards for borrowers of
all incomes and all races. In fact, you would be correct. But in the world
of mortgage discrimination the goal is to increase mortgages for certain
"non-traditional" customers, and in this case financial standards are to
be twisted or discarded if necessary.

We can go through the document's critique of underwriting standards
one at a time.

*Credit History*: Lack of credit history should not be seen as a negative factor. Certain cultures encourage people to "pay as you go" and avoid debt. Willingness to pay debt promptly can be determined through review of utility, rent, telephone, insurance, and medical bill payments. In reviewing past credit problems, lenders should be willing to consider extenuating circumstances. For lower-income applicants in particular, unforeseen expenses can have a disproportionate effect on an otherwise positive credit record. In these instances, paying off past bad debts or establishing a regular repayment schedule with creditors may demonstrate a willingness and ability to resolve debts. Successful participation in credit counseling or buyer education programs is another way that applicants can demonstrate an ability to manage their debts responsibly.

The first few sentences, to the extent they just imply that paying bills in cash should not hurt loan applicants, are largely unobjectionable. But then banks are told that extenuating circumstances should be taken into account when evaluating prior credit problems. Although this does not appear unreasonable on its face, the fact is that people with credit problems invariably have excuses for their problems, and whether those are legitimate extenuating circumstances or not is the key question. The way this is worded, a bank with an applicant who provides an "extenuating" circumstance faces the charge of "discrimination" if the application is denied. Past bad debt, the document continues, if eventually made good, should be ignored, which sounds like a recipe for inviting, well, bad debt.

More troubling is the claim that "credit counseling" is a demonstration that applicants can manage debts successfully. This is an example of the most naïve form of wishful thinking being used in place of actual thought (although one might claim that the relaxing of underwriting standards was also an instance). There is no evidence whatsoever that "credit counseling" helps applicants avoid mortgage defaults.[4] The focus on consumer education, which is a constant and persistent theme in this literature, seems to have more to due with political payoffs to "community activists" who help provide the "education" than with providing any benefits to homeowners or lenders.

*Obligation Ratios*: Special consideration could be given to applicants with relatively high obligation ratios who have demonstrated an ability to cover high housing expenses in the past. Many lower-income households are accustomed to allocating a large percentage of their income toward rent. While it is important to ensure that the borrower is not assuming an unreasonable level of debt, it should be noted that the secondary market is willing to consider ratios above the standard 28/36.

Again, the first sentence seems reasonable enough. But then the tone shifts and it suggests that many lower-income households can handle high obligation ratios, not just those applicants who have demonstrated an ability to handle high housing expenses in the past. Clearly, the Fed is suggesting that the 28/36 ratio (share of income that can be devoted to mortgage payments, gross or net) that had been historically used for most homeowners shouldn't apply to poor individuals even though logic would say that poor individuals, who are les likely to have savings (see next paragraph) or other forms of discretionary income, are more likely, not less, to have trouble handling housing expense ratios above normal. The secondary market obliquely referred to in the last sentence of the quote is basically Fannie Mae and it was willing to stretch the obligation ratios since it was an enthusiastic advocate of relaxed lending standards.

> *Down Payment and Closing Costs*: Accumulating enough savings to cover the various costs associated with a mortgage loan is often a significant barrier to homeownership by lower-income applicants. Lenders may wish to allow gifts, grants, or loans from relatives, nonprofit organizations, or municipal agencies to cover part of these costs. Cash–on–hand could also be an acceptable means of payment if borrowers can document its source and demonstrate that they normally pay their bills in cash.

This quote mixes legitimate and illegitimate sources of extra income in a dangerous way. Cash and gifts from relatives seem unobjectionable. But what this paragraph opens the door to is the "gift" from a builder wishing to sell his housing. Since these guidelines went into effect it has become commonplace for builders of low-income homes to "gift" the down payment to the mortgage applicant, often using a non-profit "front" organization to channel the funds. Since homebuilders are not charities, the price of the home is raised by an amount equal to the cash gift, with appraisers apparently willing to go along (shades of Tony Soprano).

> *Sources of Income*: In addition to primary employment income, Fannie Mae and Freddie Mac will accept the following as valid income sources: overtime and part–time work, second jobs (including seasonal work), retirement and Social Security income, alimony, child support, Veterans Administration (VA) benefits, welfare payments, and unemployment benefits.

As with the other proposals, this one is a mixture of the reasonable and the outrageous. Second jobs, for example, can be held indefinitely and thus are reasonable sources of income. Unemployment benefits, on the other hand, are time limited and it is a mistake to include temporary sources of income when the mortgage is not temporary. The fact that Fannie Mae and Freddie Mac accept these sources says more about these agencies' attempts to water down underwriting standards than it does to prove that such watered down standards make sense.

What was the impact of this attack on traditional underwriting standards? As you might guess, when government regulators bark, banks jump. Banks began to loosen lending standards. And loosen and loosen and loosen, to the cheers of the politicians, regulators and GSEs.

One of the banks that jumped most completely on to this bandwagon was Countrywide, which used its efforts to lower underwriting standards on "behalf" of minorities (and everyone else) to catapult itself to become the leading mortgage lender in the nation. Countrywide not only made more loans to minorities than any other lender, it also had the highest consumer satisfaction among large mortgage lenders, according to JD Powers.[5]

Testimonials to Countrywide's virtue abound. In 2000, *La Opinión* (the nation's leading Spanish-language newspaper) named Countrywide "Corporation of the Year" for their outstanding work in the Latino community. Additionally, LULAC's (League of United Latin American Citizens) chair of national housing said "Through the generosity of ethical businesses like Countrywide, we can make significant strides towards bringing the pride of homeownership to our communities and enhancing the quality of life for more Latinos."[6]

According to a flattering report by the Fannie Mae foundation, Countrywide was a paragon of lending virtue.[7] Countrywide was nothing if not flexible, I mean innovative, in its underwriting practices. The report stated:

> Countrywide tends to follow the most flexible underwriting criteria permitted under GSE and FHA guidelines. Because Fannie Mae and Freddie Mac tend to give their best lenders access to the most flexible underwriting criteria, Countrywide benefits from its status as one of the largest originators of mortgage loans and one of the largest participants in the GSE programs.
>
> When necessary—in cases where applicants have no established credit history, for example—Countrywide uses nontraditional credit, a practice now accepted by the GSEs.

Countrywide had even outdone itself with respect to consumer education.

> In an interesting departure from local counseling assistance, Countrywide provides centralized homeownership counseling through the House America Counseling Center. Counseling staff members who are located in California field calls on a toll-free line. Bilingual (Spanish and English) counselors are available ... the Counseling Center distributes materials to help potential homeowners achieve and maintain homeownership. These materials include the *Guide to Homeownership* and *A Feeling Called Home*, a video that is narrated by James Earl Jones.

Apparently, even the voice of Darth Vader couldn't keep defaults at bay. The report also reports on Countrywide's other great videos.

Countrywide has developed a video titled *Living the Dream: A New Homeowner's Survival Guide*, which covers the basics of loan closing, mortgage insurance, budgeting, and home maintenance, as well as how to use credit wisely, make mortgage payments on time, cope with financial crises, and reap the rewards of building equity.... The video was originally created for use in the House America program. However, following praise by industry leaders, including officials at Fannie Mae, Freddie Mac, GE Mortgage Insurance Corporation, and HUD, copies of the video have been provided to city and county libraries nationwide as an educational tool.

This hasn't stopped critics looking for villains in the mortgage meltdown from fingering Countrywide. Of course, Countrywide is really the poster-boy for flexible underwriting standards, but none of the usual critics wants to criticize the standards themselves.

There is one part of the story that has not yet been discussed. We know where the idea of flexible underwriting standards came from and we know how relentlessly it was pushed by almost every government organization or quasi-government organization associated with the industry. But how did investors, who are supposed to be cool and rational, misperceive the risk so badly? One of the questions about the current crisis is why purchasers of mortgages (i.e., mortgage-backed securities) were willing to treat them as AAA and perhaps more surprisingly, why the rating agencies were willing to give them AAA ratings.

Although it is not clear that any answer to this question can be completely satisfactory, I believe that if it is understood how universal the idea of "flexible underwriting standards" had become, how dangerous it was to suggest anything else (and risk being labeled a racist) and how strong this force is, even now, it becomes possible to understand how investors, who, just like other human beings, are prone to mistakes (the dot com bubble is another recent example), might be led by the same arguments that were being repeated by so many others.

To understand this it is useful to examine the sales pitches that were made. I was able to find a 1998 sales pitch from Bear Stearns, a major underwriter of mortgage backed securities, for loans banks undertook to fulfill their CRA obligations, which means mortgages to low- and moderate-income individuals.[8]

This sales pitch is important because it shows us the thinking being used to sell these products in secondary markets. This was also likely the pitch that was made to the security rating organizations by the underwriters of the mortgage-backed securities. As will become apparent, this sales pitch for loans based on relaxed lending standards generally follows the script laid out by the Boston Fed and followed by the entire regulatory apparatus surrounding the housing industry. Faced with overwhelming acceptance of these facts by presumably knowledgeable experts, why wouldn't an investor believe it?

Further, the housing price bubble that was caused in part by these relaxed underwriting standards tended to reduced defaults and obscure the impact of the standards while prices were rising because almost no one would default when they could, instead, easily sell the house at a profit. Rating agencies could suggest that these loans were no more risky than the old antiquated loans and provide empirical support for that conclusion, given the still low default rates at the time, although to do so was short sighted to the point of incompetence.

In fact, the rating agencies seemed overly concerned with the trees and lost sight of the forest. For example, a *Wall Street Journal* article (which is the basis for the following three quotes) reports on rating agencies' benign treatment of piggyback mortgages (taking out a second mortgage to cover the down payment required by the first mortgage).[9] In previous decades, mortgage applicants unable to come up with the full down payment and therefore thought to be more at risk of default, were required to pay "mortgage insurance" which raised the interest rate on the loan. Piggyback loans allowed borrowers to avoid this mechanism, thus presumably making the loan riskier. Nevertheless, the article reports that rating agencies did not consider these loans more risky:

> Data provided by lenders showed that loans with piggybacks performed like standard mortgages. The finding was unexpected, wrote S&P credit analyst Michael Stock in a 2000 research note. He nonetheless concluded the loans weren't necessarily very risky.

The finding was unexpected because it contradicted what had generally been known about mortgages by a prior generation of mortgage lenders—that when applicants made smaller down payments, increasing the loan-to-value ratio, the probability of default increased. This finding contradicted common sense. Further, these measurements were being made at the front end of a housing price bubble (Figure 13.1 below shows that prices were rising smartly in 2000), likely biasing downward any default statistics. Relaxed lending standards also had a short enough track record that rating agencies could not know how they would perform in the long run or in adverse conditions, meaning that it isn't clear that sufficient information existed to even rate these securities. So how did the rating agencies defend their counterintuitive ratings?

> One money manager, James Kragenbring, says he had five to ten conversations with S&P and Moody's in late 2005 and 2006, discussing whether they should be tougher because of looser lending standards.... Other analysts recall being told that ratings

could also be revised if the market deteriorated. Said an S&P spokesman: "The market can go with its gut; we have to go with the facts."

Whether such a myopic view of the "facts" was responsible for all or most of the excessively high ratings I cannot say, but these ratings were consistent with the views of the relaxed lending standards crowd. The real facts, of course, eventually soured the view of the rating agencies:

> By 2006, S&P was making its own study of such loans' performance. It singled out 639,981 loans made in 2002 to see if its benign assumptions had held up. They hadn't. Loans with piggybacks were 43% more likely to default than other loans, S&P found.

In spite of their inaccurate ratings, the rating agencies, nevertheless, were making great profits from rating mortgage-backed securities, a quasi-sinecure created by the government which required many financial organizations (e.g., insurance companies and money market funds) to invest only in highly rated securities as certified by government (Security and Exchange Commission) approved rating agencies (NRSROs). There were only three such approved rating agencies for most of the last decade (S&P, Moody's and Fitch). Given that government-approved rating agencies were protected from free competition, it might be expected that these agencies would not want to create political waves by rocking the mortgage boat, endangering a potential loss of their protected profits.

Seemingly everyone went along. And most felt morally upright doing so since they were helping increase homeownership, especially among the poor and minorities.

Returning to the sales pitch made by Bear Sterns in 1998 and quoted below, Bear Stearns claimed that LTV (size of the loan relative to the value of the home) *had been* the key consideration for predicting defaults but suggested that it was not appropriate for affordable loans (an opinion seconded by the rating agencies a few years later, as we have seen).[10] The traditional logic was sound: if someone puts 20 percent down on a house, the traditional down payment level, they would be unlikely to default. Even if the homeowner has trouble making the payments, as long as prices do not fall by 20 percent the homeowner would prefer to sell the house and get some of their down payment back. Yet in the sale pitch we encounter a feeble attempt to explain why this should not be true for low-income borrowers.

> **Traditionally rating agencies view LTV as the single most important determinant of default**.... While we do not dispute these assumptions, LTVs have to be analyzed within the context of the affordable-loan situation. Three or 4 percent equity on a $50,000 house is significant to a family of limited financial resources. In relative terms,

$1,500 to $2,000 could easily mean three to four months of advance rent payments in their previous housing situation.

Obviously, there are more delinquencies with the higher LTV loans than the lower, but there is no tight linear correlation between the LTV levels. Delinquency rates increase along with the LTV levels, but not proportionately. As a result, the use of default models traditionally used for conforming loans have to be adjusted for CRA affordable loans.

Let's take a look at this logic. LTV has been the most important predictor of default. But when it comes to "affordable" housing, LTV is not to be taken as seriously. Why? The real reason is that if traditional LTVs were imposed on applicants for "affordable" loans, most of these applicants would be unable to come up with anything like a 20 percent down payment and the loan would be rejected. That is a politically unacceptable result. The logic being put forward by Bear Stearns appears to be that a 3–4 percent (down payment) of a small mortgage is more important to poor people than 3–4 percent of a bigger mortgage for wealthier applicants. This is a mere assertion, although to question it (or most of the other claims being made at the time) was to run the risk of being called a racist. But more importantly, as we know from the Boston Fed Guide book, the down payment is most likely going to come from someone other than the applicants themselves anyway ("accumulating enough savings to cover the various costs associated with a mortgage loan is often a significant barrier to homeownership by lower–income applicants"), so there is little reason poor applicants should treat it with particular extra care.

Also, as we will see below, mortgages from the poorer portion of the income distribution have, for the last 30 years at least, have had much higher default rates than traditional mortgages, a result that is conveniently ignored in so much of this literature. Subprime mortgages have tended historically to be foreclosed at ten times rate of prime mortgages and FHA loans (limited to low- and moderate-income individuals) are foreclosed at about four times the rate of prime mortgages.

Continuing with the 4 percent down example, if the price of the affordable house goes down by more than 4 percent the homeowner would be "underwater" or "upside down," depending on your preferred metaphor. If this is due to an overall decline in housing prices, it means that the homeowner could turn around and purchase a similar house for a lower price and lower monthly payments. There is no reason to think that poor people are less likely to be swayed by this logic than middle-class people (although, as we will see, Bear Stearns considers poor homeowners to be too ignorant to figure this out).

What other nuggets of wisdom are found in this Bear Stearns pitch?

**Credit scores**. While credit scores can be an analytical tool with conforming loans, their effectiveness is limited with CRA loans. Unfortunately, CRA loans do not fit neatly into the standard credit score framework.... Do we automatically exclude or severely discount ... loans [with poor credit scores]? Absolutely not.

They agree with the Boston Fed manual that traditional credit scores are not useful for poor and moderate-income households. They don't really provide any reason for this belief except to say that credit scores are complicated constructs.

**Payment history.** While some credit-score purists might take issue with our comments in the preceding section, payment history for CRA loans tracks consistently close to the risk curves of conforming loans.... In many cases, purchasing a home puts the borrower in a more favorable financial position than renting. It is quite common for a first-time homebuyer using a CRA loan to have been shouldering a rent payment that consumed 40 percent to 50 percent of his or her gross income.

When considering the credit score, LTV and payment history, we put the greatest weight by far on the last variable.... Payment history speaks for itself. To many lower-income homeowners and CRA borrowers, being able to own a home is a near-sacred obligation. A family will do almost anything to meet that monthly mortgage payment.

Although the above quote might bring tears to your eyes, the tears should be from contemplating to the point of parody the poor economic logic being used by a leading financial firm. First, the claim, that lower-income homeowners are somehow different in their devotion ("near sacred") to their home is a purely emotional claim with no evidence to support it. It also completely ignores the fact that foreclosure rates for loans to low-income individuals (FHA or subprime) are much higher than for ordinary mortgages, sacred obligation or not. Also, whether apartments or houses are better deals depends on the ratio of housing prices to apartment prices, which varies over time and by location. At the peak of the housing bubble, for example, apartment prices were much less expensive than amortized home payments and the claims about the savings from homeownership made above would have been false in almost all locations.

Finally we have the "education" canard repeated again:

Where do most payment problems occur? Usually, the problems stem from poor upfront planning and counseling. Hence, one of the key factors we look for in a CRA portfolio is whether the borrower completed a GSE-accredited homebuyer education program. The best of these programs help the individual plan for emergencies that can arise with homeownership.

Ironically, although education programs do not impact defaults, they do impact prepayments (meaning that the loan is paid off early). The

Bear Stearns pitch is highly focused on prepayments. Lenders do not like prepayments because increased prepayments often means that interest rates have dropped, allowing homeowner to refinance at a lower rate. In that case, the lender fails to lock-in the gain from the original higher interest mortgage that is paid off (prepaid) when it is refinanced.

> CRA-backed securities are attractive to mortgage investors because of their very stable prepayment behavior. Because pre-payments are unlikely to accelerate if interest rates decline, these securities consistently outperform their traditional mortgage-backed counterparts on a total-rate-of-return basis.

Why are affordable loans thought less likely to have prepayments? There are two reasons suggested by Bear Stearns. First, they state that many such loans are heavily subsidized (usually by taxpayers unaware of their largesse), so the applicants would have no incentive to renegotiate. Second, such borrowers are considered too unworldly to take advantage of the lower rates. ("The low-income borrower population is much more likely to have limited access to funds and/or have limited desire or ability to pay the out-of-pocket expenses associated with a refinancing transaction.")

The Bear Stearns document goes on at great length about the prepayment advantages of affordable mortgages. And in a world where default is of no relevance, small disadvantages to the lender, like getting paid in-full *early,* could appear to be a major problem. But to ignore the possibility of defaults, to ignore the possibility that housing prices might someday fall and to not weigh these possibilities against the minor problem of getting paid in-full early, is nothing short of gross incompetence. Getting paid early is nowhere as serous a problem as not getting paid at all is and you should not need a Ph.D. to figure that out.

Here is a final pearl from Bear Stearns: "If you are setting aside inordinately high loan loss reserves against your balance sheet, you should consider freeing up the capital for more productive purposes." They apparently took their own, deficient, advice. R.I.P. Bear Stearns.

In closing this section a word about mortgage innovations and the current crisis is in order. Much of the evidence related to mortgage innovation that was just presented has been focused on poor and middle class borrowers. Indeed, the strongest incentive for eliminating traditional underwriting standards, as we have seen, came from attempts to help poor and minority borrowers. Nevertheless, newspapers tell us that upper income individuals are being foreclosed in large numbers as well.

There are two points that need to be kept in mind. First, preliminary evidence (Mian and Sufi, 2008) indicates that the recent increase in defaults has been dominated by those areas populated by poor and moderate-income borrowers. Further, Figure 13.9 below and the discussion surrounding it shows that poor and moderate-income areas had the largest share of speculative home buying and speculative home buying will be seen, later in this chapter, to be the leading explanation for home foreclosures. Thus the evidence is that the foreclosures are disproportionately a problem of the poor and moderate-income areas, which is entirely consistent with the weakened underwriting standards discussed above. The fact that foreclosures among poor and moderate homeowners are not receiving the greatest amount of newspaper attention doesn't mean that they are not at the epicenter of the foreclosure problem.

Second, although the original mortgage innovations were rationalized for low- and middle-income buyers, once this sloppy thinking had taken hold it is naïve to believe that this decade long attack on traditional underwriting standards would not also lead to more relaxed standards for higher income borrowers as well. When everyone cheers for relaxed underwriting standards the relaxation is not likely to be kept in narrow confines.

### 3. Empirics of the Current Crisis

The immediate causes of the rise in defaults is fairly obvious—it was the reversal in the remarkable price appreciation of homes that occurred from 1998 until (the second quarter of) 2006. Since then prices have sharply declined. The housing price bubble can be easily seen in Figure 13.1, which shows inflation adjusted housing price index since 1987.

Prices in the second quarter of 2008 are not yet available but they appear likely to drop by more than 5 percent compared to the first quarter (since we have two months of data in the quarter), which would make the average real price index for the second quarter of 2008 approximately $70,000 using 1983 prices.

It is difficult to determine why bubbles come into existence. There are often many elements, including economic, psychological, regulatory, and political ones. One element in this case was an extremely large increase in the number of families qualifying for mortgages under the relaxed lending standards, which then translated in higher ownership rates.

Figure 13.2 illustrates changes in homeownership rates beginning with 1970. Except for a small but temporary increase in the late 1970s, these rates had been basically flat until 1995, whereupon they began a steep ascent. Why did homeownership increase in the mid-1990s? It is almost certainly due to the relaxing of lending standards whose machinery, as

**Figure 13.1**
**Yearly Real (1983$) Home Price Index**

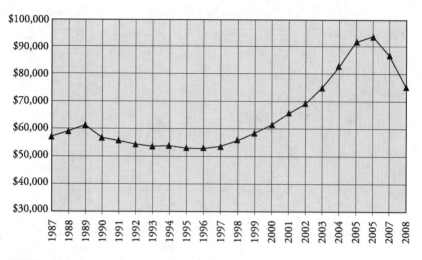

(2008 based on 1 quarter)
Source: Case Shiller National

we have seen, was starting to be put in place in 1993. This was also the conclusion of the Federal Reserve Bank of San Francisco in 2006:[11]

> We examine several potential reasons for this surge in the homeownership rate. We find that, while demographic changes have some role to play, it is likely that *much of the increase is due to innovations in the mortgage finance industry* that may have helped a large number of households buy homes more easily than they could have a decade ago [emphasis added].

Those "innovations" are the same ones discussed at length above.

If relaxed lending standards allowed more households to qualify for financing, basic economics also says that housing prices would have risen as the demand for homes increased. Some portion of the housing price bubble, perhaps a large portion, must have been caused by the relaxed lending standards.

Of course it is not the rising portion of the bubble that causes unhappiness. In fact inflating bubbles are usually associated with joy and the robust housing market was generally looked at benignly and considered good for the economy. The rising home prices would also keep the dark underbelly of relaxed lending standards from view since any homeowners having difficulties handling their mortgages, and there must have been many who would have run into trouble relatively quickly, could easily

**Figure 13.2**
**Yearly Home Ownership Rates**

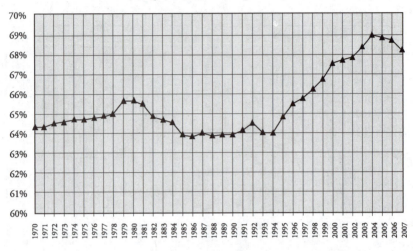

Source: U.S. Census

refinance or sell their home at a profit. Defaults would remain a rarity even for loans that should never have been made.

When housing prices started to fall, however, all the joy and happiness came to an end. The increase in home prices peaked in the second quarter of 2006 according to Case-Shiller statistics. It is probably not a total coincidence that foreclosures began to rise in the very next quarter, the third quarter of 2006, as can be seen in Figure 13.3.[12]

The increase in foreclosures began rising virtually the minute housing prices stopped rising. It did not take much of a nominal decline in home prices to have a very large impact on foreclosures, which is important to note. Nominal housing prices dropped a mere 1.4 percent in the six months from the second quarter of 2006 to the fourth quarter of 2006. Yet foreclosure-start rates increased by 43 percent, from .40 percent of homes to .57 percent of homes. At that moment in time, with virtually no price decline yet in evidence, foreclosure-start rates were already at a record high, some 21 percent higher than they had ever been in the modern (post 1978) period. This increase in foreclosures was not due to an economic recession, since the economy was still humming along. This increase in foreclosures was not due to a large price drop in homes, because virtually none had yet occurred.

It is hard not to surmise that this sudden jump in foreclosure-starts (from 170,000 to 248,000) came from homeowners who, having been

**Figure 13.3**
**Foreclosures Started**

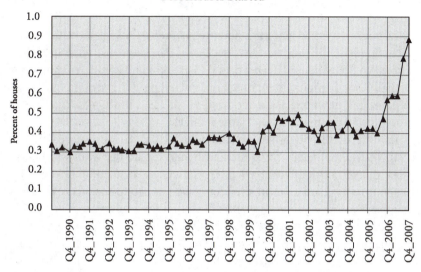

able to purchase their home without putting any money down, intended to flip or refinance their home at a profit within a relatively short period of time. Once the home appreciation stopped, so these homeowners could no longer quickly flip or refinance it at a profit, it is likely that some of them would have walked away, particularly in states like California, where lenders have no recourse and cannot go after the assets of the individual. We know, from the several television shows on the subject (i.e., "Flip that House") that there was considerable interest in short-term homeownership. Nevertheless, this is only a conjecture, although one that seems to explain the data, including more detailed data discussed below, quite well.

Through 2007 and 2008, prices have continued to fall and foreclosures have continued to rise. It is generally agreed that the enormous increase in foreclosures was due in large part to the absurdly loose mortgage underwriting that had been allowed on many approved mortgages prior to the financial panic and the stricter underwriting standards that have since been put temporarily into place. Reporters have had a field day describing the various loans that had become popular: liar loans, where the applicant made up a figure for income without verification; zero-down loans where the applicant did not have to provide any money in order to purchase a home; option ARMs where the borrower was able to choose the payments they would make each month even if the size of the outstanding mortgage kept increasing; and other variations of these types of loans.[13]

Of course, relaxed lending standards, or underwriting innovations as it is euphemistically put, were so successful that standards were loosened across the board so that even a prime loan applicant could avoid making virtually any down payment by taking out a piggyback second mortgage to cover the down payment required by the first mortgage (often both mortgages were made by the same lender).

In spite of the abundant evidence of all the various successful attempts to relax underwriting standards, almost no one wants to blame those relaxed standards for what has happened. Instead, almost all the blame is focused on subprime lenders who happen to specialize in loans that use relaxed lending standards. Unscrupulous subprime lenders, we are told, are the guilty parties responsible for financial calamity at both the macro level and the personal level. They are financial vampires, sucking the lifeblood from hypnotized mortgage applicants who have signed forms giving away their souls.[14] I refer to this as the subprime boogeyman story.

Forgotten in this story is the fact that the increase in subprime lenders helped to fuel the increase in homeownership, which was largely made up of poor and minority applicants. This is exactly what the purpose of the relaxed lending standards was supposed to be.

## 4. Problems with the Subprime Boogeyman Hypothesis

The bogeyman in the mortgage story is the unethical subprime mortgage broker who seduced unwary applicants out of their hard-earned, sacredly treated assets. The subprime boogeyman charged usurious rates for his mortgages and bamboozled his clients with artificially low teaser rates that allowed them to purchase homes that were unaffordable at realistic interest rates. This character has been pilloried by all manner of politician and pundit. Although a convenient scapegoat, this character does not appear responsible for the main part of the mortgage meltdown. This is not to say that there are not lying and cheating mortgage brokers—there are. But every profession, including economists, has its share of liars and cheaters.

There is an important problem with the hypothesis that evil subprime lenders caused the mortgage meltdown. That problem is the fact that *subprime loans did not perform any worse than prime loans.* Let's take a look.

**Figure 13.4**
**Subprime Foreclosures Started**

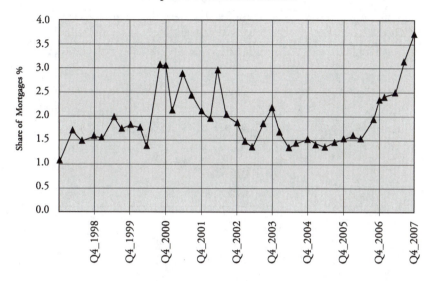

Figure 13.4 shows foreclosures started for subprime loans. Just as for overall mortgages, the increase began in the third quarter of 2006. But this wouldn't be surprising since subprimes foreclosures are a large share of all foreclosures. However, while the overall foreclosure rate was clearly in uncharted territory by the end of 2007, the foreclosure rate of subprimes, by contrast, is only somewhat above the level that occurred in late 2000 and mid-2002.

It is interesting to compare this to the performance of prime loans, which the media claimed only started suffering from defaults after the problems in the subprimes "seeped" into the prime market.

Prime foreclosures began their increase at the same moment (third quarter of 2006) as subprimes, as can be seen in Figure 13.5. Further, the prime foreclosure rate went into territory that was far above where it had been in the prior 10 years, much more so than was the case for subprimes. In percentage terms, the increase in foreclosures started, from the second quarter of 2006 until the end of 2007, was 39 percent for subprime loans and 69 percent for prime loans.

There is no evidence to support a claim that somehow the subprime market had this unprecedented increase in foreclosures and that later the primes accidentally caught the contagion. Both markets were hit at the same time and the force was at least as strong in the prime market.

**Figure 13.5**
**Prime Foreclosures Started**

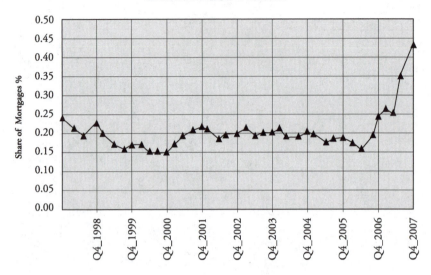

But this is not to say that foreclosures were not higher in the subprime market. They were. Historically, subprime default rates have been ten times as large as the default rates for prime loans and that has largely continued through the mortgage meltdown (just compare the numbers on the vertical axes of the two figures). That is one reason that subprime loans carry much higher interest rates than prime loans.

It has also been claimed that *adjustable* subprimes have been hit harder by foreclosures even than fixed-rate subprimes. This is true. Figure 13.6 illustrates this fact.

The foreclosures on subprime adjustable mortgages track closely with the foreclosures on subprime fixed mortgages until 2005, at which point they begin to sharply diverge. Foreclosures on subprime *adjustable* loans began to increase in late 2005 and had increased by almost 300 percent by the end of 2007 (almost 200 percent from the second quarter of 2006). Fixed subprime loans, by contrast, also had defaults rise from mid-2006 until mid-2007 (by almost 80 percent), but the foreclosure rate at the end of 2007 was considerably lower than it had been in previous years, such as 2000–2002 or the end of 2003.

The prime adjustable mortgage foreclosures, pre 2005, do not track quite as closely with the prime fixed rate mortgage foreclosures, unlike the close tracking of the two types of subprimes. Figure 13.7 shows the

**Figure 13.6**
**Fixed and Adjustable Subprime Foreclosures Started**

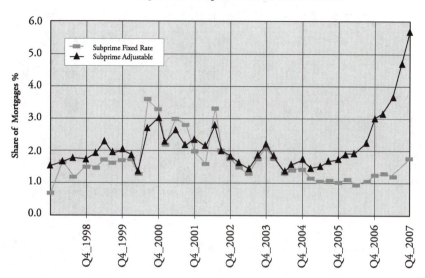

two series. Prime adjustable mortgages routinely had higher default rates than prime fixed mortgages for the first six years of data and then the two briefly coalesce in 2004–5 before diverging sharply again in 2006. As was the case for subprimes, however, when prime foreclosure rates diverge, the *adjustable* prime foreclosure rate skyrockets.

Prime fixed-rate mortgage foreclosures go up by 54 percent from the second quarter of 2006 until the end of 2007, which is not a small number, but visually the increase doesn't appear to be much because it is so dwarfed by the adjustable rate mortgages. Fixed-rate prime defaults are also at all time highs by the end of 2007, but not by much. This result is completely overshadowed, however, by the increased default rates of adjustable rate prime loans, which increase by almost 400 percent over the same period and which reached levels unlike anything in the previous decade. Again, adjustable rate prime mortgages are hit as hard or harder than the adjustable rate subprimes.

The main facts standing in the way of the subprime-boogeyman theory is that adjustable rate prime mortgages had a larger percentage increase in default rates than did the subprime market and that overall there was very little difference between the prime market and the subprime market.

Since the subprime-boogeyman, by definition, does not inhabit the prime mortgage territory, this theory is then at odds with the performance

**Figure 13.7**
**Fixed and Adjustable Prime Foreclosures Started**

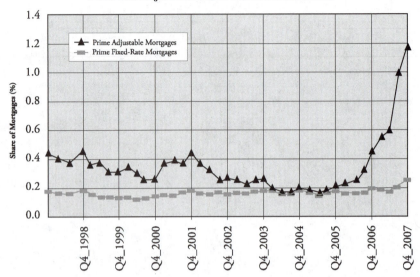

that has actually taken place in the mortgage markets. Why would mortgage defaults increase so greatly in the prime adjustable market where there was no boogeyman at work? Prime mortgage brokers do not charge usurious rates. They presumably do not face witless clients across the desk who can be easily bamboozled.

The subprime boogeyman story requires that only subprime mortgages perform badly relative to prime mortgages. They did not. Nevertheless, this story was so strongly believed that it probably explains why most news stories failed to properly note that the rise in prime defaults was occurring at exactly the same time as the subprime market and instead intoned that the subprime market problem was "leaking" into the prime market.

## 5. Interpreting These Results

So, if there is no subprime-boogeyman on whom the mortgage meltdown can be blamed, what's a politician to do?

Before answering that it is worthwhile thinking about why it might be that adjustable mortgages performed so much worse than fixed rate mortgages. The story that is popular about poor performing adjustable subprime mortgages was that the subprime customers were led by boogeymen mortgage brokers to purchase homes they could not afford because their initial lower rates would help them qualify for such a house. What adjustable rate mortgages do, of course, is to provide lower interest rates initially, at the risk of rates rising later, although they also may fall later.

Figure 13.6 makes clear, however, that adjustable rate subprime mortgages did not have higher defaults in prior years than did fixed rate subprime mortgages. This then shows another weakness in the boogeyman theory. Why would subprime customers be less susceptible to being bamboozled prior to 2005?

Actually, customers should have been more likely to be bamboozled prior to 2005. Figure 13.2 shows that new homeowners entered the market in great numbers from 1994 until 2005. Because this increase had come to an end by 2006, applicants truly unfamiliar with the mortgage process should have been less common in 2006 than had been the case in prior years. If these naïfs were steered to adjustable rate mortgages, we should have seen the higher defaults for adjustable rate mortgages prior to 2005.

Left out of the story so far is the impact of interest rates. After all, if interest rates increased then adjustable rate mortgage payments would ratchet up when they adjusted and some defaults would be likely to ensue. The timing of when the original rate adjusts in an ARM varies from one loan to another. The adjustment period for common adjustable mortgages can change within a year, or after 3 or 5 years, or at any time for option adjustable mortgages.

Figure 13.8 provides a short history of both adjustable and fixed rates for mortgages.[15] The first notable feature is that adjustable mortgages always have lower interest rates than fixed mortgages. This is for the simple reason that otherwise no borrower would ever prefer an adjustable rate mortgage. Banks can offer adjustable mortgages at lower rates since such mortgages reduce their risk. Thirty-year mortgages are commitments to receive a fixed payment for thirty years. If high inflation (and high short-term interest rates) occurs in the intervening years, the bank would take a loss since the payments they receive from these mortgages do not rise with inflation. If interest rates fall, you might think that the bank will benefit in a symmetrical way, thus evening things out, but that is not the case since the mortgagee can refinance at a lower rate, depriving the bank of the gain. Since adjustable rate mortgages change with the market, the bank is not stuck on the wrong side of an asymmetrical contract and thus banks are willing to accept lower interest rates in return.

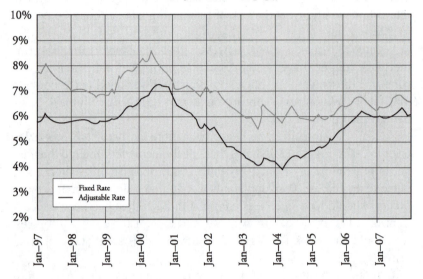

Figure 13.8
Fixed and Adjustable Mortgage Rates

The other major feature of Figure 13.8 is the drop in mortgage rates from mid-2000 until the beginning of 2004 followed by an increase in adjustable mortgage rates until mid-2006 (rates on fixed-rate mortgages remained relatively constant).

There is some evidence here consistent with a claim that higher interest rates in 2006 and 2007 might have led to defaults for mortgages adjusting in those years since the new interest rates would be higher than the old if the original rate were set in 2003 or 2004. Note, however, that a somewhat smaller but still substantial increase in interest rates occurred during 1999 and through mid-2000 yet it had a very unclear impact on defaults. For subprimes, defaults on adjustable rate mortgages rose substantially in 1999 and remained high in 2000. The problem with attributing this to the increase in interest rates is that defaults for fixed rate subprime mortgages exhibited virtually identical behavior, indicating that something other than the higher interest rates was responsible for the increase in defaults. For prime mortgages in 1999 and 2000, defaults reached a nadir in 1999 and although they did increase in 2000, this just brought them back to 1998 levels when the interest rates were not increasing. Since increases in interest rates at that time did not lead to much of an increase in foreclosures, it seems unlikely that the recent very large increase in defaults is due to increased interest rates.

It is also worthwhile remembering that much of the world, such as Canada, operates with only adjustable rate mortgages and you do not see massive defaults every time interest rates rise.

Which brings us back to the question: Why did default rates rise so rapidly for adjustable mortgages but nowhere as quickly for fixed rate mortgages? Higher interest rates seem unlikely to account for more than a small part of the increase in defaults. Declines in house prices, or more precisely, the ending of the price rise should have impacted both fixed rate and adjustable rate mortgages equally, if the population of homeowners was similar for the two types of loans since either group is as likely as the other to be underwater when home prices fall.

One possibility for the remarkable increase in defaults on adjustable rate mortgages, is that adjustable rate mortgages drew a very different types of homebuyer than did fixed rate mortgages. Fixed rate mortgages, since they charge higher interest rates, make sense for people who plan to stay in their homes for several years and who do not want to risk the possibility of rates increasing. Adjustable rate mortgages, on the other hand, are most attractive for people who intend to stay in a home for only a short period of time if at all. Such buyers get the lower interest rate without the worry about interest rates rising in the future, since they do not intend to own the home for long enough for the rates to reset.

One type of home purchaser that would be particularly attracted to adjustable rate mortgages is the speculative buyer. These would be people not expecting to stay in their house very long. One sub-type in this genre is *flippers,* as seen on several television shows. House flippers consist of people who intend to make some alterations to a house and then sell it at a profit. The other type of person looking for a short-term gain can be called *ATMers.* These are individuals or families who like to use the appreciation of a house as a personal ATM. Often, members of this latter group try to move up to larger houses so that the appreciation would be greater (assuming there would be appreciation). Sometimes someone in this latter group will purchase a second house to rent out as they wait for it to appreciate. Because of the unprecedented rise in house prices on the upside of the housing bubble, house speculation was a very successful activity drawing many new individuals into it.

Flippers never intend to hold the houses that they work on for very long and do not live in the house. ATMers often do not plan to stay in a house very long and sometimes do not live in the house. Such buyers would prefer a mortgage with the lowest possible rate, even just a teaser rate, since they plan to be out of the house before the rate resets. Since it would never make sense for these types of house buyers to get fixed rate loans, their foreclosures will show up in the adjustable mortgages, whether prime or subprime. That is consistent with the fact that prime and subprime adjustable rate mortgages each experienced enormous increases in defaults the minute that housing prices stopped rising. The foreclosures could easily be due to speculators being unable to profit from the property and thus just defaulting instead.

How many such speculative homebuyers are there? According to the National Association of Realtors, speculative home purchases amounted to 28 percent of all sales in 2005 and 22 percent in 2006.[16] These numbers are large enough that if only a minority of speculators defaulted when housing prices stopped increasing, it could have explained all or most of the entire increase in foreclosures started. Although it is unlikely that speculators are responsible for the entire increase in foreclosures, the fact that foreclosures are very high where speculation was rampant (Florida, Las Vegas, and California) further strengthens this hypothesis. The alternative boogeyman explanation does not seem to explain why foreclosures are so high in these locations.

The type of speculation described here might sound like a middle or upper class activity. In fact, the areas where this type of speculation seems most common are lower-income areas. The lower line in Figure 13.9 reveals that areas with low incomes have a larger share of homes bought speculatively. The measure of speculation is the share of mortgages made to people not planning to make the house being purchased their primary residence. The data come from the 2006 HMDA. This particular measure of speculation is actually biased against such a finding because it includes vacation homes as short-term speculative purchases (which they are not since people buying vacation homes plan to stay a long time) and vacation homes tend to be in higher priced neighborhoods.

Indeed, speculation is more strongly negatively related to income of a census tract than is subprime mortgage origination (where subprime is defined mortgages with above normal interest rates), which is the upper line in Figure 13.9. The point of this comparison is to show that speculation is more strongly related to an area's income than is subprime lending. Indeed, speculation occurs at more than twice the rate in low-income areas than in wealthier areas.

Although this evidence supports a view that the increase in foreclosures is mainly due to speculators, it is not a direct test. Whether speculators are responsible for most of the dramatic increase in defaults can be, in principle, more directly tested. Since speculators are less likely to live

**Figure 13.9**
**Shares of Spectulative and Subprime Loans by Census Tract Income**

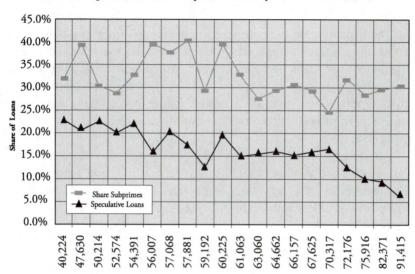

in the homes they purchase than are ordinary purchasers, a direct test would be to examine whether homes that are defaulting also have lower occupancy-by-owner rates than typical homes. In particular, how much of the increase in foreclosures would seem to be due to owners that did not occupy the house? This, unfortunately, would require data of finer granularity than found in typical data sets and whether such data even exist is unknown to me.

A second and weaker approach would be to examine the share of homes that are purchased to be lived in for both fixed and adjustable rate mortgages and see if the population of homes that are not occupied by the owner has a higher percentage of adjustable rate mortgages than owner occupied homes. This would be less definitive as a test but it would at least examine whether my suggestion that speculative purchasers take primarily adjustable rate mortgages is correct. Such data probably exist but I do not have access to such data.

## 6. Conclusions

We are experiencing one of the worst financial panics in the post-World War II era. Everyone knows that the increase in mortgage defaults has been the primary driver for these financial difficulties. The mortgages with outrageously lax underwriting standards that have been justifiably ridiculed in the press are not unusual outliers but unfortunately representative of a great many mortgages that have been made in the last few years.

The question that is being asked is the correct question: how did it come about that our financial system allowed such loans to be made, condoned such loans, and even celebrated such loans? The answers that are being given are not yet the correct ones, however. The main answer that is being given, that unscrupulous lenders were taking advantage of poorly informed borrowers, does not fit the evidence nor does it dig deep enough.

Almost completely ignored are the "mortgage innovations" that are largely the responsibility of the federal government. These "innovations," heralded as such by regulators, politicians, GSEs, and academics are the true culprits responsible for the mortgage meltdown. Without these innovations we would not have seen prime mortgages made with zero down payments, which is what happens when individuals use a second mortgage to cover the down payment of the first. Nor would we have seen "liar loans" where the applicant was allowed to make up an income number, unless the applicant was putting up an enormous down payment, which was the perfectly reasonable historical usage of no-doc loans.

The political housing establishment, by which I mean the federal government and all the agencies involved with regulating housing and mortgages, is proud of its mortgage innovations because they increased homeownership. The housing establishment refuses, however, to take the blame for the flip side of its focus on increasing homeownership—first, the bubble in home prices caused by the lowering of underwriting standards and then the bursting of the bubble with the almost catastrophic consequences to the economy as a whole and the financial difficulties being faced by some of the very homeowners the housing establishment claims to be trying to benefit.

The evidence on foreclosures is consistent with an overall loosening of underwriting standards, as I describe above, not with the subprime story being put forward by the housing establishment and its pliant political supporters.

The key facts are that both subprime and prime loans had large increases in foreclosures at the same time. The subprime vulture hypothesis story just does not fit the evidence. The main driver of foreclosures was adjustable rate loans, both prime and subprime. Therefore, any understanding of the current crisis must account for this fact. The subprime boogeyman theory does not.

The hypothesis that currently seems to best fit with the evidence suggests that housing speculators were taking out many loans with the hope of a quick and profitable turnover. These housing speculators did not much care about the terms of their mortgages because they didn't expect to be making payments for very long. But it is clear why they would prefer adjustable rate mortgages. The hypothesis also is consistent with speculators often lying about their income on their loan applications and taking out teaser rates so they would qualify for larger loans, so they could make a bigger bet on housing. Under this hypothesis borrowers are adults, not witless pawns.

When the housing bubble stopped growing, according to this hypothesis, these speculators turned and ran. Left holding the mortgage-debt bag are the investors who lent money to these speculators. The size of the mortgage-debt bag was so massive that fear of being left holding it brought the financial system to its knees.

But let's not blame the speculators here. There is nothing wrong with speculation or speculators. At fault is a mortgage system run by flexible underwriting standards that allowed these speculators to make bets on the housing market with other people's money. It was a system that invited the applicant to lie about income. It was a system that induced applicants to watch a video instead of providing solid evidence about their financial condition.

Even that would not be so bad if the people making the money available were aware of its use and knew that they would have recourse to getting their money back. But the money for the speculation was made available by lenders who believed the housing and regulatory establishment when this housing and regulatory establishment said that such loans were safe. Since the housing and regulatory establishment consisted of mighty government agencies and highly educated academics, it was not unreasonable for the lenders to assume that the claims made for flexible underwriting standards were correct. Unfortunately, the claims were not correct although most of the housing and regulatory establishment continue to argue otherwise.

Hindsight is the best sight, they say. Unfortunately, the housing establishment and our political leaders seem intent on not learning from the past. Hopefully this chapter can help move the debate in a direction that will allow for more productive learning.

## Notes

1.    Including academic winds. The article (Munnell et al., 1996) was published in the *American Economic Review* and the editor presumably felt strongly enough

about the political conclusions that he refused to run any comments on the article. Further, he allowed the Boston Fed authors to malign the work of one of their critics, David Horne, by alleging he could not reproduce certain of his results, which Horne denied. I believe Horne.

2.    All quotes were taken from "Boston Fed Finds Racial Discrimination in Mortgage Lending is Still Widespread" Thomas, Paulette. *Wall Street Journal*, Oct 9, 1992, p. A3.

3.    It was actually called: "{Closing the Gap:} A Guide to Equal Opportunity Lending" There were no authors listed but Susan E. Rodburg and Richard C. Walker, III were listed as Project Coordinators. Available at http://www.bos.frb.org/commdev/commaff/closingt.pdf.

4.    This is true regardless of whether the counseling is at the individual level, based on classroom "education" or conducted over the telephone. See Spader and Quercia (2008).

5.    Both of these stories are reported here: http://www.minorityprofessionalnetwork.com/News/Countrywide.htm.

6.    See http://www.prnewswire.com/cgi-bin/stories.pl?ACCT=104&STORY=/www/story/06–08–2005/0003824590&EDATE=.

7.    "Case Study: Countrywide Home Loans, Inc." Fannie Mae Foundation 2000. http://www.fanniemaefoundation.org/programs/pdf/rep_newmortmkts_countrywide.pdf.

8.    "Packaging CRA Loans into Securities" Dale Westhoff, Mortgage Banking, May 1 1998. http://www.allbusiness.com/personal-finance/real-estate-mortgage-loans/677967–1.html.

9.    *The Wall Street Journal*, "Credit and Blame: How Rating Firms' Calls Fueled Subprime Mess—Benign View of Loans Helped Create Bonds, Led to More Lending" Aaron Lucchetti and Serena Ng, August 15, 2007.

10.    For a recent and careful analysis showing that LTV is the key factor leading to foreclosures see Gerardi et al. (2007).

11.    "The Rise in Homeownership" FRBSF Economic Letter Number 2006–30, November 3, 2006 http://www.frbsf.org/publications/economics/letter/2006/e12006–30.html.

12.    All statistics on foreclosures come from the Mortgage Banker Association. There are several measures of delinquency and default. The measure chosen for the charts here is "foreclosures started" which differs from foreclosure inventory, which was not chosen since the latter depends on more than just what is happening in the most recent quarter, meaning that how quickly or how slowly homes leave foreclosure also impacts the inventory.

13.    An exquisite personal story illustrating these points involves one Dien Truong from Richmond California, a 35 year old water deliveryman who refinanced his home with an option adjustable ARM for $628,000 from which he promptly removed $156,000 to purchase a second house. On his loan application he and his wife claimed to make more than twice as much income as they actually earned. His loan balance on the first mortgage, since he had opted to pay less than the interest payment on the mortgage, is now $690,000 and he cannot make his monthly payments. Says Mr. Truong "I've been a good customer.... This time my credit will be screwed up for good." See Wall Street Journal "FirstFed Grapples With Payment-Option Mortgages" Ruth Simon, August 6, 2008.

14.    I apologize for mixing metaphors.

15.    These data come from HSH Associates. It is a quite imperfect measure since it is an amalgam of slightly different mortgages (points and so forth) mixed together

to come up with an average rate. The data can be found at http://www.hsh.com/
mtghst.html.

16.   See "Vacation-Home Sales Rise to Record, Investment Sales Plummet in 2006"
      April 30, 2007, National Association of Realtors. http://www.realtor.org/press_
      room/news_releases/2007/phsi_apr07_vacation_home_sales_rise.

# References

Day, Theodore and Stan J. Liebowitz "Mortgage Lending to Minorities: Where's The
      Bias?" *Economic Inquiry*, January 1998, pp. 1–27.

Gerardi, Kristopher, Adam Hale Shapiro, and Paul S. Willen, "Subprime Outcomes:
      Risky Mortgages, Homeownership Experiences, and Foreclosures" Working Paper,
      Federal Reserve Bank of Boston, December, 2007.

Listokin, David, Elvin K. Wyly, Brian Schmitt, and Ioan Voicu, "The Potential and Limi-
      tations of Mortgage Innovation in Fostering Homeownership in the United States,"
      Fannie Mae Foundation 2002.

Mian, Atif and Amir Sufi, "The Consequences of Mortgage Credit Expansion: Evidence
      from the 2007 Mortgage Default Crisis" Working Paper, University of Chicago,
      January 2008.

Munnell, A., Tootell, G., Browne, L., Mceneaney, J., "Mortgage Lending In Boston:
      Interpreting HMDA Data," *American Economic Review*, March 1996, pp. 25–54.

Spader, Jonathan S. and Roberto G. Quercia "Does Homeownership Counseling Affect
      the Prepayment and Default Behavior of Affordable Mortgage Borrowers?" Work-
      ing Paper: January 2008 Center for Community Capital, The University of North
      Carolina at Chapel Hill.

# 14

# Urban Planning:
# The Government or the Market

*Fred E. Foldvary*

A plan serves as the blueprint or foundation for a construction or action. An urban plan is a design for the physical elements of a city such as the streets, blocks, land usage, and transit, and the operational elements such as the governance and financing. Regional planning is applied to a wider area, with less detail.

Economic investments, as an increase in the stock of capital goods, necessarily involve planning, because the attempt to maximize net gains requires estimates in advance of the costs of the materials and time required, an analysis of the opportunity costs (the alternatives foregone), and the expected gains from various methods of production and the various possible products. Wise planners know that these variables are subject to change, and that the further into the future a plan reaches, the greater is the degree of uncertainty. Thus, an optimal plan economizes on the planning process itself, because overplanning can become wasteful if the plan's goals are not realized.

Complex plans, such as a city master plan, will have gaps because all circumstances cannot be anticipated. Market dynamics provides a way to fill gaps and mitigate planning errors. As stated by Israel Kirzner (1992: 12), "each gap in market co-ordination expresses itself as a pure profit opportunity." Filling these gaps is not automatic, as it requires entrepreneurial alertness, but as gaps are noticed, markets eliminate them. The market as a whole can be regarded as a means of, as Mark Pennington (2002: 39) put it, "decentralized social planning," as the plans of individuals continuously become adjusted to one another via prices, contracts, and personal relationships. Competition helps people discover how much planning is optimal.

Wise planners in a market context realize that their planning capabilities are limited by the need to have voluntary agreements with customers, employees, suppliers, and tenants, all of whom have their own autonomous plans. In contrast, government officials may believe that they have a greater control of their plans, because they can use coercion to compel people to act within the constraints of their plan. But this imagined planning power is illusory, even a conceit, to use Hayek's (1988) term, because the complete information needed to implement the plan is unknowable. The greater the scope of the plan, the less the planners are able to take advantage of economic calculations that reflect scarcity and social welfare, so the actual outcome will be far from optimal. If the aim of the governmental plan is the maximization of overall social well-being, centrally imposed plans necessarily fail.

There have been cities such as Washington, DC that were physically designed from the beginning, and there also are many urban master plans for the further development, or the preservation of status-quo land uses, in existing cities. There have also been many communities planned from the beginning by private developers operating in the market. Their plans have included not only the physical elements but also the post-construction administration of the community, such as with homeowner associations. Such relatively small-scale plans for the physical, administrative, and financial infrastructure can work well, provided that the property rights are clear and that the plans do not attempt to suppress market prices or economic evolution.

The spontaneous order of a market is not "anything goes" but, as an order, falls within the constraints of market ethics and within the physical structures that can indeed be planned, just as skaters in a rink gyrate spontaneously within the ethic of skating that forbids deliberate bumping, and is confined to the rink. Planning and spontaneity can be complementary, if each respects the domain of the other.

Private organizations necessarily include administration, decision-making, rules, and financing, thus governance. Homeowner associations elect boards of directors whose function is analogous to a city council. Hence, the fundamental contrast is not markets versus planning but between imposed government planning, ("planning by edict," as Lai (2005) puts it), and planning by voluntary governance.

We need to delve into the concept of the market to understand its method of urban planning, which is based on voluntary governance. Then we will investigate urban planning in the context of a pure free market, and can contrast that with imposed government planning.

## 1. The Meaning of the Market

The pure "free market" consists of only voluntary human action. The market consists of activity that produces, exchanges, and distributes economic wealth—goods and services. The concept of "voluntary" action implies an ethic that designates two distinct sets of acts: coercive acts, which lie outside the market, and the voluntary acts, which are permissible within the market. This market ethic, which Foldvary (1980) notes that philosophers have called "natural moral law," regards market exchange favorably because people agree to the exchanges and thus must view the result as beneficial, or at worst neutral. Coercive acts have the potential to harm people against their will, however, and constitute an invasion into the domain of a person. The market ethic recognizes that people have rights only to their property, not to the property of others.

Pure free markets imply planning by freehold rather than by the state. A "freehold" is a legal right to the possession of, and income from, real estate during the life of the owner. In planning by freehold, households and enterprises that own freehold estates are free to make their own planning decisions (Foldvary, 2005b). Such planning has four aspects: the internal planning of organizations, the contractual relationships among these organizations, the relationship between the owner and the community governance, and the spontaneous evolution of plans as circumstances and preferences change, and as people learn by trial and error. Planning by freehold, being decentralized and conducted by owners seeking to maximize net benefits, harmonizes ethics and economics. It does not coercively impose costs on others, and it provides incentives for maximizing the productivity of the location.

## 2. Governance in a Pure Free Market

Private planning is typically on a smaller scale than governmental planning. Gordon Tullock (1994) proposes that many urban services can be devolved to the neighborhood level. The typical private community is an application of that small-scale principle. There are two basic options for contractual governance by freehold estates: the proprietary community and the civic association.

The proprietary community is owned and governed by one agent. The community includes the tenants, customers, and guests. Examples include shopping centers, industrial parks, office buildings, apartments, mobile home parks, and marinas. The owner can be a corporation, land trust, real estate investment trust (REIT), partnership, nonprofit organization, or sole proprietor. The proprietor itself, such as a corporation, can have many owners, but there is one designated decision maker, either a person or a group such as a board. The residents and tenants are not empowered to make community-wide decisions, although they may have a voice. The best-known proprietary community is Walt Disney World in Florida, which includes theme parks, hotels, and wildlife conservation areas. Currently the largest proprietary residential community, with a population of 200,000, is in Wuhan, China (Webster et al., 2005). Indeed, much of the new housing in fast-growing China is being administered by private communities.

The civic association is a group of co-owners who form a community with democratic governance. Often the planned unit developments, also called common interest developments, begin as proprietary communities controlled by the developer but gradually become associational as more of the board members are elected by the residents, replacing the developer's representatives. In some residential associations (but not in a condominium), renters may also vote for the board, an owner-occupant having two votes, one as resident and other as owner. The types of civic associations include residential or homeowner associations, condominiums, and cooperatives.[1]

Purely voluntary civic associations are similar to city governments in form and in the provision of public goods, but there are two elements which makes them market-based rather than imposed government. First, private governance is based on explicit contracts, and second, the parties to the contract have an equal legal standing, with no immunity from lawsuits (Foldvary, 2006a). The voluntariness of an agreement is at the highest level of agreement, such as getting married, hiring an employee, or signing a lease. Once the agreement is made, parties to it take on certain obligations. A valid contract requires real agreement, and the mere fact that someone is located in some jurisdiction does not imply that the resident has agreed with the laws and the methods of enacting and changing the laws. Furthermore, voluntary contracts are positive-sum, with each party gaining value; otherwise, they would not enter the agreement. Imposed restrictions can be zero-sum or negative-sum.

With homeowner or residential associations, the areas not under individual title are owned by the association. In condominiums, the association owns nothing, and each member has a percentage interest in the common elements (such as the landscaping, meeting rooms, and parking), with that percentage also allocating its voting share and its share of the assessment payments.[2] In a cooperative, a member owns shares, which entitles the member to use a housing unit.

If a developer is planning a large community, he may include a mix of governance, such as proprietary governance for a shopping mall and homeowner associations for the residential areas. Governance can also encompass a greater association by making neighborhood communities members of a higher-level association, the latter governed by a board or council to which the neighborhood organizations send representatives, unless the entire greater community is to be under one proprietor.

In a proprietary community, private law is established by the leasehold contracts. Business relationships which are complex and long-term can induce opportunism, the exploitation of dependent relationships. The market response is complex contracts and private governance, backed up by tort law. In a civic association, the developer typically creates a constitutional document such as a master deed. The developer and then the association board enact bylaws and covenants, conditions, and restrictions (CC&Rs). The covenants prevent negative externalities such as noise and disagreeable visual effects, and can also mandate positive externalities such as requiring well-maintained front yards. As stated by Philip Booth (2005): "Externalities exist, not where markets fail, but where markets are incomplete or absent."

All planning and all collective goods can be produced via the market with several levels of association. Households would contract with a proprietary or associational community. A score of these communities could create a higher-level association to coordinate activities and to provide services that have economies of wider scale. These associations could in turn create a next higher-level association, and so on up to the highest level desired. Much as many counties make up a state, many homeowner associations could join together to form a super-association, many super-associations could form an even larger association, and so on to create larger associations that could produce large-scale goods and services for their members. All governance would then be contractual, and thus all public goods would be provided voluntarily, creating a "completely decentralized city" (Foldvary, 2001).

### 3. The Financing of Club Territorial Goods

Competition among private communities for property buyers, tenants, and customers induces communities to use efficient means of financing, because people will respond to incentives. They will do less of what is more costly and more of what is more beneficial. Trial and error can also achieve efficient results, and we can see what works in practice. For example, if an architect designs a park in the shape of a square, we can confidently predict that people will cross the park diagonally, to economize on time, so a plan that does not put in a diagonal path will fail, as people will tread on the grass to create such a path.

The cost-minimizing financing of collective goods avoids the dead-weight loss of typical governmental taxation. Charges imposed on users will not be based on income or sales, or on other sources of revenue unrelated to benefits. The most efficient general source of voluntary civic financing is the rentals of the affected real estate because the payments internalize what would otherwise be the externalities of civic benefits. As stated by James Buchanan and Charles Goetz (1972: 35), competitive landed clubs are most efficient when the payments by the members are "related to the size of the *locational rent* component in individual income receipts." As stated by Spencer MacCallum (1970: 50), "The objective is to optimize the total environment of each site within a system of sites in order to maximize the combined rents they will command." This is what theory predicts, and it is what is actually practiced in the market.

Better civic services—streets, security, parks, fire protection, transit—increase the benefits of the affected territory and the demand to be located there, driving up rentals and site values. This upward capitalization of civic services provides the means to finance them from the generated rentals. If the revenue is from the site value or rental, excluding the value of the buildings and other improvements, then the public finance has no deadweight loss. Within the boundaries of a community, the supply of surface space is fixed and immobile. Land does not shrink when tapped for revenue, nor does it hide or flee (Foldvary, 2005a).

A user fee can finance a service that affects specific persons and which has significant marginal costs. But where the marginal cost is not worth collecting, and the service impacts territory and induces greater rentals, the efficient user charge, in accord with marginal-cost pricing, is zero, the costs instead being paid from the rental. In a hotel for example, elevators and escalators have no user charge, as they add value to rooms, and the cost is paid from the room rentals.

The economics of horizontal community transit are similar. The cost of one more rider in a bus is near zero, and many private communities offer free shuttles and bus service, paid for from the assessments on the units owned by the members.

A third source of market-enhancing club-goods financing can be charges for negative externalities such as pollution and congestion. Besides levying effluent charges for dumping industrial waste, modern technology can be used to measure automobile exhaust using remote sensors, and the car owners who pollute can then be billed (Klein, 2003).

Contrary to "market failure" doctrines, roads and other infrastructure can be and actually have been provided and funded privately (Samuel, 2003; Roth, 2006). The entrepreneurs don't need to contract with all the individual customers, because in a pure market setting, people are not isolated individuals but are always already organized in communities, including geographical ones, such as proprietary apartment buildings and homeowner associations. The financing for roads can come from tolls, a portion of site rentals of communities served, charges for pollution and congestion, and associated services such as parking, rest stops, and utility rights of way. It is interesting to note that many cities charge people to park in "public" parking lots, whereas most shopping centers offer "free" parking, with the cost of parking being covered by the rents paid by tenants. Historically, in early America, plank roads were financed by benevolent contributions (Klein, 1990).

## 4. The Physical Elements of Private Planning

The roads, streets, transit, parks, and other physical elements of a private plan complement the financial side. Since locational benefits become capitalized into higher site values, within an area to be developed, the optimal plan maximizes the land rental of the community, and the optimal amount of particular features such as parks and recreation is the amount at which the marginal benefit equals the marginal cost. Such estimates are subject to entrepreneurial error, such as building tennis courts which get little use, but in that case, the cost is borne by investors who know in advance that they may face losses, and the cost is not imposed on an entire region or economy.

Economic efficiency is maximized at quantities for which price equals marginal cost, where the costs include all implicit negative elements such as congestion and pollution. The efficient price for a street, highway, or parking place is therefore a toll just high enough to prevent congestion, with no charge when the passage is not crowded (Foldvary, 2006b). A developer may well plan to include such tolls, but the amount of tolls cannot be precisely planned for, as it depends on uncertain future demands.

The plan for urban transit should allocate transit operators' "curb rights," i.e., property rights to locations along street curbs and turnouts, where vehicles may pick up passengers. In addition to having its own bus stops, a community could rent out such "curb rights" to jitneys and taxis

(Klein et al., 1997). A taxi cab operates on demand rather than having a fixed route, with personalized service, and it therefore has a significant marginal cost per rider and group of riders. A jitney, like today's airport vans, has characteristics between a taxi and a bus, operating more flexibly than a bus, and at a smaller scale, and so it typically charges individual fees less than that of a taxi. Jitneys and buses would therefore typically not be provided gratis to users by proprietary communities. The owners of private communities would instead profit from renting curb rights, along with providing metered parking. The optimal allocation of parking would use advanced metering technology that records the time electronically, with no time limit, the charge varying by hour to prevent congestion (Shoup, 2003).

In proprietary communities such as shopping centers and large hotels, the developer plans for complementary tenants who will maximize the expected rentals. This includes, in a shopping center, an anchor store which attracts customers. The plan also provides services such as parking, waste collection, restrooms, traffic controls, and security. "Free parking" is optimal when there are normally enough spaces for all shoppers and there would be a loss of profits if the parking space were used for more stores instead or if customers were charged for parking.

The most influential plan for civic associations was developed by Ebenezer Howard in his book *Tomorrow: A Peaceful Path To Real Reform* (1898). The second edition was entitled *Garden Cities of Tomorrow* (1902). It included a "voluntary plan of public finance" using leaseholds of land: "ground rents ... shall be paid to the trustees, who, after providing for interest and sinking fund, will hand the balance to the Central Council of the new municipality, to be employed by such Council in the creation and maintenance of all necessary public works—roads, schools, parks, etc."

A Board of Management, elected by leaseholders, would govern the city. The extent of town services would be limited by the willingness of leaseholders to pay the rents. Howard envisioned charitable institutions in the community sponsored by public-spirited residents. Some communities in the United States such as Arden village and the Reston Association have implemented Howard's plan to a remarkable degree.

## 5. Spontaneous Orders versus Government Planning

Although the initial physical layout, as outlined above, can benefit from an intelligent design, the fatal conceit of central planning should be avoided by limiting the scale of the plan, by avoiding excessively rigid rules, making it too difficult to change the rules, and by attempting to plan the individual human uses of the physical elements. Thus, the plan should allow spontaneous orders to emerge.

As Jane Jacobs (1961), critic of urban plans, pointed out, cities thrive when spontaneous changes are not blocked. Spencer MacCallum (1970) has argued that subdivided communities, including those with homeowner associations, are inherently too rigid, because any major redevelopment requires the consent of the members, and some owners will obstruct a change that would increase the productivity of the site. He argues (2003) that proprietary entrepreneurial communities provide the most effective means for private-sector planning, as the owner has the authority to change the plan. On the other hand, some residents prefer the greater control that individual ownership provides, and the security against being evicted.

Historically, cities have grown rapidly and in an orderly manner without any visible hand to control the development. Great Britain became the world's first urbanized population by 1851, with an unprecedented growth of its cities, without any centralized urban planning or land-use controls until the Housing and Town Planning Act of 1909. Urban growth was "directed by property rights and private contracts, and shaped and determined by market forces" (Davies, 2002: 19). There were no housing shortages, and the poor were provided with affordable housing. Infrastructure was provided by the landlord or the developer. Covenants were used to coordinate and allocate land-use rights, thus preventing offensive uses. Prescriptive covenants specified the types of materials used and the heights of the buildings. The absence of governmental planning was therefore not a chaos of disorder, but a decentralized profit-incentivized contract-based order that was simultaneously spontaneous and organizational. The main role of the government was to enforce the contracts.

As Friedrich Hayek (1967) pointed out, many institutions and practices have evolved as a result of the unintended consequences of human action, being neither constructed nor "natural" (based on instinct or genetics). In peaceful institutional evolution, those practices that are less effective tend to be eliminated, as profitable enterprises expand and those with losses get weeded out. Applied to urban planning, this Hayekian insight implies that while the physical infrastructure can be initially designed, the subsequent optimal use of the sites evolves spontaneously, and the original plan may need to change. Private contracts such as easements are more decentralized and flexible than city-wide zoning and less subject to political pressures.

## 6. Problems with Government Planning

Any governmental planning is subject to three principal defects: perverse incentives, the absence of relevant knowledge, and value imposition.

The two main incentive issues are well known in the branch of economics called "public choice." The first is "transfer seeking" by special interests. When the potential benefits of subsidies, privileges, and protection from competition are concentrated in a relatively small group, then the members have a strong incentive to spend money in the "market for legislation" (Wagner, 1989) in order to gain these transfers (also referred to as "rents"). With a high demand for campaign financing by candidates seeking office in a mass democracy, the special interests supply the funds in exchange for the subsidies, and vote-trading by legislators enables the transfer seekers to obtain gains even if they only influence some of the government officials. The costs of these transfers are thinly spread among the taxpayers and consumers, so they have little incentive to organize a resistance.

The second incentive issue is the tyranny of the majority, as candidates cater to the "median voter," whose position on policy is in the center of a range, as this maximizes the vote total. The incentive towards the median voter leaves those at the fringes without an effective voice or free choice.

The third defect of governmental planning is value imposition. Production in a market economy, and the production plans of private enterprise, is ultimately dependent on the preferences of households, which get transmitted up to the firms by their demands. Any intervention into the market necessarily alters the choices of individuals, overrides consumer sovereignty, and imposes values on unwilling subjects. As discussed above, the market consists of voluntary acts, which may displease others but do not invade the domains of others. Laws which prohibit private coercion—theft, trespass, damage to other's property—are market enhancing, but laws which restrict peaceful and honest human action are market hampering. Any intervention into the market necessarily changes what peaceful human action would otherwise do, imposing the value of the authority over that of the person affected.

For example, suppose a neighborhood is zoned for detached houses, and an owner wishes to replace his house with an apartment building. His neighbors object to that wish because they value the lower density and population characteristics of the status quo. The owner values the greater income he could get from the property, and potential future residents value the greater opportunity for housing that development would offer. The zoning, and the denial of a zoning variance, imposes the status quo values above the values of those who would benefit from a change. In a free market, some will be displeased by some outcomes, but none will have their property domains invaded. Those who are offended or displeased are not enslaved, because they do not have a right to be the masters of others and determine how others use their property. In contrast, those who are involuntarily restricted by government-imposed plans have had property rights that they worked to acquire forcibly taken from them, which implies to that degree an enslavement to others.

The question is not whether there is planning, but at what level and by whom. Even within firms and community organizations, the decentralized knowledge about the local and current circumstances prevents the central director from controlling all the processes and decisions, but the planning structure is agreed to by all participants. This is not so when government plans are imposed on people.

### 7. Knowledge, Economic Calculation, and Planning

The analysis of the epistemics—the relevant knowledge—of planning has been analyzed most intensively by the Austrian-school economists, principally Ludwig von Mises and Friedrich Hayek. Mises (1920, 1922) pointed out that "economic calculation," an allocation of resources which reflects scarcity and desire, requires the incentive of profit seeking as well as competitive market prices, elements missing in governmental planning. The private entrepreneur gains from judging well, and so has an incentive to minimize costs, while the government planner does not personally gain from the success of, say, zoning, so he instead seeks to maximize the budget for his office or some other private benefit. Moreover, market prices reflect the individual desires of those making bids, whereas the planner's preconceived goal such as "urban renewal" presumes a social gain but has no way to actually measure or predict it, and the social costs of the plan become somebody else's problem.

Friedrich Hayek (1945) added the concepts of decentralized and discovered knowledge. The knowledge relevant to economic decisions is dispersed in the local activities of entrepreneurs, workers, tenants, and shoppers. Neoclassical economics posits that there is simply some cost of obtaining information, but the Hayekian insight goes much deeper than mere cost.

The knowledge needed for large-scale planning is not capable of being collected, for several reasons. First, the relevant variables are too complex to be integrated into one plan. As the number of variables and their interconnections increase, the number of interactions becomes too large to assimilate in a plan. Second, the variables are in constant flux, and there is a lag in collecting the data, with another lag in using it and a third lag in the effects on society. A plan has to include planning for change, ways to alter the plan. Private firms typically handle this by endowing the owner or his agent, a manager or executive, with default control when plans need to change. Changing a governmental plan involves going through the channels of a hierarchy, public hearings, or changes in legislation, all of which take time and are typically not the outcome of expert knowledge.

Third, much of knowledge is not written down, but is embedded in the human capital of entrepreneurship, employee labor know-how, and users of facilities. Much of the relevant economic knowledge is not in a handbook or manual. The knowledge is to a large degree tacit; these agents themselves may not be able to articulate the fullness of this knowledge.

Fourth, even when facts are available, the data must necessarily be interpreted. As Ronald Reagan (1988) inadvertently stated, "facts are stupid things." Reagan meant to say, and corrected himself to say, "stubborn things," citing John Adams, who had written, "Facts are stubborn things." But indeed, facts do not speak for themselves, and are always interpreted. The interpretations depend on subjective values, cultures that differ, and on beliefs and doctrines which may not be fully warranted by logic and evidence.

Fifth, orders from the planners to the administrators will be imperfectly transmitted and followed, because the agents will also cater to their own wants, and because the orders will be imperfectly understood. Sixth, the future is inherently uncertain; some of the consequences of attempts to plan will be unintended and unforeseen.

Seventh, in a market context, people can make choices continuously; a tenant may move, an owner may sell, workers may quit, and a customer may switch a service provider. Contracts may usually be broken, at some price. In contrast, governmental planning, once a plan is set, is often stuck until the next legislative acts. In a pure market, all persons are sovereign, while under a government directive, everybody becomes a slave to the plan. Those affected cannot quit or secede, other than to emigrate. The plan can become politically difficult to change, as the vested interests resists changes that will make them suffer losses.

Another knowledge problem concerns knowledge about planning itself. There is no consensus among planners regarding optimal plans. "The contemporary planning literature is polarized between advocates of 'compact settlement' approaches ... and those who favour a more low-density alternative" to deal with pollution and congestion (Pennington, 2002: 43). If there is no clear theory of planning, how can planners presume to know better than market participants?

The epistemics of economic decision making often emerges from the very acts of production, exchange, and consumption. A consumer discovers what goods he likes by trying them out. An entrepreneur conducts market surveys, and also learns from his competitors, and the dynamics of the market—firms making profits and losses, prices moving up and down unexpectedly—are all learning experiences. As Hayek (1985) put it, competition is a discovery process. The central planner cannot discover this, and he also cannot gather and interpret and use the data fast enough, and worst of all, the government planner often does not and cannot even know what data he should be looking for.

## 8. Governmental Zoning

Zoning and other elements of a comprehensive governmental plan imply that the city council and planning commission have set objectives and goals, such as the extent and direction of economic development. But such goals at best reflect the values of a portion of the community, and most likely not even a majority. It is well established by the Condorcet Voting Paradox that the outcomes of voting are not necessarily consistent, and the "impossibility theorem" of Kenneth Arrow concludes that no voting system can unambiguously reflect a general will of the public. An even deeper problem is that people as consumers, voters, and investors, don't necessarily know what they ultimately prefer among a list of choices; they often try out various choices or experiment to see what they like or what works best. They may at first object to a new chain coffee shop, only to find out later that they like its ambiance and service. Preferences are not all given, but can emerge and be developed as acquired tastes.

Zoning is an intervention into the land-use decisions that property owners would otherwise wish to make. One rationale of zoning is the reduction in negative externalities such as noise, excessive traffic, crowding, and visual blight. But the attempt to treat an externality that accompanies higher density can itself create other externalities, such as higher housing costs and costly urban sprawl.

Zoning has been construed as a collective property right of a majority of the current residents. With zoning they restrict the property rights of those within the community who prefer other land uses as well as those outside the community who wish to enter and develop sites differently. In practice, the "collective" that pushes for and benefits from zoning can be a special interest that gains at the expense of the majority. Governmental planning decisions are made by city councils and legislatures, who may well pay attention to professional planners, but also cater to those helping them get elected. George Stigler's (1971) public-choice analysis of regulation applies to zoning and other urban planning: once government has the power to control rights, then groups with concentrated potential benefits will use the political market for legislation to transfer wealth and privileges to themselves. In effect, zoning creates a territorial cartel. Among other pathologies, "Zoning was a powerful instrument of income and class segregation" (Nelson, 2005: 145).

There is no natural collective property right to the density or a particular land use in a neighborhood. In market-based planning and dynamic evolution, unfavorable changes can be prevented with covenants and easements. An easement gives particular persons property rights in real estate owned by others. For example, an easement could give someone the right to cross another's property along a particular path, or an easement could provide a neighbor with the right to a view, prohibiting the view from being blocked. Easements, along with covenants and deed restrictions, can take the place of zoning and other governmental land-use controls. An "easement appurtenant" runs with the land, being transferred to new owners.

Because the same ends could be accomplished with such private rules, in effect zoning confers a subsidy to the beneficiaries. Instead of buying an easement, the city benefits a landowner by restricting the property use of others. By saving the cost of buying an easement or deed restriction, the beneficiary is subsidized.

Zoning is not warranted just because some people benefit. Instead we must analyze both the social costs and benefits. Zoning that prohibits greater density, for example, benefits the current residents at the expense of those who wish to move in, and raises rental costs and land prices for tenants and new buyers. But by reducing the efficiency of land use, zoning that prevents higher density can have a net social cost.

It is not entirely a free-market choice when people prefer to live in suburbs today. Their incentives have been skewed by restrictions on development, such as zoning, that shift it elsewhere, and to public-works-inflated locational values. One cannot therefore logically conclude from current land-use patterns that this is simply what people "choose." As Mason Gaffney (1964, 18) versed it:

> O, Thou, who didst with windfall and with waste
> Beset the streets where buildings may be placed
> Thou wilt not with predetermined choice propel
> Me outwards, then impute my sprawl to "Taste"!

## 9. Quasi-Governmental Planning

Planning by government edict and planning by voluntary market dynamics are not disjoint, but a continuum. For example, in Hong Kong, the government sells leaseholds of government-owned land, with conditions set in the contract. Because nobody is forced to buy a leasehold, is this, as Lai (2005) puts it, a voluntary "planning by contract"? There is a market element in the competition for the leaseholds by auction and tender. Excessively restrictive contract terms result in lower leasehold bids. In Hong Kong, the leasehold contracts permit housing development and commercial uses in many zones. But that can also be accomplished by a more permissive zoning system. The effect of the land use rules set by the contract is the same as that set by governmental zoning of fee-simple land titles. In a pure free market, the government could indeed lease land for revenue, but not condition the leaseholds with covenants. The covenants of private owners are paid for by the owners, reflecting their individual subjective values, as they seek to maximize rents and other gains. Private covenants engage local knowledge and can be altered without bureaucratic permissions. Contracts set by the government in effect implement central planning.

Business improvement districts are another mix of government and market. Although they are established by a vote of a majority of the commercial property owners, once established, membership in these districts is mandatory for the real estate within the boundaries. They often do provide beneficial services such as enhanced security and trash removal, and they are often privately directed by councils elected by the district enterprise or real estate owners, but the mission is based on city planning, and the district rules are imposed on all, thus making such districts a level of government beneath the city. Moreover, business improvement districts have tended to become permanent (Hoyt, 2005). Similar services could be provided by voluntary districts. Those who do not join it would be denied its package of services, or the city government could have a joint venture with the voluntary district to which the holdouts would contribute via assessments to the city. In a pure market setting, there would be a package of services such as security with benefits largely internal to the club, and nonmembers would have to provide them on their own.

Another type of hybrid planning is where the initial plan is set by a developer, but then the town incorporates, and the city government adopts the existing plan in its own zoning, as happened in the case of Foster City, California (Bogart, 1998).

Robert Nelson (1999) has proposed a policy for converting neighborhoods to residential associations. Approval would require an affirmative vote both of 90 percent of the total property value affected and 75 percent of the individual unit owners. All property owners in the privatized neighborhood would be required to be members of the association and pay assessments, which would make the association a quasi-governmental lower level of government.

## 10. Conclusion

Human action necessarily looks to the future. The best financial decisions are plans from which we choose the alternative with the highest net present value. Government interventions change what would otherwise be mutual gains from trade. Private communities and voluntary contracts can handle externalities more flexibly and provide public goods more effectively by using market prices, avoiding deadweight losses, and engaging local knowledge and individual values. With market-based planning, we can adapt Gaffney's verse as follows:

> O, Thou, who didst, with contracts and with voice,
> design the streets where buildings may be placed.
> Thou wilt indeed with ownership and choice,
> use market prices, to make our growth well spaced!

## Notes

1.  In some places, the government has mandated that new developments include homeowner associations, which then places them in the non-market sector as not really voluntary, becoming in effect a level of government beneath the city or county that mandates them.
2.  In the United Kingdom, the Commonhold and Leasehold Reform Act of 2002 established the "commonhold tenure" (Webster and Goix, 2005) which is similar to the condominium in the U.S.A.

## References

Adrian, Erin. 2001. *Why is Housing so Expensive in Silicon Valley?* Santa Clara: Civil Society Institute.
Bogart, William Thomas. 1998. *The Economics of Cities and Suburbs.* Upper Saddle River: Prentice Hall.

Booth, Philip. 2005. Editorial Note. *Economic Affairs* 25 (4) (December): 2–3.

Buchanan, J. M. and C. J. Goetz. 1972. Efficiency Limits of Fiscal Mobility. *Journal of Public Economics* 1: 25–43.

Davies, Stephen. 2002. "Laissez-Faire Urban Planning." In *The Voluntary City,* Eds. David Beito, Peter Gordon, and Alexander Tabarrok (Ann Arbor: The Independent Institute and University of Michigan Press, 2002), pp. 18–46.

DTLR (Department for Transport, Local Government and the Regions). 2001. *Planning Green Paper. Planning: Delivering a Fundamental Change.* London: The Stationery Office. Cited in Webster (2005, p. 4).

Foldvary, Fred E. 1980. *The Soul of Liberty.* San Francisco: The Gutenberg Press.

Foldvary, Fred. 1994. *Public Goods and Private Communities.* Aldershot, UK: Edward Elgar Publishing.

Foldvary, Fred. 2001. The Completely Decentralized City. In *City and Country,* edited by Laurence Moss. Malden, MA: Blackwell Publishers, pp. 403–418.

Foldvary, Fred. 2005a. " Geo-Rent: A Plea to Public Economists." *Econ Journal Watch* 2 (1) (April; "Intellectual Tyranny of the Status Quo"): pp. 1–12. Retrieved 11 May 2006 from www.econjournalwatch.org/pdf/FoldvaryIntellectualTyrannyApril2005.pdf.

Foldvary, Fred. 2005b. Planning by Freehold. *Economic Affairs* 25 (4) (December): 11–15.

Foldvary, Fred. 2006a. The Economic Case for Private Residential Government. In *Private Cities: Global and local perspectives.* Edited by Georg Glasze, Chris Webster and Klaus Frantz. London and New York: Routledge.

Foldvary, Fred. 2006b. Streets as Private-Sector Public Goods. In *Street Smart: Competition, Entrepreneurship, and the future of Roads.* Edited by Gabriel Roth. Oakland: The Independent Institute, and New Brunswick: Transaction Publishers, pp. 305–325.

Gaffney, Mason. 1964. *Containment Policies for Urban Sprawl.* Lawrence, KS: University of Kansas Publications, Governmental Research Series No. 27.

Gaffney, Mason. 2006. Repopulating New Orleans: How did San Francisco do what a top economist says New Orleans cannot?" *Dollars & Sense* (March/April). March/April 2006. Retrieved April 18, 2006 from http://www.dollarsandsense.org/archives/2006/0306toc.html.

Hall, Sir Peter. 1982. *Great Planning Disasters.* Berkeley, CA: University of California Press.

Hayek, Friedrich A. 1945. "The Use of Knowledge in Society." *American Economic Review* 35, No. 4 (September): 519–30.

Hayek, Friedrich A. 1967. "The Results of Human Action but not of Human Design." In *Studies in Philosophy, Politics and Economics.* Chicago: University of Chicago Press. Pp. 96-105.

Hayek, Friedrich A. 1985 [1978]). "Competition as a Discovery Procedure." In *New Studies in Philosophy, Politics, Economics, and the History of Ideas* . Chicago: University of Chicago Press. Pp. 179–90.

Hayek, Friedrich A. 1988. *The Fatal Conceit.* London: Routledge.

Heath, Spencer. 1957. *Citadel, Market and Altar.* Baltimore: Science of Society Foundation.

Howard, Ebenezer. 1965 [1902]). *Garden Cities of To-Morow.* Cambridge: The M.I.T. Press.

Hoyt, Lorlene. 1005. Planning through Compulsory Commercial Clubs: Business Improvement Districts. *Economic Affairs* 25 (4) (December): 24–27.

Jacobs, Jane. 1961. *The Death and Life of Great American Cities.* New York: Random House and Vintage Books.

Kirzner, Israel. 1992. *The Meaning of Market Process*. London and New York: Routledge.

Klein, Daniel B. 1990. "The Voluntary Provision of Public Goods? The Turnpike Companies of Early America." *Economic Inquiry* 28, no. 4 (October): 788–812.

Klein, Daniel. 2003. "Fencing the Airshed: Using Remote Sensing to Police Auto Emissions." In Fred Foldvary and Daniel Klein (eds.), *The Half-Life of Policy Rationales*, New York and London: New York University Press, 86–106.

Klein, Daniel; Moore, Adrian; Reja, Binyam. 1997. *Curb Rights: A Foundation for Free Enterprise in Urban Transit*. Washington: Brookings Institution Press.

Lai, Lawrence Wai-Chung. 2005. Planning by Contract: The leasehold foundation of a comprehensively planned capitalist land market. *Economic Affairs* 25 (4) (December): 16–18.

MacCallum, Spencer. 1970. *The Art of Community*. Menlo Park: Institute of Humane Studies.

MacCallum, Spencer. 2003. The Entrepreneurial Community in Light of Advancing Business Practices and Technologies, in F. Foldvary and D. Klein (eds.), *The Half-Life of Policy Rationales*, New York: New York University Press: 227–42.

Mises, Ludwig von. 1920. Economic Calculation In The Socialist Commonwealth . Translated by S. Adler. Originally under the title "Die Wirtschaftsrechnung im sozialistischen Gemeinwesen" in the *Archiv für Sozialwissenschaften*, vol. 47 (1920). The translation was first published in F.A. Hayek, ed., *Collectivist Economic Planning* (London: George Routledge & Sons, 1935; reprint, Clifton, N.J.: Augustus M. Kelley, 1975), pp. 87–130.

Mises, Ludwig von. 1922 [1981]. *Socialism,* translated by J. Kahane. Indianapolis: Liberty Classics.

Nelson, Robert. 1999. "Privatizing the Neighborhood: A Proposal to Replace Zoning with Private Collective Property Rights to Existing Neighborhoods." *George Mason Law Review* 7, no. 4 (1999), pp. 827–880. Rpt. *The Voluntary City*, Eds. David Beito, Peter Gordon, and Alexander Tabarrok (Ann Arbor: The Independent Institute and University of Michigan Press, 2002), pp. 307–70.

Nelson, Robert. 2005. *Private Neighborhoods and the Transformation of Local Government*. Washington, DC: Urban Institute Press.

O'Toole, Randal. 2001. *The Vanishing Automobile and Other Urban Myths: How Smart Growth Will Harm American Cities*. Bandon, OR: Thoreau Institute.

O'Toole, Randal. 2006. *The Planning Penalty: How Smart Growth Makes Housing Unaffordable*. Independent Policy Report. Oakland: The Independent Institute. http://www.independent.org/pdf/policy_reports/2006_04_03_housing.pdf

Ottensmann, John R. 2005. Planning through the Exchange of Rights under Performance Zoning. *Economic Affairs* 25 (4) (December): 40–43.

Pennington, Mark. 2002. *Liberating the Land: The Case for Private Land-use Planning*. London: Institute of Economic Affairs.

Reagan, Ronald. 1988. Remarks at the Republican National Convention in New Orleans, Louisiana (August 15). Retrieved 19 June 2006 from http://www.reagansheritage.org/reagan/html/reagan_rnc_88.shtml.

Roth, Gabriel, ed. . 2006. *Street Smart: Competition, Entrepreneurship, and the Future of Roads*. New Brunswick: Transaction Publishers, and Oakland: The Independent Institute.

Saltzman, J. D. 1994. Houston Says No to Zoning. *The Freeman* 44 (8): 431–5.

Samuel, Peter. 2003. Motorway Financing and Provision: Technology Favors a New Approach. In F. Foldvary and D. Klein (eds.), *The Half-Life of Policy Rationales*, New York: New York University Press: 47–59.

Shoup, Donald. 2003. Buying Time at the Curb, in F. Foldvary and D. Klein (eds.), *The Half-Life of Policy Rationales,* New York: New York University Press: 60–85.

Shoup, Donald. 2005. *The High Cost of Free Parking.* Chicago and Washington, DC: Planners Press.

Staley, Samuel R. 2002. Zoning, Smart Growth, and Regulatory Taxation. In *Politics, Taxation, and the Rule of Law.* Edited by Donald Racheter and Richard Wagner. Boston: Kluwer Academic Publishers, pp. 203–224.

Stigler, George. 1971. The Theory of Economic Regulation. *Bell Journal of Economics and Management Science* 2 (spring): 1–21.

Stringham, Edward P., and Powell, Benjamin. 2004. *Housing Supply and Affordability: Do Affordable Housing Mandates Work?* Reason Public Policy Institute, Policy Study 318.

Tullock, Gordon. 1994. *The New Federalist.* Vancouver: Fraser Press.

"Urban planning." Retrieved 26 May 2006 from http://en.wikipedia.org/wiki/Urban_planning.

Wagner, Richard E. 1989. *To Promote the General Welfare.* San Francisco: Pacific Research Institute for Public Policy.

Webster, Chris. 2005a. Editorial: Diversifying the Institutions of Local Planning. *Economic Affairs* 25 (4) (December): 4–10.

Webster, Chris. 2005b. The Public Assignment of Development Rights. *Economic Affairs* 25 (4) (December): 44–7.

Webster, Chris, and Renaud le Goix. 2005. Planning by Commonhold. *Economic Affairs* 25 (4) (December): 19–23.

Wesbter, C. J., F. Wu, and Y. Zhao. 2005. China's Modern Walled Cities. In *Private Cities: Local and Global Perspectives,* edited by G. Glasze, C. J. Webster, and K. Frantz. London: Routledge, pp. 153–169.

# 15

# Private Neighborhood Governance: Trends and New Options in Collective Housing Ownership

*Robert H. Nelson*

In recent years a major—if still surprisingly little noticed—change has taken place in American housing, property rights, and local government.[1] At the micro level of common services and regulations, local governance is being decentralized to a neighborhood scale and being privatized. This is the result of the rise since the 1960s of the private neighborhood association. In 1970, fewer than 1 percent of Americans lived in a neighborhood association. Today, about 18 percent do, amounting to about 55 million people living in 275,000 neighborhood associations. Fully half of the new housing built in the United States between 1980 and 2000 was in a neighborhood association. More than 1.25 million Americans today serve on the board of directors of a neighborhood association.[2] All of these numbers are rising rapidly.

There are three main kinds of neighborhood associations—homeowners associations, condominiums, and cooperatives.[3] When a person moves into a neighborhood governed by one of these associations, he or she is required as a condition of purchase to agree to the private terms of governance. These include the power to levy "assessments"—in effect, a form of private taxation. Neighborhood associations assert comprehensive regulatory controls over housing and other property within their boundaries. The association can control the color you paint your home, where you plant a bush, whether you can build a fence, how frequently you mow your lawn, and so forth. This authority is laid out in the "CC&Rs"—the Covenants, Conditions, and Restrictions.

The neighborhood association will also usually provide certain common services such as garbage collection, street lighting, snow removal and road maintenance. Many associations provide private security patrols. It is estimated that about 10 to 20 percent of associations maintain a gate—the so-called "gated communities."[4] Neighborhood associations generally mow the lawns, trim the trees, and otherwise maintain the "common areas" that belong to everyone collectively. They provide and regulate the use of recreational facilities such as swimming pools, golf courses, and tennis courts. Many neighborhood associations are now providing neighborhood park areas and other open spaces for people to go for a walk, jog on a trail, do some bird watching, and so forth.

This all amounts to the rise of neighborhood government in the United States.[5] Americans may want less government at the national level but in their immediate neighborhoods they seem today to want more. A private neighborhood association can be as small as a single building and as large as a city of 50,000. But the typical size is around 200 to 300 housing units with a population of perhaps 500 to 1,000. This does not mean, however, that there is no role for local government in the public sector. The rise of private neighborhood associations is leaving local public governments to focus on collective service responsibilities with a wider territorial scope such as sewers, water, air pollution, the court system, and arterial highways. In parts of the United States with large numbers of private neighborhood associations, county governments are now often the dominant form of local government in the public sector.

## 1. Transforming Local Government

These trends are particularly apparent in rapidly growing parts of the United States. Because homebuyers have to agree as an initial condition of purchase, private neighborhoods are found mostly where they have been created as part of the initial development process. In states such as Florida, Texas, Arizona, Nevada, and California, there are wide areas where almost every new major development is now being built in a neighborhood association. In California, at least 60 percent of all new housing today is privately governed by a neighborhood association.[6]

In those parts of the United States mainly built before 1960, however, neighborhood associations are less common. In the typical pattern of metropolitan governance in the Northeast and Midwest, there is an older city surrounded by a large number of small suburban municipalities in the public sector. Almost half the municipalities in the United States have less than 1,000 people (although admittedly these small municipalities have only 2 percent of the total of 174 million Americans who live under a municipal form of government).

As shown in Table 15.1, reflecting a widespread governing arrangement in older parts of the country, the Chicago metropolitan area has 569 general-purpose local governments (excluding school and other special-purpose local districts) in the public sector. The Detroit area has 335; St. Louis has 314; and Cleveland has 243. If they are not all at a neighborhood scale, most of these small suburban public governments have no more than a few neighborhoods.

It is much different in newly developing parts of the South and West. Nevada is today the fastest growing state; most people have arrived there since the 1960s. Although it has 1.6 million people, Las Vegas has a grand total of only 13 local governments in the public sector. There are only 19 public municipalities in the entire state of Nevada, along with 16 counties. Does this mean that Nevada residents have a special taste for large government, and do not want small governments? The answer, of course, is the opposite. Nevadans have a strong preference for small localized government but they are obtaining this privately, even as this trend does not show up in the official statistics. While it has few municipalities, Nevada is filled with many hundreds of private neighborhood associations. But the U.S. Census of Governments does not recognize a private neighborhood association as a form of government that it counts in its surveys.

Nevada is an extreme, but there are similar patterns in other rapidly developing parts of the South and West. Private neighborhood associations are playing the role in these areas that small municipalities in the public sector assume in the Northeast and Midwest. In Florida, the Orlando metropolitan area has 1.6 million people and only 40 general purpose local governments. The Tampa area has 2.4 million people and 39 local governments. These numbers can be compared to Cincinnati, where the metropolitan area has 2.0 million people and 233 local public governments. The Pittsburgh metropolitan area has 2.4 million people and 418 local public governments. Other metropolitan areas in the Northeast and Midwest show similar patterns. Overall, private neighborhoods are taking over many of the functions of local governance in the newer parts of the United States that small suburban municipalities in an earlier era would have assumed elsewhere.

Minnesota, to show another example, is an older state in the Midwest which has a population similar to Arizona—both around 5 million. But the state of Minnesota has 854 municipalities and 1,793 towns and townships (frequently the functional equivalent of a municipality). By comparison, there are only 87 municipal governments in the entire state

**Table 15.1**
**Total General-Service Local Governments**
**(County, Municipality, Town or Township), by Metropolitan Area**

| Older Metropolitan Areas | Number of Local Governments |
| --- | --- |
| Buffalo (1.2 million population) | 65 |
| Chicago (9.2 million) | 569 |
| Cincinnati (2.0 million) | 233 |
| Cleveland (2.9 million) | 243 |
| Detroit (5.5 million) | 335 |
| Milwaukee (1.7 million) | 113 |
| Minneapolis (3.0 million) | 318 |
| Philadelphia (5.1 million) | 442 |
| Pittsburgh (2.4 million) | 418 |
| St. Louis (2.6 million) | 314 |
| | |
| **Newer Metropolitan Areas** | |
| Austin (1.2 million) 49 | |
| Las Vegas (1.6 million) | 13 |
| Orlando (1.6 million) | 40 |
| Miami (3.9 million) | 62 |
| Raleigh-Durham (1.2 million) | 30 |
| Phoenix (3.3 million) | 34 |
| San Diego (2.8 million) | 19 |
| Tampa (2.4 million) | 39 |

Source: 2002 U.S. Census of Governments

of Arizona. The Phoenix metropolitan area has only 34 general-purpose local governments, compared with 318 in the Minneapolis metropolitan area—both with total populations of around 3 million.

## A. *Privatizing Local Government*

The transformation of local government in the United States thus involves two main features. It is shifting core functions of local government to an even smaller geographic scale, the individual neighborhood. And, second, it is privatizing local government at this level of micro service delivery.[7] Legally, most neighborhood associations are organized as non-profit private corporations. They are governed by a board of directors and in other key respects resemble a private business corporation.[8]

The rise of the neighborhood association is actually returning local governance to a pattern found 200 and more years ago in England and the United States. Until the nineteenth century, a local municipal corporation and a private business corporation had a similar legal status. A municipality was organized originally as an act of "incorporation" that legally followed the same procedures and requirements as incorporating a profit-making business firm.[9]

The newly revived private status of local government has various practical implications. Consider voting rights. Voting is allocated in most neighborhood associations in proportion to property ownership. Owning a unit in a neighborhood association thus is like owning stock in a business corporation. If a person has two units, he or she has two votes. If four adults share one unit, they have one vote. If I own a unit in Massachusetts where I spend the summer, and another unit in Florida where I spend the winter, I can vote in both places. A Norwegian can vote if he or she owns a unit in Florida, whether a U.S. citizen or not, and independent of the actual amount of time spent living there. Landlords vote but tenants do not.

The shift to a collective form of private property ownership partly reflects the fact that the main functions of local government include protecting and increasing the value of a private investment in a home. Home equity represents about 30 percent of the total financial wealth of Americans; a main objective of homeowners will be to see the capital value of their property rise. Unit owners thus will seek neighborhood management that has the skills to maximize this investment value. The economist William Fischel finds that in the public sector as well, municipal residents are strongly motivated to protect and increase their home values.[10] They vote for politicians and policies at the municipal level to maximize the financial return on their housing. The private neighborhood association, in this respect, carries a longstanding trend farther, now explicitly acknowledging and legally establishing the private character of much of local government activity in the United States.

In my own past work, beginning with my 1977 book *Zoning and Property Rights,* I argued similarly that local land use regulation essentially serves private purposes.[11] Although it is nominally a public function, local zoning gives the same right to exclude as a private property right; it thus amounts in practice to a collective property right to a common neighborhood environment.[12] In this respect as well, a neighborhood association makes a private status newly explicit and official.

A third key function of local government is to provide common services. Once again, this is a business-like activity. There is not a great difference between a private golf club and a municipal golf course limited to local residents. A private neighborhood association recognizes this, and delivers the collective services privately from the start. In many cases, private provision is also more efficient, partly because it is not necessary to deal with civic service unions, rigid work rules, lifetime job tenure, and other public-sector obstacles to economical delivery of services.

So, to summarize the argument here, the differences between a small local government in the public sector and a private neighborhood association are greater in form than in substance. Private neighborhood associations have carried farther and made more explicit a general privatization of local governance that was already occurring in the United States through much of the twentieth century.

## B. Private Prerogatives

There are some important practical consequences, however, of a newly official and legally declared private status for local government. Overall, neighborhood associations because they are private have wider freedom to innovate in matters of governance. There are fewer constitutional constraints, for example, on a private organization, as compared with a local government in the public sector. A local public government is bound by the one person/one vote rulings of the U.S. Supreme Court. A neighborhood association, in contrast, has the ability to allocate voting rights according to property ownership.

Another area of difference is the application of constitutional rights such as freedom of speech and assembly. In most states a neighborhood association can ban political signs on lawns. An association can deny the right to have a protest march. In general, constitutional rights that would clearly apply in a public context may not apply in the private setting of a neighborhood association. Neighborhood associations designed for senior citizens, for example, are one of the rapidly growing segments of the housing market. Permanent occupancy by children is prohibited in such associations, a form of discrimination according to family status that would be unlikely, if not outright illegal, in the public setting of a municipality.

In one example, my own family experienced the greater flexibility of neighborhood associations. My parents own property in a second-home neighborhood association in the Shenandoah Valley of Virginia. This association was having trouble passing an amendment to its declaration, even thought it was not particularly controversial—not enough unit owners were voting to meet the minimum requirement. So the association decided to convert the referendum into a lottery. Each vote submitted became in addition a lottery ticket. The first prize was $300, second was

$200, and third was $100. I heard about it because my parents won the $100 prize. With this incentive for voting, the amendment easily passed. It was, to my mind, a practical device to stimulate greater unit owner voting turnout. It was legal for a private neighborhood association but might well have been illegal in a local government in the public sector. In America, a government is not supposed to pay people to vote in public elections.

Consider another example where money payments are illegal publicly, but legal privately. Let us say a small new grocery store wants to locate in a neighborhood. A private neighborhood association in concept could sell the entry rights. It would simply be another sale of private rights, something that happens routinely in the marketplace. The revenues might be distributed to all the unit owners, or some part used to compensate the nearby property owners. The entire neighborhood might benefit as well from easy access to a conveniently located store. In the public sector, this would be impossible—at least legally and officially—because changes in zoning are not supposed to be for sale. If a public official takes money, it could even be a case of bribery, a felony.

Consider one more example. The 2005 *Kelo* decision of the Supreme Court, involving the City of New London, Connecticut, highlighted some of the problems of land assembly. The use of eminent domain—approved by the Supreme Court—is troublesome in a number of respects. But it is still the case that assembly of large parcels, potentially involving many separate ownerships, will facilitate coordinated land development. Given potential problems with holdouts and other obstacles to collective action, this raises an important issue: How can such assembly of many separately owned parcels best be accomplished?

One possibility is that, if a private neighborhood association existed, and depending on the association declaration, it might be possible for the association to sell out a full set of neighborhood properties in one transaction. The neighborhood association could vote to terminate and divide up what might be large windfall profits among all the unit owners. It might take a vote of say 80 percent, but not 100 percent, to approve such a transaction. This would have two major advantages over eminent domain. First, the neighborhood price would be set by direct negotiations between the neighborhood association, representing the unit owners collectively, and a potential developer. Second, the decision to accept or reject a developer offer would be made by the neighborhood unit owners themselves. Under eminent domain, by contrast, the wider city acts unilaterally to make these decisions. It is understandable that many property owners are upset when they believe they have not been adequately compensated or simply do not want to leave the area.

## C. Retrofitting Neighborhood Associations

Of course, at present such neighborhood control over redevelopment would be feasible only where there is an existing neighborhood association. But what if it were possible to retrofit a new neighborhood association in a previously developed area—one in which the properties are already individually and separately owned? Indeed, I have proposed this approach to land assembly in several previous writings.[13] It might work as follows. If a group of property owners in a promising area for redevelopment wanted to create a new neighborhood association, the owners would be required to gather signatures on a petition. If a high enough percentage of owners signed, representatives of the proposed new association and the local government would work out a transfer agreement for current public properties and services. It would cover streets (some of which might be turned over to the association and thus privatized outright), shifts of garbage collection and other service provision responsibilities, new assignments of land-use regulatory authority, and so forth. In the next step, and after wide opportunity for public discussion and debate, the property owners would vote. A favorable vote of say 80 percent of the property owners might be required to form a new private neighborhood association.[14]

Under this approach, and if this legal mechanism existed (which would require new state legislation), the property owners in the *Kelo* case could have pursued an alternative to eminent domain. They could have formed a neighborhood association to serve as their bargaining agent. It would then have been up to the developer to make a large enough financial offer to gain collective agreement on a sale of all the neighborhood properties. Acceptance of the developer offer would not require unanimous consent but a high supermajority such as 80 percent.

Even if whole neighborhoods were not sold in this manner, the retroactive creation of new neighborhood associations could stimulate the redevelopment of inner city and other urban neighborhoods. A new neighborhood association could provide a greater degree of security of investment in an inner-city area. The association might install gates and otherwise act to control entry—becoming an inner-city gated community. If urban neighborhoods could confidently exclude criminals, drug dealers, and other potentially disruptive individuals, many well-located neighborhoods would become more attractive for land redevelopment.

Although most gated communities are now found in the suburbs, it is in the inner cities that the security of a gate might be the most valuable.[15] Investment might even flood in to the neighborhood.

## D. Future Prospects

Overall, the rise of private neighborhood associations thus offers many attractive features.[16] It provides a tight collective control over neighborhood environments that many Americans seemingly want. It facilitates the collective provision of services in an economical fashion. There has been much concern expressed about a declining sense of community in American life. Many older forms of association such as labor unions, the Kiwanis Club, the American Legion, the Masons, and so forth are declining. But private neighborhood associations are exploding across the United States. They may represent the most important newly emerging form of American community.

Neighborhood associations are also a major development in the evolution of American property rights. By the end of the nineteenth century, the new legal form of the private business corporation had become a major factor in the economic organization of American industry. The business corporation shifted ownership of industrial property from individual proprietorships to groups of stock holders. At the end of the twentieth century, there was a similar shift in the United States from individual private ownership of residential property to new collective forms. In combination, reflecting the rise of the business corporation and the private neighborhood association, much of American economic life is today occurring under a collective private arrangement, perhaps a consequence of the greater interdependence of individuals living and working together in modern society.

The analogy with the business corporation is important in other respects. Business corporations exist within a legal framework defined by state laws but they have substantial organizational and operating autonomy in many areas. They can issue, for example, varying amounts of preferred and ordinary stock and can create different categories of stockholders with different voting rights. They can rely to a greater degree on bonds instead of stocks to finance their activities—thus giving bankers a greater role in corporate oversight, as compared with the shareholders. They can have different numbers of inside and outside directors. Business corporations can combine or separate the positions of chairman of the board of directors and chief executive officer. Partly as a result of the Enron and other problems of business oversight, the present period is one in which substantial innovation is taking place in federal and state laws and in the internal organization of many American business corporations.

Private neighborhood associations, however, are not seeing a similar degree of creativity, even though many of them have experienced significant operating and other problems. Quite a few neighborhood associations experience deep internal tensions that all too frequently result in litigation. Some unit owners speak of members of their own board of directors as "power loving," or even in extreme cases as "little Nazis."[17] Some of this may simply be inevitable when people are living and interacting with one another in close association. Some families are dysfunctional, and perhaps it should be no surprise that some neighborhood associations are dysfunctional. Yet, the institution of the family is alive and well in American society; perhaps the institution of the neighborhood association should be seen in a similar overall light, despite all the warts in some particular cases.

That does not mean, however, that the workings of neighborhood associations can not be improved—and in some cases significantly so.[18] In the remainder of this chapter, I will address some alternatives for writing (or rewriting) neighborhood association declarations—their "constitutions"—to improve the internal workings and governance of this important new collective form of housing ownership.[19]

## 2. Writing Neighborhood Constitutions

In choosing a neighborhood association to live in, a homebuyer is also purchasing a neighborhood constitution. The form of private neighborhood government becomes yet another exercise of consumer choice. Yet, as a result of various institutional factors, land developers may have neglected some important constitutional possibilities that might lead to higher profits as well as more satisfied housing customers. In the end, this is an issue that will not be settled by any theoretical debate but by market competition.[20]

The world today is witnessing a period of unusual constitutional ferment. Eastern European nations have had to write new constitutions in the wake of the collapse of the former Soviet Union, and the European Union has been writing the first European-wide constitution. The government of Kenya has been designing a new constitution, and many other postcolonial African nations are still searching for effective basic institutions of governance. Yet, the rise of the private neighborhood association has resulted in far and away the largest number of new constitutions in recent years—more than 200,000 during the past three decades in the United States alone.

The writing of neighborhood constitutions, however, has been left mainly to real estate lawyers and their developer clients who typically use boilerplate documents. According to one observer, "with no previous experience available to understand what the pros and cons would be to live in a community controlled by covenants, DABs [Declarations, Articles of Incorporation, and Bylaws] were born in approximately the 1960s. Operating within the bureaucratic framework created by VA and FHA, the legal profession created the collection of standard, boilerplate, 'canned' rules." So despite decades of experience that might have suggested new constitutional possibilities, "developers and attorneys still use wording from the original off-the-rack rules."[21]

Even for established neighborhoods that already have a constitution, a "neighborhood constitutional convention" might be convened. Thomas Jefferson suggested a rewriting of the U.S. Constitution at least every 20 years. Today, new neighborhood constitutions might include a provision for periodic review, perhaps every 15 to 20 years. Law professor Paula Franzese argues that neighborhood associations at present are falling short of their potential: "Most common interest communities put the cart before the horse, relying on elaborately prepackaged mandates to impose 'community,' rather than facilitating the development of a genuine social fabric.... We need a change in the way we draft documents." As a result, "the challenge for all of us as academics, practitioners, empiricists, CIC developers, planners, leaders and residents is not to lament the withering state of community, but to help guide its restoration."[22]

Neighborhood association attorney Wayne Hyatt similarly suggests that the initial association constitution should "contain only a limited number, perhaps a severely limited number, of prohibitions and restrictions, including only those restrictions that the developer believes to be vital to the overall community development plan." Hyatt would then gradually rewrite the rules through "a method for permitting changes and for the adoption, modification, or abrogation of regulations" of the neighborhood association. The neighborhood constitution thus should "create and institutionalize rule-making as a dynamic rather than a static process."[23] If the market sustains a popular demand for it, the private constitutions of many neighborhood associations might be tailored more closely in the future to the actual concerns of current unit owners, as determined after they move in to the neighborhood. Of course, there will always be some people—it could even turn out to be the majority—who want the security of detailed rules known in advance that are difficult to change.

## A. *The Neighborhood Legislature*

Charles Fraser, founding chief executive officer of Hilton Head's Sea Pines Plantation, believes that many American neighborhood associations are experiencing significant private governance problems. Even though these associations are democratic in theory, this leading land developer has found that too often there is in practice "control by the arbitrary few." And according to Fraser, an "unfortunate pattern in human affairs has been inflicted on most U.S. master-planned communities." Part of the problem rests with neighborhood associations' founding constitutions because the attorneys writing them have given "too little thought to the need to restrain abuses of power" that can occur in a private as well as a public governmental setting.[24]

The retired unit owners in a neighborhood association may have larger amounts of time available and may even be looking for new activities. Partly as a result, Fraser finds, the practice of democracy in neighborhood associations often results in "control over the young by the old." Indeed, in some neighborhood associations, the board of directors exhibits "a virtually unchecked focus on the self-interests of the male resident aged 70 and older." It can be a large problem for neighborhood associations of mixed age groups because "all sociological studies of differences among age groups ... show sharp differences in the life interests of people 35 years old" when compared with those who are much older. Potentially, there can be an especially large clash "between the interests of 35-year-old mothers and those of childless or empty-nester 70-year-old males."[25]

Among American land developers, Fraser is a free thinker. As a solution to the problem of the frequent "autocracy" in many neighborhood associations, Fraser proposes that private "condominium and community boards ... divide board membership into 50 percent women and 50 percent men, and then divide each half among three age groups: over age 70, ages 55 to 70, and under age 55."[26] Admittedly, this degree of specificity raises a number of practical concerns but Fraser's proposal nevertheless underscores the possible benefits from rethinking election procedures and governance structures in many neighborhood associations.

For board member elections in most associations at present, each unit owner is eligible to vote and casts either a single vote or a total number of votes that corresponds to the number of open seats. The highest total vote getters then become members of the board of directors. Under such a system, a majority of unit owners can consistently vote for the same types of candidates and policies, leaving a minority feeling unrepresented. Indeed, too many neighborhood boards, Hyatt says, "are dominated by members of a similar age, housing type, or a particular interest—e.g., golfers—and others are shut out," perpetuating "a negative governmental environment that feeds on itself." Hyatt suggests that associations may want to explore a private system of proportional representation as an alternative to the current "majoritarian win-lose exercise" in selecting neighborhood leadership.[27]

Concerns such as those expressed by Fraser and Hyatt are not limited to the democratic workings of neighborhood associations. Summarizing a common view, Alexander Tabarrok argues that in public elections as well the typical American system of "plurality voting is one of the worst of all possible choices."[28] Although most American municipal elections are based on plurality voting, he argues that "almost anything looks good compared to it [this system]."[29] In 1997, the newly elected government of Tony Blair established an independent commission to review the United Kingdom's voting methods. The commission noted that, following World War II, India was virtually the only nation that had adopted the traditional English and American systems of plurality voting.[30]

The commission recommended that a new method of voting—"the Alternate Vote," involving the transfer of votes from losing candidates to higher-ranked candidates—should "be implemented throughout the United Kingdom."[31] In a 1995 survey article, Jonathan Levin and Barry Nalebuff reviewed 16 election alternatives, ranging from simple majority rule to more complicated voting systems.[32] Unless limited by state law (which may often be the case at present but these laws could be changed), neighborhood associations thus have the option in writing their constitutions to chose among a wide range of voting possibilities.

Private neighborhood associations, as noted above, generally follow at present the business corporation model of governance. Compared with a business corporation, however, neighborhood associations typically find it easier to assemble the unit owners for full neighborhood meetings, thus reducing the burdens of direct democracy. The policy and management issues facing a neighborhood association will usually be less technically complex than those facing corporate boards. Another difference is that the "principal-agent" problem should be less severe in a neighborhood association.[33] The design of a neighborhood legislature may benefit from new constitutional approaches that reflect the particular transaction cost and other circumstances typical of neighborhood associations, as compared with the operating environments of business corporations.

## B. Neighborhood Federalism?

Students of government have long studied the ideal size for a local governance unit. They have found, for example, that African tribes historically were often made up of self-governing clans that typically did not exceed a few hundred individuals. These clans were about the same size as the ancient Grecian "deme"—a "small territorially based association, which formed the basic political unit of the Athenian polity." Indeed, as Michael Sarbanes and Kathleen Skullney observe, the deme "shared many characteristics" with the contemporary neighborhood association.[34]

Modern sociologists suggest that an ideally sized social unit will permit a member to know most of the other members personally. A desirable size for an election district thus might be a few hundred people—or a hundred or so households. If the entire neighborhood association is about this size, then separate districts will obviously not be needed. However, what about larger associations that often have a thousand or more unit owners?

Depending on geographic features, street routes, densities, and other circumstances, it may be desirable to divide a larger neighborhood association into smaller, "subneighborhood" groups of, say, 50 to 150 unit owners each. Each private subneighborhood would then elect one or more members to the higher-level association board. Within each subneighborhood, the unit owners might have their own "mini" governing associations with their own boards of directors. This most local of elected bodies would handle the most "micro" issues, such as the enforcement of covenant restrictions on land and property within the subneighborhood area.

Although it would raise the transaction costs of democratic decision-making within the wider neighborhood umbrella association, such a constitutional system of "private neighborhood federalism" might have significant overall political advantages. The private community of Reston, Virginia, started in the 1960s, is in fact organized in this privately federalist manner. There is a Reston-wide association to govern all of what has now become a full fledged private city approaching 60,000 in population. Within this broader governing framework, there are more than 130 small neighborhood "clusters," ranging in size from 11 to 231 housing units, and each with its own private cluster association to deal with internal regulatory and other matters.

One concern, however, would be that association board members who represent a particular district might show greater commitment to the interests of that district. This narrow focus might prompt each board member to become particularly well informed about his or her district, but prove a liability when the neighborhood association must consider issues affecting all unit owners together. As the number of board members increases, the collective choice problems of free-rider behavior and "rational ignorance" on the part of individual members of the neighborhood board would also increase.

If each member of a neighborhood board of directors represents a particular district, then these members might also spend much of their time seeking to redirect spending to their own part of the neighborhood (more playgrounds, for example, for a neighborhood sections with more children). As legislators compete with one another to "bring home the bacon," as can occur in a private as well as public form of local governance, they might raise taxes and governmental services above levels that the unit owners desire. Writers of private constitutions for neighborhood associations may want to establish special constitutional barriers to logrolling and other such practices, for example, perhaps requiring a supermajority to approve any neighborhood budget increase above the inflation rate.

## C. Proportional Election Methods

Aside from such practical concerns with respect to a private neighborhood federal structure, another consideration is that many minorities within a neighborhood association may not be clustered geographically. If the goal is to ensure a wide range of views represented on the board of directors, districting would then not work and some other election system would have to be found. Indeed, the writers of future neighborhood association constitutions may want to consider entirely new alternatives to traditional plurality voting. Election systems based on proportional representation, for example, are explicitly designed to elect a governing group that represents a wider range of voter opinion. Conceived in the mid-nineteenth century and then adopted for many European parliamentary elections by the end of that century, proportional representation is widely employed around the world today. In comparing standard "majoritarian" and proportional election systems, political scientist Bingham Powell concludes that the clear advantage lies with the latter "as instruments of democracy."[35]

Given the absence of political parties in neighborhood associations, proportional representation might be dismissed as infeasible. Use of proportional representation, however, might stimulate the creation of neighborhood "parties," although probably not based on traditional Republican and Democratic allegiances. Some systems of proportional representation, moreover, involve only individual candidates without party labels. In such a system, as in plurality voting, the candidates who receive the most votes win. Instead of being assigned an equal vote, however, each elected member of the board of directors would receive voting power in proportion to the total number of votes he or she received. Thus, if candidates Jones and Smith were both elected to the board of directors of a neighborhood association, but Jones received twice as many votes as Smith, then Jones would also have twice as many votes in subsequent board decision making for the association.

Such a voting system in a neighborhood association might encourage a wider number of unit owners to offer themselves—or be nominated by other members of the association—as candidates for board membership. In the nineteenth century, the British economist John Stuart Mill endorsed such a voting system for national as well as local elections:

> Of all modes in which a national representation can possibly be constituted, this one affords the best security for the intellectual qualifications desirable in the representatives. At present, by universal admission, it is becoming more and more difficult for anyone who has only talents and character to gain admission into the House of Commons.... [In the newly proposed system], those who did not like the local candidates, or who could not succeed in carrying the local candidate they preferred, would have the power to fill up their voting papers by a selection from all the persons of national reputation. ... In no other way which it seems possible to suggest would Parliament be so certain of containing the very *elite* of the country.[36]

### D. Private Election by Lottery

In ancient Athens, the Council of Five Hundred ran the city. The members of this council were selected each year by lottery from citizens over age 30 and in good standing in the community. Fifteenth-century Florence—the "Athens" of the Renaissance—also used a random method for selecting its representatives. As constitutional scholar Dennis Mueller reports, random selection "appears to have made all citizens feel that they were a part of the government, and that their interests were represented. It also appears to have led representatives to identify with the common interests of Florence."[37]

Mandatory service on boards of directors, as selected by lottery, might be an effective way of surmounting the free-rider problem common to many neighborhood associations. At present, members of many private associations complain that it is difficult to find people to run and too many "busybodies" and other poorly qualified people end up on neighborhood boards. A lottery among unit owners might significantly increase the numbers of shy and quiet people—many well qualified for board service—who are chosen. Mandatory service would support the idea that each unit owner owes something to the neighborhood. Indeed, more broadly, one legal authority has suggested making "membership and participation on an association committee mandatory, as is payment of assessments."[38] Once a person had served, he or she would be exempt from a further neighborhood "draft" for at least a certain number of years.

To be sure, many prospective homebuyers might want to avoid any private neighborhood where they could be drafted to neighborhood service. Whether or not to buy a home in a neighborhood association using a lottery election system, or other form of required service, could thus become yet another element in private choice among neighborhoods with different private constitutions and other operating arrangements.

*E. The Neighborhood Executive*

Reflecting the prevailing business corporate model for neighborhood association governance, an elected board of directors has the final authority for the conduct of neighborhood affairs. The board is directly elected by association unit owners and—subject to any limits specified in the neighborhood constitution—sets the policies for enforcing covenants, using common areas, providing neighborhood services, and conducting other areas of association activity. The board itself selects a president, secretary, and treasurer as the association's executive officers. The officers in practice are also generally board members, although this is not legally required.

Some of the current tensions within neighborhood associations, as real estate lawyer Scott Mollen reports, may reflect many unit owners' sense that "ownership and operational decisions are being made by individuals who may have no professional real estate expertise or experience."[39] Neighborhood decisions may require technical knowledge that few if any members of the board of directors have. In the future, keeping a board of directors separate from direct operational responsibilities thus may be important to improving the internal workings of many neighborhood associations.[40]

The developer Charles Fraser, already mentioned above, similarly argues for a redefinition of the relationship between association boards of directors and neighborhood administrators. In the future, he argues, neighborhood associations should make greater efforts "to hire competent and experienced management companies." Neighborhood associations should be willing to sign long-term contracts that assign much of their administrative responsibility to an outside firm. Fraser labels this approach as "'town hall' management" by an experienced, "semi-independent" private company entering into perhaps a 5-to-10-year contract with the neighborhood association.[41]

In this respect, such a step would move the private community association closer to the traditional business corporation model. As one expert in corporate governance puts it, "the main job of the directors is to hire, fire, and set compensation" for the CEO.[42] This job definition reflects the fact that, as another corporate authority states, the CEO "will have much more information than the other board members. Unless the board has lost faith in that individual, ... it will trust this more informed person" to run the corporation.[43] A powerful executive and a weak board have served many American business corporations well. One possibility for neighborhood associations would be to move in the same direction in organizing their systems of internal governance and management.

### F. Should There Be a Neighborhood "Mayor"?

If the job of chief executive of a neighborhood association is merely technical and administrative, there would seem to be little need for an elected chief executive—a "mayor." Like a business hiring a new CEO, a neighborhood association might simply hire a well qualified professional to perform in the executive role. If a neighborhood is large enough to need a full-time manager, then this top neighborhood executive—chosen partly for professional skills and experience in association management—could work on-site in the neighborhood and report directly to the board. The traditional position of neighborhood "president," filled at present by a board member, might even be abolished so as not to create a confusion of authority with the top professional manager. There would instead simply be, as in the business world, a neighborhood association "chairman of the board" who would work to select the neighborhood association "chief executive officer."

Some public municipalities in the past did try hiring their top executives. In the 1920s, Cleveland, Kansas City, Cincinnati, and a few other large American cities experimented with the hiring of professional city managers in place of elected mayors.[44] However, these cities soon abandoned these experiments (except for Cincinnati, which made the change much later), recognizing the impracticality of trying to separate policy from administration. This happened because, in large cities at least, hired professionals generally had neither the political skills nor the political legitimacy to run city governments. Large cities have diverse interests and constituencies; the job of the mayor often includes assembling a working coalition in order to solve citywide problems. The task is inherently "political." A professional administrator's formal training and special expertise might not be much help in such politically charged aspects of city government.

Even in smaller jurisdictions, and contrary to the thinking prominent in the Progressive Era, few now argue that it is possible to separate the "political" from the "administrative" sides of governance—and neighborhood associations will also have "political" sides to their operation, if now a private politics. As one legal authority states, local governments "have become too complex for a structure of government that attempts to separate policy from administration. Inevitably, an appointed manager makes policy decisions." Hence, council-manager government "increases conflict and the potential for political gridlock. Experience shows that the council expects the manager to 'get things done.' But when the manager tries to take initiative or make policy decisions, he risks offending the council and getting fired." Yet, managers who are cautious are "blamed for 'not getting things done'" and they may lose their jobs too. Thus Stephen Cianca concludes, "The executive role of government is too important to subordinate to a legislative body" in American public government.[45]

A powerful and independent executive could also potentially stand as a check against legislative excesses, even as the legislature can counteract any threats of misuse of executive powers. Given the past complaints about misuses of board authority in many neighborhood associations, greater formal separation of executive and legislative powers within neighborhood associations thus might be a good idea. Under such a model, a neighborhood mayor—taking on the role of the association president—could be chosen by a direct vote of the unit owners. There would be provisions for recall but the grounds would be limited and would require a high supermajority vote (probably of the unit owners themselves).

An elected president of a neighborhood association might have wide powers and substantial autonomy from the board of directors. This neighborhood chief executive officer might, for example, have veto authority over board actions, subject to a supermajority override by the board. He or she might have the independent authority to hire a management team or a professional management firm. The neighborhood president might administer the enforcement of neighborhood covenants, oversee the maintenance decisions for the common areas, and develop the neighborhood budget, although in most cases these actions would be subject to board approval. The term of office for an elected neighborhood association president might be from two to four years.

The case for selecting a neighborhood president by unit-owner vote becomes stronger as the size of the neighborhood becomes larger. Yet, even some smaller neighborhood associations might want to elect their own chief executive officer, thus legitimating his or her stature and power within the neighborhood—an important advantage in resolving internal disputes and representing the neighborhood in outside arenas.

## G. A Private Neighborhood Judiciary

Scott Mollen, a real estate lawyer in New York, has seen it all. In the relationships among the unit owners living in New York condominiums and cooperatives, disputes all too often "erupt into diatribes of emotionally charged words which exponentially expand and intensify the conflict. The printable vocabulary of occupancy conflicts often includes words like 'livid,' 'vicious,' 'revenge,' 'fraud,' 'arrogant,' 'pompous,' 'power crazy,' 'breach of fiduciary duty,' 'self-dealing,' 'favoritism,' 'insensitive,' 'litigious,' 'stupid,' and 'troublemaker.'" Indeed, lawyers practicing in the field of collective ownership of housing commonly "believe that after relationships involving love and/or sex, the next most passionate relationship in our society is that of ... condominium unit owner/condominium board of directors and cooperative shareholder/co-op board." Although the New York disagreements observed by Mollen often have arisen within a single building, he recognizes that the spread of such conflicts within neighborhood associations has increasingly been "national in scope."[46] Fully 41 percent of neighborhood associations in the United States have been involved in at least one lawsuit with a unit owner.[47]

In one extreme case described in a report for the Community Associations Institute, a California homeowner and a neighborhood association became embroiled in a conflict involving a $750 fence. By the end of the litigation process, the association's legal fees had exceeded $60,000, and the homeowner had spent more than $40,000.[48] The dispute obviously had ceased to be about a fence and had become a simple contest of wills between two intransigent parties that happened to be fought in a courtroom.

As Mollen believes, "the judicial system is ill suited to resolve occupancy conflicts." It is often a waste of time and money, moreover, for unit owners who bring the suits because boards of directors generally prevail; there have been "relatively few decisions" in New York City in which a unit owner won a case. There is a good reason for this; the courts understand that "a presumption of validity is essential to the orderly operation and fiscal soundness of the common interest developments. Associations could not function properly if decisions could be 'Monday morning quarterbacked' by each individual unit owner."[49]

In light of such problems, which arise today in too many neighborhood associations, alternative private methods of resolution of many neighborhood association disputes might be desirable, possibly requiring the writing of new constitutional provisions for a neighborhood "judicial" branch. Indeed, this is probably the least developed side of private neighborhood governance at present. Yet, unit owners' perception that they have access to a reasonable private process for appeal and final dispute resolution may serve as an alternative to continuing personal conflict, disagreement, and emotional outbursts. Wayne Hyatt argues that it will be important in the future to develop improved "procedures for owner involvement and owner appeals" relating to matters of covenant enforcement and other areas of neighborhood association activity.[50]

The undeveloped character of the judicial branch in neighborhood associations reflects in part the prevailing corporate legal model for these associations. It has been assumed that disputes in neighborhood associations should be resolved in the traditional framework of contract law. However, the relationship among the unit owners in a neighborhood association resembles more closely the workings of a government, if private in this case. An association's controlling document is more like a private political constitution than a private contract. A formal body of law dealing with private constitutions does not presently exist in the American legal system, although it is being informally developed in the workings of neighborhood associations (and some other areas of law).

An internal private system of appeal could take many forms. A private "judge" could be appointed to hear appeals and to resolve other "judicial" issues—perhaps a particularly well-respected unit owner or a nonresident with real estate expertise. Small private "juries" of unit owners could be convened to hear appeals. And though such a practice would violate the strict concept of a separation of powers, the association's board of directors could serve as a special avenue of appeal. A neighborhood might enter into a contract with an outside private arbitration firm—perhaps authorized to render a binding decision in some cases where the parties cannot otherwise agree.[51]

## H. A Formal Process for Covenant Enforcement

The most contentious matter facing neighborhood associations is often the enforcement of covenants relating to neighborhood land uses.[52] In order to minimize such tensions, it is desirable to have a well-defined process for the handling of proposals for structural modifications in neighborhood properties. This process should not impose large burdens of paperwork. Nevertheless, it should be formal enough that it establishes some form of written record—if perhaps very brief. These records should be maintained by the neighborhood association and should be readily available for review by other unit owners—and prospective unit owners who may find them informative about the workings of the association in practice.

Applications for "significant" modifications of unit-owner properties should be submitted in writing. Other unit owners would be given adequate notice of the proposed change, and an opportunity to comment. Without requiring great detail, the application should contain a short statement of the proposed structural changes. Any proposal rejection should at least include a brief written statement substantiating the rejection. If others in the neighborhood have previously raised objections, and yet the proposed change is approved, a brief statement as to the grounds for approval should be offered.

At present, many neighborhood associations place the initial responsibility for the interpretation and enforcement of covenants with a board subcommittee—typically the "architectural review" subcommittee. This approach has several disadvantages. Frequent turnover in board membership may result in frequent changes in the membership of the architectural review subcommittee, which can lead to inconsistent decisions from one year to the next. Furthermore, committee members (unit owners) are not likely to have much expertise in design issues. Consciously or unconsciously, they may favor—or, almost as much of a problem, appear to favor—friends and others within their own network of neighborhood acquaintances.

Hence, it may be desirable to put the initial review of proposed structural modifications in the hands of a professional. A large neighborhood association might assign one association employee with suitable qualifications to this task. In a smaller association, an outside architectural consultant might be hired. An alternative to hiring an outside professional would be to choose a well-respected unit owner to serve on a voluntary basis. He or she might have a long-term appointment, say for five years, with the goal of developing expertise and maintaining consistency in covenant enforcement. This person would not simply issue "yes" or "no" decisions; there could be a negotiation process in which mitigating actions and other changes might be discussed to make a proposal acceptable to the neighborhood association membership.

The enforcement of covenants is likely to have greater legitimacy among unit owners if the association offers a reasonable and inexpensive avenue of private internal appeal. Rather than acting as the decision-maker of first resort, perhaps the board's architectural subcommittee could serve as this appeal body. In considering an appeal, the subcommittee would meet with the unit owner filing the appeal and hear his or her objections to the initial neighborhood decision. The person filing the appeal would also be expected to present a brief statement outlining the grounds for appeal. The architectural committee would also meet (perhaps separately) with the association employee, outside consultant, or other person responsible for making the initial decision. Whatever the outcome, the architectural committee would prepare a brief written statement explaining the appeal's resolution. In order to dissuade unit owners from filing frivolous appeals, associations might exact a modest appeal fee—say $100. If a unit owner won an appeal, this fee might then be rebated. Otherwise, the association would retain the money for its own use.

As an alternative to an architectural review subcommittee, a neighborhood association might consider establishing a private "jury" system. As in other judicial arenas, a neighborhood jury would consist of fellow citizens (unit owners). The jury might be picked at random. A disaffected unit owner could ask for a short neighborhood "trial" by a group of unit owners—say five other randomly selected owners. Neighborhood jury deliberations and voting records might be kept secret, with only the final result announced publicly. Perhaps the greatest disadvantage of this approach is the large amount of time potentially required of unit owners. It might be limited to particularly important or controversial covenant issues.

A much different approach would be for the neighborhood association to hire an outside private arbitration service to hear appeals. If this approach were widely adopted, new businesses specializing in covenant arbitration services for neighborhood associations might spring up. If a unit owner filed an appeal, the owner might have to pay for the cost of the arbitration service. If he or she won the case, the money might then be returned and the neighborhood association would be required to pay.

No matter which approach is adopted for the first round of appeal, association constitutions could also provide for a second appeal to a higher level. The appeal body at this level, for example, might consist of the association's entire board of directors. In order to prevent the board from being inundated with appeals, a significant barrier—perhaps a much higher filing fee (say $1,000)—could be put in place. The board could also require more extensive written documentation. Finally, like the U.S. Supreme Court, the board might have broad discretion to reject the consideration of any specific appeals.

## 3. Conclusion

Since the 1960s, private neighborhood associations have become an increasingly important part of the American system of local governance. In many parts of the United States almost all new development of any scale includes the creation of a neighborhood association that provides common services, oversees land use regulation, and assumes other local governance tasks. The resulting transformation of local government is characterized by two main features, a shift to government at the geographic scale of the neighborhood and the privatization of this neighborhood government.

The significance of a private government is that it frees the neighborhood association from many of the existing rules for local government in the public sector. Private neighborhood government does not necessarily mean any particular type of physical design of a neighborhood, any form of social organization, or any neighborhood governing system. It is thus misleading to ask, are private neighborhoods more or less desirable than their public sector counterparts? This is similar to asking at a personal level, is individual freedom being used wisely, or would it be preferable for society to impose rules that limit individual choice, perhaps because too many people are exercising their choices poorly? Society does make such decisions in a few areas such as the individual freedom to consume alcohol, drugs and other artificial stimulants (although with considerable controversy and often with doubtful effectiveness) but in most areas the individual is left to make his or her choices wisely or poorly.

Private neighborhoods have mostly exercised their greater autonomy to impose tighter controls over individual use of property than are normally found in the public sector. It is in some ways paradoxical that, given a wider freedom of choice, private neighborhoods have chosen to assert tighter limits on the individual freedoms of property owners within the governing jurisdiction. In the end, however, if this is what neighborhood property owners really want, their liberty to surrender some individual rights in order to gain greater collective controls over the actions of their neighbors must be respected.

Yet, the institution of the private neighborhood association is still fairly new in American society. Most social arrangements involve a learning curve that may require decades of experimentation and adaptation. Property rights arrangements sometimes evolve over centuries. It is possible that the wider freedom of choice in private neighborhood government could profitably be used in the future in new alternative ways. Up to now, private land developers and their attorneys have typically used standard documents that imposed similar land use controls and systems of governance across tens of thousands of new private neighborhoods being established in the United States.

As this chapter has examined, there are many new possibilities. The purpose here has not been to recommend any one governing approach that would be common to all neighborhoods. Rather, it is to suggest that neighborhoods should offer greater variety in seeking to tailor governance systems to their specific needs and circumstances. The ultimate outcomes in terms of neighborhood governance would then be revealed as a form of market choice. An evolving system of private neighborhood governance would be shaped by consumer sovereignty, allowing for potentially as many outcomes in neighborhood governance as there are dozens of automobile models for sale in the United States.

One obstacle to such an outcome, as this chapter addresses, is a poverty of imagination thus far in terms of designing private governance alternatives—a failing among both unit owners and developers. The other leading obstacle is legal. If a private neighborhood association chooses to be incorporated, as most do, the association at present is typically limited in state law to the mandatory legal structure of a non-profit business corporation. In addition, most states impose further legal requirements on the structure and methods of operation of private neighborhood associations. Indeed, in some states such as California and Florida there is an extensive body of state law that controls even many of the specific details of the private operation and governance of neighborhood associations.

Realizing the full potential of private neighborhood government will thus require two steps. First, the participants in the market for private neighborhood government will have to show greater creativity and willingness to innovate within the rules they face. Second, state governments (and potentially the federal government, although it has not been particularly active in this area up to the present) will have to allow private neighborhoods wider flexibility to exercise a broad range of choice in constitutional design and other neighborhood governing arrangements. No doubt, some neighborhoods will use this greater freedom of choice poorly, and some of them will experience significant failures in implementing their governing systems. Just as individuals are free to fail in their personal choices, however, neighborhoods should be free to make their own mistakes. In the end, wide private freedom of choice in neighborhood governance is likely to produce a world of more diverse, more vital and better managed neighborhood governments, as compared with local governance under the current tightly limiting rules of the public sector.

## Notes

1.  For a comprehensive description, see Robert H. Nelson, *Private Neighborhoods and the Transformation of Local Government* (Washington, DC: Urban Institute Press, 2005).
2.  See the web site of the Community Associations Institute, Alexandria, Virginia, http://www.caionline.org/about/facts.cfm.
3.  Wayne S. Hyatt and Susan F. French, *Community Association Law: Cases and Materials on Common Interest Communities* (Durham, NC: Carolina Academic Press, 1998).
4.  Edward J. Blakely and Mary Gail Snyder, *Fortress America: Gated Communities in the United States* (Washington, DC: Brookings Institution Press, 1997); and Setha Low, *Behind the Gates: Life, Security and the Pursuit of Happiness in Fortress America* (New York: Routledge, 2003).
5.  Donald R. Stabile, *Community Associations: The Emergence and Acceptance of a Quiet Innovation in Housing* (Westport, CO: Greenwood Press, 2000).
6.  David Lyon, "Forward," to Tracy M. Gordon, *Planned Developments in California: Private Communities and Public Life* (San Francisco, CA: Public Policy Institute of California, 2004), p. iii.
7.  See Evan McKenzie, *Privatopia: Homeowner Associations and the Rise of Residential Private Government* (New Haven, CT: Yale University Press, 1994); Steven E. Barton and Carol J. Silverman, eds., *Common Interest Communities: Private Governments and the Public Interest* (Berkeley, CA: Institute of Governmental Studies Press, University of California, 1994); and Robert Jay Dilger, *Neighborhood Politics: Residential Community Associations in American Governance* (New York: New York University Press, 1992).
8.  They are unlike a business corporation, however, in that they can tax their "stockholders."
9.  Hendrik Hartog, *Public Property and Private Power: The Corporation of the City of New York in American Law, 1730–1870* (Chapel Hill, NC: University of North Carolina Press, 1983).
10.  William A. Fischel, *The Homevoter Hypothesis: How Home Values Influence Local Government Taxation, School Finance, and Land-Use Policies* (Cambridge, MA: Harvard University Press, 2001).
11.  Robert H. Nelson, *Zoning and Property Rights: An Analysis of the American System of Land Use Regulation* (Cambridge, MA: MIT Press, 1977).
12.  See also Robert H. Nelson, "Zoning Myth and Practice—From Euclid into the Future," in Charles M. Haar and Jerold S. Kayden, eds., *Zoning and the American Dream: Promises Still to Keep*, (Chicago: American Planning Association—Plan-

ners Press, 1989); Robert H. Nelson, "Privatizing the Neighborhood: A Proposal to Replace Zoning with Collective Private Property Rights to Existing Neighborhoods," *George Mason Law Review* (Summer 1999); and Robert H. Nelson, "Zoning by Private Contract," in F. H. Buckley, *The Fall and Rise of Freedom of Contract* (Durham, NC: Duke University Press, 1999).

13.    Robert H. Nelson, "Privatizing the Inner City," *Forbes,* December 12, 2005.

14.    See Nelson, "Privatizing the Neighborhood."

15.    Individual buildings with entry desks and security guards already have their own "gates" but a similar form of security is difficult or impossible to establish throughout an entire inner-city neighborhood with multiple owners.

16.    Fred Foldvary, *Public Goods and Private Communities: The Market Provision of Social Services (*Brookfield, VT: Edward Elgar, 1994).

17.    See Christopher Durso, "Critical Mass: Across the Country, 'Homeowner Advocates' Are Taking to the Internet, the Airwaves, and the Halls of Power to Rail—More and More Loudly—Against Condos and HOAs," *Common Ground,* May/June 2006.

18.    See Lee Anne Fennell, "Contracting Communities," *University of Illinois Law Review* (2004): 829–898.

19.    For further details on neighborhood constitutional options, see Nelson, *Private Neighborhoods and the Transformation of Local Government,* Part V.

20.    See Donald J. Boudreaux and Randall G. Holcombe, "Government by Contract," *Public Finance Quarterly* 17, no. 3 (1989); Yoram Barzel and Tim R. Sass, "The Allocation of Resources by Voting," *Quarterly Journal of Economics* 105 (August 1990); and Donald J. Beaudreaux and Randall G. Holcombe, "Contractual Governments in Theory and Practice," in David T. Beito, Peter Gordon, and Alexander Tabarrok, eds., *The Voluntary City: Choice, Community, and Civil Society (*Ann Arbor, MI: University of Michigan Press, 2002).

21.    Joni Greenwalt, *Homeowner Associations: A Nightmare or a Dream Come True?* (Denver, CO: Cassie Publications Inc., 2001), p. 37.

22.    Paula A. Franzese, "Does It Take a Village?: Privatization, Patterns of Restrictiveness and the Demise of Community," *Villanova Law Review* 47, no. 3 (2002), pp. 590, 592–93.

23.    Wayne S. Hyatt, "Putting the Community Back in Neighborhood associations: An Action Plan," in Bill Overton, ed., *Community First! Emerging Visions Reshaping America's Condominium and Homeowner Associations* (Alexandria, VA: Community Associations Institute, 1999), p. 104.

24.    Charles E. Fraser, "Condo Commandos: An Abuse of Power," in Adrienne Schmitz and Lloyd W. Bookout, eds., *Trends and Innovations in Master-Planned Communities* (Washington, DC: Urban Land Institute, 1998), p. 46.

25.    Ibid.

26.    Ibid.

27.    Wayne S. Hyatt, "Putting the Community Back in Neighborhood associations: An Action Plan," in Bill Overton, ed., *Community First! Emerging Visions Reshaping America's Condominium and Homeowner Associations* (Alexandria, VA: Community Associations Institute, 1999), p. 111.

28.    Erica Klarreich, "Election Selection: Are We Using the Worst Voting Procedure?" *Science News* 162 (November 2, 2002).

29.    Quoted in Klarreich, " Election Selection," p. 1.

30.    *The Report of the Independent Commission on the Voting System,* Presented to Parliament by the Secretary of State for the Home Department by Command of Her Majesty (October 1998), paragraph no. 76.

31.    Ibid., Chapter 9, recommendation 3.
32.    Jonathan Levin and Barry Nalebuff, "An Introduction to Vote-Counting Schemes," *Journal of Economic Perspectives* 9 (Winter 1995).
33.    David E. Sappington, "Incentives in Principal-Agent Relationships," *Journal of Economic Perspectives* (Spring 1991).
34.    Michael Sarbanes and Kathleen Skullney, "Taking Communities Seriously: Should Community Associations Have Standing in Maryland?" *Maryland Journal of Contemporary Legal Issues* 6 (Spring/Summer 1995), p. 292.
35.    G. Bingham Powell, Jr., *Elections as Instruments of Democracy: Majoritarian and Proportional Visions* (New Haven, CT: Yale University Press, 2000), p. 254.
36.    John Stuart Mill, quoted in Dennis C. Mueller, *Constitutional Democracy* (New York: Oxford University Press, 1996), p. 127.
37.    Ibid., p. 316.
38.    David C. Drewes, "Putting the 'Community' Back in Common Interest Communities: A Proposal for Participation-Enhancing Procedural Review," *Columbia Law Review* 101 (March 2001), pp. 343, 340.
39.    Scott E. Mollen, "Alternative Dispute Resolution of Condominium and Cooperative Conflicts," *St. John's Law Review* 73 (Winter 1999), pp. 80–81.
40.    See Community Associations Institute, *Governance, Resident Involvement and Conflict Resolution,* Best Practices Report no. 2 (Alexandria, VA: Community Associations Institute, 2001), 5.
41.    Ibid., 69–70.
42.    B. Espen Eckbo, remarks quoted in "Emerging Trends in Corporate Governance," *Corporate Board Member—2001 Special Supplement,* p. 10.
43.    William T. Allen, remarks quoted in "Emerging Trends in Corporate Governance," p. 8.
44.    Jon C. Teaford, *The Twentieth-Century American City: Problem, Promise, and Reality* (Baltimore: Johns Hopkins University Press, 1986), pp. 50–56.
45.    Stephen Cianca, "Home Rule in Ohio Counties: Legal and Constitutional Perspectives," *Dayton Law Review* 19 (Winter 1994), p. 542.
46.    Scott E. Mollen, "Alternative Dispute Resolution of Condominium and Cooperative Conflicts," *St. John's Law Review* 73 (Winter 1999), pp. 75, 77.
47.    Doreen Heisler and Warren Klein, *Inside Look at Neighborhood Association Homeownership: Facts, Perceptions* (Alexandria, VA: Community Associations Institute, 1996), p. 34.
48.    Mary Avgerinos, *Alternative Dispute Resolution & Consensus Building for Community Associations,* GAP Report No. 26 (Alexandria, VA: Community Associations Institute, 1997), p. 17.
49.    Mollen, "Alternative Dispute Resolution of Condominium and Cooperative Conflicts," pp. 76, 86, 85.
50.    Wayne S. Hyatt, "Putting the Community Back in Neighborhood associations: An Action Plan," in Bill Overton, ed., *Community First! Emerging Visions Reshaping America's Condominium and Homeowner Associations* (Alexandria, VA: Community Associations Institute, 1999), p. 104.
51.    Avgerinos, *Alternative Dispute Resolution & Consensus Building for Neighborhood Associations.*
52.    See Byron R. Hanke and Thomas S. Kenny, *Architectural Control: Design Review,* 4th ed. (Alexandria, VA: Community Associations Institute, 1998).

## References

Avgerinos, Mary. *Alternative Dispute Resolution & Consensus Building for Community Associations,* GAP Report No. 26 (Alexandria, VA: Community Associations Institute, 1997).

Barton, Steven E. and Silverman, Carol J., eds. *Common Interest Communities: Private Governments and the Public Interest* (Berkeley, CA: Institute of Governmental Studies Press, University of California, 1994).

Barzel, Yoram and Sass, Tim R. "The Allocation of Resources by Voting," *Quarterly Journal of Economics* 105 (August 1990).

Blakely, Edward J. and Snyder, Mary Gail. *Fortress America: Gated Communities in the United States* (Washington, DC: Brookings Institution Press, 1997).

Boudreaux, Donald J. and Holcombe, Randall G. "Government by Contract," *Public Finance Quarterly* 17, no. 3 (1989).

Boudreaux, Donald J. and Holcombe, Randall G. "Contractual Governments in Theory and Practice," in David T. Beito, Peter Gordon, and Alexander Tabarrok, eds., *The Voluntary City: Choice, Community, and Civil Society* (Ann Arbor, MI: University of Michigan Press, 2002).

Cianca, Stephen. "Home Rule in Ohio Counties: Legal and Constitutional Perspectives," *Dayton Law Review* 19 (Winter 1994).

Community Associations Institute, *Governance, Resident Involvement and Conflict Resolution,* Best Practices Report no. 2 (Alexandria, VA: Community Associations Institute, 2001).

Dilger, Robert Jay. *Neighborhood Politics: Residential Community Associations in American Governance* (New York: New York University Press, 1992).

Drewes, David C. "Putting the 'Community' Back in Common Interest Communities: A Proposal for Participation-Enhancing Procedural Review," *Columbia Law Review* 101 (March 2001).

Durso, Christopher. "Critical Mass: Across the Country, 'Homeowner Advocates' Are Taking to the Internet, the Airwaves, and the Halls of Power to Rail—More and More Loudly—Against Condos and HOAs," *Common Ground,* May/June 2006.

Fenell, Lee Anne. "Contracting Communities," *University of Illinois Law Review* (2004).

Fischel, William A. *The Homevoter Hypothesis: How Home Values Influence Local Government Taxation, School Finance, and Land-Use Policies* (Cambridge, MA: Harvard University Press, 2001).

Foldvary, Fred. *Public Goods and Private Communities: The Market Provision of Social Services* (Brookfield, VT: Edward Elgar, 1994).

Franzese, Paula A. "Does It Take a Village?: Privatization, Patterns of Restrictiveness and the Demise of Community," *Villanova Law Review* 47, no. 3 (2002).

Fraser, Charles E. "Condo Commandos: An Abuse of Power," in Adrienne Schmitz and Lloyd W. Bookout, eds., *Trends and Innovations in Master-Planned Communities* (Washington, DC: Urban Land Institute, 1998).

Greenwalt, Joni. *Homeowner Associations: A Nightmare or a Dream Come True?* (Denver, CO: Cassie Publications Inc., 2001).

Hanke, Byron R. and Kenny, Thomas S. *Architectural Control: Design Review,* 4th ed. (Alexandria, VA: Community Associations Institute, 1998).

Hartog, Hendrik. *Public Property and Private Power: The Corporation of the City of New York in American Law, 1730–1870* (Chapel Hill: University of North Carolina Press, 1983).

Heisler, Doreen and Klein, Warren. *Inside Look at Neighborhood association Homeownership: Facts, Perceptions* (Alexandria, VA: Community Associations Institute, 1996).

Hyatt, Wayne S. Hyatt and French, Susan F. *Community Association Law: Cases and Materials on Common Interest Communities* (Durham, NC: Carolina Academic Press, 1998).

Hyatt, Wayne S. "Putting the Community Back in Neighborhood associations: An Action Plan," in Bill Overton, ed., *Community First! Emerging Visions Reshaping America's Condominium and Homeowner Associations* (Alexandria, VA: Community Associations Institute, 1999).

Klarreich, Erica. "Election Selection: Are We Using the Worst Voting Procedure?" *Science News* 162 (November 2, 2002).

Levin, Jonathan and Nalebuff, Barry. "An Introduction to Vote-Counting Schemes," *Journal of Economic Perspectives* 9 (Winter 1995).

Low, Setha. *Behind the Gates: Life, Security and the Pursuit of Happiness in Fortress America* (New York Routledge, 2003).

Lyon, David. "Forward," to Tracy M. Gordon, *Planned Developments in California: Private Communities and Public Life* (San Francisco, CA: Public Policy Institute of California, 2004).

McKenzie, Evan. *Privatopia: Homeowner Associations and the Rise of Residential Private Government* (New Haven, CT: Yale University Press, 1994).

Mollen, Scott E. "Alternative Dispute Resolution of Condominium and Cooperative Conflicts," *St. John's Law Review* 73 (Winter 1999).

Mueller Dennis C. *Constitutional Democracy* (New York: Oxford University Press, 1996).

Nelson, Robert H. *Zoning and Property Rights: An Analysis of the American System of Land Use Regulation* (Cambridge, MA: MIT Press, 1977).

Nelson, Robert H. "Zoning Myth and Practice—From Euclid into the Future," in Charles M. Haar and Jerold S. Kayden, eds., *Zoning and the American Dream: Promises Still to Keep,* (Chicago: American Planning Association—Planners Press, 1989).

Nelson, Robert H. "Privatizing the Neighborhood: A Proposal to Replace Zoning with Collective Private Property Rights to Existing Neighborhoods," *George Mason Law Review* (Summer 1999).

Nelson, Robert H. "Zoning by Private Contract," in F. H. Buckley, *The Fall and Rise of Freedom of Contract* (Durham, N.C: Duke University Press, 1999).

Nelson, Robert H. "Privatizing the Inner City," *Forbes,* December 12, 2005.

Nelson, Robert H. *Private Neighborhoods and the Transformation of Local Government* (Washington, DC: Urban Institute Press, 2005).

Powell, G. Bingham, Jr., *Elections as Instruments of Democracy: Majoritarian and Propoortional Visions* (New Haven, CT: Yale University Press, 2000).

Sappington, David E. "Incentives in Principal-Agent Relationships," *Journal of Economic Perspectives* (Spring 1991).

Sarbanes, Michael and Skullney, Kathleen. "Taking Communities Seriously: Should Community Associations Have Standing in Maryland?" *Maryland Journal of Contemporary Legal Issues* 6 (Spring/Summer 1995).

Stabile, Donald R. *Community Associations: The Emergence and Acceptance of a Quiet Innovation in Housing* (Westport, CO: Greenwood Press, 2000).

Teaford, Jon C. *The Twentieth-Century American City: Problem, Promise, and Reality* (Baltimore: Johns Hopkins University Press, 1986).

*The Report of the Independent Commission on the Voting System,* Presented to Parliament by the Secretary of State for the Home Department by Command of Her Majesty (October 1998).

# About the Editors and Contributors

## Editors

*Randall G. Holcombe* is Research Fellow at The Independent Institute, DeVoe Moore Professor of Economics at Florida State University, past President of the Public Choice Society, and past President of the Society for the Development of Austrian Economics. He received his Ph.D. in economics from Virginia Tech, and has taught at Texas A&M University and Auburn University. Dr. Holcombe is also Senior Fellow at the James Madison Institute and was a member of the Florida Governor's Council of Economic Advisors from 2000 to 2006. Dr. Holcombe is the author of twelve books, a contributing author to forty volumes and the author of more than 100 articles in academic and professional journals. Among his books are *The Economic Foundations of Government, Public Policy and the Quality of Life, Smarter Growth* (ed. with S. Staley), *From Liberty to Democracy: The Transformation of American Government, Writing Off Ideas, Public Sector Economics, Public Finance and the Political Process*, and *Entrepreneurship and Economic Progress*.

*Benjamin Powell* is Research Fellow at The Independent Institute, Assistant Professor of Economics at Suffolk University, and a Senior Economist with the Beacon Hill Institute. Dr. Powell received his Ph.D. in economics from George Mason University and he has been Assistant Professor of Economics at San Jose State University, Fellow with the Mercatus Center's Global Prosperity Initiative, and a Visiting Research Fellow with the American Institute for Economic Research. Dr. Powell is the author of *Housing Supply and Affordability* and the editor of *Making Poor Nations Rich: Entrepreneurship and the Process of Development*. He has contributed to numerous scholarly volumes and journals.

## Contributors

*Matthew E. Brown* is a Ph.D. candidate in economics at Florida State University. He has been a Research Associate with the Property and

Environmental Research Center, Adjunct Professor of Economics at Montana State University and Santa Clara University, and Managing Editor of *Econ Watch Journal*. His articles have appeared in *Regulation, The Independent Review*, and *Environmental Protection*.

*John B. Estill* is a Lecturer in the Department of Economics at San Jose State University. He received his M.A. in economics from San Jose State University, and he is Founder and President of Appian Engineering, Managing Partner of GME Associates, and past President of the Association of Engineering Construction Employers. His article, "Taxing Development: The Law and Economics of Traffic Impact Fees" (with B. Powell and E. Stringham), appeared in the *Boston University Public Interest Law Journal*.

*Fred E. Foldvary* is a member of the Civil Society Institute at Santa Clara University, where he teaches economics. He received his Ph.D. from George Mason University. He is a Senior Editor for *The Progress Report* online journal, and his books including *Soul of Liberty, Beyond Neoclassical Economics, Public Goods and Private Communities, Dictionary of Free-Market Economics*, and *The Half-Life of Policy Rationales* (edited with Daniel Klein). Dr. Foldvary has received the Sir Antony Fisher International Memorial Award and was first-place winner in the Community Associations Institute Research Foundation's Award of Excellence.

*Joshua C. Hall* is Assistant Professor of Economics at Beloit College. He was Dan Searle Humane Studies Fellow and Ken and Randy Kendrick Fellow at West Virginia University, where he received his Ph.D. in economics; Economist at the Joint Economic Committee of Congress, and Lecturer in Economics at Capital University. His books include *Constraining College Costs* (with R. Vedder and A. Gillen) and *Toward a Free and Prosperous Ohio,* and his articles have appeared in *The American Economist; New Perspectives on Political Economy; Atlantic Economic Journal; Journal of Social, Political, and Economic Studies; Journal of Economics and Politics*; and other scholarly journals.

*Stan J. Liebowitz* is the Ashbel Smith Professor of Economics and Director of the Center for the Analysis of Property Rights and Innovation at the University of Texas at Dallas. He received his Ph.D. in economics from the University of California at Los Angeles, and he has taught at the North Carolina State University, University of Chicago, University of Rochester, and the University of Western Ontario. The author of numerous scholarly and popular articles, Professor Liebowitz's books include *Winners, Losers & Microsoft: Competition and Antitrust in High Technology* (with Stephen Margolis), *Re-thinking the Networked Economy, Why Health Care Costs Too Much, The Relative Efficiency of Private and Public Broadcasting in Canada, The Impact of Reprography on the Copyright System,* and *Copyright Obligations for Cable Television: Pros and Cons.*

*Robert H. Nelson* is Senior Fellow at the Independent Institute, Professor of Public Policy at the University of Maryland, and Senior Scholar for the Mercatus Center at George Mason University. He received his Ph.D. in economics from Princeton University, and he has been Staff Economist for the U.S. Senate Select Committee on Indian Affairs; Visiting Senior Fellow, Marine Policy Center, Woods Hole Oceanographic Institution; Member of Economics Staff, Office of Policy Analysis, Office of the Assistant Secretary for Policy, Management and Budget, U.S. Department of the Interior; Senior Research Manager of President's Commission on Privatization; Visiting Scholar and Federal Executive Fellow at the Brookings Institution; Visiting Scholar at the Property and Environment Research Center; Chairman of Interior Department Task Force on Indian Economic Development; Senior Fellow, Competitive Enterprise Institute; Senior Economist of the Commission on Fair Market Value Policy for Federal Coal Leasing; Staff Economist, Twentieth Century Fund; Assistant Professor of Economics, City College of the City University of New York; and Consultant to the Puerto Rico Planning Board. A contributing author to many scholarly volumes and journals, he is the author of the books, *The New Holy Wars: Economic versus Environmental Religion, Private Neighborhoods and the Transformation of Local Government; Zoning and Property Rights; The Making of Federal Coal Policy; Reaching for Heaven on Earth: The Theological Meaning of Economics; Economics as Religion: From Samuelson to Chicago and Beyond*; and *Public Lands and Private Rights: The Failure of Scientific Management.*

*Randal O'Toole* is Senior Fellow at the Cato Institute and Senior Economist at the Thoreau Institute. He has been Visiting Scholar at the College of Natural Resources at the University of California at Berkeley, McCluskey Conservation Fellow at the Yale School of Forestry and Environmental Studies, and Merrill Visiting Professor of Political Science at Utah State University. He is the author of the books *The Vanishing Automobile and Other Urban Myths*, *The Best-Laid Plans*, and *Reforming the Forest Service*, plus articles in the *Columbia Journal of Environmental Law, Journal of Forestry, Willamette Week, Passenger Train Journal, Independent Review, Forbes, Regulation*, and *Reason*.

*Matt E. Ryan* is Assistant Professor of Economics at Duquesne University. He received his Ph.D. in economics from West Virginia University, and he has been Associate Fellow at the Public Policy Foundation of West Virginia, Ken & Randy Kendrick Fellow at West Virginia University, and Fellow at the American Institute for Economic Research. His articles have appeared in such journals as *The Independent Review, American Journal of Economics and Sociology, Journal of Private Enterprise, and California Labor and Employment Review.* He is co-editor (with R. Sobel and J. Hall) of the book, *Unleashing Capitalism: Why Prosperity Stops at the West Virginia Border, and How to Fix It*, that won the Sir Antony Fisher International Memorial Award.

*Bernard H. Siegan* was Distinguished Professor of Law at the University of San Diego. He received his law degree from the University of Chicago, and he was author of the books, *The Supreme Court's Constitution: An Inquiry into Judicial Review and Its Impact on Society, Economic Liberties and the Constitution, Property Rights: From Magna Carta to the Fourteenth Amendment*, and *Land Use Without Zoning*.

*Samuel R. Staley* is Director of Urban and Land Use Policy at the Reason Foundation and Co-Founder and Senior Research Fellow for the Buckeye Institute for Public Policy Solutions. He received his Ph.D. in public administration with concentrations in urban planning and public finance from Ohio State University. Dr. Staley has been Bradley Fellow in the Center for Study of Public Choice at George Mason University and Chair of the Planning Board, Chair of the Charter Review Commission, and Member of its Board of Zoning Appeals and Property Review Commission for Bellbrook, Ohio. He currently serves as a member of the Board of Trustees for the Miami Valley School System. His books include *Mobility First: A New Vision for Transportation in a Globally Competitive 21st Century* (with A. Moore), *The Road More Traveled: Why the Congestion Crisis Matters More Than You Think and What We Can Do About It, Smarter Growth: Market-based Strategies for Land-use Planning in the 21st Century, Drug Policy and the Decline of American*

*Cities*, and *Planning Rules and Urban Economic Performance: The Case of Hong Kong*.

*Edward P. Stringham* is Shelby Cullom Davis Visiting Associate Professor of American Business and Economic Enterprise at Trinity College; Associate Professor of Economics at San Jose State University; and editor of the *Journal of Private Enterprise*. He received his Ph.D. in economics from George Mason University, and he has been the F.A. Hayek Endowed Visiting Professor at the University of Klagenfurt in Austria and President of the Association of Private Enterprise Education. Professor Stringham is editor of the books, *Anarchy and the Law: The Political Economy of Choice* and *Anarchy, State and Public Choice*, and he is the recipient of the Templeton Culture of Enterprise Best Article Award, Paper of the Year Award from the Association of Private Enterprise, Best Article Award from the Society for the Development of Austrian Economics, Second Place in the Olive W. Garvey Fellowships, and Distinguished Young Scholar Award from the Liberalni Institut and the Prague School of Economics.

*Mark Thornton* is Senior Fellow at the Ludwig von Mises Institute. He received his Ph.D. in economics from Auburn University, and he is Book Review Editor of the *Quarterly Journal of Austrian Economics* and a member of the Editorial Board of the *Journal of Libertarian Studies*. Dr. Thornton has been Associate Professor of Economics at Columbus State University, Assistant Superintendent of Banking for the State of Alabama, Assistant Professor of Economic at Auburn University, and Editor of the *Austrian Economics Newsletter*. The author of dozens of articles in scholarly journals, he a contributor to numerous volumes and his books include *The Economics of Prohibition, Tariffs, Blockades, and Inflation: The Economics of the Civil War, The Bastiat Collection*, and *The Quotable Mises*.

*William Tucker* is author of the books, *The Excluded Americans: Homelessness and Housing Policies, Progress and Privilege: America in the Age of Environmentalism, Vigilante: The Backlash Against Crime in America*, and *Terrestrial Energy: How a Nuclear-Solar Alliance Can Rescue the Planet*. His articles have appeared in *Harper's, Atlantic Monthly, Wall Street Journal, New York Times, Weekly Standard, American Spectator, National Review, New Republic, Reader's Digest, Reason* and many other publications.

*Lawrence J. White* is the Arthur E. Imperatore Professor of Economics at New York University, General Editor of *The Review of Industrial Organization* and Secretary-Treasurer of the Western Economic Association International. Professor White has been Senior Economist for the President's Council of Economic Advisers, Board Member of the Federal Home Loan Bank Board and Director of the Economic Policy Office in the Antitrust Division at the U.S. Department of Justice. He received his Ph.D. in economics from Harvard University, and his books include *The Automobile Industry Since 1945; Industrial Concentration and Economic Power in Pakistan; Reforming Regulation: Processes and Problems; The Regulation of Air Pollutant Emissions from Motor Vehicles; The Public Library in the 1980s: The Problems of Choice; International Trade in Ocean Shipping Services: The U.S. and the World; The S and L Debacle: Public Policy Lessons for Bank and Thrift Regulation; Deregulation of the Banking and Securities Industries; Mergers and Acquisitions: Current Problems in Perspective, Technology and the Regulation of Financial Markets: Securities, Futures, and Banking; Private Antitrust Litigation: New Evidence, New Learning; The Antitrust Revolution; Bank Management and Regulation*; and *Structural Change in Banking.*

# Index

*Note: Page numbers in italics refer to illustrations.*

# INDEPENDENT STUDIES IN POLITICAL ECONOMY

THE ACADEMY IN CRISIS: The Political Economy of Higher Education | *Ed. by John W. Sommer*

AGAINST LEVIATHAN: Government Power and a Free Society | *Robert Higgs*

ALIENATION AND THE SOVIET ECONOMY: The Collapse of the Socialist Era | *Paul Craig Roberts*

AMERICAN HEALTH CARE: Government, Market Processes and the Public Interest | *Ed. by Roger Feldman*

ANARCHY AND THE LAW: The Political Economy of Choice | *Ed. by Edward P. Stringham*

ANTITRUST AND MONOPOLY: Anatomy of a Policy Failure | *D. T. Armentano*

ARMS, POLITICS, AND THE ECONOMY: Historical and Contemporary Perspectives | *Ed. by Robert Higgs*

BEYOND POLITICS: Markets, Welfare, and the Failure of Bureaucracy | *William Mitchell & Randy Simmons*

THE CAPITALIST REVOLUTION IN LATIN AMERICA | *Paul Craig Roberts & Karen Araujo*

THE CHALLENGE OF LIBERTY: Classical Liberalism Today | *Ed. by Robert Higgs & Carl P. Close*

CHANGING THE GUARD: Private Prisons and the Control of Crime | *Ed. by Alexander Tabarrok*

THE CHE GUEVARA MYTH AND THE FUTURE OF LIBERTY | *Alvaro Vargas Llosa*

CUTTING GREEN TAPE: Toxic Pollutants, Environmental Regulation and the Law | *Ed. by Richard Stroup & Roger E. Meiners*

THE DECLINE OF AMERICAN LIBERALISM | *Arthur A. Ekrich, Jr.*

DEPRESSION, WAR, AND COLD WAR: Challenging the Myths of Conflict and Prosperity | *Robert Higgs*

THE DIVERSITY MYTH: Multiculturalism and Political Intolerance on Campus | *David O. Sacks & Peter A. Thiel*

DRUG WAR CRIMES: The Consequences of Prohibition | *Jeffrey A. Miron*

ELECTRIC CHOICES: Deregulation and the Future of Electric Power | *Ed. by Andrew Kleit*

THE EMPIRE HAS NO CLOTHES: U.S. Foreign Policy Exposed | *Ivan Eland*

ENTREPRENEURIAL ECONOMICS: Bright Ideas from the Dismal Science | *Ed. by Alexander Tabarrok*

FAULTY TOWERS: Tenure and the Structure of Higher Education | *Ryan Amacher & Roger Meiners*

THE FOUNDERS' SECOND AMENDMENT: Origins of the Right to Bear Arms | *Stephen P. Halbrook*

FREEDOM, FEMINISM, AND THE STATE | *Ed. by Wendy McElroy*

GOOD MONEY: Private Enterprise and the Foundation of Modern Coinage | *George Selgin*

HAZARDOUS TO OUR HEALTH?: FDA Regulation of Health Care Products | *Ed. by Robert Higgs*

HOT TALK, COLD SCIENCE: Global Warming's Unfinished Debate | *S. Fred Singer*

JUDGE AND JURY: American Tort Law on Trial | *Eric Helland & Alex Tabarrok*

LESSONS FROM THE POOR: Triumph of the Entrepreneurial Spirit | *Ed. by Alvaro Vargas Llosa*

LIBERTY FOR LATIN AMERICA: How to Undo Five Hundred Years of State Oppression | *Alvaro Vargas Llosa*

LIBERTY FOR WOMEN: Freedom and Feminism in the Twenty-first Century | *Ed. by Wendy McElroy*

MAKING POOR NATIONS RICH: Entrepreneurship and the Process of Economic Development | *Ed. by Benjamin Powell*

MARKET FAILURE OR SUCCESS: The New Debate | *Ed. by Tyler Cowen & Eric Crampton*

MONEY AND THE NATION STATE: The Financial Revolution, Government, and the World Monetary System | *Ed. by Kevin Dowd & Richard H. Timberlake, Jr.*

NEITHER LIBERTY NOR SAFETY: Fear, Ideology, and the Growth of Government | *Robert Higgs & Carl P. Close*

OPPOSING THE CRUSADER STATE: Alternatives to Global Interventionism | *Ed. by Robert Higg & Carl P. Close*

OUT OF WORK: Unemployment and Government in Twentieth-Century America | *Richard K. Vedder & Lowell E. Gallaway*

PARTITIONING FOR PEACE: An Exit Strategy for Iraq | *Ivan Eland*

PLOWSHARES AND PORK BARRELS: The Political Economy of Agriculture | *E. C. Pasour, Jr. & Randal R. Rucker*

A POVERTY OF REASON: Sustainable Development and Economic Growth | *Wilfred Beckerman*

PRIVATE RIGHTS & PUBLIC ILLUSIONS | *Tibor R. Machan*

RACE & LIBERTY IN AMERICA: The Essential Reader | *Ed. by Jonathan Bean*

RECARVING RUSHMORE: Ranking the Presidents on Peace, Prosperity, and Liberty | *Ivan Eland*

RECLAIMING THE AMERICAN REVOLUTION: The Kentucky & Virginia Resolutions and Their Legacy | *William J. Watkins, Jr.*

REGULATION AND THE REAGAN ERA: Politics, Bureaucracy and the Public Interest | *Ed. by Roger Meiners & Bruce Yandle*

RESTORING FREE SPEECH AND LIBERTY ON CAMPUS | *Donald A. Downs*

RESURGENCE OF THE WARFARE STATE: The Crisis Since 9/11 | *Robert Higgs*

RE-THINKING GREEN: Alternatives to Environmental Bureaucracy | *Ed. by Robert Higgs & Carl P. Close*

SCHOOL CHOICES: True and False | *John Merrifield*

STRANGE BREW: Alcohol and Government Monopoly | *Douglas Glen Whitman*

STREET SMART: Competition, Entrepreneurship, and the Future of Roads | *Ed. by Gabriel Roth*

TAXING CHOICE: The Predatory Politics of Fiscal Discrimination | *Ed. by William F. Shughart, II*

TAXING ENERGY: Oil Severance Taxation and the Economy | *Robert Deacon, Stephen DeCanio, H. E. Frech, III, & M. Bruce Johnson*

THAT EVERY MAN BE ARMED: The Evolution of a Constitutional Right | *Stephen P. Halbrook*

TO SERVE AND PROTECT: Privatization and Community in Criminal Justice | *Bruce L. Benson*

THE VOLUNTARY CITY: Choice, Community, and Civil Society | *Ed. by David T. Beito, Peter Gordon & Alexander Tabarrok*

TWILIGHT WAR: The Folly of U.S. Space Dominance | *Mike Moore*

VIETNAM RISING: Culture and Change in Asia's Tiger Cub | *William Ratliff*

WINNERS, LOSERS & MICROSOFT: Competition and Antitrust in High Technology | *Stan J. Liebowitz & Stephen E. Margolis*

WRITING OFF IDEAS: Taxation, Foundations, and Philanthropy in America | *Randall G. Holcombe*